MW00785692

GARDEN *of* RUINS

CONFLICTING WORLDS

NEW DIMENSIONS OF THE AMERICAN CIVIL WAR

T. Michael Parrish, Series Editor

GARDEN *of* RUINS

Occupied Louisiana in the Civil War

J. MATTHEW WARD

LOUISIANA STATE UNIVERSITY PRESS BATON ROUGE

Published by Louisiana State University Press
lsupress.org

DESIGNER: Michelle A. Neustrom
TYPEFACE: Arno Pro, text; Cochin, display

Maps created by Bobby L. Horne, Jr.

JACKET PHOTOGRAPH: Baton Rouge, 1862. Andrew D. Lytle Collection, Mss. 893, 1254,
Louisiana and Lower Mississippi Valley Collections, LSU Libraries, Baton Rouge, La.

LIBRARY OF CONGRESS CATALOGING-IN-PUBLICATION DATA

Names: Ward, J. Matthew (Johnathan Matthew), author.
Title: Garden of ruins : occupied Louisiana in the Civil War / J. Matthew Ward.
Other titles: Occupied Louisiana in the Civil War | Conflicting worlds.
Description: Baton Rouge : Louisiana State University Press, [2024] | Series: Conflicting
    worlds: new dimensions of the American Civil War | Includes bibliographical references
    and index.
Identifiers: LCCN 2023045544 (print) | LCCN 2023045545 (ebook) | ISBN 978-0-8071-8139-3
    (cloth) | ISBN 978-0-8071-8237-6 (pdf) | ISBN 978-0-8071-8236-9 (epub)
Subjects: LCSH: Louisiana—History—Civil War, 1861–1865. | United States—History—
    Civil War, 1861–1865—Occupied territories. | Louisiana—History—Civil War, 1861–1865—
    Social conditions.
Classification: LCC E510 .W33 2024 (print) | LCC E510 (ebook) | DDC 976.3/05—dc23/
    eng/20231031
LC record available at https://lccn.loc.gov/2023045544
LC ebook record available at https://lccn.loc.gov/2023045545

TO MY GRANDPARENTS,

Lester and Ilse Kuss Ward

AND

Tom and Mary Bruff Strevel

Contents

Acknowledgments

Many people, knowingly and unknowingly, were part of the intellectual genealogy of this book. During my freshman and sophomore years at Itawamba Community College, I benefited from excellent academic instruction and encouraging personal connections, especially Nathan Ward, Jo Hoots, Clinton Boals, Fisher Fleming, and Ken Bishop—all of whom shaped my intellectual curiosity, engaged patiently with me, and listened (perhaps endured) through countless office hour visits. It was at ICC where an English department faculty member encouraged me to double major in English and social studies. When I transferred to the Mississippi University for Women (accepting men since 1982), I could not have asked for a better array of scholars to shape my intellectual and creative development. In the English department, Nora Corrigan, Amy Pardo, Michael Smith, Bridget Pieschel, and my adviser Kendall Dunkelberg read countless drafts of creative writing and engaged in earnest conversation with me. Philosophy professor Brian Hilliard particularly challenged me to hone my analytical thinking. In the history department, Jonathan Hooks, Amber Handy, and Thomas Velek were valuable resources. But it was Erin Kempker, my senior thesis adviser, that merged my interest in traditional military history with gender and women's history. Although I could hardly know it at the time, this present book initially germinated under her oversight as I wrote my senior undergraduate thesis on Confederate women's evolving sense of self during the U.S. Civil War.

The war challenged women's traditional location as genteel household figures, yet also augmented the social power they wielded as moral and material representatives of the antebellum order. Under the direction of LeeAnn Whites at the University of Missouri, I continued to wrestle with the juxtaposition between southern women and the challenges of war within my master's thesis. LeeAnn introduced me to the term "household war" in her Fall 2013 course on the U.S. Civil War, and it has remained a central part of my scholarly outlook since that time. It seemed to me that women under occupation were in a unique position to implement multiple offensives from their location in the household. They could harangue their occupiers as brutes who violated their communities and degraded their privileged position as women, and they could offer support directly to the Confederate cause. The two years I spent in Columbia, Missouri, where I made many wonderful friends and worked under the superb supervision of LeeAnn, were some of the best years of my life. I owe a debt of gratitude to LeeAnn, who carefully and patiently redirected my perspective of Civil War history and introduced the nineteenth-century household to me as a defining concept for southern studies.

When I entered my doctoral program with Aaron Sheehan-Dean at Louisiana State University, I was interested in expanding my study of occupation from women alone to the entire arena of tensions in occupied territory. With his knowledge of the Civil War era's intellectual and cultural roots, he broadened and deepened the analytical framework, especially with a serious consideration of the legal precedents and international context that many Americans pondered during the war years. Aaron was an excellent dissertation adviser who fielded countless conversations, office hours, and emails with me. For that, I am very grateful. The COVID-19 pandemic cut my final year short, but I will always remember my years at LSU with fondness. I would also like to thank several scholars for their invaluable instruction and advice while I attended LSU—Catherine Jacquet, Alecia Long, Nancy Isenberg, Andrew Burstein, Gaines Foster, and Charles Shindo. I further give thanks for the expert guidance of T. Michael Parrish and Rand Dotson at LSU Press.

I want to offer special thanks to the staff of numerous research libraries I visited, especially LSU's own Hill Memorial Library. The knowledgeable staff entertained a litany of special requests and research questions and without their help I would never have completed graduate school. I also want to thank my parents for always celebrating and indulging my fascination with history and for believing in my dream of becoming a historian. My mother ferried me to the library countless times as a child and encouraged my love of reading from an early age. My father never seemed to tire of accompanying me to Civil War battlefields and historic sites. Their love and support were crucial to my love of history. Lastly, I want to thank my wife, Sarah Orler, for enduring me for years while I labored on this book. It was rarely an easy process and she loved me despite it.

I dedicate this book to my grandparents, all hard-working blue-collar people who did not live to see my PhD graduation or the publication of my first book. But beyond its intellectual pretensions, this book bears their fingerprints, for it was in them that I first witnessed how common everyday people faced decades of historical change and negotiated countless troubles. They did not know it while they were still living, but my grandparents planted in me a resolve to chronicle ordinary people in unordinary times.

GARDEN *of* RUINS

Introduction

GROUND BETWEEN THE MILLSTONES

As Union authorities bolstered their occupation of Louisiana in 1863, the prominent New Orleans preacher and ardent Confederate Benjamin Morgan Palmer found Union occupation to be an unjust exercise in power. Though he had recently fled to South Carolina, Palmer was still concerned for his fellow Confederates living under Union rule in his home state. Union commanders required that occupied southerners take oaths of allegiance to the United States, which not only generated a federal compendium of citizenry but also implicitly communicated that the federal government held ultimate authority over the status of average Americans. These oaths were essentially contracts of loyalty, a miniaturization of contract theory, on which American democratic society was nominally established. Palmer castigated Union occupation authorities for punishing southerners who did not sign an oath. Coercive and divisive bureaucratic forms of belonging, such as loyalty oaths, isolated individuals from the "organic whole" and severed their "ties of allegiance" to local and national communities. Additionally, mere political forms of belonging, Palmer believed, could not reduce higher allegiances established by God and validated by historical practice.[1]

Palmer struck at one of the central issues of the Civil War that was embedded in loyalty oaths: the power of general government versus the autonomy of local individuals. Palmer believed that "the refined despotism of the Lincoln government adopts the policy of grinding individuals between conflicting jurisdictions as between the upper and nether millstones." The Union war forced southern people to choose between loyalty to the national government, which secured immediate survival, and loyalty to the South's social order, which contained all "ties of allegiance." Palmer labeled this action as a "shameful and cowardly device of dealing with single communities, and even individual persons, as if they were independent of higher authority." Southerners had an obligation to remain loyal to region, family, and God, Palmer explained, but Union loyalty oaths abstracted away these larger frameworks of belonging, atomized the individual southerner, and forced each one to betray themselves and the social order they held dear.[2]

Isolated individuals, especially male household heads, who were compelled through treason, weakness, or pragmatism to accept a Union oath also abandoned their loyalty to the central framework of social belonging in the antebellum South—the household. "Our country! What does not the term embrace? It means our homes and the cheerful firesides, and the prattling babes that gather round the paternal knee; it means sweet neighborhood and friendship." Confederate patriots under occupation in Louisiana "enjoyed a most distinguished opportunity of rendering a service to the Confederacy quite as valuable as that of the army in the field," Palmer insisted, if only they had rejected the oath in the name of preserving their national loyalty and household honor. He demanded those who took the oath to "retrieve your position by a bold and manly retraction."[3]

When he complained about southern people crushed "between conflicting jurisdictions," Palmer acknowledged the profound shifts in power that the Civil War era produced in the United States: slavery gave way to freedom; local autonomies bowed to national authority; a household economy that subjugated dependents to white male patriarchal authority transitioned to an individual contract economy. Some New Orleans citizens, Palmer stated in his lengthy diatribe against loyalty oaths, reluctantly took the oath "in good faith, intending to keep it so long as the Federal rule should continue, but in the hope that this rule would, in due season, terminate and restore them to the civil connections from which their hearts were never estranged." Yet the oaths imposed by the Union transformed "a government of force"—military occupation—into "a government of law," which would necessarily compromise southerners' allegiance to Confederate law and their own household authority. Furthermore, the oath "transferred with the citizenship all its moral obligations, and invested the authority of [Gen. Benjamin] Butler with the sanctions of a recognized and legal government." When military authorities, North and South, imposed loyalty oaths and a host of other military restrictions on the population of Louisiana, these authorities, as ambassadors for rapidly expanding state power, demonstrated that nation states now had more authority as arbiters of communal belonging than state governments or household heads. For all his secessionist bluster, Palmer was correct in summarizing the most problematic feature of loyalty oaths. Palmer's diatribe was just one example of how Union and Confederate authorities, as well as individual Americans under their jurisdiction, debated the power dynamics of war, democracy, and household during the Civil War.[4]

Palmer's text also reflected the increasing complexity of military occupation as a project of war. In the first year of invasion, Union forces captured small portions of territory on the fringes of the Confederacy: coastal regions in Virginia, North Carolina, and South Carolina, some areas of middle Tennessee, and the upper sector of the Mississippi River. In the spring of 1862, the Union navy moved up the river and the Union army moved west. Union offensives captured sizable territories in Louisiana, Tennessee, and Virginia. These conquests included New Orleans and Memphis, whose concentrated populations posed troublesome questions of governance. Confederates in Louisiana moved the state capital to Opelousas for nine months in 1862 and then further north to Shreveport until the war's conclusion. During the summer of 1863, the Union captured Vicksburg and Port Hudson, severing the Confederacy in two.

Despite repeated offensive efforts into central and western Louisiana that met with varying results, for the majority of the war Union forces reliably maintained an occupation zone that stretched from New Orleans to Brashear City (about eighty-five miles to the west) to Baton Rouge (up the Mississippi River from New Orleans and about eighty miles north of Brashear City). Beyond this region, which Confederate forces never seriously threatened, Union and Confederate forces vied for control of central Louisiana parishes, including St. Mary, St. Martin, St. Landry, Lafayette, and Vermillion in the south, and especially Avoyelles, Rapides, Winn, Natchitoches, and De Soto Parishes in the Red River Valley north of Baton Rouge. During and after General Ulysses S. Grant's Vicksburg campaign in 1863, Union forces also exercised influence over eastern parishes that bordered the Mississippi River, namely Carroll, Madison, Tensas, and Concordia.

The tension between occupied territory and Confederate territory in Louisiana closely aligns with the paradigm established by historian Stephen V. Ash. In his book *When the Yankees Came* (1995), Ash identified "three occupied Souths": garrisoned areas where Union occupation was strong and Union sov-

ereignty largely unassailable; Confederate territory where Confederates maintained most influence; and finally a gray area or no man's land where both sides,
as well as interminable hosts of guerrillas, jayhawkers, and runaways, vied for
authority and resources. In Civil War Louisiana, these border frontier areas
were extremely fluid, with Union forces briefly penetrating into central and
western Louisiana in 1863 and far into the northern part of the state during
the failed 1864 Red River Campaign. Following that defeat, Confederates
renewed guerrilla offensives into the eastern and southern parts of the state
where Union occupation was strongest.[5]

But this book is less focused on the military history of occupation and
more concerned with its daily bureaucratic workings and cultural power to
potentially reshape southern society. The Slave South's "organic whole" that
Palmer defended entailed patriarchy and mastery for white men, dependence
and respectability for white women and children, and subordination for enslaved people of African descent. War and occupation disrupted each of those
tenets. As men and resources disappeared to the front lines, southern men
found their claims to self-mastery compromised. Thousands of men, especially
those who hailed from Confederates states in the western theater, could no
longer directly protect their households. Government authorities and the war
also drained southern households of material, which burdened women with
privation. Isolated on the home front, many southern women contended with
political systems and government bureaucracy to secure survival. With their
dependence often shifted from household heads to civil and military figures,
southern women exhibited startling levels of social independence and political
participation during the war. More than either of these gendered disruptions to
the southern social order, however, both Union military occupation and Confederate government policy reoriented southern households through policies
regarding slavery. Whether faced with Union forces, who cautiously dismantled slavery over several years, or Confederate state policies, which frequently
commandeered enslaved people for defensive labor, slaveholders experienced
a diminution in their authority over Black people.[6] When historians look to the
Civil War as a primary catalyst for government centralization in United States
history, they need to examine occupation as one of the foremost examples of
how that centralization worked on the ground.[7]

As the Union tightened its grip on occupied people through various models
of governance—recruitment, confiscation, emancipation, regulation, loyalty

oaths—Confederates, southern Unionists, and Black Americans welcomed or challenged these programs of dominion. Palmer's outrage over loyalty oaths was only one response. The constellation of social reactions to occupation in turn shaped occupation itself. The same was true of Confederate state rule, which adopted an increasingly assertive governmental role as the war proceeded. Confederate Louisiana, cut off from much of the Confederate homeland by mid-1863, featured a robust central state as well as a fluctuating and quarrelsome body public. To win the war, both Union and Confederate authorities exercised increasing bureaucratic power over their populations. In cities like New Orleans, the Union created complex systems of governance and enjoyed the secure presence of military units. But in many small Louisiana towns, generally a provost marshal and a small contingent of men alone served to maintain order.

Provost marshals were military police who served in the army and exercised authority over men in the ranks, yet also extended that authority to noncombatant populations in occupied areas during wartime. Military constables and marshals in English armies had been administering "laws of the marshal" since the early sixteenth century and earlier, and such military power, despite Palmer's impassioned distinction, was not altogether separate from common law. Over a process of centuries, especially after the Glorious Revolution, various political and military thinkers justified martial law as a validation of, not subversion of, law and order, though continued questions of legality made many modern statist authority figures hesitant to apply martial law by the end of the seventeenth century. By the time of the U.S. Civil War, provost marshals adhered to formal, written rules of justice for soldiers, especially the courts martial proceedings, but could also rely on a tradition of summary process (military decisions made without trial) for civilians, especially those that participated in unauthorized military actions or behavior. In September 1862, the War Department issued General Orders No. 140, which created the position of Provost Marshal General, headquartered in Washington, and empowered Special Provost Marshals in each state to arrest deserters and disloyal persons, recover stolen government property, detect spies, and employ loyal citizens as police. The First and Second Confiscation Acts further empowered the Union military to pursue punitive actions against southern property, including enslaved people, on the basis of treason. Many provost marshals in Louisiana were citizen soldiers and their willingness to implement punishing policies on an occupied people varied by political sensibility, geographic location, and time.[8]

Albert Stearns and Jonas H. French, two officers who served as Union provost marshals in Louisiana, illustrate varying experiences with occupation and differing outlooks on occupation policy. Captain Albert Stearns, 131st New York, described the duty of a provost marshal "to be a sort of a combination machine—part sheriff and part police justice, something of a parson, father to all the planters and mother to all the darkies, a general embodiment of all the civil authorities, backed up by all the authority of the army." However impossible the task might have seemed to anyone appointed in that position, he reminded readers of his postwar memoir that occupation duty was "a class of work . . . which must be well done to keep the wheels of war moving smoothly." Before joining the army, he was a police officer in Green Point, New York, an experience he felt enabled him to deal more effectively with common men in the ranks. Throughout the war, Stearns cultivated a reputation for discipline but also demonstrated a genuine concern for emancipated people. "The negroes looked to me to see that their rights were respected, and . . . to join them in the bonds of matrimony." In contrast to Stearns, who moved around between various rural posts on the perimeter of the Union occupation zone, Lieutenant Colonel Jonas French, 30th Massachusetts, served the entirety of the war in an urban area. He served on General Benjamin Butler's staff and became provost marshal and chief of police in New Orleans—even acting as military mayor for fourteen days in mid-August 1862. Butler later wrote that "the quiet and good order . . . of New Orleans may be largely ascribed" to French. His relationship to Black Americans stood opposite that of Stearns, however. Thomas Wentworth Higginson, the Unitarian minister, abolitionist, and colonel of the 1st South Carolina (Black) Volunteers remembered that before the war French was a leader of violent attacks on abolitionist meetings and Black communities. In early 1863, one free man of color claimed that Colonel French was "much worse than our rebel masters" because he returned former slaves to their masters and "has stopped all of our night-meetings, and has caused us to get permits to hold meetings on Sunday, and sends his police around to all of the colored churches every Sunday to examine all of the permits."[9]

The Civil War generated seismic shifts in power relations in nineteenth-century America. The contrasting attitudes and actions of Stearns and French toward freedpeople in the occupied South demonstrated only one of numerous conflicts over how to reshape American social order by military rule. Military occupation in the Civil War shattered the primacy of American localism, anchored by white male household authority, by entangling communal and personal autonomies with state bureaucracy. After the war, though traditional republican idealism remained as a potent cultural force in society, Americans configured their identity in an increasing matrix of bureaucratic systems: contract labor, pension appeals, Reconstruction policy, education, and industrialization. The Civil War fueled the growth of these systems, which abstracted individuals away from the household economy, and reduced the antebellum order to a shadow of its prewar dominance. Formerly enslaved Black Americans, now freed from household tyranny, embodied the fullest measure of this national transition and witnessed its greatest shortcomings. But this grand shift from household to personhood in the American landscape failed to effectively secure the independent material basis that many citizens, especially Black Americans, needed to prosper in a postbellum world. Most tragically, Reconstruction as a continued project of military occupation failed to reduce or transform the underlying premise of the antebellum household order: white racial superiority. White supremacists in the South effectively dismantled many of the changes enacted by military occupation and established an occupation of their own that endeavored to preserve as much of the old racial order as possible.[10]

This book can best be described as a social history of military occupation in Civil War Louisiana. Not only is occupation a military project designed to secure strategic territory, it is also a critical function of nation building because it undermines previous cultural and national loyalties and seeks to erect new state relations and institutions in their place. This book is therefore a study of power relationships between common people and military government, Union and Confederate, between women and men, and between Black and white people. Household order was a central theme or motivator for military and political authorities (Union and Confederate) in Louisiana, and military occupation as a political project was just as focused on domestic order as it was on military security. Union and Confederate authorities demanded allegiance to their respective national governments as the ultimate requirement of citizenship and property protection. In contrast, common Louisianans—Black and white, male and female—demanded that the security of family and household be a top priority for civil-military powers. Despite popular narratives of destruction that still often surround the history of the war, this study concludes that white households in Louisiana often benefited from state support, while those same state powers often undermined the ability of Black people to sustain their own households, most commonly through family separation and arduous labor policies.

Garden of Ruins examines occupation as both an institution of government power and a daily social process that altered the lives of soldiers and citizens. The fluctuating, often reciprocal relationships between the governors and the governed determined the political and social contours of life in wartime Louisiana. This book examines occupation as a political history through the policies and attitudes of occupation officials and as a social history through the relationships that common southerners, Black and white, developed with military government and soldiers. Both of these interweaving experiences were often grounded in the nineteenth-century household. Military officials and policies in Louisiana, both Union and Confederate, sought to defend, discipline, or reorient the household to suit respective wartime agendas in what Stephanie McCurry has described as the "paramilitary struggle over the terms of social and political life."[11]

Historians of the Civil War era and social history benefit from a household analysis because such a framework reveals more about the internal operations and structure of the war than do battlefield studies. From a relational standpoint, military and domestic combatants regularly intersected within the locus of the southern household. Guerrilla soldiers emerged from local homes and relied on those homes for supply. Union soldiers took up residence in southern homes or interacted with southerners, especially white women and formerly enslaved people, within local households. Antagonism emerged between Unionist and Confederate neighbors in local household networks.[12]

This book relies on the conceptual framework of "household war," a phrase created by historians LeeAnn Whites and Lisa Tendrich Frank, to investigate three intersecting ideas at once. First, the term indicates the material production of war within the household structure itself—agriculture, clothing and other small supplies manufacture, sheltering soldiers, stocking weaponry, supplying information. Second, the household was itself a site of resistance where flags, songs, speech, and action indicated regional and national loyalties. However, such loyalties could be highly fluid, indicating that household survival was often the most important strategy of all. While this resistance occasionally produced bloodshed on the threshold, it more often resulted in arrest, taxation, banishment, and policies of restriction such as confiscation or house arrest. Third, household war is a political term that refers to policies intended to control the material site of the house and discipline the kinship networks the household contained. Military policies might reduce its material stability or rearrange the power structure of the household. The most compelling examples of such rearrangement were conscription, banishment, and emancipation. Conscription undermined the power of male household members by subordinating their male authority to state power. Banishment ejected rebellious women from the site of domestic protection. Emancipation reduced both the material value that a household held in bond persons and the authority southerners exercised over the enslaved. As Frank and Whites contend, "the Civil War is best framed as the most revolutionary moment in the transformation of the nation's household order."[13]

From the early days of the secession crisis, although slavery and states' rights remained the preeminent issue within southern rhetoric, Confederates made clear that family and household, especially the masculine rights of household mastery, were priorities for an independent southern nation as well. "It is our sacred duty," Jefferson Davis intoned in his final speech to the Senate in January 1861, "to transmit [our rights] unshorn to our children." Secession was a martial and manly duty, many argued, to keep southern households pure of northern political and social radicalism. Georgia's Declaration of Causes bluntly declared that northerners' "avowed purpose is to subvert our society and subject us not only to the loss of our property but the destruction of ourselves, our wives, and our children, and the desolation of our homes, our altars, and our firesides." Property in this sense included the lucrative system of slavery, which, as Benjamin Palmer noted in his November 1860 Thanksgiving Sermon, was a part of the southern household. It was the slaveholding household that abolitionism threatened, declared Louisiana governor Thomas Overton Moore in December 1860, for the northern states promised to limit slavery's westward advance. The nonslaveholding states desired that "no new soil shall be worked by [slavery], although the inhabitants shall have carried slaves, along with the other members of their household and other property, to their new home, and shall themselves desire the existence of the institution." With personal liberty laws and repeated attacks on slavery, northerners steadfastly refused to assist masters in the recovery of slave property, Moore also complained. To slaveholders, this refusal was a violation of the Constitution and an indication that southern male household mastery over dependents and property no longer enjoyed the Constitutional protection it deserved.[14]

To a lesser extent, this book also touches on the evolving concept of American democracy in the nineteenth century. Democracy nominally indicated inclusion, republican values, and mass action, and symbolized an alternative relationship between government and people than had characterized much of centralized government power prior to the American experiment. The Civil War, particularly its most statist component of military occupation, revealed the limitations of that democratic ideal. National governments North and South exercised unprecedented control over their populations, marketplaces, and popular ideologies. Such control is not uncommon in wartime across human history, which suggests, as this study does, that democratic communities are more fragile than their most idealistic proponents suggest. The war questioned the extent of power for state governments, communities, households, and individuals. War tested the capacity of citizens to participate in their own communities and interact with government. It challenged the idea that government answered to the people and that state power remained secondary to individual rights.[15]

However, as this study also concludes, no statist project can entirely subdue a people, especially those accustomed to certain liberties. In the nineteenth century, Americans drew on a variety of political sources for individual conceptions of identity, belonging, and citizenship. These institutions included high political systems such as the Constitution, regional institutions such as state governments, and more local governing frameworks such as political parties, community councils, churches, and especially local households. The Civil War provides an excellent opportunity to see how powerful household organization was to common Americans, especially in the South, because the war largely subordinated political party partisanship and heightened the direct power dynamics between centralized government and the people.

With the exception of Tennessee, perhaps no more active or potent landscape of occupation existed during the Civil War than Louisiana, where both Union and Confederate militaries controlled substantial portions of physical terrain and populations on which they imposed years of policies in pursuit of victory. Throughout the war years, common Black and white Louisianans under Union and Confederate occupation cooperated with, operated against, and appealed to government authority. Their relationships to occupation powers and government policies depended on their backgrounds, social status, race, gender, age, and the evolving circumstances of war. Sometimes, as with secession, average citizens subdued members of their own communities to support the government. In such examples, citizens were part of the process of democratic governance, no matter the antidemocratic nature of many of its impulses. In many other cases, Civil War Louisianans took loyalty oaths that betrayed their political allegiance, traded with the enemy, challenged government authority, took up arms, or called for direct government relief. With these actions, occupied southerners endeavored to reshape the contours of increasingly statist institutions in their favor.

Additionally, no other state save perhaps Virginia endured such repeated invasion, military maneuvering, social upheaval, raiding, and environmental disruption. Such warfare depleted natural resources, intensified interaction between government and people, and stimulated internecine conflict. Louisiana's local infighting and neighborhood wars resemble the bloody struggles of Missouri, which recent historians have increasingly attributed to the Trans-Mississippi region as a whole. As a book located in the Civil War's western theater, this work echoes historians such as Matthew Stith and Joseph Beilien, who have done much to advance our knowledge that Missouri was not alone in the Trans-Mississippi theater as a place of extraordinary local discord—and that violence was grounded in specific local knowledge that often mystified traditional military commanders.[16]

The war of occupation in Louisiana was many wars at once, and for that reason it is important to understand what this book addresses and what it does not. This book is not a standard narrative work and makes no concerted analysis of major military history in the state, principally Ulysses Grant's spring 1863 campaigning through northeastern Louisiana on his way to Vicksburg, or Nathaniel Banks's Bayou Teche Campaign, Port Hudson Campaign, Texas Overland Expedition, or Red River Campaign. These events are mentioned or explained only where historical context is necessary. Though they are important moments of military history in the western theater, this book is more concerned with the social history of occupation in Louisiana and in that sense

Garden of Ruins is more topical than linear in its approach. My analytical approach considers occupation as two overlapping wars—first, a household war by and against southerners where they lived and operated on a daily basis, and second, a bureaucratic war in which military authorities, both Union and Confederate, dealt with the consequences of wartime society in manners increasingly similar to later twentieth-century procedures. By bureaucracy, I refer to the efforts to govern social order made by military and governmental authorities in occupied areas and to the human administrators of those policies, though these often appeared far less coherent or effective than the organized governmental systems of the Progressive Era and New Deal Era to come.[17]

The analytical structure of this work builds on numerous volumes of gender history, social history, community studies, and micro-history. As Laura Edwards contends, "the best social history is inherently political; like traditional political history, it is about power." A social history of military occupation in the Civil War reveals the extent to which household order was a priority for military powers. This was especially true in Louisiana for several reasons. First, the Union occupied the state for a long time, necessitating policy to maintain infrastructure and social order within the occupation sphere. Second, with limited resources to secure territory and stability in the Trans-Mississippi region, Confederate authorities undertook policies to substantiate domestic order—many of which worked at odds with traditional household order. And last, as northern authorities in Louisiana and the Mississippi River Valley worked to establish a free labor system, their efforts necessarily involved consideration of Black households, traditions of white dominance, and a reevaluation of the relationship between the two.[18]

In recent years, a small but robust historiography of military occupation in the Civil War has developed. In contrast to what Stephen Ash describes as "the Federals' policy of benign neglect," this book finds Union authorities far more assertive and critical of occupied southerners. Modern studies of the Civil War tend to divorce the material organization of war from the thornier issue of how that organization affected civil liberties, but occupied regions like Louisiana illustrated that the two were profoundly connected. Occupation was a military operation, but it was also a bureaucratic project. Like the work of Mark

Grimsley and Gregory Downs, this book identifies occupation and Union war policy as central instruments of ending the war and reshaping the South. After initial policies of conciliation and pragmatism in the early years of war, by 1864 and 1865 the Union military produced a series of materially devastating raids and campaigns into strategic locations such as the Shenandoah Valley. But long before these attacks, military occupation across the South expanded the reach of the military as well as its cultural consequences. While restrained violence and organized raiding managed the destructive effects of war on the southern people, the North implemented widespread occupation as the primary management tactic of the conquered Confederacy. Among other issues, Andrew Lang writes that occupation precipitated personal and national considerations about how honorable occupiers could be. Indebted to his work, my study contends that occupation also centered on discussions about how respectable or loyal occupied populations could be.[19]

Occupation in Louisiana affected several communities of southern women. Historians like Elizabeth Fox-Genovese and LeeAnn Whites demonstrate that the war had profound social consequences for southern women, especially as the war transformed the nineteenth-century agricultural household. Drew Gilpin Faust, Nina Silber, Stephanie McCurry, and others have discussed women's role in the war itself and how the war changed the political landscape for women. More recently, edited works by Whites, Alecia Long, and Lisa Tendrich Frank have emphasized the primary role of southern women in the home front. Southern women operated the domestic supply line, ran communication networks, and confronted Union troops. Women actively participated in the conflict. In occupied Louisiana, Black and white southern women were front and center in the war and shaped Union policy by waging an indefatigable household war. In occupied cities like New Orleans, women constituted the front line against enemy troops. Women shaped the outcome of the war by forcing the militaries and governments of the Union and Confederacy to develop more complex occupation strategies, bureaucratic interventions, and welfare programs. Black women especially reshaped this wartime social and political order by pressuring the Union occupation system in the Department of the Gulf.[20]

This book also takes seriously the efforts of historians of guerrilla war and their calls to present more cohesive, unified narratives of the Civil War. As Brian McKnight and Barton Myers cogently observe, "in much of the Confederacy

... irregular conflicts were 'the war.'" Indeed, guerrilla warfare often typified the war in Louisiana more than formal combat. Similarly, Lorien Foote has argued for historians to think more critically about the concept of "home front," which this work endeavors to meet as well. When they examine the home front, the very concept requires "that historians explore the home front's connection to the battlefield, since both are part of a 'consolidated war effort,'" Foote writes. With a capacious view of occupation—including bureaucracy, local conflict, and government regulation—*Garden of Ruins* seeks to present the kind of holistic narrative of home front and battlefield that Foote and others call for.[21]

In studies of the Confederate nation as a modern state, scholars traverse two roads to the same historiographic destination. Modernist historians find Jefferson Davis and other Confederate political administrators to be managerial vanguards of military organization, corporate negotiation, governmental centralization, and state police power. The Confederacy subordinated—or as Richard Bensel argues, channeled—its devotion to states' rights and individualism to a powerful central government that foreshadowed the twentieth-century American state. Social historians of the Confederacy present serious popular obstacles to the organizational schemes of elites, to which the Confederate government responded with increased mechanisms of general welfare and police power. Building on the historiography of internal dispute, this work contends that from its inception, the Confederate States of America was an institution of antidemocratic power. The founders of the Confederacy established a strong national government with substantial executive power, no Supreme Court, and no political parties. As the pressures of war burdened southern infrastructure and society, Confederate officials significantly enhanced national government power. Confederate Louisiana demonstrated how even the best efforts of the state to protect the southern household were hopelessly entangled with policies such as conscription and confiscation that undermined that household. Ultimately, Louisiana's Civil War was largely a household war that illustrated the frustrations of shifting racial dynamics and the complexities of a democracy at war with itself.[22]

1

To Rid the Community of Suspicious Persons

THE MILITANT CONFEDERATE COMMUNITY
IN SECESSION-ERA LOUISIANA

On the cold, gray day of January 26, 1861, the Louisiana secession convention announced the state's separation from the United States to stupendous cries from the crowd assembled outside the capitol building in Baton Rouge. In a display of democratic energy, the horde of people rushed into the House chamber to proclaim their ardor for independence. Governor Thomas Overton Moore struggled through the crowd with his military aides Braxton Bragg and Henry W. Allen. They led an impromptu procession to a flagpole outside where they hoisted a white banner with a single red star. In New Orleans, bells rang and cannons fired throughout the city. The Pelican Flag flew from public buildings and private homes. Businesses closed. The Washington Artillery paraded in the streets in full military dress. With common people in the statehouse and soldiers in the street, Confederate Louisiana exhibited a potent environment in which the already porous nineteenth-century boundaries between politics and society merged into a militarized state.

Two months after secession, the *New York Tribune* reporter Albert Deane Richardson surreptitiously observed the state legislature in Lyceum Hall in front of Lafayette Square. He described the members and the mythic paraphernalia with which they surrounded themselves: a life-size portrait of George Washington, another of Jefferson Davis, a painting of the current legislature, and a copy of the signed secession ordinance. "The delegates," Richardson wrote, "have made all the preliminary arrangements for being immortalized." Yet these grand and masculine totems of political independence in the seat of secession overlooked the local dependents—masterless men, white women, and enslaved Black people—that made the material foundation of Confederate Louisiana.[1]

Despite the fanfare, not all Louisianans greeted secession with enthusiasm. The Confederate state government would expend precious time and resources securing recruits for its army. Locally created vigilante groups threatened Unionists, northerners, reluctant recruits, and anyone else who might hamper secessionist spirit in the state. While the Civil War is often viewed as a grand national struggle between North and South, it could more accurately be understood as a cacophony of many local wars, especially in the Trans-Mississippi theater. Like most of the states that joined the Confederacy, Louisiana illustrated that secession, though adorned in the trappings of democratic process, was a contentious, coercive, even violent process. Louisiana's secession, more than a simple process of high politics, also emanated from local households, and household concerns were intimately connected to the overall politics of secession. In this early phase of household war, common Louisiana secessionists who coordinated with Confederate state power and those who opposed it made those political decisions they believed best geared to defend their households and chosen loyalties.[2]

In secession-era Louisiana, while fundamentally political ways of identifying loyalty and citizenship existed (such as loyalty oaths and state-issued licenses), identity still remained strongly rooted in the household and within the local community. Patriarchal household values emanated from local regions into the halls of power, albeit mostly filtered through elite planters. Louisiana's secession, as historian John Sacher argues, was a revolution that proceeded from the people, at least the male voting constituency, into the halls of power. From this perspective, secession was a popular movement that reflected the values of self-mastery prized by male household heads in the nineteenth century. Local Louisiana white men, whose identities were rooted in household mastery, fused that identity with the larger architecture of Confederate nationalism.[3]

From November 1860 to May 1862, state power in Louisiana flexed in conjunction with local coercion to implement bureaucratic organization, martial law, and a stable social order that reflected these imperatives of Confederate nationalism. Two key features characterized the Confederate war effort in Louisiana. First, citizens at the local household level directly participated in the war effort through public martial celebrations, military recruitment, material aid (both volunteered and requested by authorities), and coercion within communities. "We should make a stand for our rights," Kate Stone of Brokenburn Plantation declared; "a nation fighting for its own homes and liberty cannot be overwhelmed." Second, many state government policies reflected household concerns. The government issued public fiscal relief, enforced social order, and mandated an increasing array of regulations throughout the first months of war. These statewide policies continued with varying levels of effectiveness until the Confederacy dissolved in the spring of 1865.[4]

Although Louisianans divided between cooperationists and separatists during the 1860 election and the Secession Crisis, secessionist sentiment largely prevailed after Abraham Lincoln's presidential victory in November. Major newspapers shifted from a conservative position of patient discretion to open support for secession. The Union was broken and southern independence was the only antidote to northern corruption, claimed the New Orleans *Bee, Daily Crescent*, and eventually even the wavering *True Delta*. Governor Moore called a special session of the state legislature on December 10, 1860, before Lincoln took office, to consider the state's continued relations with the federal government. Addressing the legislature, Moore stated, "I do not think that it comports with the honor and self-respect of Louisiana, as a slaveholding State, to live under the Government of a Black Republican President." The state of Louisiana, like its individual households, embodied a social order dominated by white men who believed their notions of honor demanded separation from an abolitionist North.[5]

Even before calling for the election of delegates to a secession convention, the Louisiana government began building a military. At the governor's request, the state legislature created a military board, composed of Moore and four members of his choosing, who were tasked with purchasing arms and ammunition to distribute to volunteers. The legislature funded the military board with half a million dollars. Another legislative act required each parish to raise and equip a company of thirty-two men, either cavalry or infantry, to serve at the command of the state government. These were public laws signifying the secessionist attitudes of powerful state leaders, but they also demonstrated how state officials would have to rely on local participation to fight the war.[6]

Following Louisiana's exit from the Union on January 26, the secession convention took numerous steps to affirm public loyalty amidst the diverse population. The state commanded that all federal posts and duties, if in compliance with state laws, were to be continued and fulfilled by their officers. Should any officer refuse to take the oath of office, the office was declared vacant and all property, money, and effects of that officer and his position were to be seized by the state. This ordinance also guaranteed and indemnified all federal officers "who comply with the Ordinances of this Convention, against all claims and demands of the United States arising out of such compliance." On February 7, the convention issued a citizenship ordinance declaring all white persons who were citizens of Louisiana on January 26 were now citizens of an independent Louisiana. Anyone who was not a citizen of Louisiana but had resided in the state for twelve months preceding the secession date was required to take an oath of allegiance to the state to obtain citizenship. Through these edicts, Confederate Louisiana endorsed the antebellum social order and it also sanctioned coercive measures against any who opposed the secession establishment.[7]

While the government endeavored to establish a military and remake citizenship around Confederate loyalty, local Louisiana residents also began to organize for war. On November 10, 1860, a large crowd of citizens organized the Minute Men of New Orleans in the city's Armory Hall. They pledged allegiance to Louisiana and vowed aid to any southern state that seceded. Leading citizens and parish leaders petitioned the state government for funds to organize military groups, but the governor had no funding until January 1861. Almost immediately, planters and merchants on the parish level began to organize Minute Men groups, Home Guards, and Southern Rights Associations. These units marched in the streets of New Orleans, Shreveport, Alexandria, Baton Rouge, and other Louisiana cities and towns. "Throughout the length and breadth of the land the trumpet of war is sounding," Kate Stone wrote from northeast Louisiana, "and from every hamlet and village, from city and country, men are hurrying by thousands, eager to be led to battle against Lincoln's hordes." Public meetings in New Orleans openly endorsed secession. Men publicly sported blue cockades, a small pelican button with two streamers attached, to demonstrate their secessionist sentiments. Confederate women swarmed the balconies of New Orleans on February 11, 1862, to greet the unveiling of a new state flag—red, white, and blue stripes, with a yellow star in a red field.[8]

On March 6, 1861, *New York Tribune* reporter Albert Richardson observed public fanfare for General David E. Twiggs, a Georgia-born commander who chose to side with the Confederacy, when he arrived in New Orleans after having bloodlessly surrendered federal property in Texas. "The great thoroughfare was decked in its holiday attire. Flags were flying, and up and down, as far as the eye could reach, the balconies were crowded with spectators, and the arms of long files of soldiers glittered in the evening sunlight." Ladies presented numerous flags to regiments passing through the city. After a public speech, the general "rode through some of the principal streets in an open barouche, bareheaded, bowing to the spectators." In displays such as these, the body public and the militarized Confederate state complemented one another during the secession movement.[9]

Famed English journalist William Howard Russell arrived in the city in May 1861 to see the Confederate flag flying from all public buildings and from many private houses as well. "Military companies paraded through the streets, and a large proportion of men were in uniform," he reported. Departing a month later to sail upriver, Russell commented on the general aura of military celebration still emboldening the populace. "It was pitiable to see the children dressed out as Zouaves, with tin swords and all sorts of pseudo-military tomfoolery; streets crowded with military companies; bands playing on all sides." Although the common people demonstrated the politics of secession in the streets and through public symbols of disunion, Russell considered it to be an exercise in futility. Yet his account also revealed southern household members as the backbone of secession in the war's initial months.[10]

Religion and southern patriotism fused easily in the church house as well. Albert Richardson attended a service in a cathedral one Sunday morning to find "the aisles crowded with volunteers who, on the eve of departure . . . had assembled to witness the consecration of their Secession flag, a ceremonial conducted with great pomp and solemnity by the French priests." From First Presbyterian Church on Lafayette Square, Reverend Benjamin Palmer espoused Confederate extremism. He and Episcopalian minister W. T. Leacock openly endorsed slavery, states' rights, and secession. In response to Governor Moore's day of "Thanksgiving and Worship to Almighty God" on November 29, Palmer expounded that enslaved people "form parts of our households, even as our children" and encouraged southerners to observe "the principle of self-preservation" by protecting slavery, home, and the civilized world. Imagery of the ruined southern household also infused Palmer's inflamed secessionist rhetoric. With the household bonds between master and slave torn asunder, insurrections like that of Saint Domingue would arise, Palmer warned, and southern children would be homeless across the land. "The southerners had formerly been very bitter in their denunciation of political preaching," Richardson commented, "but now the pulpit, as usual, made obeisance to the pews, and the pews beamed encouragement on the pulpit." Richardson keenly noted the reciprocal nature of communication between common Louisiana people and their community institutions—and their larger influence on state politics.[11]

The prominent Episcopalian minister Leonidas Polk, bishop of Louisiana in 1861, declared secession an "indefeasible right" and took pains to assert the autonomy of the church, recognize the righteousness of the Confederate state, and outline the duty of southern Christians. Polk argued that Louisiana's separation "carried with it the political allegiance of her citizens. Their Supreme Government ceased to be that of the United States, and became that of the State of Louisiana, to which alone they owed a paramount fealty, and all the duties growing out of such a relationship." As Palmer would contend in the coming years when addressing loyalty oaths under Union occupation, Polk emphasized how individual loyalties were subordinate to the organic institution of Louisiana, an idea that reflected how household dependents in the antebellum South were subordinate to household heads. A social idea as well as a political one, secession reflected the divinely orchestrated order of society. State institutions were to be supported "not only with material aid and personal services, but by supplications and prayer," urged Polk, who would be commissioned as a major general in the Confederate army that summer. Forced into what he called "Diocesan Independence," Polk asserted the Protestant Episcopal Church "must follow her Nationality." Although he needed the decision of a General Convention to make changes to the Book of Common Prayer, Polk believed the emergency of secession permitted him to make executive decisions. A pastoral letter of January 30, 1861, to the clergy and laity of the church instructed members to replace words in formal prayers. "The President of the United States" was to be replaced by the "Governor of this State," and follow similar replacements for the people of the United States and congressional representatives. By February 20, congregations were instructed to pray for the president and congress of the Confederate States.[12]

While southern churches encouraged Confederate allegiance in direct but not abusive ways, vigilance committees practiced a harder form of power. No local institution embodied the public will of Louisiana secessionists more than the vigilance committee. Operating under various names—Minute Men, States' Rights Associations, committees of public safety, or Roughs—local elite and common men populated the ranks of these organizations and flexed social power to preserve the social order they envisioned. But vigilance committees in secession Louisiana demonstrated only the latest development in a popular American democratic tradition. Male-led extralegal gangs with a shared civic identity represented coalitions of belonging and coercion within America's various social landscapes during the nation's development. Their private, informal power was often not in conflict with the state, but rather a function of the will of the people embodied by the state. "Vigilant citizens," as Ray Abrahams refers to them, used coercion to establish who belonged in a community, including themselves. Looking to vigilance committees as a social index of secession Louisiana reveals the central components of citizenship as it had developed to that point in the nineteenth-century United States: its members were white, male, infused with a blend of local interests and larger state politics, and they shared social experiences that marked their public identity and civic self-conception. Vigilance committees emerged from an affective southern public to preserve the southern nationalism in which their identity was rooted. Vigilant citizens orchestrated public discipline and violence as a civic exercise, one that ultimately marked the boundaries of white male citizenship in secession Louisiana.[13]

When the Civil War ignited, vigilant male citizens of Louisiana emerged from the miasma of antebellum democracy, which often licensed public violence and voter suppression, to in turn exercise decidedly antidemocratic power over their local communities and households. In the political world unleashed by secession, vigilance committees took to the streets to arrest and interrogate perceived outsiders. These political actions reduced ambiguity about the nature of Louisiana's civic identity, which in the minds of Minute Men and Roughs was centered around allegiance to southern nationalism and slavery. While these southern men affirmed the political reality of the state, they also shaped the contours of citizenship. An abolitionist, a Black Republican, a Unionist, or a supporter of Lincoln and fanatical northern ideas could be no citizen of the southern order. Vigilance committees also targeted numerous merchants with northern ties and forced them out of Louisiana. These vigilant citizens reduced the privileges of citizenship for their targets, especially political access, judicial process, and social mobility.[14]

During his stay in New Orleans, Albert Richardson found threats, arrests, and interrogations of suspected abolitionists to be all too frequent and he often feared for his own safety. Sitting in the Louisiana Secession Convention every day, he relied only on his memory to record the proceedings, afterward racing to his hotel room to write in secrecy before he forgot anything. He had good reason to fear. Richardson described a Philadelphia businessman who made a joke about being a Republican in a counting-room where the nearby bookkeeper, a Minute Man, overheard. "That very evening . . . a delegation of fifty, waited on the Philadelphian at the St. James Hotel. They began by demanding whether he was a Black Republican," Richardson wrote. The businessman "at once surmised that he was obtaining a glimpse of the hydra of Secession," and refused to answer the question. The Minute Men "claimed that the public emergency was so great as to justify them in examining all strangers who excited suspicion." Pressed by the inquisitors, "who were of good social position and gentlemanly manners," the man claimed to be a Democrat and unsympathetic to antislavery feelings. The southern men demanded to know the political affiliations of the business institution that employed him and even searched his luggage for incriminating evidence. The Minute Men eventually departed, but soon after "a mob of Roughs, attracted by the report that an Abolitionist was stopping there," entered the hotel and began to cry out noisily for the Philadelphian to be presented to them. A southern merchant friend hid the hapless northerner for three days until a train could carry him North.[15]

William Russell also witnessed such community coercion. "Whatever may be the number of the Unionists or of the non-secessionists," he wrote, "a pressure too potent to be resisted has been directed by the popular party against the friends of the Federal government." The local agents of the Brown Brothers, with offices in Liverpool and New York, closed their New Orleans office due to mob intimidation—what was sometimes termed as "the excitement of the citizens"—because of the firm's associated northern branch. Other merchant houses followed the example as well. On May 23, a young artist commissioned to make sketches for an English periodical came with anxiety to Russell and the British consul in the city, William M. Mure. His life was threatened because of his previous association with a New York abolition paper. He pleaded with Mure for official dispatches to protect him as he escaped northward.[16]

Charges of abolitionism were nearly as numerous as the coroner's inquests, Russell observed with discomfort. The charges appeared in the police reports printed in the papers every morning, "and persons found guilt[y], not of expressing opinions against slavery, but of stating their belief that the Northerners will be successful, are sent to prison for six months." Generally, foreigners suffered this fate, he noted, or people of the lower class who did not support slavery. "The moral suasion of the lasso, of tarring and feathering, head-shaving, ducking, and horseponds, deportation on rails, and similar ethical processes are highly in favor." New Orleans newspapers celebrated what Russell referred to as "their new mode of securing unanimity" among the southern people of Louisiana. The papers also lauded Henry Mitchell, jailer of the city's workhouse reformatory, as a primary educator in "the course of instruction in the human institution for the amelioration of the condition of Northern barbarians and abolition fanatics."[17]

Confederate Louisianans tightly patrolled social membership along lines of race as well. Aboard the steamship *Florida,* bound from Mobile to New Orleans on May 20, 1861, Russell described a notice hung in his cabin declaring the rules for passengers, among which was "All slave servants must be cleared at the Custom House. Passengers having slaves will please report as they come [on] board." One free Black British sailor, sent overland from the Mobile Consulate to Mure, appeared before the latter with a wound sustained in the Crimean War and seeking passage to England. Louisiana police immediately seized the sailor when he entered the city, and he was taken to Mure only after his protests. Mure gave him some money and a letter to admit him to the Sailors' Hospital. "The police came as far as the door with him, and remained outside to arrest him if the Consul did not afford him protection and provide for him, so that he should not be seen at large in the streets of the city." When one New Orleans privateer captured three northern vessels, which included ten free men of color, the privateer gave them to the local recorder. The recorder in turn tried to hand them over to the Confederate state marshal, but he refused. The recorder, "as a magistrate and a good citizen, decided on keeping them in jail, as it would be a bad and dangerous policy to let them loose upon the community."[18]

As the atmosphere of celebration and repression pervaded the state, Louisiana citizens, especially women, worked on personal and organizational levels to support the war effort and provide mutual aid to one another. Both on a voluntary basis and in response to calls for aid from the state government, Confederate women in Louisiana sewed uniforms, sold donated goods to raise funds, and collected blankets and clothing to dispatch to the front lines. Around forty members of the Society of Ladies in Aid of the Confederate Army gathered daily at the New Orleans YMCA to sew uniforms for local troops. The New Orleans committee called Aid to Volunteers' Families collected $7,469.30 in contributions and announced it would pay out the money in sums of $10 to the families of soldiers. Local theater shows, fairs, and benefits also collected money for soldiers and their families. Thousands of visitors, especially women carrying homemade goods, flocked to the military camps in and around New Orleans. Some even boarded trains to travel the seventy-eight miles to Camp Moore in St. Helena Parish to visit the troops. After the firing on Fort Sumter, parish police juries donated thousands of dollars to soldiers in the ranks of Louisiana units.[19]

Residents helped one another personally, especially women, with material support as male heads of household shipped away to war and the local economy fluctuated severely. In July 1861, Samuel G. Risk wrote from a military camp to Henry Bier, grand secretary of the Odd Fellows Hall in New Orleans, about the wife of his friend John McCourt, who was struggling to support her family without her husband. She was "in a very difficult state as to means and money" and "depending on the neighbors" for support. Her husband told Risk that "he does not care about going up himself, if she can be placed upon an equality with others." Another man, David Lester, "has just heard from his wife that her landlord has given her notice to leave the house immediately." Lester asked Risk if the landlord had authority to evict his wife. Risk disagreed and asked Bier for help. In another display of community camaraderie, at least one New Orleans doctor traveled from house to house offering free medical service to families with absent military members. One Unionist wrote to her father about the husband of one of her friends in the city who worked in a printing office. After the man departed to Richmond to join the Confederate army, "His employees said they would theirselves [*sic*] allow his wife ten dollars a week, all the time he should be away . . . which they did faithfully until the Union troops took this place."[20]

In perhaps the most auspicious display of household support, the New Orleans government opened a free market for the relief of military families in the city on August 16, 1861. This market opened primarily in response to a group of three hundred hungry southern white women who had elbowed through the mayor's door on July 31. A volunteer relief committee of the City Council registered families in need at City Hall and appealed for donations, which were deposited at a building on Canal Street. Applicants gained entry to the free market with a ticket from the relief committee. Although the committee complained of fraud on a few occasions, the free markets distributed thousands of pounds of provisions to New Orleans families for months. "Steamboats would stop at the rich plantations, and would be laden with vegetables and whatever else would be serviceable," Marion Southwood wrote. These donations were for those "whose protectors had left for the war." The Free Gift Lottery Association made upward of $60,000 by selling tickets for donated goods, with all the profits going to the free market. Louisiana citizens from across the state donated to traveling agents of the market until Union forces arrived in May of 1862.[21]

The collective rhetoric of secession-era Louisiana weaponized Confederate patriotic values by expressing public derision and antagonism toward the Union. Secessionists especially targeted Abraham Lincoln, New England, and abolition. When copies of Lincoln's inaugural address reached New Orleans, newspapers denounced it. The *Delta* called for anyone who sought "to dampen, discourage, or restrain the ardor and determination of the people to resist" invasions and usurpations from the North to be "a traitor, who should be driven beyond our borders." Seated at the breakfast table of John Burnside's Houmas plantation in the summer of 1861, William Russell picked up one of the newspapers that were distributed to all present. "Do you hear what they are doing now—infernal villains! That Lincoln must be mad!" the agitated southerners proclaimed. Numerous southern households, like Burnside's plantation home, were arenas of secession where Louisiana citizens could exercise their vehemence toward the North and socially bond over a shared Confederate allegiance.[22]

Shared Confederate rhetoric also expressed violence toward southern enemies. Aboard the steamer *Florida* in May of 1861, Russell described how passengers discussed politics all day long as the steamer passed along the endless bayous approaching New Orleans. "The fiercest of them all was a thin, fiery-eyed little woman, who at dinner expressed a fervid desire for bits of 'Old Abe'—his ear, his hair; but whether for the purpose of eating or as curious relics, she did not enlighten the company." One Louisiana newspaper reported a no-doubt fictitious story of "a negro of cannibal propensities." The enslaved man supposedly beseeched his owner, who was soon to depart in the army—

"I wants to go 'long wid you massa; I wants to jis cook one ob dem abolitionists when you kill him!" Beyond the physical totems of rebellion found in blue cockades and Pelican flags, and in addition to the social policing of foreigners, outsiders, and people of color, secessionist Louisianans articulated an inclusive language of rebellion with these instances of public derision and violent rhetoric. While Confederates followed varying trajectories of loyalty within the limitations of gender and class structures, the angry southern tongue democratized rebellion and made nationalism accessible to all.[23]

Recruitment and the continual display of military organization also embodied the blending of state and local power in secession New Orleans. Military companies abounded in the streets, and placards calling for volunteers covered the walls. The public notice for recruitment was a type of nationalist totem or state script—it urged patriotism and participation, but also required the engagement of local household members. The city itself, William Russell wrote, "looks like a suburb of the camp at Chalons," though he later disparaged the unity of southern resolve based on his low estimates of Confederate recruitment in Louisiana. Tailors labored day and night to produce uniforms; seamstresses strained their sewing machines to churn out flags, even turning Russell away when he brought in some shirts to be mended. Several parish governments offered bounties to men who joined the army or local militia groups. Others offered payments to soldiers' families as incentive. Locally formed companies beseeched the state for aid, including the officers of the Third Company of Chasseurs a Pied. "We will remark to your honorable body," petitioned three officers to the Board of Aldermen of the Common Council, "that Our Company is composed of native born Citizens of New Orleans" and ready for deployment. However, many of the eighty men in the company were not equipped for war. They asked for $500, giving the company "the chance to be the first in the field and prove its faithfulness and patriotism towards the government."[24]

Recruitment in secession-era Louisiana was often coercive as well. Several times Russell heard of British subjects forced into the ranks of Confederate battalions: "In some instances they have been knocked down, bound, and confined in barracks, till in despair they consented to serve." Mure relieved all he could but his resources and abilities were limited. Russell feared many others were trapped in prison or the service. Indeed, after Nathanial Banks took command of the Union-occupied Department of the Gulf in late 1862, he forwarded to the federal government numerous complaints from the French and British consuls about European subjects forcibly conscripted into the Confederate army. Historian Roger Shugg suggested that many southern volunteers in Louisiana's Confederate forces joined out of economic privation brought on by Confederate economic policy and the Union blockade. Doubtless this was true but coercive recruitment had begun even before working-class Louisiana men felt the pressure of joblessness. Overseers were dismissed from work, as were levee contractors. The Confederate provost marshal commanded all white deck hands on steamboats to be discharged and replaced with free Black laborers.[25]

By June 1861, Louisiana had somewhere around sixteen thousand troops in the field, either in the state or throughout the Confederacy. These were volunteer forces and their numbers outpaced the quota that Jefferson Davis asked of Louisiana. When news reached the state of the victory at the Battle of First Manassas, in which several Louisiana units had participated with distinction, Louisianans celebrated wildly. The victory enticed many more volunteers to the ranks, as did rebel victories that fall in Oak Hill, Missouri, and Belmont, Kentucky. In September, Governor Moore issued an order for a registry of all men between ages eighteen and forty-five to be made. No volunteer companies organized outside the governor's authority would be recognized. Moore declared any person refusing to perform military duty as "suspicious" and subject to fines. He also recommended that banks and insurance companies close at 2 p.m. and merchants and manufacturers close by 3 p.m. to allow employees time to perform military training and preparation. By late November 1861, over 23,000 Louisiana troops were in the Confederate army, with almost double that number in the state through participation in militia or formal military units.[26]

As in prewar days, eliminating slave rebellions and maintaining the boundaries of slavery were primary concerns for Louisianans both in the army and at home. William Russell noted strengthened patrols on the streets of New Orleans in late May 1861 and overheard a woman comment on impending mischief from the enslaved. A few days later, a southern businessman at dinner blamed enslaved people in New Orleans for the numerous fires that erupted nightly in the city. Russell believed faulty flues and stoves were the more likely culprits, but the paranoia was palpable. As in Palmer's Thanksgiving Day sermon, southerners persistently feared destruction of their homes by rebellious slaves. This social trend within Louisiana society carried over from antebellum days, when armed slave patrols threaded the river roads and watchful overseers observed profitable plantation properties. But given the explosion of a gun-powder mill in the old U.S. Marine Hospital in December 1861, New Orleans Confederates also believed they had reason to fear sabotage from enslaved people or secret Unionists.[27]

While local Confederates patrolled the city streets, the Confederate state of Louisiana confiscated property belonging to the federal government and constructed fortifications along the Mississippi River and the Gulf Coast. Louisiana forces made quick work of capturing federal forts and treasuries, including the United States Branch Mint in New Orleans, containing nearly $500,000 in gold and silver. The Lone Star flag of Louisiana flew over the mint, where 120 Confederate troops were garrisoned. Even before the secession convention convened, Governor Moore ordered Louisiana troops in New Orleans to sail to Baton Rouge and seize the United States Arsenal defended by Major Joseph A. Haskins. Several "country companies" departed when Haskins refused to surrender. But on the afternoon of January 10, Haskins relented and the Confederates captured the some fifty thousand small arms, numerous cannon, and supplies of ammunition stored in the arsenal. Around the same time, Confederate forces overtook Forts Jackson, St. Philip, and Pike about seventy miles below New Orleans and turned them into southern defenses. In May, as he departed the city and sailed upriver into Louisiana's interior, William Russell noted fortifications being constructed on some of the shoreline near Grant Pass in Plaquemines Parish.[28]

Beyond New Orleans, potent displays of martial sentiment, military aid, and volunteer service flowed through the rest of Louisiana in the heady days of the secession winter, again illustrating that secession was as much a production of Louisiana households as of grand politics. In early December 1860, Adjutant General Maurice Grivot reported to Governor Moore a strong desire among the people "for the forming of volunteer corps, to protect their homes, their families, and their property, and scarcely a week has passed, but that requests, either verbal or written, have been made upon me for arms to equip the companies then organizing." On former governor Andre B. Roman's plantation, Russell noted particular animosity toward the Union among the Creole people in the region. A dress parade in Madison Parish in late July 1861 drew hundreds from the surrounding area. "Altogether the place seemed to be overflowing with people," Kate Stone wrote, "we would have had to drive over women and children to get out of the yard." In faraway Shreveport, a military unit called the Caddo Greys marched through the streets. The *South-Western* newspaper declared, "May they ever be ready to defend our firesides against abolitionists and intestine war." In Port Allen, the *Sugar Planter* celebrated the Delta Rifles, "justly the pride of our parish." A member of Company K of the 3rd Louisiana Regiment described the march from Camp Walker to transport ships docked in New Orleans as "one grand ovation, the balconies of the houses, banquets, and streets being crowded with countless thousands of men, women, and children, bidding the brave boys farewell." Similar displays occurred in Plaquemine and Lake Providence. The departure ceremony represented national patriotism and communal cohesion. In the distance from household to battlefield, the strongest connection of soldier to state was not the government but the community.[29]

The public martial atmosphere could both blend households of differing material status and accentuate their division. The *Sugar Planter* commented on the Delta Rifles: "We are pleased to notice in the ranks as private soldiers, some of our wealthiest and most influential planters. This is the right spirit, as it serves to assist in bringing many into the ranks whom Fortune has not blessed with an abundance of the world's goods." In February 1861, Assumption Parish sugar planter Alexander Pugh witnessed "a great display of military and the people" in Paincourtville. A few months later, he spent a day distributing handbills in Napoleonville for a public military meeting. He desired to arouse "a military spirit among our people." In attendance a few days later, he believed the meeting would result in "considerable good." Some of these public martial displays therefore involved the suspension of class hierarchy, or at least the pretense of its suspension. The Alexandria *Constitutional* excoriated "unblushing demagogues" who claimed class conflict ruptured racial unity between the average farmer and the wealthy planter. "The interest of the poor man and the rich man are the same in this country, one and indivisible," the paper declared. "We have but two classes here, the white man and the negro." The early days of war provided the illusion that materially unequal households could unite over shared racial and social equality.[30]

Yet Confederate Louisiana was not without class tension. In August 1861, the Shreveport *South-Western* reported discord in Winnfield, Louisiana, "There seems to be a very bad feeling existing between two classes of citizen in our parish. We are sorry to see such a condition of affairs, but it is so, and we cannot help it. The non-slaveholding population think that the slave-holders are not doing their duty, and therefore, should be made to do it." A mass meeting reportedly organized in the town on August 24 "for the purpose of devising means by which men of the parish who are able and not willing to support the volunteers, can be reached." This meeting illustrated that some nonslaveholding households did not support the war and dissented against slaveholders because of their privileged class identity, which at times distanced them from wartime sacrifices that poorer households had to face. As the war continued, the strain between wealthy households and poorer households grew more pronounced, and meetings such as these became part of a larger pantheon of state and community strategies that encouraged the militarized body public— especially the male household heads gathered in the ranks—to imagine itself more unified than it often was.[31]

Perhaps spawned from public meetings like those in Napoleonville or Winnfield, local vigilante groups in the outer parishes also exhibited the kinds of volatile social control seen in the streets of New Orleans. In St. Charles Parish, west of the city, two people were exiled from the region because they apparently "tampered" with slaves, "hurrahed" for Lincoln, and expressed "sentiments at the present hostile to the interests of the parish." In Shreveport, the South-Western reported that the local vigilance committee warned Boston piano manufacturer Lemuel Gilbert to leave the area because of his support for Abraham Lincoln. When he departed soon after, the newspaper preened, "We are pleased to see the prompt action of the committee, and hope that action will be taken to rid the community of all suspicious persons." Distant from the formal politics at Lyceum Hall, rural Louisianans still pursued political conformity in their communities. In Madison Parish, Kate Stone knew of only three Unionists, but she believed they should be sent northward "to a more congenial people."[32]

Such direct local action could prove troublesome to some who feared that an excessive atmosphere of reprisal might disrupt social order. A letter from an editor on the Atchafalaya River in St. Landry Parish that was published in the Daily Picayune complained of vigilance committees in the parish as well as throughout the state. The committees "make and execute laws in some cases, instead of acting strictly in aid of, and in subordination to, legal authorities."

Furthermore, the writer complained, judicial and other officials "suspend or evade the operation of the laws, whenever popular sentiment or some assumed exigency seems to require it." Without more information about the author of the piece it is difficult to surmise his social location, but his general attitude seems to reflect a supporter of John Bell and the Constitutional Union Party. "I'd rather suffer many evils that are now illegitimately cured (or pretended to be)," the writer continued, "than to have the barriers of the constitution broken down, and its mandates set at naught; for I know the value to liberty of maintaining law." But secessionists interpreted the barriers and mandates of the Constitution to be disgraced by Republican rule, and in choosing political separation, they announced themselves as arbiters of national discord. Whether this St. Landry writer understood it or not, in an agrarian slave society at war, local households settled issues of national politics with the same coercion they used in community disputes.[33]

As the months following secession unfolded, the drain of supplies and manpower from Louisiana, as well as the increasingly burdensome presence of the Union naval blockade, began to strain New Orleans's economy, but the agricultural community in the rural areas of Louisiana remained somewhat isolated from these market vagaries. In May 1861, Kate Stone's mother readied large quantities of vegetables to sustain her family in the oncoming war. "Our only chance for anything from this time until the close of the war will be to raise it ourselves. Strict economy is to be the order of the day." With the help of their enslaved Black laborers, her family also raised a small group of hogs and cattle. Journeying up the Mississippi River toward Natchez in June, William Russell observed how sugar plantation owners in St. James Parish had large amounts of Indian corn planted on their property, a staple food for feeding their enslaved property. They had the corn planted to prepare for the possibility for a lengthy war "without any distress from inland or sea blockade."[34]

But physical isolation did not prevent rural Louisiana household members, especially Confederate women, from organizing substantial communal support for the war effort. Confederate women in Baton Rouge established a Campaign Sewing Society, selling tickets for prizes in order to raise money for the needed supplies. In St. Landry Parish, a newspaper generated a plan to accept donations of vegetables from planters in the parish and supply them to New Orleans. The Atchafalaya Rangers, fully composed of planters, readily agreed to the plan. Other residents in the Atchafalaya region also agreed to provide and transport aid. The Port Allen *Sugar Planter* declared, "Our citizens have been liberal in their subscriptions for . . . supply" of the Delta Rifles, providing some $1,700 in aid. The Committee on Contributions in East Baton Rouge Parish operated a Volunteer Fund in December 1861. Collecting "gifts of various articles of any and every description," the Committee coordinated with the Ladies Campaign Society to sell the items at auction and send the money to New Orleans. Their "patriotic enterprise" accepted a wide range of donations including sugar, molasses, cotton, cattle, horses, sheep, hogs, jewelry, dress, patterns, needlework, cakes, poultry, books, furniture, and any other available item. To address the shortage of metal needed to create cannons, Louisianans shipped thousands of bells from plantations, schools, and churches to New Orleans.[35]

Rural Louisiana residents were particularly eager to demonstrate support for soldiers. In response to Governor Moore's appeal for blankets to send to Louisiana troops stationed in Virginia, the Ladies Volunteer Aid Association of Lafourche Parish collected over one hundred blankets in addition to sewing numerous uniforms, socks, and scarves. Kate Stone and her female kin prepared her brothers for war. "We lined their heavy blankets with brown linen and put pockets at the top for soap, combs, brushes, handkerchiefs, etc." By the end of August, Kate served on the soliciting committee for her local sewing society. R. W. Stanley of the 21st Louisiana Infantry was tasked with moving supplies to west Louisiana in the fall of 1861 when he encountered the largesse of locals in New Iberia. He wrote Henry Bier from the Lion Hotel in New Iberia, detailing the helpful patriotic activities of locals toward him and his men. "[The] residents here are the most Patriotic people I have yet met[.]" Southerners in the town facilitated the travels of soldiers passing through the region by guiding them to ships, giving them directions, and transporting them free of charge. "They took me on board and treated me as if I had been Genl Beauregard himself," Stanley exclaimed. Two local men even procured some wagons for him and his men free of charge. They packed every room in a local hotel with a company of men traveling from Texas to Virginia, sparing no expense on their lodging and supply. The townspeople brought baskets swelling with fruit and other food and slaughtered a hog to provide for all the soldiers. When the company left, the townspeople kept all the food that the Texans could not carry for the next group moving through the area.[36]

As in New Orleans, militarized male citizens performed the important military and social duty of the slave patrol. Seven men from the St. Tammany Parish militia, for example, were ordered by Captain W. D. Bagley of the St. Tammany Regiment to patrol the town of Covington on March 29, 1862. "A servant with a special pass will be allowed to go on his way, unless some suspicion be entertained regarding the pass, when in such case, one of the guard must accompany the negro to the written destination." Sergeant of the guard James Bourie later reported he and his men discovered some fifteen or twenty enslaved people off the property of their masters that night, each having a special pass. Although Governor Moore worked to incorporate as many Home Guard units into the state militia as he could, numerous local protection groups chose to patrol communities instead as the state mobilized for war. Parish leaders divided parish territory into wards and enlisted slave patrols made up of at least five men to police in assigned districts. Members of the patrols were to be between the ages of fifteen and fifty and drawn from the white male population. Parishes in Confederate Louisiana required male citizens to participate in these patrols, empowering local captains to call on any man necessary to perform the duty. The power of the slave patrol increased as war began, as they could issue commands in place of masters about travel, assembly, and activity for enslaved people. These slave patrols illustrated the compulsory frameworks underlying democracy in the South, as did vigilance committees and secession itself.[37]

The power of popular support for secession extended to property confiscation and destruction as well. On his journey up the Mississippi River, Russell commented on how "the Confederate authorities are now determined to confiscate all property belonging to persons who endeavor to evade the responsibilities of patriotism. In such matters the pressure of the majority is irresistible, and a sort of mob law supplants any remissness on the part of the authorities. In the South, where the deeds of the land of cypress and myrtle are exaggerated by passion, this power will be exercised very rigorously. The very language of the people is full of the excesses generally accepted as types of Americanism." As Russell witnessed it, the excesses of American democracy, feared by such men as the anonymous St. Landry editorial writer, animated the public spirit of secession and threatened the heart of Constitutional values—property rights. Yet many pro-secession voices like the New Orleans *Daily Crescent* reflected Russell's stern observation. In August 1861, the paper urged readers to profit from the example of George Washington and the American rebels of the Revolution, who immediately confiscated Tory property when the British army evacuated Boston, auctioned it off, and applied the proceeds "to the public exigencies." In late 1860 and early 1861, raiding secessionists burned bridges, barns, and crops on the property of two leading cooperationist delegates to the state secession convention, James Madison Wells and James G. Taliaferro, the latter of which would be thrown in a Confederate jail for his Unionist sympathy. As southern support for secession issued from the household, secessionists just as eagerly targeted the households and property of those who did not align with the new Confederate nation.[38]

Despite the presence of a few cooperationist figures who strongly urged Louisiana to remain within the Union, from the fall of 1860 to the spring of 1862, Louisiana politicians endeavored to establish a Confederate government that could effectively support the national war effort while also protecting Louisiana households. In the process, the state government demonstrated the limitations of democracy within a Confederate state. Ultimately, as the government adopted increasingly harsher restrictions and implemented martial law, Confederate leaders compromised household autonomy and individual rights to pursue military security. Just two days before the election for delegates to the state secession convention, the editor of the Baton Rouge *Weekly Gazette and Comet* complained that the convention was called in "an inflamed state of mind" and that the assembly "will claim the right to dispose of the lives and property of our citizens as may best suit the purpose of the leaders in this matter, who place no value on the Union." The January 7, 1861, election selected 80 secessionists, 44 cooperationists, and 6 "doubtful" delegates. The statewide popular vote produced 17,296 votes for cooperationist delegates, compared to 20,448 for secessionists, a fairly close vote that demonstrated persistent divisions in Louisiana's political landscape. Cooperationist delegates tended to support secession as a defense of southern property and honor, yet they believed that severing the federal Union should occur only if Louisiana could enjoy the mutual aid and protection from fellow southern states. Secessionists were the most vocal proponents of immediate separation.[39]

Even as the convention turned from secession to the ratification of the national Confederate Constitution, political debate continued over the nature of democratic involvement in the new republic. On March 17, Charles Bienvenu of New Orleans stirred trouble in the convention by submitting an ordinance

Louisiana Parishes
1860

requiring the official number counts of the delegate elections from each parish. The convention struck down the proposal. Next the convention debated submitting the Constitution of the Confederate States to a popular vote. The secession convention was "no Long Parliament to rule Louisiana without check or limit," Christian Roselius, former attorney general of Louisiana, insisted. Yet the ordinance for a popular vote on the Confederate Constitution was also defeated. The Secession Oligarchy, as the spying Albert Richardson termed it, left "the people quite out of sight." As local vigilance committees and secessionist Roughs proved, Richardson's statement applied to only some of the people, most likely many of those, especially in central Louisiana, who had voted for cooperationist delegates like Bienvenu, Roselius, and Taliaferro. Nevertheless, the elite leaders at the secession convention steadfastly pursued a consolidation of power rather than a truly democratic society wherein political minorities were uniformly protected. As Confederate Louisiana proved, secession was an exclusionary process. Despite cooperationist protests, Louisiana ratified the constitution on March 21 with a vote of 101 to 7. The convention adjourned on March 26 to meet again in November.[40]

The heavily secessionist convention reflected immense but not unquestioned elite control over Louisiana's process of separation from the Union. Many of the elite planters and politicians in the state rejected a popular referendum on secession or the Confederate Constitution precisely because they feared the results of placing such a decision in the hands of those they perceived as their social inferiors. A man named Dr. Rushton complained vigorously to William Russell about the social plague of universal male suffrage, citing numerous examples of "the terrorism, violence, and assassinations which prevail during election times in New Orleans." The architects of the "grand slave confederacy," Russell wrote, "believe themselves . . . to be masters of the destiny of the world." Russell rendered a critical appraisal of democracy in the United States when he argued that, in New Orleans and New York alike, "the opinion of the most wealthy and intelligent men in the community, so far as I can judge, regards universal suffrage as organized confiscation, legalized violence and corruption, a mortal disease in the body politic." With such conservative viewpoints, Louisiana elites had reason to simultaneously value and fear moments of local coercion that germinated in Confederate Louisiana. Used in favor of secession, as was much popular rhetoric, material support, and vigilante violence, local political participation contributed to the state's independence. When Louisiana citizens resisted conscription, taxes, and martial law, as many would do in the coming years, they bent the will of the state—normally an organ of elite authority—in alternative directions.[41]

Although elites maintained control over the arena of formal politics and often tried to channel the secessionist energy of their yeomen neighbors, immediately after secession the Confederate state government introduced a complex series of policies that reflected class concerns of both elite and yeoman Louisianans. The state government took immediate steps to align fiscal policies, land sale, state relief, manufacturing, and civil rights with the state's war effort. Overall, however, state measures were less about a balance of power or appealing to interested parties than they were about the stability and security of the state itself.

With the preparation for war, Louisiana experienced some financial strain. Louisiana banks tightened financial operations in the fall of 1860 when the general election portended national discord. They refused all loan applications in the months after the election, a policy intended to prevent insolvency, which the Louisiana Board of Currency declared in January 1861. After the creation of the Confederate state government, the money market expanded once more, though it contracted again with the attack on Fort Sumter and the resulting Union blockade. By September, under pressure from the national Confederate government to place Confederate paper currency on a sure footing, Governor Moore recommended to New Orleans banks that they suspend specie payments in favor of Confederate currency. Though the banks reluctantly complied, the availability and value of paper money plummeted in the city. New Orleans resident Clara Solomon wrote that many people "absolutely refuse to give specie for paper" and no one would part with silver money in their possession. In January 1862, the legislature went so far as to pass an act protecting state banks from civil suits for suspending specie payment and declared Confederate currency legal tender for the sale of all public land and debt. These money regulations were only the initial steps that the state would take throughout the war to direct the economy, regulatory programs that revealed the distance between the state's allegiance to elite institutions and its purported allegiance to Confederate citizens like Solomon.[42]

Louisiana's Confederate government and even members of the population conflated monetary policy with patriotic loyalty. On March 5, 1862, the New Orleans Committee on Public Safety adopted a resolution condemning all persons who refused to accept Confederate money as "unworthy of the countenance and respect of patriotic citizens, and justly obnoxious to the indignation of the community." In April, with the city of New Orleans under Confederate martial law, a newspaper announced, "All traffic in paper currency, tending to create distrust in the public mind, or otherwise to produce embarrassment, shall be held as acts of hostility against the Government, and will be dealt with summarily. . . . Delinquents will be visited by prompt and severe punishment." Just as with clothing items, volatile secessionist speech, and public military fervor, Confederate citizens could demonstrate local and national loyalty by adherence to Confederate fiscal policy.[43]

The government of the state also took broad control of land policy in Louisiana. On March 7, 1861, the legislature passed a resolution declaring all unappropriated public domain within Louisiana's boundaries to be the property of the state. By March 21, the legislature adopted a land act that established a general land office, provided for a commissioner of public lands, mandated a minimum price of $1.25 an acre for public land, and stipulated that no person could buy more than 160 acres at that price. In December, the legislature forbade any lawsuit against persons serving in the military, and that law was to remain in place until six months after the war had ended. Controversially, the legislature attempted to pass a "stay law" on January 17, 1862, requiring all appraisers appointed in cases of forced land sales to appraise all property at its value as of April 1, 1861. Planters and merchants howled. Elites petitioned Moore to veto the "Act to Regulate Forced and Judicial Sales of Property," no doubt because many anticipated cheap prices for land that would come to be, as the law stated, "depreciated by the existing war." Maybe Moore and other government figures had poorer households in mind when they tried to protect them from losing property—or perhaps the state looked to maintain high prices for any lands it might seize and sell to railroad companies or manufacturing ventures during the war. In either case, a state law that forbade lawsuits against Confederate soldiers who may have fallen behind on mortgages and land payments during their military service was fundamentally a law that protected yeoman households. By shielding its troops against lawsuits from avaricious bankers and landed elites, the state no doubt understood that it preserved the physical integrity of the army as its central war-making institution.[44]

No ambiguity of intent clouded direct financial relief from the state to the people. Severe drought affected Louisiana in late 1860 and early 1861, for which the legislature apportioned $30,000 to purchase corn and rice for "the poor who are actually in a state of suffering, or are likely to be." No parish that applied could receive more than $1,500. The Union naval blockade also began to deplete trade in the city of New Orleans as early as the summer of 1861, eventually causing an economic depression. One resident wrote in July, "There is a great deal of suffering here at this time and many families are not able to pay their rent and [are] thrown out of employment." Flour coming from north Texas flowed into New Orleans, but not much else. Speculation soared beginning in late 1861. Prices for all goods rose at an alarming rate. Beginning in October, Mayor John T. Monroe of New Orleans organized a schedule of bread prices to protect consumers from exorbitant costs. The governor, responding to overwhelming support from cotton factors in New Orleans, ordered no shipments of cotton to embark from the city's port—part of a nationwide Confederate embargo on cotton, in response to the Union blockade, intended to provoke intervention from a cotton-starved Europe.[45]

While the state busied itself providing for common people, wealthier cotton interests appealed to the government for relief as well. Excessive rain in June and July of 1861 reduced that year's cotton crop by half in the state. Unable to sell what cotton they did have, proponents of the Cotton Planters Relief Bill proposed that the state take all available cotton from Louisiana planters as security and issue $7 million in paper currency in return (five cents per pound). Opponents decried state largesse to cotton planters at a time when many suffered from loss of resources and Moore subsequently vetoed the bill in January 1862. On February 10, Moore declared any ship or train bringing cotton into New Orleans without a special permit would be seized by authorities and removed from the city at the expense of the owner. By the summer, the state offered only Confederate bonds in payment to planters for cotton. On the issue of cotton sale and public relief, it would seem that households of lesser material status experienced more security from enhanced state controls.[46]

Cooperation between Louisiana citizens and the Confederate state government in secession-era Louisiana culminated around concerns of military preparedness. With the arrival of Union forces and the breakdown of Confederate defenses in early spring 1862, Louisiana Confederates experienced a diminution in their power to coerce or protect Louisiana households. By June, William Russell noted how secession and the Union naval blockade generated destitute conditions in the city. "The municipal authorities, for want of funds, threaten to close the city schools, and to disband the police; at the same time employers refuse to pay their workmen on the ground of inability." Hundreds of shipbuilders and dock workers went on strike rather than work without pay. A few rumors circulated that Unionist workers had attempted to sabotage the ironclad *Mississippi* as it sat in dry dock, including a case of arson in early 1862. Many distraught Irish, English, and Scottish workers, Russell reported, crowded the British Consulate requesting to be sent north or to Europe. Mure could not oblige, so many enlisted in the Confederate army instead.[47]

As dread over a Union attack on New Orleans increased in the spring of

1862, civil and military authorities increased measures of military occupation. Appointed commander of New Orleans and its vicinity on October 18, 1861, Major General Mansfield Lovell attempted to bolster defenses in southern Louisiana. Lovell petitioned Confederate commanders in Richmond and Pensacola for more ordnance and began sinking chains, anchors, rafts, timber, and trees into waterways in southern Louisiana. The Safety Committee of New Orleans aided him in this process. No Confederate officials could meet his request for more artillery, so Lovell constructed a powder mill and a cartridge manufactory in the city. He also converted part of a hospital into an arsenal. He ordered trenches dug, laid rail tracks, and established telegraph lines out of the city. "I also made every effort," he reported, "through the citizens, to endeavor to accumulate a supply of flour and meat sufficient for sixty days for the whole city, to enable the inhabitants to stand a siege." The effort failed. In January 1862, the Confederate War Department dispatched $1 million to Lovell and ordered him to seize fourteen steamers and fortify them with cotton bales for defensive use. Additionally, he armed a dozen skiffs to patrol on the local bayous and canals "for the purpose of preventing marauding expeditions and to keep negroes and others from communicating with the enemy." Confederate defenses in Louisiana were as much about policing the local southern population as warding off invading Yankees.[48]

In the first two months of 1862, Lovell watched his forces drain as he dispatched troops and arms to thwart Union efforts in Kentucky and Tennessee. By late February, he had fewer than three thousand militiamen, and not even half of them possessed muskets. "These troops were commanded by their own State officers, and a part of them," he reported with disappointment, "when ordered to the support of Fort Jackson, mutinied and refused to go, and had to be forced on board the transports by other regiments." Nevertheless, Lovell believed the strength of the land defenses would be enough to repulse enemy invasion.[49]

Confederate war policy in Louisiana encompassed free African Americans as well. Numerous free men of color were arrested for supposedly stirring up trouble among enslaved people. White slaveholders and policemen surveilled Black congregations when they held service in the city. Free people of color constituted 10,939 people in the parish of Orleans in 1860, a population the state government also drew on for military recruitment. In the heat of secession, Afro-Creole leaders volunteered their service to the governor, perhaps a

public measure to ward off threats of expulsion, violence, and property confiscation. Moore enrolled some 1,500 soldiers into the 1st Louisiana Native Guard.
Confederate commanders drilled the troops, but the men supplied their own
arms and uniforms. Afro-Creole company officers later described the coercive
Confederate tactics that pressed the Native Guard into service. They were, as
one Black New Orleans man testified, "ordered out and dared not refuse, for
those who did so were killed and their property confiscated." A Creole named
Charles Gibbons later claimed a police officer threatened to lynch him if he did
not join the ranks of the Native Guard. Prominent white Unionists in the city
verified that Confederates threatened the lives, children, and families of free
Black people to pressure them into military service. Some of the Black troops
did express fealty to the state of Louisiana, indicating that they were frightened
by Confederate newspaper descriptions of crushing Yankee hurricanes who
would make no distinction between enemy and Unionist. Others hoped to
protect their property within Confederate Louisiana or perhaps even advance
their social status to be roughly equal to that of whites. Despite their service,
the Native Guard was disbanded in mid-February after the legislature issued
a law allowing only white men to bear arms in militias. The fact that the Confederate state government appointed white commanders to the Native Guards
and later disbanded the unit most likely indicates that the state organized the
Black regiment to surveil the city's free Black residents. Additionally, their presence no doubt represented tangible propaganda to the Confederate cause in
southern Louisiana. In any event, Moore valued the Native Guards enough
to reinstate the unit in late March, about a month before New Orleans fell to
the Union.[50]

As Union forces began to flex their might on the southern shores of the state,
Confederate Louisiana enacted its most assertive coercive measures. In Feb-
ruary 1862, the New Orleans City Council named sixty-four men as a Com-
mittee on Public Safety, a group that cooperated with national and state au-
thorities for the defense of the city and provision to Confederate troops.[51] On
March 13, 1862, President Jefferson Davis authorized the request of Moore and
Lovell to place New Orleans, as well as the parishes of Orleans, Jefferson, St.
Bernard, and Plaquemines, under martial law. Two days later, Lovell issued
General Order No. 10: "All grown white males in the aforesaid parishes, except
unnaturalized foreigners, will be required to take the oath of allegiance to the
Confederate States, and all persons, whether foreigners or not, who are un-

friendly to our cause, are notified to leave the district embraced by this order without delay." The order also established a registry of names and passports. Anyone who desired to travel within the parishes under martial law had to provide satisfaction of their loyalty to one of the eight appointed Confederate provost marshals. Perhaps most startling, the order encouraged "all good citizens . . . to report to those officers all who are suspected of hostility to the Government." All stores selling alcohol had to close by 8 p.m., lest they be permanently closed and their product confiscated. A few days later, Lovell issued General Order No. 11, requiring every white male above the age of sixteen in Orleans and Jefferson Parishes (soon to be followed by St. Bernard and Plaquemines Parishes), regardless of citizenship status, to register with the provost marshal within six days. All those claiming to be Confederate citizens had to "subscribe an unconditional oath of allegiance to said States" promising never to "convey to our enemies any information relative to the military or political affairs of the country." Lovell also took frequent measures to suppress trade with "Lincolnites," especially oystermen who ferried around in their boats on the state's southern edge. Many were arrested and some even hanged. These military policies, more formal and concentrated than the haphazard coercion of vigilance groups, anticipated and even exceeded the occupation measures of the Union military when it arrived.[52]

Perhaps concerned by the idea of such direct government power, Lovell attempted to balance state power with local power and appealed to the patience of Louisiana's citizens. He ordered the New Orleans police to assist the provost marshal, especially in arresting any person who came into the city since May 21, 1861, and could not obtain a signed permit to stay. "Martial law has not been declared for the purpose of annoying unnecessarily the true and loyal citizens," he assured Louisianans in General Order No. 11. "No greater restrictions will be imposed upon the community than are deemed absolutely necessary by those in authority." The primary objective of martial law, he stipulated, was to discover and remove from the general population persons "acting under the instigation of the enemy . . . endeavoring by word and deed to impede our onward progress towards independence and self-government." Lovell's words nearly bordered on sophistry as he endeavored to convince Confederate citizens that drastic military measures were for their benefit. However he pontificated, his message was clear: in Confederate Louisiana, if loyalty could not be won, it would be enforced.[53]

Despite claims of resistance to a tyrannical northern government, the Confederate government and community of Louisiana implemented many of the very undemocratic strategies they accused their northern brethren of exhibiting. Purported democratic proceedings dissipated in a secession convention that failed to heed outspoken critics of separation and specifically rejected proposals for a popular vote on secession or ratification of the Confederate Constitution. In this centralization of authority, Louisiana followed all but four Confederate states that refused to extend secession to a popular vote. Similarly, secessionists in Louisiana often dispensed with the procedural requirements of due process and judicial rights when ejecting outsiders and suspected enemies. Whether endorsed or opposed by varying factions of the population, the state government introduced broad managerial tendencies in the regulations of land and food prices, trade practices, and armament of military forces. With these measures the government hoped to fight the war and secure continued support from Louisiana households. As public fears over Union invasion heightened in the spring of 1862, the city of New Orleans and the surrounding areas were placed under Confederate martial law. With these regulatory controls, the Confederate state government fully revealed that it was willing to compromise individual household autonomy in order to prioritize conformity, military order, and opposition to Union invasion. Some Louisiana citizens, like the irascible James Taliaferro, harangued the irony of state authority abusing the rights of the people in order to protect the rights of the people. But the legislature did produce some measures to aid all the people of Louisiana—such as the stay law on property appraisals or the series of acts beginning in early 1862 which postponed payment of state taxes until February of the following year. These actions, however effective, were only the beginning of excessive control the Confederate state would come to exercise over the shrinking terrain of Louisiana as Union forces solidified their hold in the southeast and pressed further inward.

In late April 1862, as Union naval flares rocketed skyward over Forts Jackson and St. Philip, one final testament to secession's fractious and coercive foundations—especially among Louisiana's white yeomanry—developed in the Confederate defenses. Some four hundred recruits, many of them immigrants with little confidence in the Confederacy, mutinied inside Fort Jackson. Turning weapons on their officers, over half their number departed the fort on the night of April 27–28 and surrendered to nearby Union forces under the command of General Benjamin Butler. As this mutiny demonstrated, strong undercurrents of anti-Confederate spirit coexisted with secessionist enthusiasm. One northern reporter who streamed up the Mississippi River toward New Orleans with David Farragut's naval vessels wrote that "for some miles the houses on each bank [were] decorated with white flags, and in several instances tattered and torn American ensigns waved over fishing luggers and houses. We were greeted by the waving of handkerchiefs, and the people seemed glad to see us." While elites argued down the small but resolute opponents of secession at the secession convention, zealous elements of the common white population of Louisiana practiced their own coercive support for secession. But these measures would never have been necessary, as the waving white flags symbolized, if notable pockets of Unionism and cooperation had not rendered Louisiana a divided terrain in the 1860s. The contest for a loyal Confederate Louisiana took place in local households as much as through the public policy of the state government. Both institutions waged the Confederate war in Louisiana.[54]

Creating Confederate Louisiana was a contingent process largely based on reciprocal material and ideological relationships between state authority and local communities. As Confederate Louisianans built an interlocking matrix of state and local powers that relied on militarized force to coerce the body politic, they created the first military occupation of the state. Disunion was a political act on paper, but it was social work in action. Ministers preached loyalty in the pulpit, vigilance committees policed it in the streets, politicians mandated it from the legislature, people practiced it in steady crusades of material support. Those who opposed faced a political reality in Confederate Louisiana in which their national allegiance to the United States was no longer valued and in fact openly targeted. The rhetoric of loyalty framed these scenes of citizenship, and it was this mutual emphasis from the people and the state that compelled adherence to the Confederate social order. Yet when Union forces set boots on the ground in May 1862, they were commanded by a man who believed it was his duty to challenge not just the Confederate military, but also the very social order that undergirded secession and rebellion.

2

Disorder and Dominion

BENJAMIN BUTLER & HIS WAR OF OCCUPATION

During the Civil War, President Abraham Lincoln and the Union high command faced strategic decisions over how to conduct the war that were inseparable from the more problematic questions of political reconstruction. From the early days of the war, northern public opinion generated a bewildering array of reactions to secession that measured from peaceful reconciliation to vengeful belligerency. If all northerners of various political convictions could have possibly agreed on a central wartime tenet, it was that powerful southern slave aristocrats led the rebellion and therefore deserved the most acute punishment. On the subjects of emancipation, recruitment of Black soldiers, and a biracial free labor system, most northerners were more circumspect. But as the war went on, Union war policy became more aggressive. With the First Confiscation Act (August 5, 1861), Congress earmarked southern property that was used to support the Confederate war effort, including enslaved people, but within less than a year the Second Confiscation Act (July 17, 1862) targeted all southern property and later formed the legal basis for the Emancipation Proclamation. These laws, as many northerners complained, were more assertive on paper than in action. Convinced that the Confederacy's defeat would require harsher policy, Union commanders like John Pope, Ulysses Grant, and William T. Sherman adopted hard war strategies on the battlefield and in occupied territory, such as burning property, confiscating supplies, and liberating enslaved workers. As these political debates and battlefield decisions played out in the war years, Lincoln, military commanders, and northern political figures experimented with new visions of democracy and national order in sites of Union occupation. More than any other state policy, direct military rule empowered the Lincoln administration and its occupation commanders to make decisions about how to reshape the South.[1]

Though he did not possess the same national influence that a commander like Grant did, and in spite of the fact that his legacy is often overshadowed by southern animosity or suspicions of corruption, General Benjamin F. Butler played a crucial role in developing Union occupation strategy. Butler's most effective occupation policy decisions were those that targeted the southern household, and Butler's war of occupation in the Department of the Gulf can best be understood in domestic terms. With his controversial Woman's Order, he targeted women as legitimate combatants much earlier than his hard war colleagues did. When he executed William Mumford, he directly assaulted southern patriarchy and demonstrated that loyalty would be the primary identifier for renewed national citizenship. Butler disrupted southern class structure by taxing, arresting, or otherwise debasing wealthy southern house-holds and aiding poor whites. And though he was hesitant to incorporate Black Americans into his vision of a reconstituted southern domestic order premised on loyalty, his eventual transformation mirrored the changing racial attitudes of the North as well. Historians must transcend the traditional discourse de-scribing Butler either as a corrupt, distasteful political general or as a practi-cally successful but otherwise unremarkable commander, and instead see him as part of the grander narratives of occupation and national reshaping that oc-curred during the Civil War. In contrast to the often-blinkered historical per-ception of him, Butler as occupation commander accelerated Union hard war policy at a time when it remained just one policy in a constellation of possible responses to secession and he can be viewed as an avatar of changing national perspectives on race.[2]

Both in his lifetime and since his death in 1893, clouds of antagonism of-ten surrounded "Beast" Butler due to supposedly self-serving confiscations of southern property, mysterious financial dealings, nepotism toward his brother Andrew, and unlawful treatment of southern people—yet modern scholarly appraisals of the general have often bordered on heroic celebration. In the ear-liest scholarly biography of the general, Richard Holzman wrote, "Ben Butler had the attributes that should have made him one of the great American heroes of all time." Hans Trefousse believed Butler "contributed to the final victory" of the Union cause, and though "slightly tarnished perhaps . . . productive of good nonetheless." Richard West depicted Butler as an "independent idealist."

According to West, wealthy opponents castigated Butler for his progressive and populist stances as much as Confederate belligerents maligned his wartime policy. Howard P. Nash confessed that "my study of General Butler's life has led me to like him," and favorably compared him to William Jennings Bryan and Franklin D. Roosevelt. More recently, Dick Nolan and Chester G. Hearn present balanced perspectives of Butler's career, though Hearn suggestively points to Butler's extended record as a criminal defense lawyer to explain his perspicacious persona and cunning ability to avoid incriminating evidence. The most recent scholarly biography of Butler comes from Elizabeth Leonard, who also depicts him as a progressive figure, genuinely dedicated to "the kind of social and cultural transformation so many Americans still seek today."[3]

None of these historians significantly link Butler's war policies as an occupation commander to his ideas about what a properly restored southern household should look like. Several factors have most likely contributed to this perception. Arguably, his contraband policy at Fort Monroe and the international consternation that arose from the Woman's Order overshadowed Butler's long-term contributions to Union occupation policy. Likewise, northern commanders like Grant, Sherman, Sheridan, and Pope continue to be the primary representatives of Union hard war edicts. But viewed from a domestic lens rather than a battlefield perspective, Butler deserves a position among the constellation of hard war advocates who executed such policies early and often.

Butler illustrated his hard war policies on southern households in occupied Louisiana soon after taking command of the Department of the Gulf on February 23, 1862. The War Department had created the command only a month earlier, and its boundaries encompassed the coast of the Gulf of Mexico from Pensacola harbor to as much of the Gulf States as Butler could possibly occupy. While Union forces collected for an invasion, Confederate state and military commanders failed to secure a firm military perimeter on the southern coast of Louisiana. Subsequently, in April 1862, the Union's West Gulf Blockading Squadron under Flag Officer David Farragut and Commander David D. Porter spearheaded the seizure of southern Louisiana and New Orleans with relative ease. As commander of the occupied city and the surrounding areas, Butler concentrated on domestic operations over military campaigns. He confiscated property, issued edicts, cleaned the city, contended with local southerners, and feuded with foreign consuls, but Butler dispatched few of his regiments further westward. In the occupied city, Butler faced opposition from the local population, especially Confederate women, though he hardly ever resorted to violence to maintain order. Instead, he relied on a series of general orders intended to quell malcontents and restore commerce to the region.[4]

While Butler's (in)famous domestic policies demonstrated the initial radical phases of Union hard war strategy, his perspectives on slavery, emancipation, and Black recruitment in Louisiana signaled a more conservative approach still largely characteristic of the northern public and the Union war effort in the first years of the war. Waves of enslaved people poured into Union ranks in southern Louisiana, quickly straining Union supplies. In response, Butler backpedaled on the policy he had issued at Fort Monroe, Virginia, in August 1861, in which he held enslaved property as "contraband of war." He required runaways to work on Union defenses in the Department of the Gulf, resisted the creation of a free labor system for months, and even returned some laborers to white masters in Louisiana in the early weeks of his occupation tenure. By the time he was replaced by Nathaniel Banks in December 1862 and stood before the Joint Committee on the Conduct of War, Butler was quite vocal about his support of Black troops in the Union army. This transition in his perspective was a result of his command in Louisiana and a notable example of how the process of occupation altered war policy for North and South.[5]

To understand Butler's significance as a commander in occupied Louisiana, it is first necessary to locate him in the framework of the Union war prior to the moment he set foot in New Orleans in May 1862. From the beginning of the war, conservatives, moderates, and radicals in the North debated how to wage the war. From the perspective of many northerners including Lincoln himself, secession not only violated the Constitution but ushered in physical confiscation and occupation of federal properties in the South such as forts, arsenals, custom houses, and post offices. Northern public opinion helped fuel a litany of proposed punitive bills from Republican Congressmen in the Thirty-seventh Congress in 1861–62. Yet vengeful northerners who targeted southern property did not necessarily believe in emancipation. A belligerent Union man could believe that southerners had forfeited many of their property rights—which was an extreme viewpoint that grew in the North as the war continued—but remain moderate or conservative in his opinions on slavery.[6]

Benjamin Butler was such a belligerent moderate. He was adamantly antisecession, even suggesting to President James Buchanan that South Carolina secession commissioners be tried for treason before the Supreme Court in 1861. Missing no opportunity for self-promotion, he volunteered himself as prosecutor. Butler was perhaps even more eager than Republican governor John A. Andrew to rush Massachusetts militia troops to the defense of the Union. In his legal and political career prior to the secession crisis, he displayed remarkable flexibility. Initially, he was a Barnburner Democrat who associated with labor unions, campaigned for a ten-hour workday for mill workers, and battled elitist Whigs. Yet he acknowledged that the Constitution left slavery under the domain of individual states. As a delegate to the Democratic convention in Charleston, South Carolina, in 1860, he had largely neglected Stephen Douglas and voted fifty-seven times for Jefferson Davis. He then ran for governor of Massachusetts as a Breckinridge Democrat. Nevertheless, by the time he arrived in the Confederacy as an occupation commander, Butler approached occupation with the classic disposition of a political moderate: federal protection for southern Unionists, reduction of Confederate resistance through confiscation (but not destruction) of property, and limited interference with the institution of slavery without the promise of emancipation or compromising the underlying fundamental concept of white supremacy.[7]

As a Union commander, Butler practiced reconciliation, but it was a hard reconciliation.[8] He occupied Baltimore without permission, enforced federal law, and even threatened to execute the prominent secessionist Ross Winans. His run-ins with Confederate-sympathizing women in the city prefigured his policies toward women in New Orleans. His actions violated the mostly conservative early war policies of the federal government and angered Winfield Scott to the point that Butler was removed to a new command at Fort Monroe. Lincoln took the opportunity to implicitly affirm Butler's aggressive tactics by promoting him to major general, a maneuver also aimed to win the administration a close Democratic ally in Butler. In late 1861 and early 1862, while Congress debated who had authority over the conduct of the war, Butler anticipated the expanded war powers espoused by theorists like William Whiting and Francis Lieber. Installed in the fort in late May, Butler introduced his contraband policy, which deprived the enemy of property in Black labor without pursuing emancipation. Although Radical Republicans and abolitionists, as well as later generations of historians, looked to Butler's policy as a welcome antislavery intervention into federal war policy, Butler himself did not use the term "contraband" in his probing letters to the Lincoln administration. A notable defeat at the Battle of Big Bethel on June 10, 1861, blemished Butler's reputation, but the general soon orchestrated a renewal of public veneration by claiming victory in another occupation venture. In August, he coordinated with naval forces to capture Fort Clark and Fort Hatteras on the North Carolina coast, giving the Union a much-needed victory after the Union loss at Bull Run in July and once more elevating his status in the eyes of the Union high command.[9]

When viewed in context with his previous operations, Butler's occupation of the Department of the Gulf appears as a continuation of his hard war tactics, not as an inhumane aberration of international law that Confederates, and even some northerners or foreign observers, reproached. While Butler arrested people, confiscated Confederate property, and made bold declarations of power in Louisiana, he still offered simultaneous claims to moderate or conservative policies. He respected the private property of those who produced no trouble for the occupation force, punished Union troops who acted out, supported Unionist southerners, and claimed that non-Unionist southerners responded with enthusiasm to his policies. "The general's basic strategy," argues Peyton McCrary, "was to assert federal power vigorously, but then reassure the local population that their cooperation would be rewarded with moderate policies." This mixed approach alarmed conservatives like George McClellan but won Butler favor in Radical Republican ranks.[10]

Despite favor from those who endorsed hard war tactics and emancipation as a war measure, Butler was largely moderate or conservative on antislavery polices before the end of his time as occupation commander in Louisiana. Although he displayed no overt proslavery sympathies, he hardly articulated any firm antislavery viewpoint. Some historians assert that Butler's contraband order was the perfect moderate response to slavery, for it straddled the line between retribution against southern property and outright emancipation. He typified a northerner who opposed the aggrandizement of slave power but held prejudicial views toward people of color. He demonstrated his conservative antislavery feelings by declaring that he would use military force to suppress any slave insurrection in occupied Annapolis—which he claimed to do in order to protect women and children. He also openly discussed his fears of arming Black men in Louisiana and initially resisted the implementation of a free labor system on Louisiana's plantations. When he did create a free labor system, he maintained the racial status quo by requiring that Black workers continue to work under white property owners. In effect, Butler sometimes did more to substantiate the antebellum racial order than to undermine it. Yet before the end of his tenure in the Department of the Gulf, Butler relented and began arming and training a few regiments of Black men. He also issued General Order No. 91, which established a rudimentary wage system for formerly enslaved laborers in the Lafourche District.[11]

Ultimately, it was not Butler's hard war occupation policies that led to his replacement in Louisiana, but rather his ego, his supposed self-enrichment in Louisiana, and, most of all, his confrontation with foreign consuls in New Orleans. Butler left conflicting legacies. As a representative of military power, Butler spearheaded a more resolute occupation policy toward white southerners, but he failed to embrace profound alterations to the racial structure of American democracy. Through his exercise of occupation power, Butler consequently transmitted a vision of democracy that enhanced federal power at the expense of the southern household without a concomitant expansion of biracial democracy. Regardless of his checkered character and evolving racial perspective, his potency as a figurehead for Union policy remains unquestioned. An examination of Butler's most notable policies in occupied Louisiana reveals his concentration on the domestic home front, beginning with expectations of loyalty.[12]

In late April 1862, Union naval forces crashed through Confederate defenses at the mouth of the Mississippi River, Fort Jackson and Fort St. Philip. As Union ships taxied up the Mississippi River toward New Orleans, the levees blazed with burning cotton and other property. The streets erupted into chaos and residents streamed from the city in a downpour of rain. At 2 p.m. on April 25, Union Captain Theodorus Bailey and Lieutenant George Perkins labored through a boisterous mob to reach City Hall. Angry New Orleans men and women beat on the doors and windows while Mayor John Monroe deliberated the surrender of the city. The two officers demanded that the flag of the United States be raised over the post office, the custom house, and the U.S. Mint—all federal government structures. At this early date in the war, these officers were prepared to demand only surrender of federal property. Not until Butler arrived did the Union army begin to target domestic property under the general's direction. Monroe deferred surrender to Mansfield Lovell, who also claimed he had no authority to surrender the city. Fearful of the raging mob, prominent New Orleans politician Pierre Soule conferred with the crowd on the steps of City Hall while the two Union officers slipped through a side door and back to Flag Officer Farragut.[13]

As Monroe continued to delay, Farragut dispatched two more emissaries, protected by a guard of twenty marines, to demand surrender. Meanwhile, a squadron of Union marines hoisted the U.S. flag above the mint. This action heightened antagonism. Confederates poured through the city and down to the riverfront with banners and songs while several men, led by a local man named William B. Mumford, tore down the U.S. flag over the mint and rent it to pieces. While the Confederates vacillated for two more days, Farragut busied himself with reducing Confederate defenses at Carrolton and capturing a few ships. On April 28, Farragut threatened to bombard the city into submission, giving women and children forty-eight hours to pack and evacuate. With that ultimatum, Farragut transformed the surrender of the city into a domestic war operation. As Butler traveled up the river toward New Orleans, he wrote to Edwin Stanton, "I find the city under the dominion of the mob." Fresh from Union victory over Forts Jackson and St. Philip, Butler perhaps did not expect that most of his military strategy in Louisiana would be oriented around restoration of social order rather than combat plans but his statement about dominion preceded a prolonged battle for authority in the state. Impatient for the arrival of Butler, Farragut sent 250 marines and two howitzers ashore on April 29, where they lowered Confederate banners over the custom house, the mint, and the post office and replaced them with U.S. flags. They also lowered the state flag over city hall, but as that building was not federal property, they left the flagstaff empty.[14]

When the main bulk of Union forces under Butler arrived in New Orleans on the evening of May 1, a boisterous crowd thronged the wharf, hurrahing for Jefferson Davis, throwing rocks, and threatening to kill anyone who approached. A company of the 31st Massachusetts pushed back the crowd at bayonet point as they disembarked. "We were insulted and called all kinds of names by the filthy mob," one Union soldier wrote. When Butler himself set foot on the shore, the crowd renewed its vigor, hurling verbal insults at the general and his troops. Through this torrent, Butler made his way to the custom house, a large granite federal building that served as a symbol of Union authority and would also function well as a fortification if needed. That night he returned to his ship and prepared a proclamation to the city, known as the Civil Code, which appeared as a handbill the following day. Butler and his wife, Sarah, established Union headquarters in the Saint Charles Hotel on May 2. When the *True Delta* refused to print Butler's code, the general had Union troops seize the paper's printing apparatus.[15]

In Butler's proclamation he claimed that "the armies of the United States came here not to destroy, but to restore order out of chaos, to uphold the government and the laws in the place of the passions of men." Already Butler was calling for social order to rest on national allegiance. The Code also proclaimed martial law, required the surrender of all arms, demanded all flags other than that of the United States be taken down, called for oaths of allegiance, prescribed licenses for alcohol purveyors, established military courts for crimes against Union authority, suppressed the Confederate press, and forbade public assembly in the streets. Graciously, he allowed the circulation of Confederate money until the local economy could be stabilized once more (a practice he discontinued on May 27). He allowed civil courts to remain open in order to handle minor disputes and did not close public businesses or churches. The civil order that Butler restored looked much like the city always had, only specifically geared toward Union sentiment. He invited "the efforts of all well-disposed . . . to have every species of disorder quelled." Butler would immediately confront such disorder in the city and prescribe Union correctives, beginning with the arrest of William Mumford and other disloyal men.[16]

Butler's regime was part of a larger realignment of white male authority in the household during the Civil War. During the first several weeks of his command, Butler signaled to white southern men under occupation that loyalty to the Union was paramount. Part of this perspective was ideological—secessionists had violated the Union and must demonstrate their dedication to it once more. Another part was practical—occupation commanders such as Butler needed a shorthand, such as loyalty oaths, to make administration of occupation territory more manageable. Butler's war for Union privileged white manhood but reclassified masculine honor and identity as a function of nationalist allegiance, not local community loyalty or an individualistic gambit for status. As the Reconstruction years would prove, Union occupation in the Civil War did not entirely erase regional identity and white violence, but it did sanction a political system in which southern states and individuals could maintain many of their racial values as long as they met certain criteria for national allegiance.

Within the first several weeks of occupation, Butler arrested numerous men for disloyal acts. Although Mumford was not executed for the crime of treason and "an overt act thereof" until June 7, Butler had him arrested soon after his arrival. On May 8, he arrested one man for hurrahing for Jefferson Davis and sentenced him to three months of hard labor at Fort Jackson. Charles H. Lee was placed in custody for insulting Union troops and sentenced to sixty days' imprisonment on Ship Island. In Baton Rouge, Stephen Roberts was convicted for the attempted murder of a Union officer. Two New Orleans storeowners, John W. Andrews and Fidel Keller, were arrested for publicly displaying skeletons that they claimed were the remains of Union soldiers. Both were given two years of solitary confinement on Ship Island.[17]

Butler's most dramatic reinforcement of Union authority was the execution of Mumford, who was the only culprit involved in the removal of the U.S. flag from the mint foolish or unlucky enough to have his name published in the papers. Mumford claimed that others had torn up the flag, but Butler was convinced of his guilt or determined to make an example of Mumford. The general received around fifty anonymous threatening letters, which only strengthened his resolve to prove his command over the city. Although many southerners castigated Butler for the decision, Mumford's death came after Butler made a last-minute decision to stay execution orders for six other political prisoners, members of the "Monroe Guard" who had contemplated breaking out of the city and joining Confederate forces further north in Louisiana. Butler demonstrated leniency in pardoning the six Monroe Guards, whose offense was a military matter, but applied restrained harshness to Mumford, whose individual act represented a much profounder treason. When Butler made a precision strike at rebellious Confederates in New Orleans, he chose Mumford, a regular man whose nonmilitary identity stood in place, however liminal, of the treasonous southern household patriarch.[18]

In an example of the domestic war that Butler found himself waging, Mary Mumford and her children appeared with tears streaming down their faces as they begged the general for the life of their husband and father. Tears were a small but nevertheless potent weapon on the domestic battlefront, but Butler resisted—an outcome perhaps just as symbolic of Union authority as Mumford's public death. By the time Mumford's body swung from the gallows in front of the mint, Butler had elevated his decision from a punishunishent of a crime to a judicious exercise of power. If the pressure for Mumford's clemency had persuaded Butler to back down, he would have undermined his own authority. If he had switched Mumford for another citizen, as at least one southerner suggested, or executed the six Monroe Guards as well, he feared risking a spectacle not unlike the Reign of Terror in Revolutionary France, where state sovereignty rested upon the bodies of the executed. For Butler, Mumford's death was a tactical decision as much as a moral one. Butler validated his own command and reinforced respect for the Union. He also preserved the image of the northern effort to subjugate treason as a righteous orderly crusade, not a bloodthirsty regime change. This was a battle that he won as much in the Mumford household as he did in the courtyard of the mint. Even if angry southerners embellished his beastly nature, Butler followed a careful logic of order and authority that reflected his own policy of aggressive moderation.[19]

The Mumford incident served as a vessel for conversations about honorable behavior and loyalty in wartime. When he violated a sacred symbol of Union, many northerners believed, Mumford demonstrated his treason and justified Butler's hostile response. "No good man petitioned for his release," Butler moralized, "but the bad men, the blacklegs and blackguards, assembled in large numbers and voted that he should not be executed." Conversely, Mumford claimed that "he was impelled by the highest patriotism." Mumford was a symbol of martyrdom to Confederates and many viewed his death as part of a larger assault on southern honor and property. Together, Butler and Mumford were part of a national dialogue about heroic and villainous behavior during the war, which was largely manufactured by press media in the months following Mumford's execution. Using the language of honor and loyalty, this dialogue produced a popular conception of treason at a time when the federal government's prosecution of the war wavered between conciliatory and hard war measures. Numerous northern newspapers defended Butler's actions as necessary to reassert federal authority and enforce national allegiance. As a *New York Herald* commentary declared, Butler had more resolve to execute the war than the government.[20]

These dialogues about the proper role of honor under occupation, as well as whatever behavior that honorable resistance might produce, stemmed from and often occurred within the arena of occupation itself. Occupation precipitated conversations about national and personal honor, about what was and was not proper conduct in wartime. Butler understood the national conversation about loyalty, honor, and behavior that the war had generated by the summer of 1862, and he understood his occupation policy was a public commentary on that conversation. "I called upon every soldier of this army to treat the women of New Orleans as gentlemen should deal with the sex," Butler claimed. Taken as a whole—his condemnation of disrespectful rebel women, his hanging of a disorderly traitor and household head who attacked a national symbol, and most egregiously his confiscation of southern property—Butler's occupation policy constituted an attack on Confederate domestic order. In the instance of Mumford's execution, Butler killed a family man and household head, symbolically assaulting the southern household itself. It did not take long for Confederates, and even some foreign observers, to associate Butler's verified actions with unverified accusations of sexual assault—the most egregious attack on southern homes imaginable.[21]

Butler and Confederate America also waged an ongoing propaganda war over Mumford's death and his widowed family. Outraged southerners declared that Butler was a bloodthirsty tyrant whose "savage instincts" were hardly rivaled by supposedly uncivilized Native Americans. Governor Moore venerated Mumford's martyrdom and declared Mary Mumford and her children to be a public trust, enveloping southern dependents into the protective bosom of the Confederate state. With Mumford unable to care for his own household, the state would take up his responsibilities. However, Butler himself would ironically serve more in that capacity than cheap Confederate scrip. Butler helped the widow pay off a lien on her house in 1869. He also secured a job for her in the internal revenue office, then in the post office. Years after the war, Butler was aiding a household he had been instrumental in dismantling.[22]

Despite bitter public outcries over Mumford's execution and other policies from Butler, the seizure and occupation of New Orleans did not prove to be a bloodthirsty crusade against Confederates, nor was occupation a military disaster for the Union war effort. If Jefferson Davis and other prominent Confederates had strengthened southern defenses along the coast and especially the forts guarding the river—as Lovell and other Louisiana Confederates beseeched—the Union attack fleet might have been completely or partially destroyed, injuring the northern naval blockade. Butler was also a largely incompetent field commander, who arrived with fifteen thousand untested troops in a humid climate surrounded by a hostile population. If southern citizens had exercised unrestrained violence against Union troops from the moment of their arrival, or if enslaved people had taken up arms in a vengeful crusade against white oppressors, then Union occupiers would have adopted an aggressive response or perished. Mumford's execution could have been one of many under Butler's command if he had chosen to send a more severe message about national traitors. Instead of conspicuous displays of violent defiance, Louisiana residents choose verbal antagonism and modest public actions of Confederate support rooted in their local households. Unquestioned Union military sovereignty in New Orleans produced a relatively stable domestic occupation from the spring of 1862 until war's end.[23]

In addition to male loyalty, Butler also arrived in New Orleans with very specific ideas about women and civility that informed his domestic occupation war. He believed men and women were supposed to behave in certain ways that not only reflected personal character but that of Union allegiance as well. Within days of Union arrival, Confederate women took up resistance where formal Confederate military defenses had failed. So many New Orleans women avoided walking under the Union flag, displayed Confederate symbols, verbally assaulted Union soldiers, and even spat at Union officers, that Butler decided to take action. In response to repeated venomous attacks from Confederate "she-adders," Butler issued his now notorious General Order No. 28 on May 15, 1862: "As the officers and soldiers of the United States have been subject to repeated insults from the women (calling themselves ladies) of New Orleans in return for the most scrupulous non-inference and courtesy on our part, it is ordered that hereafter when any female shall by word, gesture, or movement insult or show contempt for any officer or soldier of the United States she shall be regarded and held liable to be treated as a woman of the town plying her avocation." Decorum, it seemed, was also a weapon of war. The men under his command had behaved appropriately, he contended, so now it was time for southern women to verify their status as ladies or bawdy prostitutes based on their behavior.[24]

As with Mumford's execution, supporters and opponents of Order No. 28 implemented language of virtue and respectable behavior. Sarah Butler supported her husband, declaring to a friend, "This *city will be governed,* and made to wear the *outward* forms of *decency,* however much they struggle against it."

When Mayor Monroe protested the order as an attack on "the honor of the virtuous women of the City," the general retorted that virtuous women would never demean his troops, so the order did not affect them. In response to rebellious women, Butler issued an order that balanced the competing federal war policies. His threat to treat uncooperative women like prostitutes—by jailing them—reflected Butler's own penchant for hard war tactics, yet his emphasis on respect in exchange for good behavior reflected the conciliatory methods of more conservative supporters. The order also employed the gendered domestic ideals of northern society. Butler's occupation war was a household war.[25]

However, despite the enormous protests of the Confederacy, the infamous Woman's Order, as it came to be known, did not indicate that Butler inherently devalued women. On the contrary, as Jacqueline Campbell writes, Butler had many strong women in his life that he admired. Butler's order, Stephanie Mc-Curry argues, was a part of a series of efforts on the part of Union generals to control the troublesome Confederate women under their authority. Despite all of its flash in the press, Butler's order indicated "the new accountability imposed on Confederate women by enemy soldiers: a new estimation of the value of women's loyalty and of their political salience." Men and women in the Civil War, occupiers and occupied, understood that women who demonstrated obstreperous behavior against Union occupation also undermined traditional assumptions about women's moral character. In New Orleans, Butler and his men faced verbally abusive women who cursed and spat at Union troops and even poured soiled water on their heads. For Butler, their presence was a challenge to his authority as an occupation commander, and the authority of the Union to restore order in the South as it envisioned. When they resisted, Confederate women presented a military threat to Union order that they grounded in the southern household.[26]

The order was explicitly about women as domestic combatants, one that played on cultural assumptions about sexual propriety and social status, but implicitly the order also became about gendered spaces and the power of the state. Butler hoped his order would encourage the Confederate community of New Orleans to self-police, an avenue of social order that other Union commanders like John Pope had pursued. Seen in context with early war policies—which sought social discipline with minimal physical abuse—the Woman's Order was less an egregious affront to womanhood than a savvy command that targeted the weak gender and class joints of the Confederate social body. In order for Confederate women to continue resistance, they had to potentially abandon one of the foundational attributes of their southern identity—class respectability.[27]

From street to statehouse, outraged Confederates excoriated Butler's order for expanding regular military warfare into the southern household and issuing, as many erroneously saw it, a license to rape. Monroe decried the Woman's Order as "a war upon women and children, whose only offense had been to show displeasure at the occupation of an enemy." Such outrage as he believed the order kindled was "a reproach to the civilization not to say Christianity of the age in whose name I make this protest." For his insolence, Butler had the mayor removed to Fort Jackson, placing Colonel George F. Shepley at the head of a military municipal government. From a southern perspective, Union men were not just dishonorable combatants who violated the laws of war but were also inhuman brutes. Confederate General P. G. T. Beauregard, whose home and wife were under Union rule in Louisiana, excoriated Order No. 28 as an attack on southern households and southern women. In June, Beauregard read the order to his army stationed in Corinth, Mississippi, and described Yankees as "violators of our family ties." Despite the hyperbole of Confederate leadership, their rhetoric did follow a careful line of logic rooted in the household war—honorable and effective warfare could proceed from domestic combatants and any sexualized assault on southern white women was an immoral counterattack on their honorable resistance.[28]

National and international responses to the Woman's Order also targeted the integrity of northern masculinity, revealing that an order supposedly about women also had much to say about men. Some pro-Confederate politicians in England essentially declared that the United States was not a civilized nation because of Butler's intolerable treatment of women. "An Englishman must blush to think that such an act has been committed by one belonging to the Anglo-Saxon race," Lord Palmerston exclaimed. Butler was barbaric, another British politician proclaimed. These declarations were explicitly gendered assaults on the character of northern men. The fallout about the order and its consequences reflected a larger debate about what kind of warfare was appropriate. Physically, Confederate women shifted their battleground from the streets to the household itself, but on a larger scene, Butler and company faced a new host of enemies.[29]

While many debated the morality and implications of Order No. 28, few probably linked the order to the more substantial results that Butler's edict produced for Union occupation in Louisiana. Within a month of his infamous order, the military government under Butler and Shepley had reorganized the city's Confederate schools with new pro-Union personnel and textbooks, placed Colonel Jonas M. French over the municipal police force, which was now filled with Unionist men, and established a large public works project employing two thousand men to clean the streets and drain ditches. The city paid each man fifty cents a day, while Butler distributed daily rations to them. Married men gained preference in the hiring process because Butler reasoned he could support more of the city's dependent population that way. Butler also established a tight quarantine of the city to prevent the spread of yellow fever. Meanwhile, no reported rapes or assaults resulted from the Woman's Order. While it would most likely be unreasonable to assume that Butler intended the Woman's Order to bloom into a wider array of social policies, it is conspicuous that an order controlling the militant behavior of white southern women precipitated the creation of a military government in Louisiana. Shocked by the order's supposed sexual threat to southern women, political men like Monroe refused to abdicate their patriarchal position as defenders of women's safety and virtue. With their removal, the order unintentionally produced other edicts about reorganizing the southern social order in Louisiana. Butler used his foremost piece of occupation policy as a platform to execute a domestic war.[30]

While Confederates across the South raged about the order's threat to white women, Benjamin Palmer decried Butler's domestic policies as part of a larger system of northern tyranny and declared that, despite its informal name, the true target of the Woman's Order was southern men. The edict was "part of a premeditated system to strike universal terror into the heart of the community," Palmer reasoned. He interpreted Order No. 28 as an assault on southern households because "the blow was threatened just where the affections were most sensitive; and the violation of the sweetest sanctities of home was set forth as the penalty of resistance to the tyrant's will." The Woman's Order attacked the home, Palmer alleged, and "though directed in form against the women of Louisiana, its evident design was to reach through them their intractable guardians of the other sex. The husband and the father were called to look upon their imprisoned households, and then to survey the hounds of the despot by whom they were held at bay." Palmer suggested that New Orleans's in-

habitants feared the familiar and entirely untrue accusation that northern soldiers barely restrained their sexual lusts in the occupied city. "Doubtless these
fears were, to a large extent imaginary; for they were never realized by those
who openly defied the tyrant's power, who seemed rather to amuse himself
with playing upon the fears of and with imposing tests of their moral courage,
and with mocking those who faltered and trembled under his frown." From
Palmer's perspective, the Woman's Order was not just about one commander's
disregard for the sanctity of southern women's bodies, but also a northern cultural assault on the southern household that arranged those female bodies under the authority of men. The Woman's Order and Butler's occupation regime
undermined the capacity of southern men to defend their homes and families.
Consequently, Palmer accused, Butler's tyranny undermined southern moral
courage. He constructed that logic on gendered terms that centered men, not
women, at the heart of the war's political and cultural crisis.[31]

Measuring the success of the order depends on perspective. Based on his
own appraisal of gender conventions, Butler claimed that the order enforced
itself because no southern white woman wanted to socially disgrace herself.
But the domestic battlefront actually continued to evolve under his command.
The order may have curtailed some public resistance from Confederate women
in New Orleans, but it certainly did not prevent all crinoline rebels from taking to the street. More importantly, Confederate women simply weaponized
their households by singing Confederate songs, producing war materials, and
taunting Union men within earshot. Eugenia Levy Philips was carted off to
Ship Island for laughing at a Union funeral procession from her balcony. Far
from being entirely subdued, southern women continued informal resistance
through resilient systems of supply, sabotage, and mail.[32]

Perhaps Butler recognized the wide spatial context of household war when
he issued General Order No. 76 in September 1862. This order required, among
other demands, all southerners, including women, to take an oath of allegiance
or be qualified as an enemy of the state, which expanded the requirements of
his earlier General Order No. 41 (issued in June), requiring all military, civil,
judicial, executive, and legislative state officials to take the oath of allegiance
if they wanted to remain in office. Both of these orders, reviled by southern
women especially, were not so much attacks on womanhood itself as they were
a gendered reorganization of public order in occupied Louisiana. Butler knew
that most of the occupied population was female, so his orders indicated a

military response based on that understanding. First, the Woman's Order announced the moral gaze of the state upon women's rebellious activity. Next, having categorized their behavior as disorderly, Butler effectively expanded the body politic to women with Order No. 76. By requiring women to take an oath of loyalty, they and not their men became formally responsible for their own bodies, property, and public behavior. Under Butler's hand, as in other locations across the wartime South, occupation hammered out a larger body politic by reconfiguring the gender values of the antebellum era.[33]

In addition to challenging the gendered southern social order, Butler also targeted class relations in Louisiana. His plan was twofold. First, he sought to dismantle the authority of Confederate culture in Louisiana and replace it with Union allegiance by assailing the wealthy class of Confederates that he believed to be the primary impetus for secession. Soon after taking New Orleans, for instance, Butler ordered the graves of Confederate generals Albert Sydney Johnston and Daniel E. Twiggs opened and searched for silver. Horrified Confederates declared that Butler was defiling even the dead to enrich himself. Perhaps Butler was padding his pockets with graveyard silver or perhaps he was devaluing sacred Confederate sites as a public message about the consequences of treason. Second, Butler hoped to win over common southerners by fostering public displays of Union sentiment that would encourage Louisianans to return to the federal fold and by providing military aid to many poverty-stricken by war. He commanded all religious congregations and school classrooms to pray for Abraham Lincoln and the United States, replacing their regular prayers for Jefferson Davis and the Confederacy. Many refused. By the end of the year, Marianne Edwards, an Indiana-born wife of a northern ship captain who was living in New Orleans at the time, railed against Butler for imprisoning a pastor whose only offense was "spending all his money in keeping open [the] free market to supply the poor with something to eat." Butler, she added sarcastically, "wanted the pleasure of feeding the poor himself." The free market established by Confederate city authorities in New Orleans had indeed nearly collapsed after the turmoil that precipitated Union arrival. But Butler could hardly be personally blamed for this, especially given that Confederate authorities and zealous southerners burned up many crops before Union troops arrived.[34]

Butler used the humanitarian crisis in New Orleans as an opportunity to further undermine a Confederate social order premised on the political and social influence of southern elite. Despite Edwards's cynicism, Butler followed an explicit class analysis when he proclaimed on May 9 that he would issue confiscated beef and sugar to the "mechanics and working classes of this city." The leaders of the rebellion, he alleged, executed the war without regard for the material consequences of that conflict on "the starving poor, the working-man, his wife and child." By configuring household order into his class analysis, Butler revealed the domestic strategies that underpinned his vision of Union military occupation in Louisiana. Substantiate the working poor, he figured, and they would willingly unseat the slave aristocracy. While he sponsored the working class with one hand, he struck at the wealthy with the other. On August 4, Butler issued General Order No. 55, in which he assessed certain wealthy Confederates at 25 percent of their original contributions to the New Orleans defense fund. Butler considered this action "a question in justice" that should fall "upon those who have brought this great calamity upon their fellow citizens." The middle and working classes, Butler contended, never had a chance to voice their opposition to secession at the ballot box. "Those who have brought upon the city this stagnation of business, this desolation of the hearthstone, this starvation of the poor and helpless, should, as far as they may be able, relieve these distresses." Butler not only laid the blame for economic deterioration at the feet of wealthy Louisiana secessionists, but the ruination of the southern household in Louisiana as well. It was a language he hoped would resonate with the city's middle and working classes.[35]

Governor Moore repudiated the efforts of Butler as that of a typical avaricious Yankee capitalist. Honorable, chivalrous southerners should ignore Butler's divisive comments. Moore believed that the real contention in the proclamation, as historian Peyton McCrary argues, "was the preservation of the Southern social order." Class division as devised by Butler, the governor declared, would unleash servile war. According to Marianne Edwards, Butler had at least two other reasons for "break[ing] up that free market, so as to reduce the people to starving point." First, poor, hungry men were more likely to join the regiments that Butler attempted to recruit in the city. Once these units departed, it reduced both the dependent population and gave Butler credit for supplying more manpower for the Union war effort. Second, he wanted "an excuse for putting a tax on the rich people," with which proceeds he supposedly fed the poor of the city. Some historians suggest that Butler kept that taxation money for himself and instead used government stores intended for the army to feed the poor. Eventually, he would be forced to explain what became of many military stores and southern property to his superiors in Washington. Regardless of the personal consequences to himself, as an occupation commander Butler used class politics to attempt a realignment of the power dynamics of Louisiana's households.[36]

Butler also silenced much of the Confederate press and private communication in New Orleans in order to disorganize Confederate resistance. No publications or communications about Union movements or intended "to influence the public mind against the United States" were permitted. Articles, editorials, correspondence, and telegraphs about the Union army had to be examined by officers Butler appointed. Within a day of seizing the city, Butler suspended the *True Delta*, only to open the paper again when the owner apologized for not printing Butler's proclamation to the city. Two weeks later, a military commission shuttered a local paper called the *Algeria News Bay*, confiscated the printing property, and sentenced the editor A. B. Bacon to a year in prison at Fort Jackson unless he paid a $5,000 bond and signed an oath of allegiance, with which he did not comply. This followed Butler's shuttering of *Le Propagateur Catholique*, the *Bee*, the *Daily Crescent* and the *Daily Delta*, which he turned over to the army. In August, Butler suppressed another paper, *L'Estafette du Sud*, but allowed it to reopen a few days later. Without a rebellion press, Butler recalibrated the Confederate space of New Orleans into an environment where Union dictates had supremacy. Yet his censorship was not so stringent as to permanently close most presses. Butler's suppression of the press extended only to Confederate papers, indicating that Union occupation in Louisiana was not a wholesale attack on constitutional rights, but rather a targeted management of democratic values that privileged pro-Union speech at the expense of secessionist speech.[37]

Ultimately, Butler's hard reconciliation tactics and his unique flare for household war alarmed both Americans and Europeans. Butler generated tension for the Union High Command because of his supposed underhanded business deals in Louisiana and the considerable strife he caused with European nations. England, France, Spain, Holland, and other foreign states enjoyed profitable economic relations with the South, especially via the numerous foreign merchants living and conducting business in New Orleans. Butler not only disrupted trade relations, but he arrested foreign nationals who sympathized with the Confederacy or refused to follow occupation regulations. English and French politicians publicly questioned Butler's treatment of New

Orleans women, a critique that threatened to blemish northern manhood and national sovereignty in the international arena when the Lincoln administration could not afford more tension. Butler's contentions with European nations came a mere seven months after the Trent Affair, in which U.S. naval vessels halted the British Royal Mail steamer and forcibly removed two Confederate envoys to England. Even if Butler was an effective occupation commander who targeted southerners where they lived in an effort to end the war, he generated too many headaches for the Lincoln administration, one of which might have been his persistent letters seeking direction over the fate of slavery, Black free labor, and Black recruitment.[38]

Added to a long list of Confederate denunciations of occupation, many considered Union occupation a threat because of the numerous enslaved people that went free in southern Louisiana. In November 1862, Union General Godfrey Weitzel, engaged in the Lafourche region west of New Orleans in one of Butler's few offensive operations, complained about the quality of Black troops under his command and also expressed his fears of servile insurrection. Such insurrections would endanger the local population, Weitzel wrote Butler, and by extension, his own offensive lines. Should he remain in offensive operations, Weitzel warned, he would be unable to protect Louisiana citizens from insurrections should they arise.[39]

Butler disagreed. The disintegration of slavery was a result of the war, he claimed, and "I do not see how you can turn aside from the armed enemy before you to protect or defend the wives and children of these armed enemies from the consequences of their own rebellious wickedness." "The more terror-stricken the inhabitants are that are left in your rear," Butler reasoned, "the more safe will be your lines of communication." To prevent such terror, the fathers, brothers, and sons of the "terror-stricken women and children" must surrender and return home to defend their families, Butler declared. Butler claimed that Confederate General Braxton Bragg, recently defeated in Kentucky, was "at liberty to ravage the homes of our brethren of Kentucky because the Union Army of Louisiana are [sic] protecting his wife and his home against Negroes. Without that protection, he would have to come back to take care of his wife, his home, and his negroes."[40]

Union Advances in 1862

Bayou Lafourche Campaign
October–November

Approximate Union Occupied
Territory

While the last statement was a bit farfetched, Butler's letter to Weitzel outlined another piece of Butler's household war. In this exchange, the Union army remained critical to restoring a wayward southern society and the loyalty of restored southern men was crucial to defending their homes from servile insurrection. Yet, despite Butler's assurances that Black troops were able and sufficient for Weitzel to continue his offensive and that they "must be commanded by Officers . . . like any other Regiment," Butler's November letter left unquestioned the assumption that enslaved Black people might prove volatile. Butler's response, which imagined Confederate soldiers who surrendered would be "returned peaceably to their homes," did not mention the fate of enslaved people or speak about peaceful Black households guarded by Union forces.[41]

Ironically, given heated rhetoric about race and servile war from Confederates, Butler's policies concerning enslaved people in Louisiana did not initially demonstrate a profound sympathy for Black people. As Butler endeavored to reshape occupied Louisiana, Black people did not really figure into his vision of restored southern households. While he had no issue with suppressing Confederate property rights, he was also aware of Lincoln's response to John C. Fremont's decree in the Western Department in August 1861 as well as David Hunter's General Order No. 11 in May 1862 in South Carolina—decisions that followed Butler's own contraband policy and thus signaled definite limits to emancipation as military policy at that point in the war. Additionally, he could not have been ignorant of prevalent conservative attitudes in the North that bristled at any thought of emancipation. Despite early belligerent rhetoric toward secessionists, northerners also feared that radical military commanders, backed by a standing army, might subordinate civil matters to military control and subvert the republic. Emancipation, enacted by a commander of any political persuasion, might portend economic competition with Black people at best and servile war at worst, many northerners feared. Along with thousands of vengeful though racially conservative northerners, Butler embodied the racial perceptions of his time period, which he soon demonstrated in his ambivalent treatment of formerly enslaved Black people and Afro-Creoles in southern Louisiana. Butler's racial politics foreshadowed the Union military's failure to truly radicalize the demise of slavery. Though he regarded traitors with animosity and eventually softened his opposition to arming contrabands, Butler did not reward Black loyalty with full social inclusion. Though his perspectives on Black freedom and Black soldiers were changing near the end of his time as occupation commander—as his letter to Weitzel indicated—his occupation policies helped contribute to an unequal Reconstruction society because they did not include Black Americans as legitimate equals in the restored American household.[42]

Without the guiding light of federal policy, Butler faltered on the question of slavery in Louisiana when General John W. Phelps, an abolitionist commander from Vermont, set about emancipating and even recruiting formerly enslaved men around the Union defenses at Camp Parapet, west of New Orleans on the east bank of the Mississippi River. Unlike at Fort Monroe, Butler tried to send back some enslaved people to loyal slaveholders in Louisiana. "Is

it not best that a boy of thirteen who has not discretion enough one would suppose to know how to take care of himself be allowed to go back to his mistress,"
Butler wrote to Phelps about one runaway in July 1862. "He can hardly be called
a 'fugitive of labor.' The widow is a loyal woman has taken the oath of allegiance
and in my judgement should have back her servant." A week later, when a slaveholder demanded the return of several runaway laborers in Fort McComb,
Butler informed his subordinate at the fortification that "of course we cannot make them return but you may allow all to go back that are willing to."[43]

As Phelps and Butler continued to spar, the commander sought direction
from Secretary of War Edwin Stanton. Slaveholders in Louisiana were generally obedient to Union commands, he reported, meaning they were subject to
property protections that Butler had assured in his Civil Code. Furthermore,
Butler and Phelps struggled to feed the many freedpeople who moved within
their lines. Butler aptly recognized that Phelps intended to make his actions a
test of federal policy regarding slavery and freedpeople, which he encouraged
Stanton to elucidate. When Butler sought clarification from Washington, he
did not denigrate Phelps, but in a private letter to his wife in early August, he
declared that Phelps was "mad as a March Hare on the 'n—— question.'" Butler claimed that his respect for Phelps "will lead me to treat him very tenderly
but firmly," but his difference of opinion with the abolitionist subordinate was
clear. Because the Lincoln administration was not forthcoming with a specific
policy statement, Stanton instructed Butler to use his own discretion, while
avoiding "any serious embarrassment to the Government, or any difficulty with
General Phelps." Rather than pursue racial policies as assertive as his domestic
controls over gender decorum and social order in New Orleans, Butler instead
sought to contain "saucy and troublesome" freedpeople whom he feared to
arm. By mid-July, some seven hundred contrabands were within Phelps's lines,
a growing population for which the Union army had inadequate supplies and
organization. To solve this issue, Phelps began organizing Black men into five
military companies. "Society in the South seems to be on the point of dissolu-
tion, and the best way of preventing the African from becoming instruments in
a general state of anarchy is to enlist him in the cause of the Republic," Phelps
explained as he requested arms for his new recruits. When Butler would only
permit contrabands to clear land and build fortifications, Phelps balked at the
idea of becoming a "mere slave driver" and resigned his commission.[44]

Although Butler urged Phelps to reconsider, he still believed recruitment and armament of Black Americans would compromise Unionist sympathy in Louisiana, which remained his paramount concern. Union figureheads in Louisiana such as Reverdy Johnson and Thomas Durant agreed. But secretly, the Lincoln administration—in tandem with the Second Confiscation Act— desired emancipation and Black recruitment as war policies. In a July 31 letter, Salmon Chase hinted as much when he suggested that Butler emulate Andrew Jackson and summon Black recruits to the defense of New Orleans. With northern public opinion shifting in favor of more decisive strikes against the institution of slavery, "You can hardly go too far to satisfy the exigency of public sentiment now," Salmon wrote Butler. This encouragement from the Lincoln administration seemed to assuage Butler's anxieties about remaining in step with federal policy on the Black question. Meanwhile on the ground, repeated instances of Black violence from enslaved and contraband laborers may have convinced him that recruitment could serve as a tool to channel insurrection rather than instigate it. On August 4, some twenty-five to thirty plantation workers armed with cane knives and pistols marched up the levee in military fashion and engaged in a tremendous struggle with municipal police who confronted them. In the fighting, five runaways were wounded, one killed, and thirteen captured. Four police officers were also badly wounded. As occupation persisted, Black laborers continued to challenge those who claimed authority over them both inside and outside Union lines. Perhaps with this in mind, Butler wrote his wife on August 12 that he was leaning toward armament, which he also communicated to Stanton two days later.[45]

On August 22, even before he received reply from Stanton, Butler invited the Native Guard to enlist in his forces. Perhaps inspired by the martial performance of the runaways on August 4, he also organized two regiments of contrabands. Even the officers were Black or of mixed racial heritage. Assigned to Weitzel's Lafourche expedition in the fall of 1862, the 1st Louisiana (as the Native Guards were now known) was tasked with bringing order to a region rife with runaways, refugees, outlaws, and deserters. As Butler recognized in his November 6 letter, Weitzel despised having the troops under his command and claimed their presence frightened local white women and children and might even incite servile war. But Butler insisted that the Black troops remain.[46]

Butler's shift in his racial attitude from spring 1861 to fall 1862 followed the trajectory of Congressional Republicans' strengthening resolve during that time to destroy slavery. To undo slavery—which the Constitution protected as property rights—Republicans in the 37th Congress began to distinguish between the labor and the physical body of an enslaved person. In the first session in the summer of 1861, Congress had adopted the Holman Resolution, restricting the members to topics only immediately relevant to the war, but in the second session in the winter of 1861–summer 1862, Republicans passed twenty-six antislavery laws, including a prohibition on Union military figures returning enslaved people (April 13, 1862), emancipation in the District of Columbia (April 16), abolition in the territories (June 19), and military service for Black men (July 17). Yet antislavery laws did not translate into protections of Black freedom or civil liberties. In 1862, Republican antislavery measures were a legal revolution without a concomitant emphasis on a social revolution in racial equality. As an occupation commander in the first half of the war, Butler's hesitancy to dismantle slavery and endorse Black freedom reflected a general government that was still debating how the Union would fight the war and shape the war's consequences.[47]

While Butler eventually softened his opposition to Black recruitment because of the changing tides of northern opinion and subtle pressure from the Lincoln administration, he was still reluctant to provide room in his household war for Black Americans. Black troops remained under Union military supervision, where their more belligerent tendencies, as Butler and many other northern officers believed, could be curtailed. Building the Black household was another matter altogether. Not until November 1862 did Butler issue General Order No. 91, which sequestered all property in the newly conquered Lafourche region and appointed a three-man Sequestration Committee to make a detailed review of loyal and disloyal property owners. Movable property belonging to disloyal property owners was to be transported to New Orleans and sold at auction. Some of this money supposedly disappeared into Butler's pockets. The committee was also authorized to establish a free labor system on the plantations of loyal and disloyal owners, wherein owners were to pay Black men $10 a month (minus $3 for clothing) and lower wages to women and children. In addition to maintaining meticulous records, owners had to provide food, medical care, shelter, a ten-hour workday, and an environment free of physical punishment. Those who did not comply could have their property seized by the Union army, who would operate the plantation as a free labor site or lease it to a loyal citizen who would follow the dictates of Order No. 91.[48]

Here Butler faltered in his household war. Numerous planters refused to cooperate with Order No. 91 even though the general promised Union soldiers would "preserve order and prevent crime." Dissatisfied laborers began walking off plantations once more when they did not receive payment or fair treatment. Some Union guards behaved as scurrilously as antebellum overseers. Butler was even forced to implement the labor of the 3rd Louisiana, made up of contraband laborers anyway, to operate some properties in the Lafourche District and stock them for the coming winter. George S. Denison, a federal customs inspector dispatched to account for the finances of the Butler administration, alleged that the general's brother, Andrew, quickly made enormous profits by buying up plantations or plantation crops. Supposedly he sold many southern properties and crops at auction but the money never quite made its way to the Treasury Department.[49]

This supposed malfeasance with Confederate property was another reason that made Butler's placement in Louisiana difficult for the Lincoln administration to countenance, but it arguably generated more ire with Confederates than even the hated Woman's Order. In General Order No. 111, issued on December 23, 1862, Jefferson Davis declared Butler to be a "felon deserving of capital punishment," a "public enemy of the Confederate States of America," and moreover an "outlaw and common enemy of mankind." In other words, Butler's attacks on southern homes, dependents, and property had removed him from the shared circle of humanity. The Union forces under Butler's command, Davis proclaimed, "have borne no resemblance to such warfare as is alone permissible by the rules of international law or the usages of civilization." Among the "atrocities and outrages" that Davis outlined, he included a litany of attacks on the southern household and its most vulnerable members, women and children. He decried sexual outrages committed against southern women, including "helpless women . . . torn from their homes and subjected to solitary confinement." Union forces also unlawfully plundered New Orleans and issued tax levies. To prevent such loss, Davis charged, southerners felt compelled to take oaths against their conscience, a troubling process that Palmer also condemned. Nevertheless, numerous women and children had been "ejected from their homes and robbed of their property."[50]

While he alluded to the supposed effects of the Woman's Order, Davis did not directly name that policy, but he did specifically reference Butler's Order No. 91. That order had authorized the Union army to sequester for confiscation much of the personal property of southerners west of the Mississippi River and later sell it at public auction—a literal scheme to dismantle southern households. "If executed," Davis pronounced, the confiscation order "condemns to punishment by starvation at least a quarter of a million of human beings of all ages, sexes and conditions; and of which the execution although forbidden to military officers by the orders of President Lincoln is in accordance with the confiscation law of our enemies." While Davis exaggerated the effect of Butler's order, he was correct when he directly associated Butler's confiscation policy with the Union war effort writ large. Yet before he named that assault on Confederate property, Davis grounded his critique in its effects on southern households and women in Louisiana.[51]

Notably, only then did the Confederate president proceed to condemn the effects of Union occupation policy on slavery. "And finally the African slaves have not only been excited to insurrection by every license and encouragement," Davis renounced, "but numbers of them have actually been armed for a servile war—a war in its nature far exceeding in horrors the most merciless atrocities of the savages." As Civil War historians have noted, Davis and other Confederates castigated the Union war effort and the Emancipation Proclamation for instigating race war upon the Confederacy. But Davis specifically connected Butler's occupation policies to race war. Butler and the officers under his command "have been in many instances active and zealous agents in the commission of these crimes." Subsequently, Davis declared that Butler and all his commissioned officers were no longer to be considered "as soldiers engaged in honorable warfare but as robbers and criminals deserving death." He promised to execute any who were captured, though he did not extend such a draconian consequence to enlisted men and noncommissioned officers in Butler's command. After condemning the chief architects of the Union war on southern homes, Davis then wrote that all Black men under arms for the Union who were captured would be returned to the control of state authorities. Most chillingly, he announced that all commissioned officers who served with Black troops would be executed. From the Confederate perspective, such were the consequences of a war on slavery and southern household security.[52]

Had he remained in Louisiana, perhaps Butler could have developed another dramatic order or social mechanism for compelling occupied planters to participate in a contract labor system that benefited Black laborers. Or perhaps he would have issued a flamboyant reply to Davis's disconcerting edict. But Butler was recalled by the Lincoln administration in December 1862. Stories of unseemly profit, even if they more accurately reflected his brother's behavior, and Butler's unflattering battles with European consuls damaged his reputation. Nathaniel Banks, a Massachusetts Republican with his own flare for personal glory, replaced the infamous and perhaps ingenious occupation commander. Even if he gave lip service to social equality for Black Americans, Banks ultimately minimized social transformation in Louisiana in favor of several formal military campaigns and a conservative Unionist reconstruction government.[53]

On December 24, Butler made a brief and resolute farewell speech to the citizens of New Orleans. "I found you captured, but not surrendered; conquered but not orderly," he declared. He reiterated the conciliatory component of his occupation policies—no one who cooperated with Union authorities experienced any retribution. Referring to Order No. 28, he asked the "just-minded ladies of New Orleans to say whether they have ever enjoyed so complete protection and calm quiet for themselves and their families as since the advent of the United States troops." He also repeated his emphasis on loyalty to the Union as the identifier for restored southern society. His rule over the city could have been much more aggressive and bloodthirsty, Butler affirmed, referencing among other historical examples the atrocities of Napoleon's Spanish Peninsula War and the slaughter of the Sepoys at Delhi.[54]

Admittedly, he had taxed wealthy Confederates, but Butler reminded Southerners that his policy was to feed the poor and reduce the power of elites. "I saw that this rebellion was a war of the aristocrats against the middling men, of the rich against the poor; a war of the land-owner against the laborer; that it was a struggle for the retention of power in the hands of the few against the many." Butler departed in peace knowing that "I carry with me the blessings of the humble and loyal, under the roof of the cottage and in the cabin of the slave." He was equally content to "incur the sneers of the *salon,* or the curses of the rich." Butler then listed his accomplishments in the city, such as cleaning the streets, restoring free elections, and ensuring fair adjudication of law.[55]

In his concluding remarks, Butler issued one last plea for southerners to return to national allegiance. A fruitful economy and a stable constitutional government awaited. Only slavery blocked the way. "I have given much thought to this subject," Butler admitted, referring to how his time in occupied Louisiana had reshaped his thinking about slavery and Black Americans. "I came among you . . . inclined to sustain your domestic laws," however, "months of experience and of observation have forced the conviction that the existence of slavery is incompatible with the safety either of yourselves or of the Union." Slavery should be removed, Butler encouraged, rather "than it should longer vitiate the social, political, and family relations of your country." He accused slavery of destroying the framework of southern society. With that destruction in mind, Butler urged southerners to "take into your own hands your own institutions; remodel them according to the laws of nations and of God." By targeting the rebellious southern household with social rules, taxation, even confiscation, Butler had done more perhaps than any other Civil War occupation commander to reshape Confederate society in the image of northern ideals of loyalty, honorable behavior, and free labor. But he left his most famous posting with a clear impression of the cultural work still to be done.[56]

Military occupation demonstrates how victory, peace, and social order are not just won, they are manufactured. Butler entered southern Louisiana with an idea of the social order he wanted to create and he championed unprecedented social and economic regulations under Union civil-military authority. Through occupation strategies more than military campaigning in the state, he formalized the Union war as not one just of battles and strategy, but of administration. Above all other military concerns, administrative war targeted the southern social order organized in the household. Although his overbearing personality eventually unseated him from the Department of the Gulf, Butler's assertive model of occupation aligned with the more aggressive wartime strategies of Union commanders in the western theater and contributed to the overall shift to hard war as a Union war on household order and production. There were limits to Butler's efforts, especially in the realm of slavery, but enslaved people themselves continued to press at the material and moral boundaries of the Union war.[57]

Butler understood occupation as a social problem, to which he responded with administrative measures to clean New Orleans, feed the poor, implement loyalty oaths, confiscate southern property, and disrupt foreign connections to the Confederacy. He disorganized rebellion and marshaled loyalty on a social level. He battled Confederate women on their own terms and even if he did not win a total victory over them, he recognized that southern white women could at times be as formidable as any man. To win a war of domestic politics, he turned to tools of management, not simply the bayonet. Though he eventually came to understand occupation in more liberal racial terms, he hardly ameliorated racial inequities with his own responses to slavery's gradual undoing. Entering the department behind Butler, Nathaniel Banks demonstrated a more lenient attitude toward white southerners, a greater interest in military campaigns, and more diplomacy (or compromise) in constructing a plantation system.

Military occupation, as a project both of conquest and national reorganization, reoriented the gendered nature of American citizenship. With a reconstruction of the republic in mind, the Union reorganized national belonging around individual loyalty. Butler embodied the attitude of many occupation officials who were eager to implement loyalty as a requirement for citizenship and federal protection. When governmental figures like Butler validated national loyalty over regional loyalty and household authority, they redirected the seat of white male power away from the site where their mastery over dependents "made" them autonomous. Southern white women, who had been visible but often liminal in the prewar household order, made themselves into political subjects by resisting Union authority with such fervency that occupation commanders turned to formal political measures such as loyalty oaths and military justice to quell them. Through his occupation policy, Butler essentially made himself like a patriarch, overseeing the power relations and material conditions of occupied households. In order to repudiate a patriarch they considered to be unlawful and disgraceful, southern white women in Louisiana paradoxically broke with their traditional status and entered the public sphere.

Overall, this transition from local belonging to national allegiance accompanied larger (inter)national transformations in civil rights, nationalism, and personhood in the nineteenth century, especially concerning the status of enslaved people. Yet even as they tampered with the autonomous conditions of white male citizenship and contended with southern women, Union authorities rendered occupation a conservative project on racial grounds. Union commanders were generally not inclined to extend this national vision of loyalty and belonging to Black Americans, much less arm formerly enslaved men. All but the most radical of Republicans spent much of the war considering how to attack slavery without dislodging white supremacy. Meanwhile, as elites and politicians debated these issues in the North, common Union soldiers in occupied Louisiana had to wrestle on a daily basis with the complex issues of state control and personal autonomy.[58]

3

Administering (Re)Union

COERCION & POLICY IN THE RANKS
OF UNION OCCUPATION

As a Union officer in occupied Louisiana, William B. Allyn was unimpressed with his military duties. Encamped near Thibodaux, west of New Orleans, Allyn wrote to his sister that smoking his pipe was "my *sole comfort* here in Dixie." He gained weight, had his photograph taken in New Orleans, and watched his fellow officers smoke and drink. In the fall of 1862, Allyn's unit pushed into central southern Louisiana, where Union troops repulsed Confederates in the area and established Camp Stevens "in one of the richest sections of the country." Lafourche Parish, he observed, was "the best sugar district in fact in the state and [the] Government will make several of millions by our encamping here. A great many traitors have plantations in the vicinity which with the sugar is of course confiscated, also the crop standing which is converted into either molasses or sugar by Government employees & Uncle Sam pockets the dollars realized by the sale." When some fellow Union officers prepared "a little expedition after some traitors," Allyn wrote, "I am going to try and accompany it for I do like to clear out all these little bands of . . . rebels which travel about in the Parish doing more harm than good." In a few paragraphs, Allyn described two of the primary objectives of Union occupation—securing resources and dispersing guerrilla bands—but he also described a casual domestic front that would come to shape the nature of household war as much as Butler's stern directives and Banks's military campaigns had.[1]

While it was certainly not always true of relationships between Union soldiers and southern citizens, Allyn fostered polite social relations with his southern counterparts in occupied Louisiana. "I have made several very pleasant acquaintances since being on the Bayou," he reported. A nearby planter named Ledet had several pretty daughters "who play lively upon the piano and are great at cheating playing Euchre." Amused with their company, Allyn went on horseback rides with the ladies, where he found "they sit on a saddle splendidly." He often dined with the family as well. "They are very polite and kind and seem to enjoy my company as much as I do." He enjoyed hunting and dining on local wildlife, which one of the soldiers in camp prepared. "I often ride the country in a buggy which we have confiscated. I have plenty of horses." Whether his unit would stay at Camp Stevens or enter winter quarters in New Orleans, Allyn could not predict. "It is immaterial to me where I am ordered." As bored or ambivalent as he seemed to be, Allyn represented many of the essential characteristics of occupation's front line: battling Confederate raiders, seizing supplies for military and personal use, associating with local southerners, and protecting government economic investments. Lincoln and other Union figures hoped to use Louisiana as a wartime exemplar of Reconstruction and Union soldiers on the ground like Allyn served as critical diplomatic warriors, shaping the social environment from which renewed Unionism might spring.[2]

Another Union soldier, stationed in the Commissary Department in Brashear City (present-day Morgan City in St. Mary Parish), indicated some of the racial and political implications of Union occupation. Signing his letter, "S.F.S.," this Union administrator wrote his wife about his conditions in the lines. All of his furniture was confiscated from the rebels and "I have a n—— to wait upon me to, yes and a colored women for a cook." If he was hungry, "I can go to the store room and take anything I want and have it cooked all up nice." He also paid the cook to make a dress for his wife, which was very affordable, he related with delight. Aside from his material comforts, he had political observations. "This war seems bad-hard-cruel-unendurable—but there is being brought about one of the greatest eras in the history of the world. But I just as much believe that God is ruling this all for the best and 3 and one half millions of people are to become Free men & women of America." The formerly enslaved people around him knew nothing of the joys of life, he wrote. They had endured much punishment for "petty crimes" and experienced arduous labor under the sun. "All this has been done within the very towns and cities where we are now . . . [but] thanks be to the glorious old Union laws—we, our army, have made a bold push and have done great things—yes this blow has done more to the crushing out of rebellion than any other thing during the whole war." Not only did the soldier recognize how slavery and southern culture was quickly altering during the war, but he identified Union military occupation and the social order it designed as the foremost agents of transformation. What this commissary agent most likely did not realize was that Union occupation, like his own perceptions of the Black laborers who serviced him, spelled out conservative parameters for reconstruction.[3]

At the ground level, bureaucrats in blue managed these designs in social order. Tasked with subduing Confederate territory, regulating and winning over the locals, suppressing guerrilla activity, and emancipating and controlling slaves, the Union army faced a reality as difficult and fluctuating as any army mobilized for combat purposes on a strategic battlefield. Occupation would stabilize the Union military effort as it pressed deeper into southern territory on all sides, reduce southern household resistance that constituted a kind of warfare in itself, and ultimately shape the postwar cultural landscape of the American South. Yet as part of the long-term military goal of conquering the Confederacy, the Union army was forced to manage a nexus of pressing social issues in the areas it permanently, or even partially, occupied. To understand the full scope and meaning of the U.S. Civil War, historians must understand how the Union's longest large-scale military occupation conflated military strategy with the maintenance of social order.[4]

Union occupiers shared two primary social relationships with southern people in Louisiana. First, Union forces engaged in relationships of discipline, like Butler's Woman's Order or William Allyn's pursuit of guerrillas. This civil-military atmosphere of discipline dismantled many features of the prewar South, but also shielded certain conditions from radical change. Slavery, as Butler indicated in his farewell speech, was the largest obstacle to restoring national harmony. As the anonymous Brashear City administrator believed, one of the greatest cultural reconfigurations won by Union arms was the destruction of slavery. As Union soldiers reduced slavery, however haphazardly, they transformed the southern labor system, depleted the enormous profit values that slaveholders possessed in enslaved people and agricultural products, and signaled, for a short time, that large-scale land ownership would not be the single greatest determiner of status and social value in America. With the control of wealthy southern elites thrown into question, Union occupiers troubled the structure of patriarchy. Before the Civil War, white southern men—as masters and husbands and political leaders—maintained a wide jurisdiction of authority over dependents, but occupation reduced their authority in favor of Union military soldiers and bureaucrats. In addition to the challenges of administration, Union forces debated the morality of property destruction as a means of disciplining southern society.[5]

Second, despite these profound social changes and the southern antagonism they often produced, Union forces also shared relationships of mutualism with white Louisiana civilians, such as Allyn's hospitable relationship with the Ledet family. Southern civilians often looked to Union administrators to trade supplies, obtain property protection, secure jobs, and satisfy numerous other requests. Just as secession itself was a cooperative process between government and household, Union occupation also featured local household support, not only in terms of the relationship between Union soldiers and friendly southerners, but moreover in the shape of Unionist recruits that joined the ranks. Butler and Banks actively recruited among Louisiana men, Black and white, and lower-level commanders also pursued this strategy to increase ranks decimated by disease, combat, and expired service terms. Even as Union occupiers disciplined southern behavior and altered Louisiana society, these friendly relationships with southern household members proved beneficial to occupier and occupied alike.[6]

Occupation in Louisiana became more complicated as the war proceeded, due to increases in Black emancipation, civilian impoverishment, Union offensives, and Confederate guerrilla operations, which further bureaucratized relationships of discipline and mutualism between Union forces and Louisianans. As will be seen more clearly in chapter 5, the army and the high command dismantled slavery in pieces. Whereas Butler oversaw an occupation regime that embraced largely moderate antislavery policies in 1862, from mid-1863 onward Banks and other Union authorities liberated more enslaved people and established more complex systems of Black labor and recruitment. These endeavors produced mixed results for Black Americans, but Union occupation forces also shared complex relationships with white Louisianans. Under the Banks administration, the Union army launched several large-scale military campaigns and increased the federal bureaucracy to secure federal command of Louisiana. Unionist cooperation was key to this success, especially on a political level. Rather than compel more Louisianans into Confederate-controlled territory, the Union military government emboldened Unionist sentiment in the state and ultimately empowered Unionists to create a new civilian state government in 1864. Banks's crowning bureaucratic achievement, however shakily accomplished, was the creation of this Unionist government, though it promised disparate consequences for Black and white Louisianans.[7]

As occupation expanded across the state, the Union army engaged Louisiana residents in a variety of ways that made civic-military relations more complicated. For as much property as they destroyed through war or retaliation, destruction was not a permanent feature of occupation. While the Union army could not help battlefield destruction as a natural consequence of war, in highly garrisoned regions Union forces built and maintained much infrastructure. However, Union administration was not without corruption and internal discipline problems as well. Most disturbingly, Union forces faced a frustrating guerrilla war that intensified in 1864 and 1865, especially in the Lafourche region around Brashear City, eighty-five miles west of New Orleans. To facilitate a more coherent occupation and strengthen the hand of the state, Union administrators adopted complex management technologies such as registers, loyalty oaths, military orders, taxes, trade restrictions, and prisons to regulate the loyalty of southerners under their command.

As Union occupiers pursued relationships of discipline and relationships of mutualism, they shaped the occupation order in tandem with southern citizens, demonstrating how American democracy was a production of the dialogue between state and people. Whether they favored occupation or not, white citizens embedded themselves in the project of bureaucratic administration that kept much of Louisiana organized under Union authority during the war. The military made itself part of the state, establishing territorial dominance, securing borders, regulating trade, and policing the behavior of those in the occupation zone. White southerners under occupation confronted the federal government in direct ways they had never before experienced. While these interactions unfolded, Union occupiers (sometimes consciously, sometimes unknowingly) laced their loyalty management systems with the rhetoric of respectability, loyalty, and race, which helped determine social status in the occupation regime. By actively shaping social values within occupied Louisiana, administrators in blue identified the conditions of national and community belonging as they might appear in the reformed Union. They remade public and private spaces into state spaces and negotiated with the white inhabitants of that state space to mutually determine the values of belonging and the parameters of state authority. Ultimately, Union occupation in Louisiana implemented a sophisticated managerial regime that subverted Confederate political autonomy but preserved the primacy of white citizenship over Black.

An overview of Union broadsides plastered in Baton Rouge, mostly throughout 1863, demonstrated how Union authorities established the parameters of daily life in occupied Louisiana. The provost marshal required all steamboats to report to the harbor master to have their manifests approved. This order was no doubt intended to discourage smuggling that occurred regularly throughout the war. In March 1863, Colonel T. E. Chickering declared that no persons would be allowed to leave the city without a pass, and a later public broadside declared that all citizens, white and Black, were forbidden to carry concealed weapons within city limits. All public gatherings, "for amusement or other purposes," were forbidden without authorization from the provost marshal. That same month, Major General C. C. Augur also commanded: "ALL persons occupying houses in Baton Rouge, to which they are not entitled, will report immediately such occupancy to the Provost Marshal." Union authorities also forbid "Hawking, peddling fruits, goods, wares, or merchandise without license," and issued numerous prohibitions of the public sale of alcohol. In September, Captain Edward Page urged citizens of the city to organize "for the purpose of organizing a Citizen Police Force for the protection of property." Protection from whom was not specified. On November 26, Lincoln's proclaimed day of Thanksgiving and Prayer, the Union command closed all businesses. As part of Lincoln's hopeful effort to establish a new government in the rebellious state, all voters in Baton Rouge were required to register with the provost marshal as of December 1863. In July 1862, a broadside even authorized the police "to kill all Dogs running at large in the streets."[8]

Gun control presented the most immediate problem and probably the most routine regulation issued in occupied territory. Butler's May 1 proclamation to New Orleans required "all persons in arms against the United States" to surrender weapons, equipment, and munitions. However, he thanked the European Legion, a body of foreign-born militia numbering some ten thousand men, for preserving order before the arrival of Union troops in the city. These men were allowed to keep their guns. Most nonmilitary personnel in occupied Louisiana were forbidden to keep firearms without a registered permit. "Permits to keep & carry arms will be given only to persons who have furnished evidence of active and sympathetic loyalty toward the government of the United States, and the provisional Government of the State of Louisiana," one Union order read. Union troops who confiscated weapons, as with much other property or provision, were required to issue a certificate to peaceful citizens with a description of the items seized and then turn in the weapons to ordnance officers. Violators were arrested, which entailed an array of paperwork and prison conditions. The order also called for a confiscating officer to assess the loyalty of those who bore firearms. In some areas, such as the Lafourche District, railroad employees and lessees of government plantations were exempted from these restrictions.[9]

To reduce resistance while maximizing military effectiveness, the Union army created an extensive, if at times haphazard, bureaucracy that sought to balance civil and military order. Often, Union officials managed the politics of loyal space by issuing commands to local provost marshals with specific injunctions not to distress the populations under their jurisdictions. Even after conciliatory policies faded as a war strategy, Union occupation forces did not seek to generate more trouble than necessary. As late as the summer of 1864, various provost marshal officers ordered the seizure of local weaponry, "avoiding all unnecessary annoyance and irritation of the inhabitants." Simultaneously, Union commanders had to keep the military itself organized and operational. Butler and Banks fielded military operations while thousands of formerly enslaved people poured into the territory occupied by the army. Louisiana citizens also beleaguered the Union occupation structure with requests for protection, property, and provision. From every military outpost, provost marshals had to dispatch monthly reports accounting for their actions and expenditures to Union headquarters in New Orleans, including enrollment expenses as recruitment officers infused the ranks with Black and white Unionist troops.[10]

Supply and transport also represented another pressing issue to the Union army. "To give *one look* at what we are doing here towards *feeding the troops*," wrote Sergeant Mills Barnard to his wife in mid-1863, he listed the many supplies that he and other Union soldiers had loaded onto ships at Baton Rouge. Through strenuous manual labor, the men loaded 22,000 loaves of soft bread baked in the city, 100,000 pounds of rice, 150,000 of beans, 80,000 pounds of bacon, 180,000 pounds of beef, and 160,000 pounds of pork and pickles. All these supplies were sent upriver to supply the Union army as it besieged forts, suppressed guerrillas, and attacked the Confederate army in northern Louisiana.[11]

To aid the Union military in its complex efforts of occupation, commanders demanded loyalty from southerners and they engaged in daily assessments of authenticity. At the most elemental level, southerners under occupation testified to their fealty by signing loyalty oaths. More than just a bureaucratic form of accounting the population, the loyalty oath was also a textual statement of citizenship. Paperwork made the loyal citizen legible to the Union army. On June 10, 1862, Butler issued General Order No. 41, requiring all civil officials to take the oath of allegiance. Like many of the military orders and social environments produced under occupation, Butler's order aligned civil and martial order. The order referred to the oath as a sacred obligation and American citizenship as "the highest title known." Under General Order No. 76, issued four months later, all citizens had to take the oath of allegiance, declare themselves a friendly foreign national, or be classified as an "Enemy of the United States," subject to property confiscation and banishment. After Banks took over, he issued the more lenient General Order No. 9 in January of 1863, allowing "public enemies" to regain protected status if they finally agreed to sign the oath. Treasury secretary Salmon Chase dispatched several associates, especially Louisiana Unionists driven out by the Confederates, to the state to organize Unionist sympathy in hopes of resurrecting civil government. "More was at stake than a battle for control over domestic space," historian William Blair contends; "it was also a battle for the political will of the Confederate populace." On the domestic home front, political will could be a powerful weapon in favor of or opposition to Union authority.[12]

As a political tool, oaths of loyalty followed an inconsistent process from modest statements reserved for political prisoners in border states to profuse declarations for all southerners, a trajectory congruent with how political attitudes toward loyalty shifted throughout the war. In the early days of the war, when Lincoln and other moderate to conservative northern authorities valued reconciliation, Union forces required no oaths at all from a southern population many believed would happily reenter the national union anyway. Eventually, Union commanders on the ground reframed loyalty as a more active condition of personal allegiance. Edicts such as Butler's Orders No. 41 and No. 76 grew more elaborate and demanding as the war progressed. But Butler had no capacity to enforce these orders outside the occupation zone he commanded. In 1862, Radical Republicans conjured up the Ironclad Oath, which accentuated the signer's past by requiring the oath taker to never have supported the Confederacy. Such a statement would have eliminated most white southerners from the body politic of the United States. Republicans eventually incorporated it into the 1864 Wade-Davis Bill, which Lincoln pocket vetoed. Instead, his more forward-looking Presidential Amnesty Oath, issued in December 1863, offered full pardon and restored citizenship to all southerners and proposed a lenient pathway to reestablished Union state governments.[13]

Whatever form it took, the oath itself was only a measure of loyalty, not its complete embodiment. Union officers regularly depended on face-to-face interactions to confirm the loyalty of travelers or local citizens. "The fact of having taken an oath of Allegiance will not alone entitle parties to this permit [for firearms]," commanded Brigadier General John McNeil. "Loyalty is an active virtue & its possessors will be known by their public professions, and the example of their lives," he contended. Union officials had good reason to suspect many southerners who took the oath of allegiance. One southerner in St. Charles Parish met with disfavor from the provost marshal because of suspect community relations. "The owner had taken the oath of allegiance," reported Major H. O. Bradley, "but has two sons in the Rebel army. He had not taken the 'Iron Clad.' I have very little confidence in his loyalty. He is always hand in glove with the reputed disloyal men of this parish." Unionist Dennis Haynes referred to such men as "double-distilled traitors" and claimed that many Rebels "did not regard the oath as binding on their consciences." General T. W. Sherman complained that he believed many southerners who entered Union lines for safety were actually spies. To fulfill their duty as an occupation force, Union provost marshal officers had to continually judge southern citizens for their loyalty and respectability.[14]

Louisianans under occupation understood the "active virtue" of loyalty because it affected their social status and material property. In November 1862, two residents of St. Tammany Parish appeared before Butler claiming that no competent officer existed in their parish to administer the oath. They had traveled far to reach Union lines and asked for consideration of this trouble and respect for their loyalty to the Union. Like many who took the oath, these St. Tammany men understood that only loyal status entitled southerners to the protections and rights generally guaranteed to a national citizen. First, loyalty or disloyalty determined access to civic rights and social inclusion, such as personal mobility, voting, and membership in social public like police forces or church congregations. Second, loyalty affected property ownership, including homes, estates, businesses, and personal property. Southerners were acutely conscious of the communal politics involved with taking the oath. With a simple signature, a person might win friends in blue but earn enemies in gray. Yet many signed anyway, even if that statement of loyalty did not represent their true personal feelings, because to be registered as an enemy of the state essentially estranged them from their communities and exposed them to hardship.[15]

Northerners and southerners during the Civil War contemplated loyalty documents as part of a larger political dialogue about the conditions of national belonging. Loyalty oaths, for all their political potency, were far from a precise barometer for Union sentiment. Union occupiers at the time and many historians since the war have determined that southerners under occupation frequently took the oath not because they nurtured Union sympathies but to prevent themselves from being arrested or banished and to protect their property from confiscation. It is difficult to determine to what extent Union commanders differentiated between various loyalty oaths. Most seemed to adopt an attitude like that of General James Bowen, who told one provost marshal in Louisiana: "A person who will not take the oath should be to you as one dead." For occupation forces deep within Confederate terrain, oaths were part of a more involved process of measuring allegiance by degrees.[16]

Beyond the personal paperwork of loyalty oaths, southerners within Union-occupied territory appealed to local testimony to validate their political loyalty and good character. Local white residents referenced neighbors and friends to prove their loyalty to Union officials, such as one southerner who wrote Union authorities in New Orleans that his friend was "a *good union* man." Such appeals were a communal process with roots in the antebellum period as well, when neighbors called on the opinions and characterizations of their neighbors to validate their status. When the provost marshal of St. Charles Parish ordered William and Sarah Pickard to build a new levee on their plantation, they balked at the heavy cost. They gathered fourteen signatures, including Joseph Walker, owner of Good Hope Plantation, and Henry B. Fitch, superintendent of Hermitage Plantation, to attest to the sturdiness of their levee. In their letter to the provost marshal, they made reference "to the certificate of many respectable citizens who are neighbors and who *are therefore most interested* in the maintenance of a good levee on the plantation referred to, for the purpose of supporting their opinion and of assuring that it is not suggested by a wish to avoid a public duty." Fitch's signature demonstrated how Union occupiers merged military identity and social responsibility. Another southerner pleaded with Jonas French, chief of police in New Orleans until 1863, not to occupy his friend's house. A man named W. G. Robertson appeared before French with a reference letter from a friend which claimed Robertson "represents Yankees who have had Tobacco seized and who are in no wise identified with the present troubles." With such communal assurances of national loyalty, southerners hoped to preserve as much of their pre-occupation lives as possible. Others hoped to forge mutually beneficial avenues of economic profit with Union forces.[17]

Community support could work in the opposite direction as well. A man named J. H. Burris sent a hostile letter to the provost marshal defaming E. Murphy, recently appointed by Union officials as inspector of weights and measures in the First and Fourth Districts of New Orleans. According to Burris, Murphy was "an unprincipaled [sic] Scoundrel, his Own Brother States this fact[.] [H]e was On the police previous to the arrival of the United States Army—was a Loud mouth abusive Secessionist." If that information were not enough, Burris identified another policeman who could testify to Murphy's disloyalty. Sillvester Cameron protested his imprisonment because a man with "an animosity against me . . . Made a charge on me as being a Desperate character" and even threatened to shoot Cameron. Imprisoned for almost two months, Cameron insisted on his innocence to the provost marshal. He requested a trial and permission to find witnesses "to prove my character through out the city." By associating loyalty to the Union with public moral character, these southerners aligned martial values with civic values more familiar to them, much like Union occupiers. Whereas Radicals in Congress appeared to pursue loyalty as an objective condition, Union occupation authorities contended with a murky social terrain in which local community ties obscured or corroborated national loyalty. Whether they were truly loyal to the Union or not, southern whites often aspired to correlate their domestic order with Union military order.[18]

In urban areas, especially the seat of Union power in New Orleans, white men called on this language of loyalty and community belonging when they beseeched Union authorities for jobs and government support. Typically, historians have focused on the physical exigencies of white southern women, who often lived on the domestic home front without the presence of their men, or displaced Black laborers, who pressed for freedom, jobs, education, and supplies from nearby Union forces. But in occupied Louisiana white men who remained behind Union lines also found themselves facing joblessness and privation that threatened their positions as providers and heads of household. "You have given us a long speech," a former policeman named Peter Becker wrote to Jonas French, "wherein you said that as long as we do our duty faithfully and comply with your order strictly and promptly we can retain our positions." Nevertheless, his lieutenant had released Becker from duty without explanation. Becker appealed to be reinstated on grounds of his unquestioned obedience and because his brother was a captain in the Union army. Only an imperfectly healed arm, Becker informed French, kept him from joining the military as well. Maurice Adams claimed that he and his large family were subjects of France and appealed to the provost marshal for permission to reopen his distillery in order to support his family. Another man implored French for employment because he needed money to care for his elderly mother. He included a reference to verify his loyalty. One British-born American citizen informed the provost marshal that he and his family "have suffered privations in consequence of our Union feelings, which has thrown me in deep distress and want." He and his sons were willing to do any job French could offer and willing to offer references to substantiate their respectability and capability. Louis Carella included two signatures "to furnish the required security" when he applied for a job. For white patriarchs under occupation, pledging their allegiance to the Union allowed them access to the financial security that they had once been accustomed to as a matter of their gender.[19]

New Orleans residents Fred Courret and Frederic Collins appealed to Union administrators directly on the grounds of their own impoverishment as household heads. Courret, employed as a policeman in New Orleans, sent a lengthy letter to a Union officer after he fainted on duty in the fall of 1862. He had "long endured misery before his appointment," he wrote, "not having the proper means to get such food what would have strength and the health of his body instead of weakening the same by mini privations he had to undergo." To increase his woes, he was behind in his rent and had not slept in days, to the point that his landlord brought Courret before Union officials to pay what he owed. Including two signatures "to certify that the petitioner is of steady and moral character," Courret pleaded with Union authorities for "generosity of heart" and to gain his job back. A few months earlier, Frederic Collins, brought by

Union troops to New Orleans to face unspecified charges, petitioned Jonas French for a pass to return to his family. "I am the poorest of the poor, if was not for the officer of the U.S. Navy, now having charge of Fort Livingston (who know now that I am innocent) and who have sent provisions at my home; my wife & children will now be starving." Collins's misfortune not only revealed how military occupation could sever white men from the household but also demonstrated the beneficial material and emotional relationships that Union authorities could sometimes foster with occupied enemies. As the war progressed, more and more white southerners recognized this reality and called on the Union army for help.[20]

As occupation grew more complex, Union administrators created registries, or "enrollments," of white citizens and their property to enhance the visibility of the populace. These enrollment forms included conscription rolls as well, as the Union army recruited white and Black men into home guard units in Louisiana. Union commanders wanted an accurate understanding of planters, lessees, cultivated plantations, and abandoned plantations in each parish under occupation. In the fall of 1863, General Bowen ordered Captain J. L. King to make an enrollment of all white male citizens twenty years and older in St. John Parish, as well as the number of able-bodied Black males between eighteen and fifty. Two years later, Captain George Darling was ordered to make another enrollment of all white and free colored residents between the ages of eighteen and forty-five years in the parish. Similar accountings of white and Black populations occurred in other parishes. Provost marshal officials in Brashear City made a complex census of all white residents in town. Going from house to house, they recorded the name, sex, age, and employment of every person over fifteen, as well as the number of each person under that age in each household. "Ascertain which have taken the Oath & record the *kind & date* thereof," their orders read. Officers marked a "P" next to those who had taken the presidential amnesty oath, "A" for the Alien Oath, "41" for the oath prescribed under Butler's General Order No. 41, and "I" for the Ironclad Oath. In November 1864, a military circular to all provost marshals in the Department of the Gulf ordered them to compile lists of all planters, their plantations, their distance from the nearest military post, their status of loyalty, if they were original owners or lessees, who lessees were leasing from, and the number of hands employed on all plantations. Union officers used these enrollments for a variety of purposes, especially to chronicle the transition of Black labor, but they never strayed too far from the original purpose of these managerial instruments: accounting for the loyalty of occupied people.[21]

In a highly populated area subject to frequent fires like New Orleans, Union commanders pondered the loyalty of New Orleans firemen. After a series of suspicious fires in 1863, Union authorities extended the charter of the Pioneer Fire Company because "public safety requires that this organization should Be continued in force." Two months later, New Orleans police officers issued a detailed report for each of the four districts in the city to the chief of police concerning the number of each fire company and how many were loyal or disloyal. In the First District, an officer reported that in Fire Companies 1, 2, and 12, nearly all of the firemen had taken the oath of allegiance. In Companies 13, 14, 18, and 20, most had not. Fire Company No. 6, as well as three other stations, including Louisiana Hose, were divided in loyal and disloyal membership. An officer in the Fourth District reported numerous firemen were paroled men formerly in the Confederate army. In Engine Company No. 23, with over sixty active members, the investigating officer found "the majority are paroled and some taken the oath," but nevertheless, "their disposition is sesech [sic]." Most firemen in the Second District were loyal save a few, Lieutenant W. D. Miller found, including two in the Pelican Hook and Sadder Fire Company No. 4 who were "Registered enemies." Some were foreigners. In the Third District, too, an officer believed many fire company members to profess loyalty except those belonging to the Hope Hook and Sadder Company No. 3 and the Phoenix Fire Company No. 8. By measuring the loyalty of firemen in the city, Union officials could perhaps determine their own level of endangerment.[22]

Stationed far from northern soil with a finite number of troops to perform the tasks of occupation, Union commanders used loyalty registries to their benefit by staffing a large bureaucratic infrastructure with loyal southerners. Many southern men who had not taken the oath were fired from public positions and even detained by provost marshal officers. For civic and governmental positions not directly fulfilled by a military figure, Union commanders appointed loyal southerners. In September 1862, George Shepley—promoted to the rank of brigadier general and appointed military governor of Louisiana in July 1862—authorized his first nonmilitary appointees. He designated civilian oversight for levee inspection and repair. James E. Dunham was authorized to administer the oath of allegiance to one man, Marshal White, in Orleans Parish. Within three weeks, Shepley ordered that T. Druett, the fifth justice of the peace for Orleans Parish and city of New Orleans, "being a loyal citizen will continue to discharge the junctions of his office exercising civil jurisdiction in accordance, the laws and customs of Louisiana not inconsistent with the orders of the military authorities or the functions of the Provost Judge or Provost Marshal." Although he started with a small number of civilian appointees, Shepley and other Union commanders expanded the role of loyal citizens exponentially as the war continued. These appointments alleviated the pressure on the Union command in Louisiana, but they also staffed the reconstruction effort with white men, many of whom were racially conservative despite their pro-Union sentiments.[23]

Primarily, Union authorities appointed loyal civilians to administrative positions to manage oaths of allegiance and oversee voter registration, but they also wanted local civic positions like sheriffs, judges, and record custodians to be staffed by loyal southerners. Throughout the war, the provost marshal appointed and aided loyal attachés in order to cultivate a stable social order in occupied Louisiana. In November 1862, Shepley authorized Thomas Cottman to administer the oath of allegiance to the sheriff in St. Charles Parish and to P. B. Marmillion, sheriff of St. John the Baptist Parish. A few days later, Marmillion received permission to administer the oath to any person in his parish, as did individual police authorities in surrounding parishes. At the same time, Shepley authorized the state treasurer to receive roughly half of the tax collections from the sheriff of Jefferson Parish, those funds to be used for any state payments for the parish. Numerous loyal civilians like George W. Jones in Assumption Parish or C. S. Martin in St. Charles Parish or James Graham of New Orleans were appointed as clerks, recorders, and notary publics to keep community records in order and streamline the collections of taxes and fees. Shepley also appointed southerners as school directors, court officers, board members to state departments, and executives to local institutions like banks and railroad companies. R. B. Lang was appointed special officer in service to the Executive Department of Louisiana and ordered to report directly to Shepley. Every time a loyal management figure such as a parish-level justice of the peace administered the oath of allegiance, he reflected the influence of Union power over Louisiana's social order, illustrated the governing alliance between management figures and the military during occupation, and multiplied the population of loyal citizens under Union control. Many of these loyal citizen managers were middle- and upper-class Louisianans who hoped to preserve their prewar material and social status by siding with the Union.[24]

Rather than entirely reorient the state governmental infrastructure of Louisiana, Shepley frequently instructed Union officials and loyal managers to follow Louisiana state law, especially relating to revenue collection. Civilian harbor masters in New Orleans were ordered "to be in conformity with the Statutes of the State of Louisiana." In Orleans Parish, the sheriff was "authorized and directed to charge for the service of any process only the fees established by the Laws of Louisiana. Before service of any process he may require the legal fees to be paid or secured." The most important regulation on state revenue collection was Shepley's Special Order No. 43, issued February 28, 1863, which instructed tax collectors to abide by Louisiana state tax laws already in effect. "The assessment made by the State tax assessors has been adopted as not only the most equitable but the least burdensome mode of meeting the expenses of the State Government," Shepley announced. All citizens were to pay their "due proportion of the expenses of protecting their property and affording them the benefits of civil tribunals and other safe guards of persons and property." "Contumacious recusants," as Shepley referred to them, would face military action. Military authorities would "resort to a more summary process in case of recurrent owners who refuse to pay their taxes." However antagonistic Shepley's tone appeared, a few months later he assured employees in the city government that their wages could not be seized or garnished.[25]

When Louisiana whites appealed to Union authority for protection, recognition, and employment or when they obtained managerial positions in the occupation regime, they demonstrated that Union authorities could cultivate positive, mutually beneficial relationships with southerners in occupied regions. These alliances contrasted sharply with the fearsome characterizations that many Confederates launched at Union soldiers and commanders. Though the Union army was a force of conquest, it was also a managerial body. The Union occupation in Louisiana proved that administration was as important as battlefield victories, lest the infrastructure of conquest collapse. By assigning local white men to loyalist positions, however, Union authorities also vindicated the gendered and racial nature of power in the nineteenth-century American state. Many of the white Louisiana men who joined the military management structure did so to obtain protection or provide for their households. Yet, as the loyalist appointees of occupation expanded into a Unionist government in 1864, they would do more to support traditional structures of social and political power in Louisiana than align themselves with radical visions of the future.[26]

While Louisianans scrambled to preserve their communal order along lines of military obligation, Union forces occupied southern buildings and confiscated property to facilitate military needs. Union troops often converted structures to accommodate their duties. With the sheriff's building occupied as a military hospital in December 1862, the clerk, sheriff, and recorder for the city of Jefferson obtained permission to find another suitable building. They did not return to their original offices for four months. The U.S. navy seized four brick buildings between Erato Thalia and Front Streets in New Orleans, from which naval agents operated during the war. In early September 1864 in Brashear City, the surgeon of the 11th Vermont complained that he did not have enough room in the building in which he operated. "It is quite necessary that I have the use of the whole building," especially since he had injured men that he needed to move upstairs. Additionally, the army bakers on the second floor "make more noise than is necessary or beneficial. Please order it vacated." Within a month, Captain E. J. Lewis took over another building in Brashear City for a hospital. Perhaps that was necessary because at the end of September, General Robert Cameron ordered Union engineers to dismantle four houses, three already occupied by Union troops (one of which was a hospital), and use the pieces to erect defensive works around the city.[27]

Occupiers respected or reused property as much as they destroyed it. Though property destruction appeared on the growing list of hyperbolic invectives that Confederates arrayed against northern invaders, the Union army followed careful logic when it came to southern property. Union property destruction, as an act of war or an act of occupation, did not undermine social order during the war or seriously enervate democracy after the war, even as the chief consequence of such destruction was to destabilize slavery. Also, contrary to the apocalyptic images generated by Union military escapades such as Sherman's March through Georgia or Sheridan's Raid in the Shenandoah Valley, the Union also maintained or rebuilt infrastructure in occupied areas like Louisiana.[28]

Even from the beginning of the war, Union officials in occupied Louisiana targeted the property and households of disloyal citizens for confiscation. A month after Union arrival, the provost marshal seized a coffee shop in Algiers belonging to a Confederate lieutenant. A Union general ordered Samuel Montgomery's New Orleans property seized in September 1862, because he was a soldier in the Confederate army. Such seizures multiplied in the months following Order No. 41, as thousands of resistant or absent southerners had their property confiscated. One New Orleans resident, P. J. Conway, sent two extensive lists of Confederate citizens and their property holdings to Jonas French in July 1862. A widow named Augite Costa complained that her boarding house had been seized by a man under Union authority. For Confederates in Louisiana, Union occupation might threaten or even destroy their property, but rarely their life. By attacking property but not persons, the Union army struck at the foundation of secession without reproducing previous carnages in human history. Occupation was a measured statist initiative that transformed the southern household without eradicating it.[29]

Ensconced in a watery region where levees were crucial to maintaining water travel and supply, Union administrators took special care to maintain levees. In 1862, Shepley appointed various civilian superintendents to inspect levees in and around New Orleans and "report as soon as possible all defects and crevasses with the ownership of the Plantations where they occur and what means if any are being taken to repair them and under whose directions and what force is being employed." The Union army continued to use civilian inspectors under military auspices throughout the war. Bowen ordered parishes divided into levee districts and "intelligent loyal planters" appointed as superintendents. If practicable, he added, they should go unpaid. "The planters will be held to a strict accountability for the proper repairs of the levees in front of their respective plantations," another Union order read. As the war proceeded, the military also noted the increasingly dilapidated condition of local levees. One Iowa officer in St. John Parish reported twelve plantation levees in need of repair. "All the levees from Mrs. M. Haydel to Ed Webre must be strengthened and fascined [sic]," he determined. Others were "much dilapidated by hogs & are full of crawfish holes." Another officer estimated levee repair costs in St. John, Jefferson, and St. Charles Parishes to be between six and seven thousand dollars. Southern property holders, especially planters, were often held financially responsible for parish infrastructure repairs.[30]

Of course, some instances of personal property loss occurred regardless of careful commanders. One French subject complained to Colonel French that a Union colonel had taken over his stable, seized his fodder, taken away his poultry, and carried off several cases of wine as well. He sent a bill of $372 to French and a second copy of his complaint to Shepley. Despite having paid a bribe to French to keep open a gambling house throughout 1862 without signing an oath of allegiance, by the end of the year J. J. Bryant found himself deprived of the building, his house and furniture confiscated, and himself thrown in jail for trying to leave the city without a pass. E. K. Bryant carried a letter of endorsement from a friend in New Orleans that claimed him to be "a loyal citizen and good Union man, residing in rather an isolated part of the City, is desirous to obtain his revolver deposited with the United States authorities, to protect himself from Burglars." Another man pleaded with French on behalf of his wife for the return of her pianoforte, which had been gifted to another family but lost to Union officers when they seized that family's home. Moments of theft or destruction behind the lines, though painful for those who lost property, were minimal compared to the considerable efforts that the Union army made to preserve property.[31]

Union military authorities utilized local prison properties in Louisiana throughout the war. Union forces used prisons as institutions of discipline, labor, and even recruitment. On the first day of September in 1862, Shepley ordered Deputy Provost Marshal C. W. Killborne to "make examination into the condition and character of the State prisoners brought from Baton Rouge." Shepley instructed criminals convicted of aggravated crimes such as murder and arson to be placed on chain gangs. He wanted a list of prisoners subject to execution, clemency, and pardon. He also wanted a list of any prisoners suitable to enlist in the army. Three days later, he dispatched a list of twenty-two men to be recruited from the Orleans Parish prison; within a week, another fifteen names were ordered to be recruited. "They will let anybody out of prison if they will enlist," one Massachusetts soldier griped.[32]

The practice of prison recruitment continued under Union occupation, as federal officials looked to increase the ranks, but also likely looked for ways to ease the burden of a weighty prison population. In mid-September, Shepley pardoned William Howard to enlist in the U.S. army, clemency that also made Howard "restored to his civil rights." The same restoration of civil rights applied to John Rice, pardoned a month later upon agreement to enlist. For men imprisoned prior to or during Union occupation, mostly white but some of Spanish ancestry (most likely Mexican) as well, enlistment was a primary mechanism of freedom and restored citizenship. Shepley released Joseph Cohn from Fort Jackson, "in consideration of his past fidelity to the Union" and Nathaniel Ingraham because he had a son in the Union army. John P. Chambers was released on condition he supply a $500 bond for good behavior over three months. Janus Gallagher was in poor health and near the end of his term anyway when Union officials released him. Within days of Butler's arrival, James Cogan claimed to have been pressed into Confederate service and begged for release. Shepley also released a large number of civilian prisoners throughout the war with little or no clear indication as to the nature of their crime or the conditions of their release, likely an effort to clear the crowded city prisons as much as he could. Beginning in 1863, his release records also reveal numbers of Union soldiers released from New Orleans jails and reintegrated into military service.[33]

To maintain prisons, Union forces had to provide money and supplies to those institutions, which also housed Union soldiers who committed various military violations. As he recruited scores of men from prisons in September 1862, Shepley also ordered Colonel H. G. Butler to deliver three bales of Ogdenburg cloth, a ball of fine shirting, and twenty-six bundles of batting to Thomas Orpin, warden of the State Penitentiary. A few months later, he ordered the auditor of public accounts to authorize $150 for clothing and stipends for five men released from prison. Each man was to receive clothing valued at $20 and receive an additional $10 in cash. Shepley authorized these stipends of cash and clothing to outgoing prisoners throughout the war. In mid-1863, Shepley appointed Lieutenant Colonel J. A. Hopkins as supervisor of the Parish Prison and ordered him to oversee rations distributed to Union troops. Hopkins was to report to Shepley "for approval any further rules necessary to secure proper treatment and suitable food for soldiers therein confined or for the suppression of seditious conduct a treasonable compensation." As late as February 1865, Union authorities still provided clothes to prisoners held in the city.[34]

As the number of imprisoned people fluctuated under Union occupation, the military was forced to devote more bureaucratic oversight to the prison population. In July 1863, Union authorities appropriated the New Orleans Police Jail to house Union soldiers only. The parish sheriff was ordered to report directly to Shepley and bill expenses to him. By the end of October, the army was billing the City of New Orleans for the upkeep of the City Workhouse, which it christened as the new State Penitentiary. At the Parish Prison, where civilians were housed, the provost marshal commanded Sergeant J. S. Eakins to provide night buckets and kettles for all cells and repair a broken water pipe in the fall of 1864. A month later, another directive commanded him to repair the water pipe and the gas pipes. Colonel Harai Robinson ordered the keeper of the Police Jail to allow "citizen prisoners," as he referred to them, the liberty to walk around on the gallery to receive light and air. A few months later the provost marshal office ordered the prisoners vaccinated. Union guards removed smallpox patients to local hospitals, burned their bedding, and scrubbed their cells. At least one rather sophisticated escape attempt forced Union troops to repair a wall in one of the city prisons and watch the prisoners more closely. In Brashear City, the inspector general of the Lafourche District found the provost guard house a dismal affair. Confederate prisoners slept in the cramped attic of the one-story building with no fire and poor ventilation. "They are also in the habit of mingling with the guards in the lower rooms," the inspector general commented. "I regard it as a very insecure, miserable place to keep prisoners, and totally unfit to keep safely anyone inclined to escape." He reprimanded inattentive guards who also kept the books very poorly. Some of the prisoners had been in the jail for nearly three weeks and had no charges against them.[35]

Union authorities implemented imprisonment as a punishment largely involving men and predominantly focused on loyalty. Civilians and soldiers languished in various jails throughout southern Louisiana during the war, and while the inmates did not suffer like those in Andersonville or Camp Chase, their confinement reflected the capacity of the Union army to dictate civil and military order based on male submission. Not only did Union authorities imprison and release men at higher rates than women, but they also released a number of women from New Orleans jails, suggesting that the Union military was unprepared to deal with a high influx of prisoners and that they imagined prisons as predominantly a male space. As men were more likely to commit more immediately threatening offenses against Union occupation, namely guerrilla war and contraband trading, the military focused on disciplining their behavior more sternly. Confederate women engaged with the Union military in public social settings like churches and city markets and adopted confrontational but nonviolent tactics to beleaguer the Union war effort. Many directives in the Union occupation regime, like Butler's Order No. 76, conflated civil and military life and compressed gendered boundaries that separated male and female civic identities. Yet by distinguishing the space of male punishment from the female space of domestic participation in the war, Union occupiers continued to produce specific forms of masculine and feminine identity through their prison policy—primarily, that male behavior was more socially legible and therefore more threatening.[36]

During occupation the Union military did not seek to use imprisonment as a rehabilitative strategy. No major military or public figure in the Civil War discussed prisons as sites in which to reform national traitors. Rather than reforming the social behavior of delinquents, military officials hoped to manage resistance. Imprisonment was a war tactic. All war prisoners were political prisoners, and those people were rarely marked as socially distinct because of their incarceration. Rather, loyal behavior determined social status in the Union occupation regime. Promises of loyalty released many prisoners, especially men, to the streets or to the Union ranks. In a larger sense, Louisiana prisons under Union control were subsidiary institutions within the larger governing space of Union occupation itself. Michel Foucault used the notable phrase "great carceral network" to describe how other public social institutions and behavioral norms adopted the disciplinary techniques that emerged in early nineteenth-century prisons, namely observation, critique, and physical punishment. Military occupiers avoided larger dialogues about reform and incarceration by expediting personal status through loyalty oaths. Prisons were momentary stages, not static institutions, in the wartime production of loyalty.[37]

By extending food, clothing, and shelter to thousands of Black and white Louisianans, the Union army filled the gap left by southern patriarchs who were dead, imprisoned, in the Confederate ranks, or impoverished by war. In the immediate days following Union invasion, indigent southern civilians in southern Louisiana relied on Butler to alleviate the extensive effects of the Union blockade and spring flooding on the local food supply. "The town is fairly and squarely on the point of starvation," John De Forest recorded. Irish and German immigrants hovered at the perimeters of his regiment and begged for even "the refuse of our rations." Immediately upon his arrival in July, internal revenue collector George Denison noted, "Thousands in this city are almost starving for food, and well dressed men and women beg bread (frequently) from Uncle Sam's boys, to keep themselves and children from starving." Butler made his relief program highly notable through General Order No. 55, which taxed wealthy Confederates and used the money to distribute some $50,000 of relief per month to around 11,000 families. By the end of the year, the city's Relief Commission reported an approximate 35,000 people supported by the Union administration, including 1,042 families of Confederate soldiers.[38]

Alarmed at the rate of refugees, especially formerly enslaved people, who crossed the lines as the war continued, Union forces did their best to catalog the number and identity of refugees, as well as provide limited aid. "You will be pleased to make returns to this office monthly the numbers of males and also of females coming into our lines in your parish as refugees," Bowen wrote to Provost Marshal George Darling in early 1864. He was also ordered to note the number of Confederate deserters. All refugees from beyond Union lines who entered New Orleans had to appear before the provost marshal, "who will immediately examine them with a view of determining their character and their motive in giving them selves [sic] up." After December 1863, Union officers were required to read Lincoln's Amnesty Proclamation to all refugees in case any of them desired to take the oath. Even as they provided relief and worked to incorporate southern refugees back into national society, Union officers still appraised the loyalties of refugees to prevent Confederate spies from infiltrating the occupation zone.[39]

To secure the occupation zone from Confederate infiltration and optimize their relief efforts for southern citizens, the Union army increasingly implemented banishment. This war tactic affected men and women across the occupied South who chose to maintain Confederate allegiance. Ardent Confederate supporters or simple public nuisances could be ejected from the occupation zone. As Banks informed a subordinate in May 1863, "All persons have had opportunity in New Orleans at least, to determine whether they can live under the government of the United States. The hour has now come when they must choose their destination." That same month, Union police in New Orleans banished W. Van Winkle, alias W. C. Allen, for counterfeiting Confederate money. Union officials confiscated some $84,000 in false bills from him and destroyed them. Banishment also served to further reduce southern patriarchs from their positions of household authority. One New Orleans woman also observed in May, "every man who is a registered enemy will be obliged to leave the city, but . . . their families will be allowed to remain." Due to the "great service rendered by his wife in the care of sick and wounded soldiers," Shepley released Charles Read, convicted of a violent act, from prison on the condition that he leave the Department of the Gulf for the duration of the war.[40]

The military also supported private institutions and even used private funding to do so. Union authorities funneled state funds totaling at least $16,000 to Catholic, Protestant, and city social organizations during the war. These establishments included the Catholic Society for the Education of Indigent Orphans, the New Orleans Orphans Home, the Ladies of Providence, St. Mary Catholic Orphan Asylum for Boys and Girls, and numerous others. Of those funds, $1,500 went to schools and an orphanage for free people of color, established in antebellum New Orleans by revolutionary reformist Creoles. Union officials also aided the public school system in Louisiana and subsidized Unionist newspapers. From 1862 to 1864, Shepley authorized funds totaling some $11,000 from the Louisiana state treasury for Charity Hospital in New Orleans. Most aid of this kind developed in urban areas, especially New Orleans, because the Union military was most established there, but Union troops distributed aid in more rural areas as well. Over twenty officers and enlisted men in Brashear City donated a total of $51 from their own pockets to refugees who entered the city in spring 1864.[41]

Union administrators demonstrated the power of a growing national state in occupied Louisiana when they superintended projects of financial support for social institutions and those injured by the war. Southerners who benefited from federal aid experienced a new relationship to the American government, which had largely left charity to the private sector before the U.S. Civil War. Union authorities used confiscation as a war tactic and provided the federal government with millions of dollars of revenue from the occupation regime, especially in confiscated sugar and cotton crops. They also foreshadowed future statist operations of social relief by requisitioning state funds for local institutions and by taxing the southern population to fund the occupation effort. Some Union officials went so far as to assess damages to Confederate sympathizers in order to pay restitution to Unionists who lost property or lives to Confederate attacks.[42]

The Union command also forbade trade with the enemy, unless sanctioned by the government (as with the cotton trade), in order to starve the Confederacy of vital supplies and to occlude Confederate opportunities to infiltrate

Union lines. "You will prevent all illicit trade," General Bowen ordered the provost marshal of Brashear City in August 1863, "and the action of all individuals the tendency of which is to give aid to the enemy." A month later, Bowen granted exclusive charge of trade permits to the Internal Revenue Department, with stipulations. The Internal Revenue Department could grant permits only in parishes designated weekly by the provost marshal general; those permits could go only to those presumably loyal persons approved by parish provost marshals; and Bowen expected a weekly report from George Denison detailing the amount of goods shipped and to whom. The following year, Bowen began regulating drug sales in the parishes immediately outside New Orleans. Every purveyor had to report the amount of drugs they had on hand. Additionally, the provost marshal required purveyors "to give the names and residence of every purchaser of any considerable amount plainly written, so that we may know who sells and who buys contraband drugs in undue quantities." General Stephen Hurlbut also commanded provost marshals to inspect all packages arriving for Union soldiers before delivering them. By early 1865, Union commanders closed all trade stores on the east bank of the Mississippi River from College Point in St. James Parish to Red Church in St. Charles Parish. Only military stores were allowed to stay open. All goods in the closed stores were to be remanded to New Orleans.[43]

In August of that same year, the provost marshal in Baton Rouge structured the local marketplace to alleviate the financial strains of the poor in the city. "All persons now in occupation of the Baking business, and every person intending to commerce the same" were commanded to declare themselves and their goods to the Street Commissioner's Office on Pike's Row. In order to keep the high price of flour within an affordable range for the citizens of Baton Rouge, bakers were ordered to sell forty-eight ounces of bread for twenty cents, twenty-four for ten cents, and twelve ounces for a nickel. Any violators would suffer a fine between $10 and $20 each time they failed to comply. Intriguingly, the provost marshal also required that anyone who bought bread at a higher price report their names, the names of the baker, "and leave a loaf of the bread purchased" along with a statement of the price at the Street Commissioner's Office. Price controls such as these also resonated with Union policies of welfare relief, for they aimed to make basic food staples accessible for as many people as possible.[44]

Despite the numerous restrictions on trade, people well positioned within the occupation regime could make substantial profits. Allied with Union occupiers, northern investors, loyal southern businessmen, and cooperative property owners also profited from supplying the Union war effort and fortifying a labor system premised on export products. Weed, Witters, & Co., a wholesale grocer in New Orleans, supplied the Hermitage Plantation with castor oil, Epsom salts, pork, borax, potatoes, brushes, collars, corn, cod fish, coal oil, lime, strawberries, lima beans, butter, ducks, molasses, shoes, and eating utensils. In 1864 alone, the grocer billed the government for over $8,000. Members of the Phoenix Inn Company in New Orleans, "whose officers are loyal citizens," Shepley determined, applied for and received permission to sell ten thousand barrels of coal confiscated from M. J. Bryce. These trade alliances between the Union military and local merchants kept the occupation regime supplied during the war. But when Union officials forged economic partnerships with locals they also privileged older forms of power in Louisiana through which white merchants, land owners, and tradesmen maintained unequal relationships to laborers, especially formerly enslaved people who sought avenues toward self-actualization promised on the free market.[45]

Union soldiers themselves collected personal profits during occupation, both from legitimate fees and business dealings as well as an array of covert enterprises and bribes. While Union commanders like Butler and Banks supposedly pilfered money and property in occupied Louisiana, average northern men in the ranks also embodied a culture of enterprise that arose from their own perceptions of democratic privilege, as Andrew Lang writes. Participating in local markets gave soldiers some avenue toward the autonomy they desired and potentially unmoored them from dependence on army wages and the lethargy of occupation. As independent marketeers, Union soldiers reclaimed their manhood from the debilitating managerial occupation order. While many Union officers worried that informal bartering would demoralize and disorganize the ranks, enlisted men often scorned officers who used the army's hierarchy to garner more profit than regular troops did.[46]

Extralegal economic endeavors numbered among a variety of internal problems that Union occupation commanders faced in Louisiana. Banks had the quartermaster of the 13th Connecticut arrested for "allowing or causing the public wagon animals and teamsters in his charge to be used for the transportation of cotton for private purposes." George Darling, provost marshal in St. Charles and St. John Parishes, frequently suffered rebuke from his superiors for high administrative expenses and using unauthorized civilian employees in his office. On March 15, 1864, General Bowen issued Special Order No. 28 directly to Darling: "From and after this date, all taxes on licenses to trade, and fees for passes imposed by you will be abolished. You will grant passes to persons under the existing regulations." The following day, Darling was ordered to settle all claims against his office and send a final statement to headquarters in New Orleans. Yet by November, Darling was in trouble again when he was once more caught charging southerners for passes.[47]

Discipline problems extended to property destruction and theft as well, which divided Union occupiers more than any other issue. In his May 1 proclamation of occupation, Butler had promised to punish any Union soldier who violated the property of a southerner who had taken an oath of loyalty to the United States. Banks reiterated Butler's position, chiding one officer that "peaceable inhabitants of the enemy country are entitled during its occupation by our army to the same protection against violence and plunder as if they had taken the oath of allegiance." Barely three months into Banks's administration, the owner of Belle Chaise Plantation complained that Union troops were pulling up his cane crop. In March 1863, Banks ordered the arrest of 2nd Lieutenant Samuel E. Hunt and fifteen soldiers for "quitting their colors to plunder or pillage." Hunt was charged with conduct unbecoming an officer and a gentleman. In the summer, a woman accused some enlisted New Hampshire men of stealing two horses that belonged to her children. Banks also expressed anger with Colonel Lewis M. Beck, 173rd New York, for stealing a piano, books, paper, and other valuables from a southern widow.[48]

Oftentimes these incidents of destruction and theft arose from the boredom, mean-spiritedness, or vindictiveness of some individual Union soldiers, but on a larger scale, Union troops seriously debated the nature of property destruction as an appropriate form of warfare. During the Red River campaign in the spring of 1864, William H. Stewart, a captain in the 95th Illinois, lamented the destructive tendencies of some of the soldiers under his command as unwholesome and dispiriting. "Strange with what ardor soldiers jump at the chance of burning and destroying something & grumble if they are not permitted," he wrote in March 1864. "Their bump of destructiveness must be large or else grows active by use until it becomes morbid and a power." Stewart found such destructive tendencies frustrating. "I can't bear it, and it requires the strongest kind of provocation to make me consent to it. It looks so wanton and outrageous. General has issued strenuous orders against meddling or destroying any property on pain of death and holds officers responsible." A few days later, Stewart and his regiment offloaded from a steamer carrying them up the Mississippi River, but "the boys had one building burning within an hour of landing and as a Consequence [sic] were piped aboard again—so it is— a few whose fingers burn to destroy something or steal something until it becomes a mania makes it necessary to enforce the most rigid rules." He was also "never more disgusted and outraged in my life" when some Union soldiers robbed an elderly couple of everything they owned. Other Union soldiers lamented that they were sometimes no more than "cattle-drivers and government horse-gobblers."[49]

Despite his frustrations and moralist rhetoric, Stewart and other Union soldiers often enacted what they considered to be legitimate violence and destruction on southerners as retribution, military necessity, or as part of hard war tactics intended to deprive the Confederacy of the material means to continue the war. During the campaign, Stewart and his troops burned cotton gins, bales of cotton, a Confederate fort, and buildings from which Confederate troops attacked Union troops. When his regiment reached Campti, Union troops removed a large supply of salt from the place and General J. K. Smith wanted to burn the town. "I pity these poor people who are to be turned out houseless yet it is one of the fazes [sic] of war and a necessity. We cannot leave a garrison and will not do to leave a place for the Rebs to congregate and fire upon our transports." Stewart was torn over such extensive destruction but ultimately he blamed the Confederate military. "It is what their own soldiers have brought upon them and they must endure it the best they can." Nevertheless, Smith decided to spare the town and Stewart celebrated. "Humanity prevailed," he wrote as the Union army departed, "For this destruction of property and heaping misery upon those already helpless and miserable is to me exceedingly annoying." Unfortunately for the inhabitants of Campti, other Union troops later burned the town anyway to protect their line of communication and supply.[50]

Union occupation commanders attempted to curtail instances of unsanctioned violence and theft by soldiers. In 1863, one Union commander forbid provost marshal officers to enter public buildings or private houses in Baton Rouge and search them without a written order. A year later, General Philip St. George Cooke instructed all military personnel who were in possession of Confederate property (aside from "supplies which are necessary in military operations") to immediately turn it over to the provost marshal. In New Orleans, a member of the special military police reported Union soldiers in a confiscated house on St. Charles Street were selling items from the house for a profit. Most likely, Union authorities issued these orders not just to protect southern property but also to prevent a constant stream of southern citizens from clogging the offices of the provost marshal. Although it is not readily apparent that Confederate citizens consciously thought of badgering the Union occupation bureaucracy as a form of resistance (by preventing the Union army from more pressing duties), it is not difficult to imagine that Union officials issued commands that aided southern citizens in hopes of streamlining their own duties. On some occasions, as with the theft on St. Charles Street, Union officers repaid the losses to original property owners or to the federal government. Some provost marshal officers even seized property or livestock from Black laborers to reimburse white property owners.[51]

Restrictive commands and moral language like that of William Stewart demonstrated that Union soldiers held varying attitudes about their behavior during occupation. Numerous Union soldiers directly targeted households in occupied areas as a strategy of war. As Lisa Tendrich Frank argues, "Throughout the home-front campaigns, Union soldiers explicitly treated female civilians as the enemy and as military objectives unto themselves." Yet at times Union troops exercised a "sense of discriminating righteousness," as Mark Grimsley writes. In occupied regions, thefts of food or livestock might suggest that sometimes Union soldiers were more interested in sustaining themselves or their private economic enterprises than attacking Confederates. Stewart believed that the destructive behavior of a few Union men limited the privileges of many. "These same reprobates are the ones that cry loudest on account of the restraint—calling it protecting rebel property and all that, claiming a great deal of principle and Patriotism [sic] in committing their depredations." Stewart rejected those reasonings. "Fudge and fudge to a large mass of the same kind of talk in Northern papers," he quipped. Even when destruction occurred under orders, Stewart argued, such behavior "tends more to demoralize and injure our army than all the injury it does the Rebel cause." If destruction had to occur, he compromised, officers should oversee the process and punish, even with execution, those who pressed too far. On the other hand, Stewart was happy to feast on beef and sugar liberated from a plantation occupied by his regiment during the campaign, and he had no qualms about burning down houses from which Confederate troops fired on his men. While it was a site of enhanced state power and of experimentation with reconstructed democracy, occupied Louisiana also proved to be a location where Union military men decided what kind of war they were fighting. Their decisions just as often targeted southern homes as spared them.[52]

Despite the proactive efforts that the Union military took to establish hospitable relations with Louisianans and protect private and public property, prolonged Union occupation increasingly disrupted community economies. Especially as guerrilla warfare and illicit trade intensified in the later years of the war, Union forces zealously guarded the Mississippi River and its numerous tributaries. "A system of smuggling is being carried on, at or near the foot of Orange Street," one Union officer informed Captain John Burke, chief of special detectives, "by which cotton is being conveyed from some captured schooners to a picket near by." The shore police were complicit in the action because they looked the other way as smugglers received cotton from skiffs sent down the river. Burke was ordered to arrest the pickets and the smugglers. A few days before that incident, Burke was seeking to arrest a mysterious officer on board a ship called the *Pierce*. Ship officers who traded passengers on the river or deposited passengers on shore without authorization could be fined as much as $1,000. In the summer of 1864, the provost marshal escalated tactics by seizing all the boats without permits around Brashear City, which was seated at the end of the Lower Atchafalaya River amid a network of lakes and bayous. Such an action could not help but have a deleterious effect on local relations and economics.[53]

Tension between Union occupiers and southern citizens could produce acts of sabotage or violence. On May 6, 1863, New Orleans police discovered multiple house fires in the Second District of New Orleans. "At about 8 1/2pm fire was Discovered in a kitchen in the rear of house No 220 Bienville St owned & occupied by Mr Smith[.] The inmates of the house was [*sic*] absent during the evening and on returning home found fire had been set in the kitchen in a box containing some corn shucks." Fortunately they doused the fire before too much damage occurred but the police surmised that "it was evidently the work of an incendiary. Mr Smith is I understand a loyal citizen." That same night police rushed to a fire on Canal Street. "The alarm was given by the private watchman on the opposite side of the street. The fire was put out with but slight damage to the building." The building had been vacant for several months the police determined, but they suspected that an incendiary generated this fire as well. In an inspection of the surrounding areas, police found in another vacant building across the street "a lighted candle with some matches on a piece of paste board in a bundle of straw & rubbish." Police eventually caught a man named Thomas Robertson as he tried to set fire to a woman's house on the corner of Love and Bagatelle Streets that night. They removed several burning rags from under her home. Records do not reveal further investigation or arrests, or if Robertson was a Confederate, but the fact that Union authorities ordered an exhaustive catalog of loyal and disloyal firemen within days of Robertson's arrest indicated they probably had reason to suspect attempted sabotage from Confederate sympathizers.[54]

Other local acts of resistance plagued the managing infrastructure of Union occupation. In May 1863, provost marshal officers in Donaldsonville arrested two men for cutting telegraph wires near Union lines but promised them release if they led Union soldiers to other guilty parties. Apparently the men objected. Banks then ordered the provost marshal "to arrest the owner of any plantation upon which the telegraph may be interfered with unless he points out the guilty party." Other troops arrested a Catholic priest in Baton Rouge for observing Union operations, even though he had a pass signed by the provost marshal. Subsequently, Banks warned the commanding officer of Baton Rouge to be careful of "depredations" committed by Confederate sympathizers. Suspicious police officers even arrested four Union officers in New Orleans as they walked home late one night. One was an aide to Banks and the police officers received quite a scolding the following day.[55]

Beyond smuggling and acts of sabotage, Confederate guerrilla bands actively forestalled Union advances and afflicted the occupation zone. Although some irregular troops were marauders without loyalty to either side, most guerrilla troops arose from local Louisiana communities and they fought the war guided by community strategies of supply and resistance. In the fall of 1863, a newly stationed provost marshal in Houma, Louisiana, reported to a superior that "most, if not all the inhabitants were rank rebels and I should not be able to get along without trouble if I did not have a guard." Faced with destruction, imprisonment, or impressment under Union occupation, many southern men more than likely joined guerrilla groups not just to oppose the Union but also to shield their communities and protect their status as southern men. As Union forces pressed deeper into northern and eastern Louisiana, formal military and local resistance stiffened. As in other parts of the war-torn Confederacy, guerrilla warfare and domestic resistance thrived despite the nebulous web of Union military surveillance and security. Union troops could not be everywhere at once. Dense Louisiana bayous shrouded rampant guerrilla activity. Despite persistent efforts, Union forces never managed to completely quell informal resistance, domestic supply lines, illicit trading, or secret mail services.[56]

By the fall of 1864, after Banks's defeat in the Red River Campaign and the reduction of Union forces in the state, guerrilla warfare forced the Union military to assume a largely defensive posture. Confederate guerrilla forces penetrated the Union-held Lafourche District, plagued Union military maneuvers, raided Unionist homes and stores, and especially targeted plantations that had been repurposed as free labor sites for freedpeople. Harassed by guerrillas who burned bridges and destroyed rail lines earlier in 1862, Butler offered a bounty of $1,000 for any guerrilla's head. Union commanders sometimes responded with destruction as retribution. Rear Admiral Farragut issued a statement to the town of Donaldsonville in the summer of 1862: "Every time my boats are fired upon, I will burn a portion of your town," which he did on August 9. Despite these early acts of retribution, in 1864 guerrilla forces accelerated attacks in southern Louisiana, stressing already beleaguered Union forces. Confederate partisan attacks kept the Union occupation forces spread thin and increasingly vigilant about internal security. Confederate and Union forces in the state fought one another as well as hunted various rogue contingents of runaways, backwoods partisans, and guerrilla bands like that under the St. Landry Parish jayhawker Ozème Carrière.[57]

More than mindless killing, guerrilla war was culture war. In the eyes of harassed Union troops, guerrillas were rebellious American sons who had broken with the American national family and, by exercising uncivilized tactics like bushwhacking, invited punitive retribution from loyal citizen-soldiers. Killing or capturing guerrillas was the ultimate manifestation of Union discipline tactics on a rebellious southern society. From their own perspective, guerrillas responded to an oppressive state project of occupation. If Union occupation reduced the economic sustainability of rural communities and reoriented rural spaces to adhere to Union loyalty, rural southerners implemented irregular war to reclaim their own community space. Guerrilla forces could envision themselves fighting not so much for the Confederacy as for Louisiana or their local communities.[58]

In response to guerrilla attacks and general fears of disloyalty, the Union army implemented three strategies to reinforce its security state. First, the military imposed more rigorous reports and supervision to surveil occupied areas. Reporting some two hundred guerrillas near plantations in Bonnet Carre, provost marshal headquarters in New Orleans ordered Captain Winslow Roberts to keep a proper record of all allegiance oaths. Near New Orleans, an officer on Bowen's staff wrote to George Darling, "If you administer the . . . oath, and fill out the Descriptive List, and send it in every ten days, it will not be necessary to send the deserters here but you must look out that you do not administer it to any *spy*." He ordered Darling to be very particular in his administration of the oath.[59]

While the Union military did not always perceive distinctions between Confederate irregulars and local antagonists, Union troops were not unaware of the local politics involved with domestic resistance. They understood not every secret cotton trade or stolen mule was a sign of subversive military activity. They also understood, as one Union soldier commented, "The Jayhawkers are bands of Robbers neither Sesech nor Union & the sesech *ever* fear them." Loyalty and survival were complicated matters, and because Union occupiers could not always distinguish between loyal and disloyal locals they kept an eye on those whom they considered to be actively disloyal. In October 1862, Union authorities were alerted to secessionist meetings held in a New Orleans home. "They receive then and read newspapers and letters," a house servant reported, and "sends papers and letters three times a week to Guerrillas over the river." Another southerner reported on Samuel Lee and others who entered New Orleans as much as twice a week to bring secret arms and ammunition back to Confederate forces. In late 1863, Albert Stearns sent two applications for sutler clerks to his superior in Brashear City. "Hawley I think is all right," Stearns commented, "Moore I think may be after cotton, but I have no proof of it in hand." Upon the recommendation of a previous commander, General Cameron, commanding the Lafourche District in the fall of 1864, employed a local resident named O. Martin and his friends as scouts. By late October, the general had "lost all confidence in them and revokes all orders employing them." Their papers were to be taken up at once, he commanded. Similarly, Asa

Douglas and James Syers lost their commissions as branch pilots for the Port of New Orleans for several days until they could prove their loyalty once more.[60]

Second, the Union military also restricted mobility and commerce among residents of south Louisiana, an action that often applied to Black Americans more strenuously than whites. Throughout the months of 1862, commanders and provost marshals endeavored to strengthen the parameters of Union-controlled territory and establish a pass system. In September, Shepley ordered the provost marshal of Plaquemines and St. Bernard Parishes to prevent all persons Black and white from entering or leaving either parish without authorized passes. A month later, one Union officer wrote to provost marshal headquarters in New Orleans for instructions about fishermen and boatmen passing by Fort Macomb, northeast of the city. Many who sailed by had passes from the commander of the guard at Lakeport and other commands, but "of late fishermen and others have had passes coming from various persons and it is hard to tell the genuine." The following year, Union officers continued to heighten their security protocols. In the summer of 1863, Shepley ordered all captain pilots in the New Orleans port to "examine all boats and all persons cruising in boats about the Passes of the Mississippi and detain all suspicious persons and report the same to the proper authorities." Rural Union commands completed registries of residents in the parishes outside New Orleans and endeavored to stabilize a free labor system in which Black workers had limited mobility and personal rights.[61]

As a final method for combating local resistance, Union forces regularly employed southern white men as part of the occupation security state in Louisiana, often to the disadvantage of Black people. Just as they had filled numerous administrative roles with loyal southerners, Union commanders sometimes relied on local whites for guidance, information, and support. In particular, provost marshal figures harnessed the power of slave patrols when they made local agreements with white property owners to expand and maintain that security state. In St. John Parish, the provost marshal divided the parish into three districts and gave civilian patrols wide latitude in security measures. Appointed by the provost marshal, patrol chiefs had authority to create detachments "of those subject to patrol duties." They were "enjoyned [sic] to patrol often and where-ever they shall think it necessary eather [sic] during the day or night, above all or the eve of a Sunday a holy-day or day of assembly at Church . . . as to keep Negroes in good order and for the purpose of asserting runaway Negroes and suspicious persons." Patrols were required to deploy at least once a week, "at irregular times," or at any time day or night that the provost marshal called upon them, upon penalty of a fine between ten and twenty-five dollars. Patrols required at least five white men, armed, with at least ten rounds of ammunition. Planters were required to furnish managers, overseers, or "other White persons under there [sic] orders" lest they be subject to a fine, as were white men who refused service without providing a substitute. Patrols were to be made on public roads and crop roads. Patrol chiefs could visit Negro quarters without permission. "Any strange Negro who shall be found" had to present a pass or face the provost marshal. Any mule or horse they might be riding was to be returned to the owner or confiscated. If the patrols discovered any Black person who had a permit from a master but "found pursuing a contrary direction to that indicated in the permit," that person was to be hauled before the provost marshal. Though firearms were restricted to moments considered absolutely necessary, the patrols were authorized to arrest vagabonds, suspicious persons, anyone disturbing the peace, and even shoot those resisting arrest or attempting escape.[62]

The racial component of these military protocols demonstrated an inherent racial unity among white men in occupied Louisiana, regardless of their loyalty. Even if white southern patriarchs faced a reduction in their own self-mastery because of occupation, patrol regulations such as these signified how many could re-establish those old authorities under the auspices of Union authority. Racially charged civil-military service like parish patrols simulated the cultural militarism endemic to southern slave society prior to occupation and empowered white southern men to maintain previous racial hierarchies. Loyal southern men cooperated with Union occupation not only by articulating the rhetoric of moral character in service to public order, but also aligned with Union concerns about racial security as well. Concurrently, even as an army of liberation, many soldiers in blue did not look favorably upon Black people. They too used the apparatus of occupation to curtail Black social inclusion. Captured in the grasp of the occupation state, formerly enslaved people experienced severe judgments on their public character and limitations of their human rights.

Unfortunately for newly freed Black Americans, the greatest managerial triumph of Union occupation in Louisiana—the creation of a new Unionist state government in 1864—largely cemented a conservative political reality that was inhospitable to radical visions of an improved American democracy. As the war progressed and Lincoln sought to draw Louisiana back into the United States, Union commanders used their bureaucratic state, infused with paternalist racial bias, to host local and state elections. When Lincoln issued his Proclamation of Amnesty and Reconstruction on December 8, 1863, Banks hoped to register as many loyal voters as possible for a February 1864 election. "It is of public importance that a large vote be cast at the elections ordered by the Commanding General on the 22nd," Bowen wrote. Union authorities discovered that many loyal voters planned on staying home because they lived too far from provost marshal outposts and voter registration sites. To solve this issue, Banks ordered Bowen and subordinates to appoint parish agents and invest them with the power of administering the loyalty oath under Lincoln's new terms. "You will be pleased to report to me," Bowen ordered, "the names of such number of loyal citizens of good moral characters, as in your opinion will be sufficient to have in your parish & afford every citizen an opportunity to take the oath of allegiance for the purpose of voting at the ensuing election." He authorized provost marshals to fulfill the duties of local sheriffs if they failed to administer the oath or register voters. Not only did Union commanders continue to fuse public moral character, national loyalty, and civil rights, they were also willing to supplant nonmilitary leaders in the process. Shepley appointed at least six civilian attachés to administer oaths of office and oaths of allegiance in days preceding the election. Union authorities even halted all boat traffic to register voters and give all passengers an opportunity to vote on February 22.[63]

The 1864 election was an important example of how the bureaucratic operations of occupation directly shaped the course of the war in Louisiana. Lincoln's pressure on Banks for a hasty election after his Proclamation of Amnesty delayed the general's invasion of the Red River Valley. Banks was delayed several weeks as he oversaw the election. In addition to the fact that he had to return ten thousand men on loan from Sherman's army in Mississippi, Banks no doubt felt rushed as he hastened northward to Alexandria. When he entered the city in late March, Banks was again beset with bureaucratic problems as scores of distressed southern citizens descended on his office with complaints of property loss and Union mistreatment. This delayed Banks another few crucial days.[64]

With Banks's influence, Michael Hahn swept the election for governor and a coalition of moderate and conservative politicians took control of the new government being established in Louisiana. "The election of State Officers is important only as a commencement of the work of restoration," Banks celebrated. Yet few of the newly elected men believed in Black suffrage. At the constitutional convention, the radicals seated only four delegates. After five days of debate, the convention outlawed slavery, though the body deliberated at length over the question of compensation before settling in favor of federal compensation to loyal and disloyal owners. Conservatives resisted taxes to aid Black education. Despite initial high hopes for political citizenship, Black suffrage activists in Louisiana had increasingly little faith in the Unionist state government. Instead, they looked to the Radical Republicans in Congress to push through Black suffrage on a national level.[65]

As Union occupiers traversed the conflicted terrain between an army of deliverance and an organization that suppressed democratic rights, they demonstrated dual motivations. On the one hand, Union men cherished a heritage of restraint and a suspicion of standing armies as agents of abuse. In contrast, they exercised restrictive or even destructive tactics against an increasingly belligerent enemy population. Occupiers troubled democracy. On the other hand, they restored the republic through lawful coercion and social relief policies. Simultaneously, they threatened social order, gender decorum, free speech, and property rights, which ultimately served to prolong the cultural struggle between North and South for many decades after the Civil War. For as much as many Union occupiers resented southerners for violating the sacred tenets of national union, they also collaborated over shared racial assumptions of social order. Emancipation loosed shackles but it did not alter the political atmosphere for Black people. Union occupiers destroyed the Confederate state, but they also (re)constructed a national order that buttressed racial antipathy.[66]

The Union's bureaucratic military state also functioned as a general welfare state. Union authorities distributed clothing and funds to released prisoners, refunded many southerners who lost property, and provided extensive public aid to refugees and formerly enslaved people. Through this aid, Union soldiers and commanders could often anticipate harmonious relationships of mutual support from some Louisianans. Yet because the Union army was fighting a war to restore national unity, not mend class inequality, Union aid did not precipitate a sustained state project of social uplift along racial or class lines.

Without a substantial redistribution of land or a reorientation of the market-place away from large cash crops, Union occupation presented an unappealing cultural change to poor whites, one that reduced them to dependents without even the limited antebellum avenues of self-advancement. As poor whites be-grudgingly signed loyalty oaths, resisted occupation, or sprang from the bushes to attack Union troops and Unionist neighbors, they fought a war for communities and households where they maintained power as men.

In occupied Louisiana, the Union military stumbled toward a statist order. The use of military coercion to maintain social order was nothing new to the American state by the outbreak of war. However, the use of military power to enforce social and economic policy among white people was something of a newer feature in the American democratic experiment. By orchestrating the politics of loyal space through evolving relationships of discipline and mutualism, the Union army managed inclusion in the body politic of occupied Louisiana. Military occupation in Civil War Louisiana demonstrated in microcosm the tensions around national belonging that are endemic to democratic states. The Union military fixated its gaze on white men, as seen in the numerous requests for jobs and government support from white southern men, as well as in the extensive registries of white men generated by Union occupation bureaucrats. For southern women and formerly enslaved people under occupation, they pursued alternative but equally visible avenues of inclusion and resistance.[67]

Benjamin Morgan Palmer: As a prominent Presbyterian minister in New Orleans, Palmer publicly endorsed secession and later declared that Union authorities had no right to require loyalty oaths from the occupied southern population. A portrait of Benjamin Palmer, Images from the Civil War and Reconstruction, 55-FF Box 21, Tulane University Special Collections, Tulane University, New Orleans.

Governor Thomas Overton Moore: The first wartime governor of Louisiana. Moore organized as much support for the Confederate war effort as possible but lamented that the Confederate government did not prioritize the defense of Louisiana. William Emerson Strong Photograph Album, Duke University Libraries.

General Benjamin F. Butler: Butler earned a reputation for duplicitous and cruel behavior among many southerners because his domestic occupation policies targeted the southern household so effectively. Courtesy of the Library of Congress.

General George F. Shepley: Commissioned as colonel of the 12th Maine in late 1861, Shepley was promoted to brigadier general and military governor of Louisiana in summer of 1862. He remained in that position until March 1864. Courtesy of Maine Special Collections.

Harper's Weekly Illustration of New Orleans Ladies, July 12, 1862: This humorous cartoon depicted rebellious New Orleans women who supposedly altered their behavior in response to Butler's General Order No. 28. Viewing this image, northerners could imagine that their culture war on the Confederacy was having good effect. Courtesy of the Library of Congress.

Harper's Weekly Illustration of Starving New Orleans Citizens, June 14, 1862: Despite angry Confederate depictions of Union occupation in Louisiana, the Union military made many efforts to support the dependent population, especially women and children. Courtesy of the Library of Congress.

Harper's Weekly Illustration, "Registered Enemies Taking the Oath of Allegiance at the Office of Gen. Bowen, at New Orleans—From a Sketch by Mr. J. R. Hamilton," June 6, 1863: Oaths were no guarantee of Union loyalty among the occupied southern population, but it was a public ritual of submission and a practical mechanism by which Union authorities could maintain social order. Courtesy of the Library of Congress.

Captain Albert Stearns: A former police officer from New York, Albert Stearns served in a variety of provost marshal positions in occupied Louisiana from 1862 to 1864. This photo of Stearns, his wife Martha Louis Snow Stearns, and daughter (most likely Mattie Stearns) was taken on Camp Street in New Orleans. Courtesy of the Library of Congress.

Baton Rouge Contraband Camp: This former female seminary became a contraband camp in 1863. Such camps provided a modicum of freedom yet also produced familiar material and racial dependencies for emancipated people. G. H. Suydam Photograph Collection, Mss. 1394, Louisiana and Lower Mississippi Valley Collections, LSU Libraries, Baton Rouge, Louisiana.

General Nathaniel P. Banks: Banks replaced Butler in December 1862 and although he handled domestic issues like his predecessor, he was more concerned with military campaigns to capture Port Hudson in 1863 and Shreveport in 1864. Courtesy of the Louisiana State Museum.

General James Bowen: Bowen took occupation policies very seriously. As provost marshal general of the Department of the Gulf, he demanded loyalty oaths from southerners, cracked down on illicit trade, monitored the mobility of Black labor, and helped organize the free state election in February 1864. Courtesy of the Library of Congress.

Adjutant-General Thomas addressing the Negroes in Louisiana on the duties of freedom: Numerous Black men in the Mississippi Valley joined the Union army, but household and family concerns remained paramount to them. Courtesy of the Library of Congress.

NAME	CLASS	PAY PER MONTH	REMARKS.
Ann Shaw & 2 children 6, 12 years old	1st	$8.00	
Carmelit Prov & one children, 2 years old	4th	$3.00	

Norbert Bodin

Witness

Albert Stearns
Capt & Pro. Mar.

Labor Contract: This labor contract signed by Norbert Bodin was countersigned by Albert Stearns as provost marshal of St. Mary and St. Martin Parishes. The form specified male workers at the top, so one of the signers shoehorned "and women" into the print, a practice repeated on many forms. Norbert Bodin labor contract, March 25, 1864, Entry 1519, Letters Received, Department of the Gulf, Box 2, Part 4, Record Group 393; National Archives Building, Washington, D.C.

"General Banks Addressing the Louisiana Planters in the Parlor of the St. Charles Hotel, New Orleans": Banks and conservative Unionist planters in Louisiana formed a political bond that shaped a restrictive labor regime for formerly enslaved people. Courtesy of the Louisiana State Museum.

General E. Kirby Smith: Smith was essentially a benevolent military dictator in the Trans-Mississippi Department. He worked in cooperation with Confederate governors and butted heads with General Richard Taylor over military strategy in Louisiana. Courtesy of the Louisiana State Museum.

Governor Henry Watkins Allen: Often praised as the most able administrative leader in the Confederacy, Allen was a former general who became governor in 1864. He embodied the merger of military and civilian concerns within Louisiana's Confederate government during the war. Andrew D. Lytle Collection, Mss. 893, 1254, Louisiana and Lower Mississippi Valley Collections, LSU Libraries, Baton Rouge, Louisiana.

4

Sentinels of the Household War

BLACK & WHITE WOMEN CONFRONT OCCUPATION

As a state project of subjugation, Union occupation was a male endeavor that concentrated on reducing male military resistance, enlisting or imprisoning men, and reappropriating male-dominated government structures. In the classical western tradition, men who bore arms were the enemy. Women, most nineteenth-century militarists and thinkers would have agreed, did not bear arms and did not constitute enemies of the state. But in Civil War Louisiana, as the Union military discovered across the Confederacy, women were able foes. Southern women (white and Black) and Union soldiers understood that public and private space translated into public power. Subsequently, southern women and the occupation forces endeavored to influence or enforce the will of occupied regions in their favor. Occupied women reoriented power relations in occupied territory by forcing Union officials to regard them as domestic combatants. White women challenged Union prohibitions on Confederate loyalty, and Black women undermined the social system of white dominance as well as white assumptions about racial inferiority. Their actions compelled Union authorities to (re)construct a state that simultaneously recognized women as dependents in need of relief and citizens in need of regulation.[1]

In nineteenth-century America, men believed in women's natural inferiority at the same time as they valorized their own calling to protect the invaluable dignity of women. This gendered double standard—women as inferior subjects but valuable objects—produced strange contortions in law and social custom. Under American law and within the minds of many American women in the nineteenth century, coverture laws effectively meant that women's obligations to male family superseded their obligations to the state. The Civil War, and military occupation especially, troubled these established ideas by revealing the limitations of male power to "cover" their women while highlighting the capacity of females to bridge the interstices between their legal identity and their lived reality. When Union occupation authorities regulated the political participation of southern women, they inadvertently recognized women as potent political subjects even as they relied on prejudicial gender assumptions to build their regulations. Black women were often beheld as doubly inferior for being female and Black. When white people asserted primitive or animalistic renderings of Black women, they suggested Black women were sexually immoral and inherently given to vice. Yet these women too pressed the state for recognition and material assistance.[2]

Historians such as Amy Murrell Taylor and Stephanie McCurry have identified a realignment of household relations between men and women during the Civil War. Notably, soldiers' wives—comprised of the wives of small slaveholders, yeomen, and laborers who served in the Confederate ranks—interacted with the state through letters, petitions, and even riots. Civil War women, Black and white, had more access to the state and vice versa than previously in the nineteenth century, when such interactions had been filtered largely through household men. The war mobilized women's everyday organic lives into visible discourses of inclusion and power. Most potently, southern white women, especially soldiers' wives, exercised a "politics of subsistence" in which they pressed the material and political infrastructure of the Confederacy to recognize their presence and restore the entitlements of household independence. Like generations of women before and after them, southern white women implemented "culturally recognizable gender roles to draw attention to masculine performances of state power." They also exercised their own everyday power, even as they simultaneously valued traditional female virtues of restraint and decorum. As soldier's wives, southern white women used confrontational or transgressive behavior to defend, not defy, their gendered location and demand state obligations be extended to them.[3]

As persistent as soldiers' wives made themselves within the Confederate interior, occupied women, white and Black, faced "the state" in the form of the Union military far more directly and on a daily basis. In wartime Louisiana, occupied women adopted some strategies similar to those of soldiers' wives. Because they moved more visibly and with more political status than prior to Union arrival, women utilized Union occupation as a space to exercise wartime gendered power. Although they still could not vote or hold public office, they could challenge Union authority in ways that only women could. They be-seeched Union authorities with written letters and confronted them in person on the streets and in the halls of power. If the state came barging into the door-ways of the household, occupied women barged back. Confederate women complemented the politics of subsistence with the politics of opposition, in which they supported the Confederate war effort and their own households in open defiance of nearby Union troops.[4]

Southern Black women also established their political presence in occu-pied Louisiana. Arguably, for free and enslaved Black women in the South, their lives always contained the politics of subsistence. Often like their white counterparts, they struggled for wages, material relief, and connection to their families. As in other regions of the South, especially urban areas that experi-enced Union occupation and an influx in population during the war, Black women in Louisiana pursued material substance, cultural expression, and pub-lic personas that defied assumptions of racial inferiority. By their own hand and through their systems of labor, they built their own meaningful freedom. But Black women also understood the political environment of occupation and ex-ercised their own politics of opposition within that space. For Black women—who ostensibly had no say at all in the antebellum social contract—occupation presented an environment where they could request, appeal, and affirm their own presence in the imagined community. They called on Union authorities to follow through on the promises of emancipation and the prerogatives of state (re)construction under occupation.[5]

Paradoxically, as the war progressed, southern women's resistance to oc-cupation order increased, but so did their dependency. When Union forces arrived, New Orleans was in a state of disarray, but southern women quickly recovered and initiated daily operations to sustain themselves and their households. Throughout the war of occupation, white and Black women im-plemented their own understandings of community politics to preserve their households. For white women, the household war was exterior—opposing Union forces and aiding Confederate forces—and interior—obtaining ma-terial aid from the Union bureaucracy and endeavoring to preserve the do-mestic slave system. For Black women, their household war tended to be more abstract, less rooted in a physical home than in maintaining family ties, per-sonal freedom, and material subsistence. Both white and Black women ad-opted these strategies early in Union occupation and intensified them as the war progressed. Women enhanced their political presence by manifesting their participatory power in wartime communities. By the fall of 1862, white women were required to take an oath of loyalty to regulate their presence as domestic foes, a public sign that Union forces recognized these women as political actors. During the next three years, they devised increasingly complex methods of resistance, such as the domestic supply line and secret communication. Black women increased pressure on Union authorities to provide protection and aid. By the end of the war, the Union army developed a sophisticated if still haphazard general welfare state in response to the demands of occupation duty in Louisiana—that is, a gendered occupation zone in which white and Black women comprised the majority of the domestic inhabitants.[6]

Military authorities and southern women also contended with another gendered consequence of prolonged occupation, rape and sexual assault. Men, typically soldiers, who breached the household and its adjacent grounds to commit depredations against white and Black women revealed the household itself as the most central battlefield of gendered power dynamics and physical autonomy. In response to increased sexual assault charges, the Union bureaucracy exercised an imbalanced racial justice—it punished Black male offenders more than white men and disregarded the suffering of Black women more than that of white women. With this imbalanced justice, Union occupation authorities revitalized the disproportionate gendered obligations and reinforced the racial polarity of American society in the nineteenth century.

Limited though their civic rights and autonomy were under the traditional conceptions of public male power, southern white women in the mid-nineteenth century exercised personal power within the private spaces of their households. Under occupation, white women sought to shield their private space from incursion and even carry the domestic power of that space out into the public sphere. They called on the army to provide material aid and offer protection to their homes and property, and it fielded endless requests to maintain family and community relations. Southern women also understood public space as an opportunity and a resource. When Union troops arrived, southern white women immediately initiated oppositional politics by endeavoring to dominate occupied space with displays of Confederate loyalty. Leaving rail cars, sliding out of church pews, sneering down from balconies, southern white women marked Confederate space by fluidly moving their own Confederate identity to spaces unpolluted by the presence of Union troops. They endeavored to attenuate Union authority by belittling or even assaulting Union men. Though the Union army recoded southern space to become a site of national loyalty, Confederate women used public demonstrations to demoralize Union men and frustrate their objectives.[7]

As physical locations, diverse southern households were sites of provision, which the Union army sought to invade or regulate, and sites of protection, which southern women sought to maintain. Confederate women endeavored to share this provision and protection with neighbors, family, and soldiers. As wartime guardians of the household and its benefits, Confederate women weaponized their own domesticity and exported it to the public sphere. Community politics and military regulations also circumscribed southern households. Southern women lived in communities shaped by social networks of kin and friends, culturally prescribed traditions of behavior, and calls to national and familial loyalty. In occupied Louisiana, especially in the urban location of New Orleans, the military added to these local politics a mixture of spying, material privation, and novel legal requirements. Even though occupation was staffed and operated by male figures, it created a bureaucratic space that was largely gendered female. Southern men, Black and white, faced a disempowering public sphere because of imprisonment, recruitment, house arrest, or banishment. Alternatively, southern women, Black and white, entered the public sphere in sizable numbers. While they too experienced military restrictions, women's material and emotional investment in the war was just as potent as that of men, and arguably produced longer-lasting effects on statecraft in Civil War–era United States. On a personal level, southern women's occupied household war was an effort to balance traditional gender decorum with military regulations and their community resistance to those regulations. On a public level, the household war gendered occupation by (re)fixing the state's gaze more clearly on women and shaping the state's actions to address the presence of women.[8]

For Confederate citizens who lived in the daily presence of Union soldiers, occupation required precarious acts of balance between loyalty and submission, resistance and compliance. When her father died early in the war, Annie Jeter, a young, wealthy southern woman, moved to New Orleans with her mother, younger siblings, and enslaved property, many of whom, for the time being, chose to remain with the Jeter family. Without the abiding presence of a male patriarch, the family abandoned their isolated plantation in St. Landry Parish for the relative safety of the city, where they were closer to the Confederate community and could sustain themselves better. Engaged to a Confederate officer who was imprisoned in the city, Jeter often traveled to the prison where she negotiated, sometimes unsuccessfully, with federal officers for passes to visit him. Once she even renegotiated to extend the allotted time she was permitted. Carefully concealing notes in the flowers and cakes she brought, she maintained communication with her imprisoned lover. She also persistently rebuffed the attention of a Unionist neighbor, Mr. Daniels, who desired to court her. In a household war shaped by community politics, she and her mother fretted over the bothersome man's continual presence around their home. Fearing what their Confederate neighbors would think, Annie rebuffed her would-be suitor on several occasions, declining his carriage rides and only reluctantly accepting his bouquets.

However, she did gratefully accept Daniels's offer to provide bail for her imprisoned brother, who refused to leave his fellow Confederate comrades. Eventually, she arranged with Union authorities to marry her fiancé, Lieutenant Emile Carmouche, and she used that newly established social relation to permanently repulse the Unionist suitor. As demonstrated by Jeter's travails, occupation shifted the gendered power relations of Confederate citizens. Imprisoned southern men depended on southern women for supplies and morale, to arbitrate with Yankees, and covertly communicate with Confederate forces. In the occupied city, performances of political loyalty—like Annie's repeated repudiation of her Unionist neighbor—were also vital to communicate allegiance and identity to a larger social and military body. After all, Annie Jeter was not simply marrying a man: she was marrying a Confederate soldier as well. The marriage was a feature of a household war that fused martial and social ethos. Resistance and self-presentation became coupled in the occupied Confederacy.[9]

Southern white women under occupation used self-presentation to demonstrate Confederate loyalty not only to Union authorities, but to their southern neighbors as well. For Annie Jeter, the frequent visits of Mr. Daniels caused considerable consternation for her family among their southern neighbors. Even associating with Daniels was cause for suspicion, as Jeter's little brother Warrie reported one day when he arrived home from school. An indignant

Warrie "informed me he wished I would marry Col. Daniels and go away for the boys at school called him Yankee and he was furious." Eventually, although loathe to marry without her brother present, she married Carmouche in early 1864. He obtained a pass to leave jail for an evening and was accompanied by a minister to the rented house where the Jeter family resided. Several Confederate neighbors scraped together a meager reception for the two, mingling and eating cake before Carmouche was escorted back to jail. While the young couple were doubtless eager to be married, their union and the support from the small Confederate community around them also demonstrated the loyalty and cohesion of the local Confederate community.[10]

Faced with years of material privation, Confederate women implemented material strategies for personal survival and community support. In the first of many examples of how traditional community relations assumed political consequences, Confederate women developed confidential lines of communication. These secret communiques, like Annie Jeter's marriage, were both social and martial. As William Blair argues, "Information did more than influence moods or the psyche: it had an impact on people's actions and on policy making." Marianne Edwards, the pro-Union wife of a Massachusetts sea captain who lived in New Orleans during the war, wrote to her father that the only information many of her southern neighbors could receive from their sons and family members outside Union lines had to be smuggled in by Confederate women. When a little boy showed up on the doorstep of her neighbor Mr. Brentford's house one day with a letter from Brentford's son Thomas, the young deliverer refused to give up the name of the person who had transported it across the lines. The boy told Brentford only that it was one of several ladies "with there [sic] cloaks lined between the wadding with letter[s] for the friends and family here." Although she supported the Union, Edwards congratulated these Confederate women—"there has been as much heroism displayed by women on [the] Secesh side as ever was displayed by the women of the Revolution." If only they would use that heroism "in a better cause," she commented, "it would be a lasting honor to them." Under Edwards's reasoning, patriotism provided the avenue by which southern women could transform traditional domesticity into public honor.[11]

Confederate women did not trust Union information, which provided another reason for maintaining communication lines with other Confederates. Confederate women were well aware of arrests that Butler made in the city, including editors of Confederate papers. Union authorities censored the papers and did their best to control information that flowed in the city. Julia LeGrand detested "tiresome" New Orleans's newspapers because "they do not dare to speak of anything that interests us." When he took command of the Department of the Gulf, Banks outperformed even Butler's use of power by transporting his own editorial staff and renaming *The Delta* to be *The Era*, which was geared specifically toward Union news. The paper, which ran from February 1863 to January 1865, beat Confederate women at their own game by regularly criticizing their rebellious behavior or making fun of them. One such account claimed that a white woman, "may be a heartless wretch," had left her infant boy in the care of a Black woman in the Fourth District of New Orleans over three months, never to return. The paper joked that the provost marshal should advertise for a wet nurse in *The Era*. "At all events," the paper quipped, "don't drown it." Just as offensive to Confederate citizens were stories that made light of Confederate military losses, celebrated slavery's demise, and promoted freedpeople's activities. Secret letters and published newspapers reprinted wild rumors and scurrilous information with the same frequency as genuine reports, but information, however dubious, was power. Occupied Confederate women and Union presses waged a rhetorical and informational war within public and private spheres.[12]

Despite the efforts of Union occupiers to provide social relief, many southern women endured widespread wartime privation and devastation in Louisiana. Union occupation quickly reduced the financial and physical security of wealthy families such as the Jeters. When Butler occupied New Orleans, Annie Jeter reported, perhaps with some exaggeration, "his soldiers searched private dwellings for arms, would turn everything topsy turvy in a house, slit open the fine ... furniture and featherbeds with their swords, then sweep the chimneys and leave." Union troops inflicted similar devastation on many wealthy southern homes or "confiscated the fine houses to live in." Before he was captured, her would-be husband Lieutenant Carmouche wrote to Annie from New Iberia, "The country here is quite laid waste. It is heart-rending to see so much property destroyed." Several months later, freed through prisoner exchange, he had occasion to pass by the Jeter plantation. "The Yankees," he reported solemnly, "have almost destroyed your plantation entirely."[13]

Under these constrained material circumstances, southern women had to develop strategies of survival. When Norman Murray, quartermaster of the

31st New York, attempted to occupy what he believed to be an empty house in Brashear City, he found a Confederate woman in the place who "defied the whole federal force to take it." Murray claimed, "She is occupying the House by no right as I can learn[.] The house I now Hold will be vacant and she can take it with you[r] consent." To make matters worse, the woman was apparently in possession of some federal property hidden in the house. "By having her removed you will be doing me a great favor," Murray requested from the local provost marshal. Instead of antagonism, widow Augite Costa used supplication to prevent Union troops from seizing one of her rental properties. Without the property, Costa would be "deprived of Said rent, necessary for the Maintenance of Petitioner and her Children."[14] John Hawkes, a soldier in the 50th Massachusetts, expressed disgust that he and men from his unit were assigned to guard a widow's property. "She pretends to be union [but] she has a brother and brotherinlaw in the rebel armey [*sic*]," he complained. During the Port Hudson Campaign in the summer of 1863, Banks still found time to answer requests for supplies from southern women. "The women must not starve," he wrote to a Union officer in Baton Rouge in June 1863. A month later, the general directed Captain E. E. Shelton, an officer in Commissary Subsistence outside Port Hudson, to issue a barrel of flour to a Mrs. Fluker and a Mrs. Newport. That same month he ordered a Union officer to return a piano, books, and paper stolen from a widow named Mrs. Huston.[15]

In addition to using the physical household itself as a battleground to resist Union occupation, Confederate women had financial decisions to make about survival. The Jeter family women moved into New Orleans because they believed they could not take care of their plantation on their own, and because they dared not remain alone on the property. They began their troublesome time in the city by first reducing their financial obligations. Finally settling into a rented home on St. Andrews Street, Jeter's mother freed some of her enslaved people—a man named Henry and his family—stating they "were no longer able to feed so many." Still rent proved difficult to pay. Because they refused to take the oath of allegiance, they were compelled to register as enemies and were issued passes to move about freely, a particular shame for them because it was standard practice to treat enslaved people in such a way. Two enslaved women, Polly and Henrietta, and their children remained with the Jeter family.[16]

Other southern families experienced more dramatic reductions in status than the Jeters and implemented alternative survival strategies. The wife and children of one Mr. Batchilden, apparently held prisoner at Fort Pickens without charge, "are in the woods," wrote Marianne Edwards, "where they have been living for months in one of the log houses built for the Negroes while out cutting lumber." Already reduced to a material and social status akin to enslaved people, most of the Batchilden's enslaved property deserted them as well, save for "one woman servant run out there with her." "Everything they had in the world [is] destroyed," Edwards said—their mills demolished, their new house ruined, and their new furniture, still in crates shipped from New York, chopped up with hatchets before their eyes. Their residence in an isolated log house was beyond federal lines, "so they cannot get back again," Edwards wrote. Unlike the Jeter family and their precarious financial strategies, the Batchilden women and children faced a more severe material situation. War and occupation had literally reconstituted their world of privilege and relocated their household to the exterior of society.[17]

The situations of these two families demonstrate how Union occupation affected rural and urban populaces differently. In rural areas, white and Black southern women endured even greater material privation due to foraging parties on both sides. In Thibodaux, Ellen Bragg, wife of Braxton Bragg, watched federal troops march into town, acquire keys to public buildings, search for ammunition, and depart. "They say they will return in a little while to seize cattle," she reported, a particularly disturbing thought because "no place is provided with provisions. The households have not supplies." For places like Thibodaux on the outskirts of occupation, Union soldiers squeezed southern households by confiscating property and diminishing the food supply. In Madisonville, Louisiana, where the Union army shipped hundreds of refugees from New Orleans, a resident named Annette Koch lamented, "there is hardly enough food to go around for those of us already here, the new arrivals are certain to starve." In urban areas, southern women were not entirely free of material and financial exigencies, but women in rural areas were far more likely to experience privation or have their property confiscated or destroyed by raiding troops, especially if they aided Confederate guerrilla forces.[18]

Even as they faced material privation or social isolation, many Confederate women also chose to resist Union occupation. Some, like a woman Julia LeGrand knew, might stay at home with "a hatchet, a tomahawk, and a vial of some kind of spirits with which she intends to blind all invaders." But for the women who demonstrated public resistance and helped generate Order No. 28, they implemented patriotic domesticity both as a public strategy of resistance as well as a private strategy of survival and community cohesion. At the beginning of the war, crowds swarmed the rail stations in populated areas, primarily New Orleans, as troops went away to war. Southern ladies organized dances and parties, performed concerts for public benefit, and sewed clothing for the troops. They wore small Confederate flags made of silk and put bows or cotton blossoms in their hair. They visited the camps during weeks of training and stood on balconies and platforms waving goodbye as trainloads of uniformed men rolled away. In these ways, southern white women mobilized their domestic abilities to supply the war effort. When Union invaders occupied their neighborhoods, they also extended war from their domestic social location into the public arena.[19]

Josephine Moore, a young woman living in occupied New Orleans in 1863, outlined how public space became a battleground between Union troops and Confederate women. She was pleased one Sunday because her church congregation "lacked the usual most disagreeable inter sprinkling of blue coats and brass buttons." Just as she and her female kin were leaving church though, three Union men "came cantering by on their stolen horses, and holding their heads as high as if they were 'monarchs of all they surveyed.'" She laughed when one of the horses tripped and nearly toppled the Union rider. Her only displeasure in walking to school, she lamented, was in passing two houses that "have been stolen by the Yankees." She considered taking an alternative route to avoid the occupiers but decided against it, declaring "I wouldn't want to go even a half square out of my way for any Yankee that ever lived." Union authorities might have been aware of the public politics of occupation that Moore highlighted when they hung two U.S. flags close to Benjamin Palmer's church. "Those persons who wish to go there, will either have to walk under them, or go a very round-about way to avoid it." Many of her fellow crinoline rebels were unsure of how to handle the situation. "They did not wish to walk under such a disgraced flag as that has become, and they were unwilling to please the Yankees so much as to go out of their way to avoid the flag." Moore and most of her friends eventually chose to avoid the flags.

Union authorities further interrupted her church public when two officers showed up one April Sunday with a copy of the Emancipation Proclamation that they required their pastor to read. "I hope they were flattered by the attention bestowed on them," Moore wrote, "for so many contemptuous glances, curled lips and elevated noses, I never saw in my life." The Confederate parishioners also cast spiteful looks at "a notorious Yankee family" in attendance. As their pastor refused to read the Proclamation, Moore feared that Union administrators would close the church. "The Yankees assume to be the directors in religious as well as military and political affairs," she quipped. Her comment illustrated how northerners interfered in local southern public spaces as a strategic function of military occupation.[20]

While Confederate women contemplated how best to publicly refute emblems of Union dominion in public, Union authorities faced a persistent problem in the form of captured Confederate troops, their families, and the numerous southern ladies who sought to aid the imprisoned. Aiding Confederate prisoners was a critical portion of the domestic supply line, though it is often overlooked in the historiography. After the fall of Port Hudson, Albert Stearns claimed a constant stream of visitors poured into the local custom house to visit some two hundred imprisoned Confederate officers. Women in Baton Rouge appeared at the state penitentiary to provide fresh clothes to the bloodied captives of St. Martin's Rangers in March 1864. According to Annie Jeter's 1913 memoir, Union authorities frequently turned away women like the mother and siblings of William Jeter in New Orleans.[21]

Confederate women also fused their roles as domestic caretakers and their patriotic allegiance by caring for Confederate wounded in New Orleans hospitals. The Unionist Marianne Edwards was shocked to enter the St. James Hospital, a large hotel converted to a medical center, and see that "the Confederate soldiers . . . were entirely taken care of by the ladies," but "our poor soldiers had no one to care for them." She did the best that she could, acquiring a pass to visit the hospital, where she fed Union soldiers and spoke with them to lift their spirits. Perhaps influenced or inspired by Confederate women in New Orleans, one Union general recommended to Banks that he send forty wounded Confederates out of a hospital crowded with Union wounded from the Port Hudson Campaign to Clinton, Louisiana, "where they can be cared for by the people." As the war proceeded, Union authorities increasingly recognized the communal ties that formed the backbone of Confederate resistance.[22]

The most dramatic display of Confederate women's domestic support came in February 1863, as Confederate women lined the docks and levees of New Orleans to supply prisoner ships bound for Mobile. Marianne Edwards watched "a constant stream of baskets, buckets, and tin kettles brought down by the ladies" and sent on board the ships. "If that was where it ended," she wrote, "not much harm would be done," but the Confederate women of New Orleans made a far more memorable scene. Whenever a ship passed by, presently "it was of course known and the levee began to be thronged mostly with ladies, their servants with them, carrying loads of good things and clothing." Every day was like this, Edwards wrote, and gradually the rebel women grew bolder. As the steamer USS *Crescent* pulled away from the levee, "such shouts as they [the women] sent up you never could imagine." The Confederate prisoners all were "waving a white handkerchief, all dressed well thanks to the ladies, and cheering them in action" as the Confederate women followed along the shore "until they [the prisoners] were clear out of sight." Then the women returned home to prepare fresh batches of supplies.[23]

Days later, the Battle of the Handkerchiefs reached a climax. An immense crowd gathered at the levee as another prisoner ship passed by, and the persistent Confederate women began to press their way on board the ship itself. One said "she was up all the night before cooking and getting things ready for the poor fellows and she should set up again all that night" as well. As the day progressed, the crowd of women began to grow unruly. The Confederate ladies called out to the prisoners, "Boys when you get to Mobile go back again into the army and fight for us and we shall come out all right yet . . . thats our home boys fight for us to the last." Frightened by this display, the meager Union guard sent for their commanding officer, who appeared and "begged the ladies to be more quiet or he should have to disperse them." Undeterred, the Confederate women "only sauced him" with provocative speech. The overwhelmed officer even "tried to awe down one lady by showing her his pistol" but it had no effect. Only when Union cavalry arrived did the recalcitrant ladies disperse. Banks kept the unit posted as a guard until Monday. Even as they retreated, the Confederate women yelled out—"How can you expect us to be Union women when you won't let us tell our friends goodbye." Family and community ties provided southern women a potent base from which to launch oppositional politics.[24]

As the Battle of the Handkerchiefs demonstrated, Confederate women asserted their politics of opposition through demonstrative language. While some Confederate women did practice violence—most notably the Bread Riots of spring 1863—overwhelmingly, they assailed systems of power with written and spoken words. New Orleans women like Marion Southwood referred to

"Picayune Butler," a term by which they meant that he was diminutive or contemptible. Some sang Confederate songs in their homes and schools within earshot of Union troops. Southern white women sparred with Union men, negotiated with them, and howled support for Confederate prisoners from the levees. White southern women implemented what one scholar has called "self-rhetorics"—spoken and written rhetorical agencies that women prepared for their own self-confidence. Armed with these self-rhetorics, southern women asserted self-protection, demonstrated political allegiance, addressed audiences, and offered up prayers for victory during the Civil War. Language became a crucial means of empowerment, agency, and resistance for southern women, which included free and enslaved women who called out Confederate masters and badgered Union authorities. Union men might even return fire in these rhetorical battles, as William Stewart and some of his Illinois men did on the Red River Campaign. Somewhere in the vicinity of Alexandria, the Union soldiers entered a hotel where some Confederate women were staying and stood in the hallway loudly singing the "best Union songs which they were forced to hear, but heard in silence." Occupation was as much a war of words as of guns and policy.[25]

As an extension of the domestic home front, Confederate women supplied southern military forces, both those directly in the Confederate army and local bands more concentrated on community defense. In mid-1862 Governor Thomas Moore, eager to repel the invaders, urged the southern populace to offer "every possible assistance" to local companies and partisan bands that formed in response to Union occupation. "Let every citizen be an armed sentinel to give warning of any approach of the insolent foe," he declared. "Let all our river-banks swarm with armed patriots to teach the hated invader that the rifle will be his only welcome on his errands of plunder and destruction." Though he spoke to the state of Louisiana without specifically gendered language, masculine tropes pervaded his call to arms. Moore also understood that behind every armed (male) sentinel stood a family of dependents who materially supported that patriot. The Union army would also discover that they faced far more female opposition than just the insolent ladies on the streets of New Orleans.[26]

Union officials, despite the official military mandate of emancipation, often displayed paternalistic or restrictive views not unlike the southern planters that emancipation policy was intended to dispossess. The journalist Thomas P. Knox indicated similarities between slave management manuals and Banks's orders concerning the containment and control of freed slaves, especially laws restricting movement by passes and contractual labor. "Their condition," Knox stated of freed slaves under Union control in the Gulf Department, "is not greatly changed from that of slavery, except the promise of compensation and the absence of compulsory control." A broadside in Baton Rouge declared that after January 17, 1863, "no contrabands to be allowed about the streets of the city, without a pass, signed by those in charge of them, or some officer of the Provost Guard." Freed persons of color were also forbidden to go out after 9 p.m. or to occupy houses other than those arranged for them. Another order forbade anyone from hiring contraband labor except through the provost marshal office. Anyone who already had "Colored Refugees in their employ, not thus hired, will, if they wish to keep them, call at once and sign the government contract." All freed people "not employed by the Government, nor thus hired," were removed to the city's contraband camp, where they were contained and hired out "at Government prices" to whoever signed the contract.[27]

Since New Orleans's colonial days, enslaved people could move more anonymously in a dense population, especially as overworked municipal officials could not maintain strict vigilance over the entire city. Free and enslaved Black women had long participated in New Orleans markets, especially in street marketing and the distribution of foodstuffs. During the Civil War, rapid population increase, including more enslaved people for urban labor projects or refugees from rural areas, contributed to a breakdown in the traditional strictures of social control under slavery. Enslaved people ran away in the mayhem; they took greater liberties of mobility; they earned their own wages with more frequency; they performed duties poorly to fatigue southern masters. Enslaved domestic servants escalated demonstrations of defiance during the war, including an avoidance of work altogether, which undermined white authority, especially that of white women in southern homes. In the antebellum period, the hire-out system had democratized slavery for white wage earners who could access enslaved labor more easily than rural yeomen; under Union occupation, freed people in urban areas utilized this hire-out system for themselves to command their own labor as best they could.[28]

Emancipated people endured a paradox of status under the Union army. In contraband camps mostly located in Baton Rouge and New Orleans, freedpeople, most of whom were women and children, enjoyed protection, housing, food, and limited education. While Black males were routinely impressed into labor service for Union forces, women generally had a choice to go work or remain in the camps. These were basic rights that Black Americans rarely experienced under southern slavery, and the idea of serving in the Union military bequeathed a status of masculinity and citizenship to Black males that was previously unavailable. However, the fact that freedpeople were still referred to as contrabands indicated that they did not possess the same civil rights as white citizens. They existed somewhere between the status of property and person. Union occupation disrupted the slave system but largely did not replace the labor system that exploited Black workers. Aside from military service and some limited education, occupation also failed to fully induct Black Americans into the arena of American citizenship.[29]

Like white women, Black women recognized how occupation altered the politics of space around them. Union occupiers dismantled slavery in fits and starts according to military needs and established in its place a patchwork environment where Black women sometimes gained justice and sometimes suffered similar degradations as they had experienced in slavery. In rural areas, Black women were often confined to plantations or contraband camps. The Union army was loathe to see Black people operate freely, where they might ignite racial disputes that the military bureaucracy would have to settle. In urban areas, principally New Orleans, Black women operated more freely. They often turned close proximity with Union forces to their advantage by utilizing the military bureaucracy as a means of justice and personal opportunity. Black women immediately took advantage of the market diversity that the urban center of New Orleans presented. Domestic labor increased in value as the war proceeded as southerners struggled to maintain their customary domestic identity. Empowered by occupation to some degree, Black women renegotiated labor and social relations in the South.[30]

Black Americans had very limited choices. They could follow the Union army as refugees, which included severe labor at times. Black males could join the military, though enthusiasm for this action varied among Union commanders. Federal policy concerning slavery and freed persons changed just as attitudes and policies toward resistant Confederate whites changed during the war.

Or enslaved people could remain where they were. That the Jeter family could no longer afford to feed all of its slaves is no surprise, but neither was Polly and Henrietta's decision to remain with the family. In the austere conditions that prevailed in much of occupied Louisiana, freedpeople faced the dismal choice between privation or working for the Union army. For enslaved people who had the opportunity, remaining with the family that owned them—or formerly owned them—could be a shrewd choice, at least until the future prospects of freed people became more certain. Remaining in the Southern home did not necessarily mean that Black women experienced a lack of autonomy, however. Annie Jeter found that by the war's end the Black women in her household "ran the household affairs pretty much as they chose." Under Union occupation, a state project to reconstruct loyalty in the South, Black freedwomen could practice their own kind of occupation, reorienting the household around their order instead of submitting to slaveholder commands.[31]

Whether southern white women remained slaveholders or not, they still found the domestic household a battlefront of occupation. By the end of 1862, Marianne Edwards wrote that many white people of status in New Orleans rarely left their homes. "It looks like a deserted city," she said; "you don't see one respectable person in a mile, nothing but flouncing Negroes and the lower class of whites. The people don't even associate together . . . people are afraid of each other for they don't know who is in the pay of the government to carry information." With occupation tactics, the Union army effectively reoriented the power of the urban southern household from a place of unquestioned white domestic authority into a refuge from a dramatically altered outside world. Edwards hoped Banks would "restore a better order of things, it is truly dreadful." In rural areas of Louisiana, southerners had all the more reason to fear internal and external threats to their homes. Union confiscation or partisan raids aimed directly at the material foundations of southern society.[32]

On this battlefront of contested homes, many more enslaved people chose to leave rather than remain, and some even adopted their own militant strategies to confront whites. When Butler offered freedom to any enslaved person who turned in their masters for aiding the Confederacy, Marianne Edwards did not think any enslaved person would do so. "But Negroes are easily influenced," she concluded with chagrin. Many white families in New Orleans immediately freed their enslaved property when they heard Butler's order, but Edwards's friend and neighbor Mr. Brentford "said he felt conscious of not having or said anything so he did not tell his [slaves] they could go." In response, his female servant "began to grow so ugly it was all they could do to live in the house with her." The servant was so angry that she went to Butler on three occasions to report her master for suspicious activity. The first time she told the Union commander that her master had weapons in his house but a thorough search yielded nothing. Next, she told authorities that arms were buried in the garden, so Union soldiers came and dug it up. They found nothing but wrecked the garden, which may have been the servant's intention all along. In a final oppositional effort against her owner, she informed Butler that Mr. Brentford and his son-in-law had helped set fire to cotton when Union forces first landed.[33]

Both Brentford and his servant used the community politics available for them to wage this household battle. Arrested but not charged, Brentford strongly protested the accusations. He now found the power dynamics of his household reversed, but he had another reservoir of domestic power to draw from. Brentford strategically invoked community relations to defend himself, claiming he could call numerous witnesses who could place his whereabouts on the day in question. But Butler rebuked Brentford and sent him to jail. Brentford's family was only informed of this when the Black servant "came with an officer with a permit from Butler to demand her clothes, and her husband's, and all that belonged to her." Bending Union occupation in her favor, the now-freed woman returned to the house with a dray to use as transportation. She claimed the bed and pillows she slept on, three trunks of clothes, and even demanded the house be searched for an item of clothing she claimed was stolen from her. The Union officer who accompanied her refused this request, saying, "you have got more clothes there now than thousands of poor women at the North have." The Black woman, now free, sold cakes and other baked goods to the soldiers while her husband, Edwards wrote, "is hanging round one of the camps." In this domestic contest of authority and property, Union occupation afforded both parties misery and success. Perhaps looking to their former servant's example, one of Brentford's daughters twice went to see "the Old Tyrant," as Edwards referred to Butler, hoping to secure her father's release. She was unsuccessful.[34]

In occupied urban areas like New Orleans, Black women regularly called on bureaucrats in blue to intervene on their behalf on the domestic battlefront. In April 1864, Reverend Thomas Conway, soon-to-be Superintendent of Negro Labor in Louisiana, conveyed a wrathful message to then-superintendent

George Hanks. A New Orleans woman reported to Conway that a U.S. officer "came to her house and took the child of her colored servant back to its former owner Mrs Tiffin." The mother of the stolen child appealed to Conway. "The child is virtually returned to slavery by a U.S. officer!" Conway exclaimed. "In the name of the liberty which crowns the achievement of our arms; in the name of Justice and humanity, I beg that this case be presented to the [action] of Genl Bowen, in order that he may punish the offender in the surest and most peremptory manner." Inspired in part by the ire of the Black community surrounding the case, Conway related to Hanks, "The colored population is being moved by a deep and intense feeling on account of these abuses. I know from personal experience and observation that they are in a state of the utmost . . . excitement." For the Black community in New Orleans, Union occupation demonstrated a troubling duality—it generated familiar injustices yet also provided an authentic space for their urgent claims to justice and advocacy. With the theft of this child, the specter of slavery again gained corporeality in the very homes where Black women worked as free laborers. Their voices of protest moved Union officials like Conway to action. "They are willing to die for the Government," he wrote, "but consider that this sort of abuse is not what they deserve."[35]

Conway's outraged letter revealed the gendered distinctions of Black labor. Isolated in the private homes of white people, in physical proximity to former owners, Black women daily disrupted established power dynamics. As independent laborers, Black female household workers in New Orleans stood at the fringes of social inclusion; as emancipated persons contending for representative value, they called at the doorways of Union authority to challenge reincarnations of the slave regime. Hanks forwarded Conway's letter up the chain of command with an added note that "this is not an isolated instance; the difficulties attending the detection of the guilty parties are multifarious." Dealt an injustice by the police power of Union occupation, the child's mother pressured and utilized that police power, however complex, back in her favor. When the child was returned and the officer arrested, it was the work of Union officers, but also the voice of the formerly enslaved, especially Black women, that fashioned justice from grievance.[36]

As much as Union occupation empowered Black women to make more choices for themselves, many federal men also mitigated against enhanced Black freedom, sometimes even through violence. "Cause all women and children both white and black who had not their homes within the lines [at Camp Parapet] before the occupation of our troops . . . to be excluded therefrom," Butler ordered at the end of May 1862. This order kept potential white female enemies outside his line, but for the Black women, they were relegated to remain in slavery until a future date. When Union managers organized plantations into work sites, they imposed on Black women many of the same restrictions they experienced under slavery. "I have to report one of my women Mona," a Union overseer on Landen Plantation complained, "who on several occasions has refused to go to work and from no other reason than that she did not feel like it." The record did not bear out what happened to Mona but the Union report signaled that she had called attention to herself for defying Union expectations. In the fall of 1862, Union officials searched for a soldier who shot an enslaved woman named Victoria near the barracks in New Orleans. When the coroner questioned the men at the barracks, they all professed to know nothing. Several months later, Banks requested an investigation into the flogging of Black woman on a Union-held plantation in the Lafourche District. Unfortunately for Black women in Louisiana, Union occupation did not readily translate into emancipation, and when it did come, emancipation did not readily translate into equal freedom. Sometimes supported, sometimes inhibited, Black women received mixed signals about their social value from the Union military.[37]

With tactics of supply, public demonstration, and negotiation, Black and white southern women under occupation, consciously and unconsciously, beleaguered the Union occupation bureaucracy so extensively that they often redirected the gaze of the state from the front line of combat to the domestic home front. Even if Confederate women never explicitly spelled out how they planned to obstruct Union occupation as a war strategy, Union authorities left a trail of responses to southern women in the historical record. Butler issued Orders No. 28 and No. 76 to combat the physical actions of rebellious women and to categorize their identity in politically legible ways through oaths of loyalty. Banks called out Union troops to directly restore order in the Battle of the Handkerchiefs. "The people of New Orleans understand or ought to understand well that their conduct," he warned during his absence in the Port Hudson Campaign, "will be the measure of their treatment hereafter by the military authorities of the United States." Women appeared at the local jails and Union offices, requesting approval from an increasingly frustrated bureaucratic system. As the war continued and Union commanders faced more rebellion and burgeoning numbers of refugees, they began shipping more women directly out of the occupied zone to places like Madisonville, north of Union lines across Lake Pontchartrain. Likewise, Black women pressed on Union authority figures, sometimes using occupation to their advantage to secure enhanced rights and recognition.[38]

The Woman's Order, though it only shifted the domestic battlefield rather than concluding it, was partly successful in that it proceeded from a larger gendered military structure that empowered men over women. While Union occupation forces focused on white men, some soldiers also galvanized masculine pride through combating women in domestic warfare, which primarily consisted of rhetorical and psychological battles. When Confederate women criticized or troubled them, some men teased or ridiculed them back. Others expressed dismay. Consciously or not, when Butler backed up his men during these domestic battles, he also reasserted traditional gendered order in New Orleans. Order No. 28 was part of a much wider nineteenth-century discourse on the social location of women versus that of men, especially military men, who were the embodiment of order in the wartime cultural landscape. More than just a criticism of recalcitrant southern white women, Butler's order retaliated against domestic combatants on gendered grounds.[39]

Butler's policies made southerners fume and even discomfited some northerners. Even Union citizens like Marianne Edwards disliked Butler. "Ain't I glad that old Wretch Butler has gone," she wrote to her father; "it is my opinion and belief he only needed the time to make him a second Robespierre." While she reassured her father that she had not turned "Secesh," she was sure her parents would hate Butler too "if you was here and see and heard what that fellow has been doing." As she would demonstrate in more than one letter back to her home in Evansville, Indiana, it was Butler's senseless violation of white people's civil rights that made him so vile. But perhaps Edwards's northern citizenship affected her understanding of the military and social relations in occupied Louisiana. From her perspective, no honorable commander could treat white civilians with the draconian measures he imposed. Yet, from Butler's position, and that of many military and political thinkers, Confederates had few civil rights he was responsible for protecting. They forfeited those rights with secession.[40]

If Butler really wanted to oppress Confederate women, he could have placed many more of them in prison, but the Union army did not utilize the local prison system in Louisiana as an institution of discipline for women to the extent that it did for men. If he had arrested women for every minor offense, Butler wrote an associate, the jail and workhouse would have been quite full, and furthermore the outcry against his beastly nature would have been amplified to a greater extent than that elicited by Order No. 28. Moses Bates, superintendent of the Louisiana State Penitentiary, reported the number and condition of prisoners to General Shepley. Of the 352 prisoners in the penitentiary, twenty were women, and only two of those were not enslaved. One named Delia Swift he recorded as being born in Ohio and of "very good" character. "She is the only American white woman among the convicts," he wrote, convicted by a French and Creole jury for having "murdered her husband under circumstances of great provocation, consequent upon his connection with another woman." He recommended unconditional pardon for her. Within two weeks, Swift appeared before Colonel French in New Orleans with a pass from Bates. "If you have any confiscated furniture that you can aid her in furnishing, a room until she can return to her friends and the North I have no doubt it will be worthily restored," her pass read. Few other prison records for Louisiana women exist in the war. In an undated letter from her cell, Aimee Costillon claimed that she had been in the parish prison for five weeks for disparaging the U.S. government. She declared that she was "perfectly unprotected" and requested to be released and "let her once more enjoy the liberty of life & her opinions." Even the notorious Eugenia Phillips—who had already experienced three weeks of house arrest in Washington D.C. in the fall of 1861—only spent a matter of months on Ship Island before her husband obtained her release and moved the family to Georgia. Ultimately, despite the castigation of Union military government by numerous southerners, Confederate women faced few if any state-mandated punishments of violence or imprisonment for their resistance to occupation.[41]

The most disturbing attack on southern women, white and Black, came not on the formal battlefield or from hotly debated Union policy orders, but from Union soldiers who unlawfully invaded households and violated female bodies. No military body or commander in the Civil War explicitly condoned or exercised rape and sexual assault as a means of warfare as later developed in the twentieth and twenty-first centuries. However, sexual attacks did occur at the hands of Civil War troops, especially on Black women. On the ground level in occupied Louisiana, Union commanders frowned on sexual violation as disorderly and immoral, but they never issued any policies specifically intended to shape a society in which women received consistent gendered state protections.[42]

Southern women regularly traded rumors and reports of sexual and physical abuse. In the fall of 1864, Louisiana resident Francis Lawrence received a dreadful letter from a cousin that reported wild attacks on southern women. The relative claimed that Union troops had cut out the tongue of a Kentucky woman who cheered for Jefferson Davis, while in Missouri the enemy killed babies and ripped out toenails to coerce southerners into giving up information. "Oh God my heart and mind are full of such horrid sets," Lawrence's cousin lamented. "Women raped to death by these fiends." Even the Confederate governor who followed after Thomas Moore, former general Henry W. Allen, responded with sexual terror to the formation of a Unionist state government in 1864. "If a negro . . . should insist upon coming into your parlor and visiting your wife or daughters on terms equally can you prevent it," he questioned ominously. In addition to the veiled sexual threat to southern women, Allen used the imagery of the parlor to signal a violation of the household. Such stories and imagery were for the most part egregiously untrue, but they generated continued foreboding among southern women. "We hear this evening that the enemy have been to Mrs. Fluker's & committed depredations," Ellen Power wrote in May 1863. She did not specify what exactly occurred, but rumors or incidents of household violation struck fear into the hearts of southern women in Louisiana. Perhaps that is why the widow that John Hawkes begrudgingly guarded requested military protection. "All we hav to doo is to ceep the darke and solgers from coming onto the place," he wrote.[43]

When men entered households and threatened or attacked women, they also contributed to an environment wherein women felt unsafe. "If a Federal approached the house I was in terror from head to foot," Francis Lawrence wrote from St. Mary Parish. When William Stewart's unit passed "a ladies Seminary" during the Red River Campaign, "2 of the soldiers straggled and went in. The girls seemed to be terribly frightened at the sacrilege, but guess they were not so bad off as they pretended." In Pineville (just north of Alexandria), Stewart eyed two women "out on a display promenade." One of them caught his attention in particular. For whatever reason, she "had a beautiful black squirrel which ran all over her, up her dress sleeves and under her lace cape into her bosom with a familiarity that made me envy the little favorite and sent a thrill that did not feel very bad through all the little veins in my body exciting desires not over complimentary to the fair exhibitor." *The Era* reported a Black man named George Adams was arrested in the home of Nelly Gray one Saturday night in New Orleans. She complained that "he was in her house under suspicious circumstances at a late hour." Since the newspaper gave no further details of Adams's intent or Gray's experience, historians are left to wonder what happened, but Adams's presence in Gray's home added tension to the general unease that white people, including many Union men, held toward Black men. Such instances revealed why southern women might request Union soldiers like John Hawkes to guard their property. In Stewart's case, however, Louisiana women might view Union soldiers themselves as threats.[44]

On the occasions in which it happened, Union soldiers in occupied Louisiana used rape and sexual assault for personal gratification and masculine dominance, not as a military technique of conquest. In June of 1862 Corporal William C. Chinock raped a twenty-three-year-old Black washerwoman named Mary Ellen de Riley, who was supposedly under his custody for transportation. In a very drunken state, "He told me to lie down and let him ride me," de Riley stated. "He beat me with his fists, pulled my clothes over my head and rode me—for an hour." His abusive presence as a Union soldier demonstrated that the blue uniform was by no means a universal symbol of justice and protection for southern women, especially Black women. Chinock's physical attack before the rape also signified the overbearing power of the military, mostly represented by men, which was as often used for harm as for help.[45]

In a brutal household attack, Fowler Willis, a formerly enslaved person now a recruit in the Union army declared, "It is the rule that Black men must sleep with white women because white men have slept with Black women." He and six others forcibly entered the Point Coupee plantation home of Frank Neff in January 1864, shot Neff and his son to death, then raped his daughter

Aloysia. The action of Willis and his vindictive cohort exemplified an even more malignant assertion of male military power: the ability to assert coercive authority over bodies, property, and life itself. While attacks from formerly enslaved people were extremely rare, Willis and his comrades used the power of their Union uniforms to reenact on white people what had been for them a disturbing reality under slavery. Slaves experienced frequent bodily harm, including sexual assault, and both African American men and women endured the ghastly sight of watching abuse and death come to their loved ones and fellow slaves, all while generally helpless to resist. For Willis and the other soldiers—once slaves, now free, empowered men—rape was a political act of self-assertion against a regime that had wielded so much psychological and physical oppression against the enslaved race.[46]

An exploration of rape and military justice during Civil War Louisiana is incomplete without understanding the gendered, racial, and class context of nineteenth-century ideas about rape and personal character. Court cases dealing with the charge of rape and sexual assault emphasized the idea of consent. If a woman consented to sexual intercourse, regardless of the physical violence or threat used to subdue her person, the attack on her would not be considered rape. In fact, she herself would most commonly be shamed for allowing the sexual digression to occur. Common medical opinion in the nineteenth century often asserted that a healthy, adult woman could not be raped. Even into the late nineteenth century, some states required proof of male ejaculation before a case could be tried as rape. Common knowledge and state laws then fostered a specific rape narrative and a particular image of a rape victim. If a woman was "fond of dress" or did not provide adequate "evidence of unwillingness," others questioned her story and impugned her character. Of course, if a white woman of sufficient wealth were assaulted, then the woman was "disgraced." A misfortune had befallen her; she had not invited the attack by spurning traditional values and moral character. Nineteenth-century cases centered on rape could be weakened or dismissed entirely if the woman were accused of lewdness or other gendered misbehavior such as prior sexual history. Poor women were most likely to have their cases questioned or thrown out because they were labeled as prostitutes. Enslaved Black women, who experienced rape and sexual assault at higher rates than white women, had little recourse for justice. Regardless of race or class or character, nineteenth-century rape law defended women primarily as the physical possessions of men. As little more

than property of male owners or protectors, women were simultaneously responsible for their victimization yet often considered weak and passive. Slave
owners also employed gendered assaults on the character of women to prevent their accused enslaved persons from being imprisoned or executed, which
would have been a blow to their financial investment in enslaved property.[47]

Military justice in the Civil War operated on the precedents of these dis-
tinctly gendered principles and also with specific martial objectives in mind,
such as keeping the peace and maintaining unit cohesion. Many Union troops
in Louisiana, especially those stationed in New Orleans, made no secret of
their fondness for prostitutes. Union commanders in Louisiana never legalized
and regulated prostitution as occupation officials did in Nashville, Memphis,
Norfolk, and Portsmouth, but more than likely they accepted the presence of
prostitution in New Orleans as a given.[48] When incidents of rape and sexual
assault could be verified, military punishments meted out in those cases were
not so much decisions of justice as decisions of order. These policies often
marginalized survivors of sexual trauma. Union occupation in Louisiana did
little to alter the prevailing ideas surrounding rape in the nineteenth century,
and often reinforced or complicated them. William Chinock was reduced to
the rank of private and fined $10 a month for four months for raping Mary El-
len de Riley, "conduct to the prejudice of good order and military discipline."
Nothing was done for de Riley. Fowler Willis, who followed his rule to rape
white women in retribution for slavery's sexual abuses, was hung in November
1864. The records bear no indication of what became of Aloysia Neff. Racial
distinction effected a disparity in punishment between the two cases that is
analogous to all cases of rape and sexual assault in the Civil War. Although
Willis and his companions did kill two male citizens in addition to the rape, a
crime of considerable magnitude that in some opinions outweighed Chinock's
offense, Black men were routinely punished with more severity than white men
among the ranks of the Union army.[49]

Like any other historical period, the performance of masculinity in the
Civil War was a contested process, and determining how male soldiers as an
occupying force should behave changed over the length of the war. Historians
of the nineteenth century generally rely on the Victorian mores of masculine
restraint and moral purpose that so typified the era as the most fundamental
explanatory mechanism of gendered behavior. Reid Mitchell, for instance, argues that "Few Northern soldiers raped. . . . True manhood was characterized

by sexual restraint not sexual assertion. . . . Letting anger toward women break out in unsanctioned violence against women would have been unmanly." But these conclusions do not engage the power differential between soldiers and civilians, especially women, in occupied regions. Union soldiers possessed power over southern women by their very nature as armed, invading combatants. Furthermore, northern cultural narratives cast them as moral characters acting out against oppression and treachery, a heroic sheen that could disguise lustful activities and property theft. Lastly, Union soldiers could generally but not always rely on the unbalanced nature of rape laws and rape knowledge, which systemically disadvantaged women while largely preserving the privilege of white males.[50]

White men occupied the pinnacle of nineteenth-century social order and the actions of white men in the Union military centered about personal honor. When Union soldier William Gardner assaulted a southern white woman, for example, he dishonored himself and his command. Martha Davis accused Gardner of rape because he forcibly entered her home, "undid his pants, took out his privates and wanted me to take them in my hands." When she refused, Gardner pulled off her clothes and "effected an entrance." When he finished his assault, he threatened to return with another soldier, most likely a warning to keep Davis silent. At his court martial, three men testified for Gardner claiming that Davis did not possess chaste character. When Gardner was "honorably acquitted" of all charges, General William Franklin was outraged at what he called Gardner's "highly reprehensible" conduct and ordered the term "honorably" to be struck from the record. While Gardner may have sullied his own masculine character in the general's eyes, Franklin nevertheless took no further action. The honor politics of white male soldiers could shield them from severe punishment.[51]

The advantage of being a white male in the Union army endowed those soldiers with the privilege of often having their crimes absolved more readily than those of Black men and white women. John H. Crowder, a young Black recruit in 1863, complained to his mother that his good opinion of his white officers was much reduced from his time under their command. "They are the most pusillanimous dirty low life men that I ever seen. Like many others they have no respect for no one, they seem to think there is not a woman that they cannot sleep with, every woman seems to be a common woman with them." Crowder was outraged when a Union soldier exposed himself to a woman and her child; she had nursed Crowder through a serious sickness the previous year. His commanding officer refused to do anything about it. When Corporal William Hilton shot and killed a "little yellow girl" after he raped her on the Pelton plantation in Bayou du Lac, General Stephen Hurlbut reluctantly "remitted the death sentence on a legal technicality," because his rank was listed on court records incorrectly.[52]

In contrast, Black men were more often charged than white men and their punishments were far more severe. Godfrey Weitzel hung a Black man named Granson (or Granville) in the Lafourche District for attempted rape in February 1863. Eighteen-year-old Evan Williams of the 48th United States Colored Troops (USCT) raped Georgianna Bryant, a white woman, in Shreveport, Louisiana, in September 1865. The war was technically over but Union occupation remained in force. "He . . . knocked me down," she reported, and "said if I made a noise he'd kill me." Williams admitted his assault on Bryant and was sentenced to be shot. He escaped custody before the judgment could be carried out, however. Fowler Willis and his six companions who killed Frank Neff and raped Aloysia Neff were hung for their transgressions. Repeatedly, Black soldiers in the Union army faced far more severe sentencing than white men for the same crime—an indication that Black men were not understood to possess honor in the same way as white men and also perhaps that white men resented potential sexual contact between Black men and white women. The inherent virtues of military service and the systemic value placed on the male gender in the nineteenth century failed to administer justice to Black soldiers in Louisiana in a manner equal to that of their white comrades.[53]

White women in Louisiana, though they suffered rape and sexual assault from Union soldiers, were more likely than women of color to be recognized and protected in the military justice system. Georgianna Bryant found not only a voice under martial law, but even justice against Evan Williams, though he eventually escaped. As a white woman, Aloysia Neff saw her Black attackers perish. Although the military acquitted her white assailant William Gardner, his court martial reveals that Martha Davis still received consideration for her assault that Black women could not always rely on. Only the public assault on her character by three of Gardner's comrades prevented her case from closing in her favor, an example of how women's socially constructed moral character often worked against them. Although justice for white women fluctuated based on race, and the attacks on their moral character were frequent, the relative stability of Union military occupation in Louisiana did provide a public court where the voices of white women could nominally be heard. And, as John Hawkes's letter indicates, the Union army could act in defense of white women and their property. In the moral and social order that the Union army set out to craft and preserve as an occupying force, white women maintained a position higher than that of Black Americans, even if it was within a paradigm that valued their status primarily as social subordinates and sexual property.[54]

Consequently, Black women suffered greater harm than white women, and were less likely to find any redress in the already narrow avenues of military justice, though the Civil War era did produce fresh crusades of Black women who pressed for bodily rights at a political level and sought sexual justice through military law. Black women, slave or free, made prime targets for predators. Under the influence of alcohol, men of the 159th New York entered a hut in southern Louisiana where some Black workers lived, held a bayonet to a young woman's head, and repeatedly raped her while her parents watched in horror. On picket duty in occupied Baton Rouge in December 1863, Wisconsin soldier Sylvester LaMotte robbed a white woman named Louisiana Jones, although she had both a pass to travel and a signed loyalty oath on her person, and then raped her Black servant while Jones sat in her carriage, forced to watch. Jones submitted a written statement of LaMotte's misconduct, but did not appear in court, so the case was dropped. The racial status of the young Black girl that William Holton raped and killed in Bayou du Lac meant that she could perish without much concern from the ranks of the Union Army.[55]

Nevertheless, rape against Black women did not always go unpunished. First Lieutenant Charles Wenz of the 4th United States Colored Cavalry had the husband of sixty-year-old Ann Booze arrested and held without charge in Port Hudson, perhaps an effort to socially isolate her for purposes of sexual predation. Afterwards he drunkenly ordered an enlisted man to carry Booze to her cabin where Wenz proceeded to rape her. "He told me if I didn't take off my clothes, he would have the rest of his men come and do it to me," she reported. When Wenz released her, she took her clothes and ran to the woods. Wenz was dishonorably discharged for his conduct and given five years hard labor, along with his officer insignia torn off before the regiment. Although his behavior was reprehensible, it is possible that the Union military command deemed his

abuse of power or his drunkenness, especially as an officer, as more disrepu-
table than the rape of an older Black woman. As Booze herself stated, "I'm an
old crippled colored woman who can't walk without a stick. I ain't no count."[56]

At least one scholar argues that Butler's Woman's Order was a piece of public policy that created a larger sense of anxiety for women during the war. "The
geographical reach of Butler's Order ensured that the threat of sexual violence
and the fear of rape were common to Southern women and central to how
they experienced the Civil War," Crystal Feimster contends. Importantly, no
reported cases of rape emerged during Butler's tenure, but the language itself
had more influence than Butler perhaps expected. Women without morality,
the order implicitly suggested, could not expect the protections of a moral
(male) society. To accomplish social order Butler utilized the inflexible nature
of public morality, as well as how the nature of sexual politics weighed in favor of male order and female subjectivity. On a larger level, however, the 1863
Lieber Code defined rape as a war crime, with no distinction based on race.
Such a definition provided legal opportunities for Black women to seek justice.[57]

Both the personal attacks of Union soldiers and the public policy of the
Union military structure in occupied Louisiana during the Civil War reveal
that rape and sexual assault as political acts operated on prewar conceptions of
male dominance and female submission. As an institution the Union military
did much to alter the social system of the South, but little to fundamentally
change the underlying racial and gender implications of sexual violence. The
attack of Fowler Willis and other Black Union soldiers represents how victims
of an oppressive system, in this case southern slavery, could themselves per-
petuate violence and victimization. Yet those who suffered rape and assault
were not entirely disempowered. Throughout the Civil War, as Feimster notes,
military and civil courts conceived of rape as a crime against property, honor,
and troop discipline—not against the intrinsic personhood of victims. The
Union military controlled southern women as sexual property, though its everyday considerations of sexual violence were steeped in cultural mores about
the personal honor of men and women as moral agents, a viewpoint that obscured the class, race, and gender frameworks that upheld the marginalized status of women, Black Americans, and persons of limited economic means. Yet
as Susan Barber and Charles Ritter contend, the fact that Union courts-martial
endeavored to hear cases of sexual injustice and punish them at all, especially

for Black women, was a progressive step. Rape also represented a violation of social order and military decorum, the antithesis of the peaceful regime Union military figures desired as they remained deep in Confederate territory. As an armed force of occupation, the Union military shaped its justice system to suit its political and martial needs.[58]

In battles of spatial authority, protection, provision, and bodily autonomy, southern women both fought against and allied with Union military occupation. The military bureaucracy that responded to their presence increased the political status of southern Black and white women within a patriarchal society by validating their political obligations to the state and extended greater welfare to them. But occupiers did not extend increased rights to them as female participants in American democracy. Occupied women, especially Black women insistent on justice, family cohesion, and economic opportunity, troubled the (un)democratic space of Union occupation. If authorities in blue were remaking the Union, Black women wanted a place in it. While some instances of material support and racial justice occurred, the Union military left no lasting legacy of democratic inclusion.

Black and white women under occupation demonstrated that the household war was not just about survival, even if that was the part most discernible and concerning to them on a daily basis. The war also unsettled the grounds of their membership in American society. Southern women made themselves visible and Union commanders categorized them as political agents subject to property seizure, loyalty oaths, and even imprisonment. Southern women also made race and gender feature prominently in the remaking of the republic that occurred under occupation. Viewing occupied Louisiana from a racial and gendered lens reveals a three-way conflict between white women (who opposed Union power yet called on it for material support and opposition to Black freedom), Black women (who opposed Confederates and Union troops who tried to maintain racial inequality yet called on Union authorities for aid), and Union soldiers (who opposed Confederate women as domestic belligerents and often attempted to limit Black freedom and mobility). Women Black and white carried the politics of the household into the streets and into male-coded public space. For Black women, that space was traditionally marked by unfreedom as well, so they battled both Union limitations and the Confederate household order. Women's local political culture demonstrated alternative value systems to Union troops and portended a larger national discourse about belonging. Likewise, Black Americans struggled to assert their belonging in a southern society altered by war and Union occupation.[59]

5

Small Pieces of Ground

BLACK FAMILIES & FREEDOM UNDER OCCUPATION

Thomas Knox was a Union soldier and reporter for the *New York Herald* who traveled extensively in the western theater of the war. He battled Confederates in Missouri, witnessed war in Arkansas, reported on the Sioux uprising in Minnesota, and traveled with Ulysses Grant's army in campaigns against Fort Donelson, Memphis, and Vicksburg. His experiences also included frequent interactions with formerly enslaved people and the efforts of the Union army to organize labor systems in occupied Louisiana and Mississippi. In the spring of 1863, when Grant's army breached the interior of northeast Louisiana, Knox described the flight of numerous white planters. He provided excellent first-hand evidence of how Union occupation forces in the Mississippi Valley transformed and regulated the lives of enslaved people. First came victory over Confederate planters. When slaveholders disappeared, they abandoned sizable swaths of prime southern land and forfeited the racial birthright of southern men: white mastery over enslaved Black dependents.[1]

Had the Union army facilitated a permanent overthrow of the elite class, it might have been social revolution enough, but the second stage of Union occupation involved paternalistic regulation of freedpeople. Instead of releasing enslaved people to lives of material and communal freedom, Union administrators immediately established bureaucratic systems of control over Black Americans. "When the negroes remained, and the plantations were not supplied with provisions," Knox wrote, "it became necessary for the Commissary Department to issue rations for the subsistence of the blacks." In many cases amid the devastation of war, immediate provisions for sustenance might have been "necessary" as Knox described. But Union wartime provisions smuggled in larger racial social controls. "As nearly all the planters cared nothing for the negroes they had abandoned," Knox assumed, "there was a very large number that required the attention of the Government." Despite Knox's characterization, enslaved and free Black Americans had battled for freedom and autonomy since the colonial era, and they would continue to do so for decades after the Emancipation Proclamation. Freedpeople were capable agriculturalists who, as some in Louisiana proved, could take care of themselves if allowed.[2]

Knox was observing the troubled birth of free labor in the Mississippi Valley. Especially after the summer of 1863, Union occupation forces occupied enough territory in eastern, central, and southern Louisiana to begin establishing a more sophisticated network of free labor plantations and trade routes.[3] To build a functional free labor system in the midst of a war in a state that was rooted in slavery, the Union military pursued three strategies at once. First, it enacted emancipation, a haphazard process that threw traditional structures of southern agricultural profit and household authority into disarray. Second, to make order from this social upheaval, occupation authorities, especially Nathaniel Banks, issued military edicts to organize emancipated people into laboring communities and soldiering units. Lastly, as the burden of this system was tremendous, military bureaucrats allowed white landowners and employers to once again command Black labor, provided they adhered to regulations that guaranteed their loyalty to the Union and did not treat Black workers as enslaved people any longer. The last two parts of this approach to free labor often worked at cross purposes. Union occupiers sought to impose culturally familiar white household structure and values onto Black Americans even as they simultaneously countenanced the prerogatives of white southern employers, a paradox that constrained the efforts of formerly enslaved people to assemble their own household order. This polyvalent Union policy often undermined Black families or at best atomized individual laborers to the detriment of traditional Black subsistence strategies like cooperative labor and household kinship networks. Union military figures often treated formerly enslaved people little better than they had been under slavery itself. Union recruiters regularly siphoned off Black men to join the ranks or compelled them to labor on public works projects and military defenses, leaving a majority of Black women and children in contraband camps and plantation fields.

Union administrators could curtail or augment the power of white property owners to maintain control over Black laborers. Just as they emphasized loyalty as the primary requirement of citizenship, Union commanders prioritized loyalty and faithful relations to military order as prerequisites for renewed agricultural efforts within occupied Louisiana. As a managerial and coercive institution of government power, Union occupation in Civil War Louisiana engineered a military state in which white southern residents, despite novel social restrictions from the U.S. army, generally maintained a portion of inclusive citizenship rights and material substance larger than that of formerly enslaved Black Americans. The Union military maintained the architecture of the past while it forged the uncertain future.[4]

Confederate war policies also weakened Black household networks, especially guerrilla attacks that plagued the waterways in the eastern part of Louisiana in 1864–65, which targeted plantations where nominally loyal planters or northern lessees hoped to turn a profit under the government-sanctioned free labor system. Guerrillas purposely uprooted, displaced, and recaptured Black laborers. Pressed at the edges by Confederate forces, signed by Union military figures and employers into individualistic contracts that attenuated their collective labor capacity, and forced to labor in a contract system that maintained many of the restrictions of slavery, freedpeople in occupied Louisiana endured a reality that stymied their incipient households. Delivered from the lash, from degrading ownership, and from lifelong characterizations based on skin color, formerly enslaved Black Americans often faced familiar patterns of exploitation in occupied Louisiana.[5]

The Union army pursued an unsteady trajectory from conservative war policy that wavered on the idea of emancipation to liberation as a war aim accompanied by sprawling free labor operations on the east coast and throughout the Mississippi Valley. Not until Butler felt the political winds shift in the latter half of 1862 did he try his hand at a labor program of limited success in the fall. In 1863, the Union managerial bureaucracy under Banks took some time to get organized, but eventually Union officials began transferring runaways from contraband camps onto government-confiscated plantations in southern Louisiana that were leased to northerners, loyal southerners, and even a small number of free Black people. Throughout 1864 and 1865, administrators continued to stock these free labor plantations with emancipated workers, but many Union officers recruited soldiers extensively from these properties, much

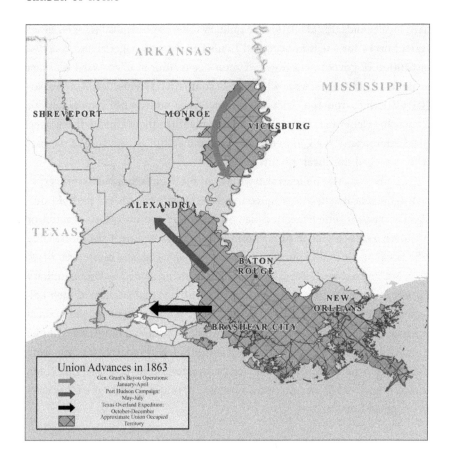

to the frustration of white employers and Black families once again separated by white authority figures.[6]

To diminish tensions and streamline a burdensome free labor system, Banks issued a series of general orders that outlined the moral and practical parameters of his vision for emancipated labor. He had been in command a little over a month when he released General Orders No. 12, which forbade Union troops both from encouraging enslaved people to leave their masters or forcing them to go back. "Those who leave their employers will be compelled to support themselves and families by labor upon the public works," he added. This iteration of coercion signaled the suspicion with which many northerners regarded independent Black people and communicated the Union army's determination to shape free labor by force if necessary. After an unimpressive planting year of 1863—marred by unchecked recruitment, mistreat-ment of workers, and rampant corruption—Banks mandated lengthy reforms with General Orders No. 23 (February 3, 1864), which, among numerous other commands, forbade recruitment from plantations without specific orders, dis-allowed family visitation, limited laborers' mobility, outlawed physical pun-ishment, and appointed provost marshal control over contracts and labor dis-putes. A few months later, he issued General Orders No. 92, which required plantation owners to supply twelve staple provisions to workers on a weekly basis in addition to adhering to the work hours and nonviolent labor condi-tions stipulated in the contracts.[7]

Banks and others issued such orders in an attempt to balance the disjointed relationship of power contained in labor contracts, yet his prohibitions on fam-ily unity and extraordinary limitations on independent Black land ownership (one acre at most) produced unreasonable hardships on Black household strat-egies. Banks also authorized the creation of the Bureau of Plantations and the Bureau of Negro Labor in 1863, which cooperated to subordinate Black free labor to a plantation system that resembled slavery. By the end of the war, the Bureau oversaw some 1,500 plantations run by various figures. Approximately 95,000 emancipated people labored on these properties. In addition, the Bu-reau oversaw four Home Colonies, which were federal properties specifically dedicated to "vagrant and helpless freedmen." Union officers also recruited over 24,000 Black male laborers into the Union army, more than any other state. That force represented nearly one out of every three workers in the Black male population between the ages of 18 to 45, a sizable intervention into the labor force of Louisiana and a serious obstacle to Black household unity.[8] But Banks's vision of free labor never encompassed Black workers as a fully inde-pendent, self-realized class. Rather, he vaunted a plantation system that re-mained highly paternalistic and eventually led to the sharecropping system. Like many Americans North and South, Banks assumed Black dependency on white administrative guidance and philanthropic largesse. Under his authority, Union forces continued to construct a regime of Black dependency with little scope for full citizenship.[9]

Even before the arrival of Union soldiers, the mere idea of their presence unsettled slavery in Louisiana. "The runaways are numerous and bold," Kate Stone wrote in June 1861. Confederate citizens in Madison Parish suspected that enslaved people would attack and seize a local mine on July 4 but the assault never materialized. The excitement of such a prospect, Stone judged, infected enslaved people. "The house servants have been giving a lot of trouble lately—lazy and disobedient." One of her neighbors endured two servants "who are worse than useless—one sick and the other contrary." Stone proposed to send her disobedient house servants to the field as an antidote for impudence. Even without local rebellions, enslaved people connected the politics of war to their enslaved condition. "In some way they have gotten a confused idea of . . . the war," Stone wrote dismissively; "they think it is all to help them, and they expected for 'something to turn up.'" Although no July 4 uprising took place in Madison Parish, two days later she could still hear enslaved people celebrating in the fields. "From the quarters I hear the faint scrape of the fiddles and the thump, thump, thump of the dancers." Those distant celebrations, however benign slaveholders imagined them to be, were a musical prelude to Union occupation, emancipation, and social transformation in Louisiana.[10]

The arrival of Union troops precipitated mass departures of Black people from southern properties, but those who remained altered the power dynamics of the southern household. "Mr. Stockett has not got a negroe [*sic*] on his place, every one left last night," Ellen Louise Power wrote from East Feliciana Parish in mid-1863. Around the same time, Francis Lawrence wrote a letter to a relative complaining about "these negroes!! Whom we thought most of were the first to take their departure." To make matters worse for Lawrence and family, some of "our contrabands who were taken up the country, returned and after remaining here for two weeks doing nothing I told them." She found one of her formerly enslaved people to be very insolent. "I asked why he behaved so ill. Said he was at liberty to talk as he please[d]." As time went on and Lawrence grew more fearful of Union troops, some formerly enslaved people tried to "make it worse by telling me the Feds were going to shell my house and hang my husband and all such stories." Such treatment hardened Lawrence, who wrote she had "no kind feeling for any except those who have been tried and still remain." In other words, upon cessation of personal loyalty, Fanny relinquished emotional connection. She abandoned the civilizing power of white sympathy.[11]

Under Union occupation, southerners renewed complaints about Black recalcitrance, even as they paradoxically enjoyed the benefits of Union protection and labor management. "The arrival of the Yankees alone turned the negroes crazy," John Ransdell, the Whig editor and Elmwood planter near

Alexandria, complained in 1863; "subordination and restraint was at an end." An Alexandria newspaper accused Union troops of "invading family firesides," where they "sowed the seeds of dissatisfaction and insurrection among the servants." Despite such allegations, the Union military enacted stiff restrictions of Black mobility and labor alongside emancipation in occupied Louisiana. On the final day of 1862, for example, New Orleans resident Julia LeGrand fearfully wrote of a supposed New Year's Day insurrection. Yet she also claimed that the provost marshal issued orders that "disarmed Confederates may now arm again and shoot down the turbulent negroes (like dogs)." The Union military undermined slavery but did much to uphold white control over Black Americans in occupied Louisiana because it feared the potential instability of racial violence within occupied territory.[12]

Beyond military security itself, the Union army sought to control Black people within occupied Louisiana because Black labor—in the ranks and in the fields and within private homes and on the levees—undergirded the success of Union occupation. Almost immediately upon arrival, Butler and other Union officials began assigning Black labor to local projects. Perhaps more than any other managerial task that preoccupied their mind, Union commanders fixated on levee repair. In September of 1862, General Shepley instructed Jacob Weizel, syndic of Jefferson Parish, to convene a planter jury to "assemble without delay and act and decide in accordance with the usages under the Statutes of Louisiana relating to levees." The same day he ordered the commander of Camp Parapet to employ a force of no less than eighty contraband laborers to repair the levees around New Orleans under direction of Weizel and the planter jury. Two days later, he commanded a captain in the 31st Massachusetts to assemble two hundred contraband laborers to repair levees. One Union officer even dispatched a circular to provost marshal outposts stating, "You will be pleased to immediately report to these HeadQuarters [sic] the number of unemployed negroes in your Parish with a view of their being ordered to labor on such levees as may require repair." Lamentably, while Black workers could demonstrate knowledge and skill on the levees, Union commanders like Shepley emulated the forced labor of slavery by extracting Black industriousness and investing it into public works projects.[13]

Black men provided substantial enterprises of labor for both military and private civilian use in occupied Louisiana. One quartermaster requested a lieutenant in the Brashear City provost marshal's office to compose a group of soldiers "for the purpose of gathering idle contrabands" to unload vessels at the city wharf. "If you have any more vagrants on hand," Colonel George Hanks wrote from New Orleans to provost marshal Albert Stearns, "I would be obliged to you if you would send them here, as there is a great demand for laborers." In late 1862, Shepley gave permission to C. N. Boofish and J. W. McMillan, owners of Willow Wood plantation, to employ all enslaved people belonging to disloyal southerners in Jefferson Parish, only if those laborers agreed. If the laborers lived within a military camp, the employers had to obtain permission from the camp commander and relieve the government of pay and rations to the Black laborers. As Boofish and McMillan traversed the terrain of Civil War Louisiana, both in regions subject to federal rule and those still autonomous, they embodied the managerial, coercive power of the Union occupation state. Their capacity to negotiate with Black laborers, some still enslaved, signaled a significant alteration in southern social relations under occupation; yet their authority to command Black labor resembled the traditional power structure of slavery, only with the state as master rather than independent white men.[14]

Shepley's order to the Willow Wood owners also illustrated the multivalent policies of the Union army concerning slavery, property, and Black freedom. Because southern Louisiana was already an occupied region when the Emancipation Proclamation was issued, that document did not clarify Union policy concerning Black people in the state. Subsequently, Union policy was always subject to lapses in bureaucracy and idiosyncratic interpretations by individual commanders. Shortly after Banks's January 1863 order, General James Bowen, provost marshal general for the Department of the Gulf, issued his own iteration of Order No. 12 to Union forces in Louisiana: "You will abstain from giving any encouragement or aid to slaves to abandon the service of their masters, nor will you compel, by force or threats, fugitive slaves to return to masters. But while you will carefully avoid interfering in any manner with the relation of master and slave, you will employ all vagrant negroes in your District in repairing the Levees, roads, and other public works." For those able-bodied contrabands who did labor for the Union, he demanded work every day except Sundays. "The refractory and indolent you will compel to work, by such slight punishment as may be effective," he added. However, if escaped slaves preferred slavery to Union labor, soldiers should allow their return. With a single order, Bowen had spelled out a number of possible actions that also spanned the matrix of northern political opinion about how the military should handle the institution of slavery.[15]

Bowen's order temporized because Union war policy was still developing, even in early 1863, but the plethora of possible actions it authorized toward enslaved and emancipated people also spoke a high rate of mobility among Black Americans in wartime Louisiana. Much to the frustration of white property owners, Black laborers did not recognize the unquestioned authority of white masters under occupation and they severed their relationship to slavery when they departed the plantations where they previously worked in bondage. Departure was perhaps the most salient of Black reconfigurations to racial household relations in the white South, an action that exasperated some Union officials as well. Formerly enslaved people, though their status remained malleable under occupation, rejected the outlines of the previous system of bondage, the conservative parameters of emancipation policy, and even the contract system established by the Union army. Black laborers refashioned their own communities first by changing their views of themselves from enslaved workers to hired laborers and again by emphasizing their relationship to each other more than their relationship to white authority. When Black laborers contested wages or departed for better wages and conditions elsewhere, they also demonstrated a desire to mitigate their own economic dependency.[16]

Union occupation officials often viewed mobile, unemployed Black men with the same anxiety as had white slaveholding society in the antebellum South. Within weeks of the army's arrival in Baton Rouge in the spring of 1862, a Union soldier named William Whitney observed "every male negro who was found about the streets was taken and put in the Penitentiary or State Prison House." An enslaved man named Arthur, whom the *New Orleans Daily Delta* reported as belonging to former sheriff E. T. Parker, was arrested early one August morning in Poydras Market for "disturbing the peace." The newspaper claimed that Arthur had "a fierce looking bowie knife" and that he was "a desperately inclined fellow." In September, Shepley committed one young enslaved man named Simeon to the parish prison as "dangerous and unruly." In St. John the Baptist Parish, a provost marshal officer arrested and imprisoned a Black man named Alexander for stealing a bedstead valued at $30, which he was removing to his own cabin. The officer also noted that Alexander "belonged to" Marcian Belford Haydel. He was found guilty and sentenced to thirty days of bread and water. This provost marshal officer, like the *Daily Delta*, Colonel

Jonas French, and Shepley, continued to recognize the social connections of slavery despite the government's ambivalent emancipation policies in 1862–63. Arrests like these undermined the autonomy of Black men in a location where slavery was beginning to unravel.[17]

The Union military also worried that Black mobility, much of which came from enterprising Black merchants, would produce internal trade disputes that might undermine social order or military security. R. E. Jackson singled out the Black people on board a schooner coming into Brashear City to be searched, in case they participated in "contraband trade." Albert Stearns reported a perturbing offense to Colonel Charles L. Harris in the spring of 1864. "I have discovered that some of the negroes who keep small stores . . . are in the habit of allowing gambling in their back rooms." Union soldiers participated in the vice as well. Stearns proposed sending away the guilty persons or moving them to New Orleans, and even suggested destroying some of the establishments where gambling occurred. "One or two examples of this kind would I think effectually stop the evil." Harris approved the tactics. A few months later, Harris confronted two problems of internal trade at once. No punishment would be too severe for persons caught selling whiskey to Union soldiers, he commanded. More challenging, he fretted over large numbers of people selling fresh beef and pork in the city. Local owners accused Union soldiers of slaughtering their cattle for profiteering. Harris suspected "that other hands than soldiers have had something to do with these depredations," and ordered a deputy provost marshal to assign some men to interrogate the meat purveyors. Edward Lewis wrote to Union headquarters in New Orleans with questions about Black laborers who appeared in Union lines with produce they had grown on local plantations and sold for cash or traded for clothing. Lewis also asked about fishermen who sailed into the local port to sell oysters. Nothing was wrong with Black laborers selling local goods, his superior wrote back— "the object of the order is to prevent *dishonest* people from purchasing the pilferings from Negroes during harvest time." Whether white or Black persons violated trade regulations, the Union military sought to reduce the frequency of these local transactions.[18]

As with white prisoners who posed threats to social order under occupation, Union officials used local Louisiana prisons as institutions of discipline in which to confine mobile Black men. Whereas Union occupiers used prisons to punish and circumvent white male resistance to the Union war effort, they generally placed Black men in prison on a temporary basis until those Black inmates were assigned to labor objectives. "I have to request that all negroes now confined in the Prisons of the various Parishes not charged with crime or misdemeanor, but confined merely on the charge of vagrancy may be released and sent to Lieutenant Hanks the Superintendent of Negro labor at his receiving depot," Banks commanded Bowen in early March 1863. In language that ominously presaged postwar Black Codes, Banks also commanded "that all unemployed negroes hav[ing] no regular habitation or employment may be arrested by the Provost Guard and sent also to this Depot in order that they may under his direction either be placed at work upon the plantations or upon the Government works." These arrangements—by which Banks meant arrest and assignment—"would avail much to the peace and comfort of the City." Prisons were stations of power where Union authorities contained and then dispersed subjects, primarily male subjects, to assigned roles. Through imprisonment and assignment, Union occupiers inscribed Black men with inferior social meaning and secured a social order premised on white security and command of labor.[19]

Just as Union commanders recruited white soldiers from Louisiana prisons, they enrolled Black soldiers and troupes of contraband laborers, from prisons as well as local plantations. In October 1864, Thomas Conway, who replaced George Hanks as superintendent of the Office of Negro Labor in August after Hanks was accused of fraud and corruption, requested the provost marshal of St. Mary Parish to deliver notices to certain local planters "to call at this office without delay for their settlement with the conscripts from their plantations." When Black laborers on local plantations under Union authority joined the army, planters were required to pay those men whatever wages they had earned to that point and end their contracts. Planters were also required to sign a certificate relinquishing the services of Black laborers to the Union army. "The certificate should embrace the time of commencing service, the class of laborer, the wages agreed to be paid per month, the [amount] paid if any, and the [amount] due at the time the parties were recruited." Conway sought equitable payment for the recruits under the authority of his labor bureau. He also requested any as-yet-unreceived conscript certificates from the provost marshal to assure that the army issued proper payment to new recruits.[20]

Despite the enhanced opportunity for inclusive citizenship and self-confidence that military service provided, Union recruitment hardly proved to be a favorable institution for all Black men. In 1862, the Lincoln administration had been coy with Butler about recruiting and arming formerly enslaved men, but after the Emancipation Proclamation, the administration dispatched Brigadier General Daniel Ullman to Louisiana with orders to raise a brigade of four Black regiments. Afterward, he was to report to Banks. Even before Ullman's arrival, Banks impressed vagrant Black men into the ranks, an action that seemed to be as much about social order as military manpower. One of his aides boasted, "This policy [led to] their speedy removal from the streets and town." Ullman's recruiters practiced harsh tactics, forcing men to join the ranks at gun point, pulling men from their families or homes, and seizing any Black man without a pass. William Whitney, who watched Black men rounded up and imprisoned in Baton Rouge, wrote that all able-bodied Black men in his region were "scared" into the ranks.[21]

Under these Union recruitment practices, Black men could suffer fates eerily similar to the worst indignities of slavery. Affidavits provided by Valgrand Verret and his son August to military investigators in September 1864 spelled out a gruesome tale for one Black recruit. Cruising up the Atchafalaya River next to Bateman Island, Union troops aboard Gunboat No. 49 discovered a sick Black recruit near the shore. He had been in the woods over a month without medical care or any food beyond raw corn and potatoes that he purloined from nearby fields. Within days, Union officers had the statement of Verret, a local citizen who owned a skiff. On the first day of August, he testified, Union pickets near Berwick City saw Verret and his son in their skiff and hailed them. Verret found the pickets guarding a Black man soldier with smallpox. Under orders from Colonel P. Jones of the 93rd USCT, the pickets (whom Verret identified as white cavalrymen of the 18th New York) commanded Verret to take the diseased man across the river and deposit him in the woods on Bateman Island without food or supplies. Just days before he left for a new assignment in the Shenandoah Valley, provost marshal Albert Stearns dispatched urgent investigative letters to the commanding officer of the 18th New York and to General Robert Cameron. Yet Stearns's immediate superior, Colonel C. L. Harris, dismissed concern over the matter. "I think it would be better for one negro to suffer than the disease get into the Colonel's regiment," he wrote. For this unwell and ill-treated Black man, Louisiana remained a dangerous landscape even after the Union army arrived.[22]

Banks, among others, feared the end result of disagreeable recruitment practices—the disruption of the labor system. Over the course of 1863, Union officials like Banks and George Hanks faced a crusade of Black men who complained in person or in petitions about Union recruitment abuses. By September, one Union officer chided a St. John Parish provost marshal for allowing recruitment to undermine labor in his jurisdiction: "You will not allow any officer to recruit, conscript or in any way interfere with persons of color, formerly or now held in service with the intention of enticing them away from their employers." Treasury agent Benjamin Flanders also worried that recruitment on local plantations would undermine the labor system and the loyalty of southern planters, who complained assiduously when Black laborers, willfully or under force, broke contracts to join Union ranks. Union officials in the Department of the Gulf also openly opposed Ullman, who interfered, whether he intended to or not, in local military operations with his cruel recruitment practices. Banks responded with a careful balancing act in which he dispatched Black troops into the fields once more if planters in the occupied parishes required more labor.[23]

When Banks responded to the complaints of local planters and furloughed conscripts back into the fields, he illustrated two precepts of Union occupation that would shape Reconstruction. First, Union officials valued economic stability and moderate political reconstruction more than personal and political Black autonomy. Second, to those ends Banks also used recruitment as a form of labor exploitation. By resisting recruitment, Black men in occupied Louisiana demonstrated their distrust for a military institution that often treated them little better than enslaved people. With the fearful discipline and violence committed by many white officers in the Corps d'Afrique, Black troops did not always view their service with zeal. As James Yeatman noted in his 1864 Western Sanitary Commission report, "The fear of being drafted into the army is preventing thousands from coming in." For Black troops in Louisiana, a blue uniform did not preclude them from extensive labor on dams, levees, roads, fortifications, and other physical duties. The punishing practices of Union officers, the alliance between planters and Banks, and the physical labor performed by Black men in the ranks proved that, in the fields and in the army, Black labor was a token of Union occupation.[24]

Black Americans were hardly submissive to such mistreatment from Union officials and white Louisianans who clung to the power dynamics of slavery. As historian Louis Gerteis has argued, "Union occupation stimulated rather than deterred Black uprisings" precisely because Union labor policies so closely re-sembled antebellum slavery. Some formerly enslaved people even took advan-tage of the disorganization on the edges of Union occupation, such as when Union forces advanced through the Bayou Teche region in early 1863, to orga-nize themselves into independent groups. One such group led by a Creole man named Theodule Melancon attempted a rebellion in the town of St. Martins-ville (near Lafayette in St. Martin Parish) in April 1863. The townspeople over-came them and even hung ten of the captured Black men from a local bridge. "In the night their friends came and carried their bodies away," one regimental history stated.[25]

Black garrison soldiers in Louisiana also faced stern resistance from local white citizens. While Black men in uniform demonstrated the altered racial reality enabled by Union occupation, they also experienced the earliest repri-sals of white conservatives in the Reconstruction era. During the Red River Campaign, William Stewart witnessed a white resident strike a Black soldier with "a whack over the head and a kick behind, calling him an infernal rascal to talk of n——s garrisoning their town." Encouraged by onlookers to thrash his opponent, the Black soldier struck his assailant "a whack between the eyes dropping him like a log." He then drew his bayonet and "the citizen made tracks." The assailant was seized and sent off to the guard house. Though he was outmatched, this white Louisiana citizen and others like him turned to violence to protect traditional racial boundaries of social inclusion. Even more than Union regulations over labor, property, and trade, the presence of Black military occupation signaled the most profound cultural shift in southern so-ciety. "I never had such feelings as I did, to think that we must be ruled by a set of black negroes," scoffed Ellen Power in East Feliciana Parish in August 1863. Stewart understood the moral power of occupation's cultural reconfiguration. "They have got to learn," he said of white Louisiana residents, "that the Amer-ican flag covers *all* American soldiers color & all."[26]

Many Union troops were not as high-minded as Stewart, giving Union commanders additional headaches. "This sacrificing a white man's life for sake of a n—— goes against my principles," one soldier wrote after the Emanci-pation Proclamation was issued. That same month J. Harvey Brown wrote his wife from Baton Rouge, "Thare [*sic*] is one thing the men in general dont like[,] that is freeing the n——s." He claimed that freedpeople fared better than soldiers or poor white people. "Thare [*sic*] is a Reg of n——s here they strut as thoe [sic] the ground was not gooden [sic] for them to walk on," he wrote disparagingly. High-ranking Union officials and bureau figureheads attempted to curtail vile behavior among white Louisianans and Union officers by using command structure and honor culture. When reports of abuse finally trickled up the chain of command, offending officers generally experienced court martial. Banks insisted that officers under his command were to be governed by the articles of war, his own orders, basic humanity, and manly honor. Officers who "indulged in punishments" were "barbarous" and "indecent." These condemnations were important, but Banks and other high-ranking officials did not pursue Black liberty so much as they chastened white masculinity. Often, even as they punished misconduct among Union ranks, military officials did not connect those offenses to the larger problem of Black household stability. Both Union officials and white Louisianans misunderstood the Black struggle to materialize their own households.[27]

Beyond contraband camps, prisons, and military recruitment, contract labor represented the most widespread and effective means of organizing emancipated people. While the free labor program proved burdensome for Union command, the bureaucratic forms and military reports issued by the army revealed the extent of occupation power as well as rendered visible the personal activities of Black laborers and white employers. In late April 1864, Thomas Conway dispatched fifty blank registration forms to the provost marshal headquarters in Brashear City to be distributed among the officers, government employees, and even private citizens who "employ colored persons." Intended to fulfill the directives of Banks's Order No. 23, the forms would contain information that Conway would build into a registry of Black labor. "All colored persons living about town or about the Camps should also be enrolled on these blanks," Conway instructed, "whether employed by others or for their own private good." As a tool of military occupation, this registry mapped Louisiana's social landscape. Registration informed Conway and other Union officials not only of the numbers and context of Black labor, but also depicted the compliance of white citizens to Union authority.[28]

Union occupation created a managerial state that could simultaneously affect both white citizens and Black citizens-in-becoming in negative or positive ways. The "blanks" Conway referred to were loose form sheets with military information printed on them, followed by a fill-in-the-blank paragraph designed to specify the employer, the location, and the workers being hired. If the numerous labor contracts packed into the provost marshal records in the National Archives are any indication, Conway's registry probably never materialized as a bound volume. Still, the loose forms, as the minutiae of occupation administration, reflected larger truths about the vision of state control. They held white employers to essential standards of pay and behavior but did not dismantle a labor environment where white property owners possessed power over Black labor. Often, the contracts indicated discernible improvements in labor and social conditions for formerly enslaved Black people but did not deliver them from continued racial disadvantage at the hands of both white southerners and the Union army. The contracts rarely translated into independent Black land ownership and stable households. Lastly, the bureaucratic forms manifested the presence of Union military occupation as arbiter of social relations in wartime Louisiana.

Union labor contracts signified new interlocking, tripartite relationships between formerly enslaved Black Americans, white citizen employers, and the Union military. All three of these groups shared certain social and organizational values with each other, especially stability behind the lines. Conversely, each group held its own economic and personal considerations that diminished mutual interests. Alongside other controversial occupation practices such as property confiscation and loyalty management, federal intervention into the arena of labor regulated the dominance of employers by requiring contractual obligations. "The contract ostensibly reconciled free choice and social order," Eric Foner argues, "and epitomized the principle that legitimate systems of authority must rest upon consent rather than coercion. By voluntarily signing and adhering to contracts, both planters and freedmen would develop the habits of a free labor economy, and come to understand their fundamental harmony of interests." Perhaps more than any other social intervention of occupation, Union authorities intended contracts to reshape slaveholding society. Detailed in handwritten columns on the contracts and scrawled in countless military exchanges, the commands of Union administrators called on employers to explicitly name their Black employees, specify their wages, and maintain some semblance of human respect for workers. By reconfiguring plantations from sites of Black enslavement to sites of semi-autonomous Black labor,

Union occupation managers also reconfigured the exercise of white mastery. However much control they maintained as employers, when planters signed labor contracts they compromised their previous assertions of white mastery. While the relative dominance of white landowners did not vanish, employers did have to customize their command of labor to fit the protocols of Union oversight. Conversely, even as Black laborers disrupted the rhythms of slavery through mobility and resistance, labor contracts recodified the schematic of racial power within slavery: white landowner, Black laborer.[29]

Union occupation also needed to synchronize with the gendered reality of Black labor in Civil War Louisiana. Out of some 333,000 enslaved men and women in Louisiana in 1860, historian Karen Cook Bell estimates that nearly 44,000 Black women between the ages of fifteen and sixty labored in the twenty-three parishes of southern Louisiana where Union occupation was strongest. Fair treatment, payment, and family stability were priorities to liberated Black women, and they recognized that, as Thavolia Glymph argues, "the institution of a free wage economy in domestic work was inseparable from the larger struggles of emancipation." Yet employers routinely underpaid Black women, forcing them to look for other work or appeal to the Labor Bureau. Given that many more women labored in Louisiana's fields than men during the war years, military authorities soon felt the gendered effect of their recruitment and labor policies. "There are but few men among the laborers," James Yeatman noted in his Western Sanitary Commission report, "most of them having been carried far into the interior or drafted into the service, so that lessees will have to rely mainly upon the labor of women, unless the Government should establish non-interference by the military with such men as should come in to labor on the plantations." With or without their men, liberated Black women made sure that Union occupiers were aware of their altered status as independent laborers. "I offended a colored woman by calling her a 'contraband,'" wrote Massachusetts soldier Henry Johns. "Be it understood that 'contrabands' are supported by the Government. *She* supported herself."[30]

The bureaucratic form of the labor contract itself illustrated myopic gendered vision. The word "women" had to be written into the phrase printed at the top of Union-issued labor contracts: "I the undersigned have this day hired the following colored men to work." Repeatedly, the historical record contains forms with "and women" shoehorned into the phrase, scrawled near the word "men," or with "men" struck out entirely and women written overhead in its place. The labor contracts reveal fragmented Black communities under occupation. This fragmentation was no doubt a product of antebellum slavery, in which Black families suffered repeated fracture and fusion. During Union occupation, the variety of names on labor contracts illustrated this splintered social environment. Names of family members hired as a unit, single men, and single women (sometimes with children) all appeared on the lists with regularity. With many Black men on the move, whether in the Union army or in search of more favorable work conditions, Black women and children often found themselves isolated in the fields. Not only did male-centric labor forms rhetorically exclude women, but writing in their presence hardly acknowledged the disadvantages of the more immobile and materially poor Black female laborer. Government forms also demonstrated the gendered assumptions of northerners, who considered the field a man's location. Northerners misunderstood how enslaved women performed much of the same labor that men did under slavery. Later forms, like that proposed by James Yeatman in his report, adjusted the gendered language to simply read "freed laborers." Though their gender status was considered to be inferior to that of men, women (and men) behind Union lines had somewhat more mobility, more access to economic opportunities, and generally more success appealing to Union bureaucracy for redress of grievances.[31]

While white employers no longer wielded the unquestioned mastery of slave owners, they worked closely with the Union army to countersign their authority as property owners and facilitate plantation production with free Black labor. Under the organizational gaze of Union occupation, white employers might find local provost marshal outposts helpful or hindering to their traditional objective of self-mastery. "We are much in want of a good Provost marshal at Houma," W. L. Minn wrote from William Minor's Southdown Planation in Terrebonne Parish. "Our negroes are stealing everything & selling in Houma at a fourth of its value." He requested a guard from the army to watch over his sugar production in the approaching season. After repeated trouble from a man who hung about the Utopia Plantation without a permit, manager J. L. Billiu took matters into his own hands. "I have had him arrested hoping that your Honor could teach him a lesson which he would not forget on his return to our neighborhood," Billiu wrote the provost marshal. Distressed by perceived assaults on their economic systems, social stability, and personal autonomy these owners and employers appealed to Union occupying forces to validate their security efforts. In concert or conflict, the authority of the Union army and white employers combined to compromise but not dismantle the plantation labor system, a prospect that predicted a conflicted future for Black Americans.[32]

When men like Adam Hawthorn, a manager on the Glen Orange Plantation owned by L. F. Daires in St. Mary Parish, objected to Black self-determination, they represented white southerners intent on restoring the racial power they had previously enjoyed. Yet their interactions with Union commanders also illustrated the dependence of white property owners on Union authority. "We have tried to conform to the Regulations & Laws by which we are to be governed & hav[e] in all instances done all that is required of us," Hawthorn assured Albert Stearns before launching into a long series of troubles. Hawthorn found his operations frustrated by "Medlers [sic] who are & have been trying to interfere with our people & have Succeeded in Seducing off Several of our hands." One of his workers had run away with another man's wife. Another had apparently lost or stolen a new axe. Three others departed for the Ramon Plantation without notice, despite having signed year-long contracts. Because Black laborers were under Union protection, Hawthorn urged Stearns to make the workers return. Directives from the Union command also prompted employers to encourage laborers to save half their wages, a prospect Hawthorn found difficult. "Unless they get goods or money for their full earnings they are dissatisfied & in fact they are anxious to overseen their wages." Hawthorn also disputed whether he had to furnish clothing in addition to wages, as commanded by Banks. Daires would hire no more workers under those terms, Hawthorn wrote, especially after one laborer named Daniel Lillery left without paying for the clothes he was provided. A thief named John Battieu also plagued the Glen Orange Plantation and surrounding properties by stealing chickens, pigs, and ducks. Hawthorn complained of "idle people with bad character," such as a man who hung around the property and swore loudly and another man who frequently badgered his former wife. He requested Stearns to discipline these men.[33]

If white property owners refused to comply with Union directives, they could have their profits garnished or find themselves without laborers altogether. To prevent just such an outcome, Oliver Pence had to account for the physical condition and location of his laborers to the provost marshal. "The only proof I have is from my foreman's report. You can question him," Pence insisted. As harvest season began in 1863, one Treasury Department agent halted all shipments from a plantation when he discovered the property renter falsely represented himself. A year later, Thomas Conway ordered the provost marshal of St. Mary Parish to identify and stop all shipments of farm produce raised by Black workers in all cases where "the lien established by general orders on all produce for pay of laborers has not been complied with and the labor paid." His approval alone permitted sale. Instituted by Banks's Order No. 23, crop liens were intended to assure payment to laborers first, before planters or leaseholders could see profits. Conway's order was no doubt to prevent leaseholders from selling all the goods before they settled with laborers then absconding with all the money. Dr. R. W. Washington, "as if to defy the authorities and disregard the order of the commanding general regarding labor," obstinately returned blank contract forms to the office of labor superintendent George Hanks. Hanks requested General Bowen to remove all workers from the property.[34]

Even Union authorities complained about the autonomy of Black people, especially when it appeared to encourage disorderliness in the ranks. During the Butler-Phelps emancipation debate of 1862, Captain Edward Page, who later became a provost marshal, reported that enslaved people regularly disrespected local slaveholders near Camp Parapet and injured their property. "It is utterly impossible to call upon the negroes for any labor, as they say they have only to go to the Fort to be free, and are therefore very insolent to their masters." Likely Page was less concerned with how enslaved people treated slave owners than with what such dismissive treatment represented. Too often, he wrote Butler, Union soldiers under Phelps not only supported disorderly Black behavior but seemed to amplify it. Alarmed to find three enslaved people confined in an outbuilding on Mrs. Fendeair's plantation, Union troops released the people and "also broke into the house and stole therefrom silver spoons, dresses, and other articles." Few Union soldiers shared Phelps's taste for social upheaval in race relations. On July 17, 1862, less than two months after Phelps squared off with Butler, Colonel James W. McMillan ordered all contrabands out of Union lines at Baton Rouge and disallowed all Black women from government buildings or camps. As Union occupiers disagreed over the content of Black freedom, they signaled the divided heart of the Union's emancipation project.[35]

With such divided intentions, Union authorities sometimes made circumstances more advantageous for Black laborers, but just as often left workers stranded with familiar dependencies. Shipping a large quantity of books, desks, and other school supplies to St. Mary Parish, the Board of Education for Freedmen ironically displaced a Black family by removing them from a building on a plantation that was to be used as a school. The Board made no provision for the family but assured the property owner "justice as to rent" for the schoolhouse. In a prolonged court case concerning Confederate forays on an Iberville Parish plantation, Union officials carefully questioned Black laborers over supplies with which they had fled the property during the raids, but left no record of aid to the displaced workers. Near Brashear City in late 1864, Captain E. J. Lewis reported to his commander the arrival of "twelve of Judge Bakers hands. They have not been paid nor have they any thing to eat." Lewis requested permission to feed the hungry workers from Union supplies until a representative of Baker, a man named Brown, came to pay the men and reimburse the army. Lewis noted an alternative course as well: "I might send some . . . to the city to work on the Levee." Lewis received instructions from his commander to "draw rations for them as destitute citizens" and ensure repayment from Brown.[36]

The telling phrase "destitute citizens" indicated that emancipated people were devoid both of civil rights and material substance. Despite the term, Black Americans were not officially citizens of the United States, so they did not enjoy legal status or civil rights under Union occupation. But as physically destitute people as well, many did not possess the material foundations necessary for their own household stability. Ostensibly, the Union army extended protection to refugees from slavery as a policy of war. Yet, as an order issued by Major General E. R. S. Canby in mid-1864 demonstrated, Union policy had specific stipulations. "Refugees in good faith will be received and kindly treated. If destitute, their wants will be supplied as far as the means under the control of the Commanding Officer will permit. They cannot however be allowed to remain in or about any Fort or garrison where their presence would embarrass military operations." Burdensome refugees were to be transported with subsistence to Cairo, Illinois. "The Commanding Officer at that place will make the necessary arrangements for the purpose of receiving and caring for these persons, aiding them in securing employment, and indicating to the Relief Associations such of them as may be in need of assistance." Too often, whether from lack of material aid or because of paternalist attitudes, the Union bureaucracy prioritized military necessity and merely shuffled freedpeople around rather than establishing their freedom through permanent social institutions such as landholding and home ownership.[37]

In addition to qualified refugee relief, the Union military also sought to offer provision and protection to Black laborers where it could. To combat poverty among Black families of women and children whose male figures had enlisted in the army, the military government issued a directive to provide rations in late summer 1864. "Where they are not employed at labor by the Government, and who may have no means of subsisting themselves," contrabands and refugees will "be provided with rations by the nearest issuing Commissary, approved or ordered by the Provost marshal of the Parish, or by the Commanding Officer of the Post or District, in which such families may be located." In the summer of 1864, in St. John and St. James Parishes, the army also designated specific locations to gather Black laborers during Confederate raids. "In order to protect the Colored people from being driven into captivity," George Hanks commanded, "upon the first indications of the approach of the enemy . . . send couriers to the plantations and direct them to provide themselves with three days rations and blankets and collect at the following designated places where they will be under the protection of our guns." He listed Donaldsonville and Bonnet Carre Church as protective garrisons. Scrawled in the margin of the order, Hanks also wrote one last suggestion: "The buildings on P. B. Marmillion's Plantation will make good shelters." Hanks even armed and trained some Black laborers, who repulsed a Confederate attack on a Donaldsonville plantation in the previous summer.[38]

While Union military officials, white southern landholders, and Black laborers certainly viewed occupied Louisiana as a labor problem, for freedpeople it was also a family problem. Black men forced into the ranks of the Union army or dispatched to public works projects, even if they volunteered, complained that they could not see their family members. Routinely isolated from male kin, Black women and children labored in contraband camps and plantations in conditions that largely resembled slavery. In other words, the Black family was not a priority within a reconstituted labor system in the Mississippi Valley. In contrast to the imperatives of national Union policy, which emphasized contract labor systems, traditional household structure, and programs of state legibility, emancipated people in the South approached freedom with their local knowledge—geographic familiarity, relational networks, individual labor capacity, and negotiation skills. While family connections were an important resource of morale and material subsistence to Black workers, military authorities and employers more often viewed those familial connections as obstacles to social order and profit.

As in the cases of Alexander, arrested for carrying away Marcian Haydel's bedstead, and W. L. Minn, who complained of emancipated people selling plantation goods in Terrebonne Parish, Union officials and distressed southern citizens often noted that Black laborers targeted households and household property, but they failed to note that formerly enslaved people were not so much dismantling white households as constructing their own. John Ransdell, who lived next to Thomas Moore's Elmfield Plantation, claimed that all enslaved people near Alexandria who did not join the Union army in the spring of 1863 "remained at home to do *much worse*." He wrote to Moore that emancipated people from numerous plantations mingled together and often drove livestock from the woods to their cabins, and that many of the governor's formerly enslaved people even redistributed plantation furniture among themselves. As many departed southward for more stable Union lines, they carried off mules, horses, wagons, carts, and numerous supplies. Formerly enslaved people even removed pictures of Moore's wife from the wall and carried them away. These incidents demonstrated that, in the Black household war of wartime Louisiana, enslaved and emancipated Black people fought not only to rid themselves of slavery's oppression, but also to give shape to their own households and protect their families.[39]

In one of the most frequent efforts to safeguard their families, Black laborers and recruits verbally demanded accountability and protection from Union occupiers rather than silently suffer under negligence or abuse. In August 1864, Black recruits in the 93rd USCT balked at the mistreatment of their family members on the government-operated Wofford Plantation, overseen by Enos Smith. "Numerous complaints [have] been made to me by men of my Co in regard to the treatment [of] their wives and children," Captain J. M. White reported from Berwick City in St. Mary Parish. Smith had apparently denied rations and medicine to one soldier's wife, named Katrina, because she was ill and could not work. "The woman has been for weeks subsisting on what she could beg from others." Smith committed other sins, the soldiers "excitably informed" White. The overseer cut wages, refused to issue rations to children, and charged exorbitant prices for provision to the extent that many of the laborers were in debt to him and incapable of buying their way to solvency. White requested Stearns investigate, "as a friend of humanity and an officer of U.S. . . . see justice done." Ironically, perhaps in response to other reports circulating about Smith's behavior, Stearns had dispatched Deputy Provost Marshal Lieutenant W. W. Mason the day before receiving White's missive. Mason found the allegations to be only somewhat exaggerated. More alarming, Mason reported, Smith issued to Black workers just three of the twelve essential provisions dictated by Order No. 92. On the contrary, Smith protested, "allowing them to have small pieces of ground to cultivate they can raise such articles . . . will be of as much benefit to them as the articles not issued." Under Smith's racial calculations, freedpeople needed little. But Black Americans demanded more than small pieces of ground.[40]

As with labor contract forms, the martial vision of the occupation state privileged the male laborer-as-soldier, but this emphasis on male recruitment had gendered consequences for isolated female family members and their children. Divided by gender—Black men in the army, Black women in the fields—the Black families of St. Mary Parish experienced a weakened capacity to support one another. Black soldiers in the 93rd USCT turned to the military hierarchy to reach out to their family members who labored on the Wofford Plantation. As they worked their way to inclusive citizenship under arms for the U.S. government, Black men illustrated their ability to potentially turn the gears of occupation to their favor.[41]

Many Union men were surprised to see how dedicated and familial Black people were. From the beginning of Union occupation at Fort Monroe, Butler noted the large number of Black men entering Union lines with "their women and children." In Louisiana, Lieutenant George Hepworth wrote, "I wished that the stolid logicians, who prove by slate and pencil, that the black has no parental regard, had been there. They pressed in crowds about us; and the first question was, 'Young master, now we'se free, can we go up to Massa Smith's plantation, and get our wives?'" Hepworth was also stunned at how willingly formerly enslaved people sought to give away their meager possessions to liberating Union soldiers. Newly freed Black people immediately surrendered the hidden property of their masters as well. Within moments of emancipation, Black Americans were eager to secure kin networks and ready to make material contributions to the war effort.[42]

In response to the situation on the Wofford Plantation, Stearns printed up a specific memorandum to counteract future deleterious behavior toward Black workers on government plantations and outline the responsibility of planters under Union authority. "I have heard rumors that on some of the plantations in this parish," the dispatch read, "the laborers are charged for their rations and medicines during the time they may happen to be sick, also that some are charged for the rations during stormy weather, when they are unable to work upon the crops." Such profiteering violated Union orders. "The planters and not the laborer must take the risk of the weather." Children were to be issued one-half of an adult laborer's ration. Laborers could not be discharged without first notifying the provost marshal. Stearns's memorandum also castigated the practice of selling merchandise to Black laborers at unreasonably high prices. "It is with pain that I learned that many laborers are kept constantly in debt to their employers," which Stearns considered to be "as bad as the Peonage System which prevails in Mexico." Stearns finished his dispatch to St. Mary Parish planters with a moral affirmation of the Union army's mission: "The Negro has been downtrodden and oppressed long enough, and it is time that he should receive some just reward for his labor, and I trust that you will aid me in accomplishing this just result." Other Union officials, including Banks himself, ordered investigations into how white lessees and Union managers conducted plantation labor in 1864. Unfortunately for Black Americans in Louisiana, stalwart allies of racial justice like Stearns were too often outpaced by avaricious Union men like Enos Smith.[43]

In addition to badgering Union commanders for justice, Black people testified in court as another public forum in which to validate their personal character and speak their own narratives. In a court battle between an antagonistic plantation manager, Benjamin Shattuck, and the owner of Bellgrove Plantation in Iberville Parish, Emilie Schiff, Shattuck hurled numerous complaints against Schiff, including that her trusted servant William Talbot delivered Confederate mail and she aided Confederate troops in her area. Talbot and other Black workers who lived on the property took the stand to renounce both claims. "I never told Shattuck I had been employed by her to carry letters to the rebels," Talbot strongly reproached. "I never had any conversation in regard to my taking any letters, and I never carried any letter for Mrs Schiff outside the lines. I never told any body I had carried letters to people out of the lines." Mary Jones and John Willis testified that they saw Confederate soldiers approach Schiff's house, but the soldiers never entered it. They said they saw Schiff also attempt to persuade the troops not to confiscate her mules because she needed them to make the crop. Morning Willis declared she had never seen Schiff and Confederates conversing at all, as did John Marshal. Contrarily, another worker, Sophy Jones, testified that she had indeed witnessed Confederate troops in Schiff's home. "They eat and drank every time they came," she stated. It is difficult to understand the discrepancy in testimony of these workers. Perhaps Mary Jones, John Willis, Morning Willis, and John Marshal hoped to escape further scrutiny in a provost marshal courtroom by evading the issue of Schiff's political allegiance. Perhaps Sophy Jones was not telling the truth but saw an opportunity to exact revenge on her employer by publicly associating Schiff with Confederate raiders. Regardless of their individual reasoning, the testimony of these Black laborers in a Union courtroom represented a public voice previously denied to them. Whatever limitations circumscribed Black people under Union occupation, opportunities such as the Schiff case did provide some space for Black people to advocate for themselves.[44]

When these Black laborers testified in the case, they not only spoke for themselves in novel displays of autonomy; they also disclosed a violent feature of the household war in which they took part. As the Union army pushed further west along the coast of southern Louisiana and further north into central Louisiana, they established more free labor plantations. Confederate assaults on Union-operated plantations were a war on the community of Blackness and the locally produced foundation of the Union supply line. These attacks on plantations, previously the seat of slavery's power, also demonstrated how occupation had shifted the southern household. No longer the bastion of white authority, Confederates aimed to diminish households now geared toward Black autonomy. Employed for a time on Bellgrove Plantation, Mary Jones reported frequent sightings of Confederate soldiers. In particular, she reported, they sought out Shattuck, no doubt because he was a northerner by birth and was a local able-bodied white man who refused to side with the Confederacy. Shattuck fled to the woods still owing Jones payment for her labor. But Confederate appearances produced collateral damage. On two or three brief forays to Emilie Schiff's plantation, guerrillas frightened off several overseers and carried away carriages, mules, tobacco, cotton, supplies, and Black laborers themselves. "They went on and came back and tried to catch the colored people, and then went away," John Willis asserted. Albert Gaillard, a planter neighboring Schiff, stated that Confederate raiders attacked his plantation and many other properties in Iberville Parish. "It would not have been possible for anyone to have protected their property there," he lamented. "Besides the mules they took some of my Negroes. I had 30 hands. Some run away. They also took some off Mrs. Randall's place." Local Confederate raiders appeared several times on the Schiff plantation, threatening the overseers, stealing provisions, and destroying property on each occasion. "The last time they took our bedding and carried away my father," Sophy Jones told the court. The rebels also seized a young child named Stephen who managed to return the following day. Perhaps it was this child that brought Jones tragic news. "I have heard they killed my father." Confederates did not only wage a war against Union occupiers, as Jones understood; they also attacked the stability of the Black family and its economic independence.[45]

As previously stated, Union military officials and, especially, white Louisianans often viewed Black mobility with apprehension, yet local mobility became a key feature of Black community in occupied Louisiana. Black people went on the move to escape slavery or avoid Confederate forces. "As soon as there were any confederates in the neighborhood, the colored people left," William Talbot asserted. After a number of Confederate raids, John Willis and four other Black laborers decided to leave the Bellgrove Plantation. Despite the protests of an overseer, A. H. Arthur, Willis selected a remaining mule and a cart and departed for a nearby Union outpost at Donaldsonville. "Nobody gave us permission to take it, or the mule," Willis testified, but "I wanted to save the mule and myself." Willis and company rode straight to the provost marshal, who immediately rebuked them for traveling without a pass. Arthur followed after the laborers to retrieve the mule. "The PM told him he could not have it nor take us back," Willis testified, but Arthur made a second journey with a pass for the mule and convinced Willis and the others to return. Even though Arthur told the provost marshal that all danger had passed, Confederate raiders were on the property when the travelers returned to Bellgrove. The Rebels took the remaining mules that night. Despite his efforts to return the laborers, Emilie Schiff lacked work and wages for them and ordered Arthur to release Willis and twenty-five other hands.[46]

Mobility was also an essential function of the informal Black economy. Released by Schiff in the face of Confederate raids and financial privation, the

Bellgrove workers had few options for survival open to them. "Mrs. Schiff said they (the hands) must go to their owners & to give them a pass," Mary Jones testified, "Those belonging to the place stayed, those that Shattuck brought went away." Without work, Black laborers became mobile. Even without passes, jobless Black laborers often turned to the nearest Union outpost or roamed to another plantation in search of work. One Union solider came across a Black man riding a bay horse during the Red River Campaign and asked him if he was a cook. The mounted man replied yes and said, "Might as well turn in with you, as anyone. Don't care where I go anyhow." Black people displaced by war searched for labor, including self-employment, for which personal mobility was crucial. By his own admission, John Marshal had no house and sometimes operated a wood yard on the road near Bellgrove Plantation, but "I was away most of the time working for myself on the river." Plantation laborers also liberated provisions to survive. With the frequent absence of overseers, Black laborers carried cotton away from Bellgrove. "I don't know where to or how much," Mary Jones testified; "they pretended to be picking and would not fetch half of it home. . . . They [sic] hands said it was all the pay they would get and took the cotton." John Willis denied that he had carried away any cotton, but confirmed others had, including a woman he knew who lived across the Mississippi River. For emancipated people facing repeated Confederate raids and impecunious landowners, these irregular times mandated irregular payments.[47]

Mobile Black people also provided the Union military with strategic information on the enemy. Escaping enslavement on a plantation near Centerville, Louisiana, a man named Michael James arrived in Union lines in St. Mary Parish in early March 1864. He reported troop strengths of Confederate companies near Franklin and Pattersonville to First Lieutenant S. E. Shepard of the provost marshal. He even relayed rumored information about a large rebel force in Opelousas. Then James asked to enlist. A year later, a man named Thompson escaped from the same area and Shepard again received him and the information he brought. Thompson reported the location of Confederate pickets on the Hudson Plantation and identified the company to which they belonged. A different motive compelled Thompson toward Union-occupied territory. "He came in to see his Family who are [in] our lines[.] He wishes to find them and remain with them," Shepard reported. Thompson's request forwarded up the chain of command, General Cameron received it and ordered that he "be allowed to hunt up and remain with his family." Mobility had multiple uses for liberated Black people, including reunification of their scattered households.[48]

In addition to verbal protest, physical resistance, and mobility, liberated Black Americans in occupied Louisiana pursued various levels of education to augment their transition into postslavery agricultural households. Union bureaucrats employed familiar tactics to craft an education system for formerly enslaved people, especially children, such as knowledge acquired through mapping and registry, property confiscation, and labor management. In late August 1863, Banks established a Board of Education for Freedmen to oversee schools created in the various parishes under its control. Secretary of the Board Edwin Wheelock believed schoolhouses to be more effective and humane than jail houses. "Behind the advancing lines of our forces follows the small pacific army of Teachers and Civilisers, and the school-house takes the place of whipping post and scourge," he informed the readers of the *Liberator* in September 1864. To properly district each parish, the board required certain information from local provost marshal outposts. Officers were ordered to identify the number of plantations in each district of their assigned parish, determine the population of children between ages five and twelve, and create another list of all persons over the age of twelve, divided by gender. Furthermore, they were "to specify in what districts buildings can be had suitable for schools, their dimensions, repairs needed if any, the place where the teachers can be boarded, with price." They were to determine which school districts needed schoolhouses and where the buildings could be built, establish how many acres of property in each district were under cultivation and with what crop, and identify tax records or lists of taxable property in each parish. The primary purpose of this information was to establish districts according to the population of school children, so that schools would have sufficient pupils for tutelage.[49]

Once Union officials established districts in occupied territory, the tedious work of procuring buildings and teachers began. Albert Stearns was at pains to renovate buildings, coordinate carpenters, fix window frames, assign pupils, and receive teachers in Brashear City. He ultimately established seven school districts in St. Mary Parish, where 206 male and 194 female children resided. Just as Union military officials employed loyal Louisianans within the occupation government in order to encourage Unionism, only 32 of 162 teachers at work in Louisiana's freedmen schools were not southern Unionists. Yet the Board of Education often wasted efforts to locate quality teachers, since Banks stipulated only "rudimental education" in order to deny Black pupils access to professional trades. Wheelock also authorized Stearns to determine what portion of school building maintenance was to be borne by the teachers themselves. In St. John the Baptist and St. James Parishes, the Board prompted the provost marshals to repair schools as quickly as possible, as they had "teachers now awaiting employment." The army even briefly considered a tax break to certain Louisiana residents who contributed funds to schools in their district. Instead, Banks targeted disloyal Louisiana planters with the heaviest school taxes in hopes of bending them to his will.[50]

Whereas local Louisiana residents often cooperated with the Union for economic stability, white opposition to Black schools was more robust. Enos Smith, later reprimanded for his cruel actions at the Wofford Plantation, asked for the removal of the local teacher. "By all means let a *Lady* be substituted in her place," he complained. From St. James Parish in March 1865, Board of Education agent Nathan Willey wrote the provost marshal to account for numerous incidents of opposition. "I find that many children are prevented from attending school because the white people for whom [their parents] labor turn them into the street if they send their [children] to the colored schools." On several occasions, Willey inveighed, he saw Black families forced off local properties with all their furniture in the road simply because parents sent their children to school. "The teachers are often greatly annoyed by the people," he continued. As "guardian of the children," he requested more definitive authority from the provost marshal to handle such cases.[51]

Like white southern resistance to emancipation and Black garrison troops, their recalcitrance toward Black education reflected opposition to the potential of a new racial culture that evolved under Union occupation. Because labor contracts and Union regulation, though restrictive to white authority, maintained the bare outline of slavery—white property owner, Black laborer—Louisiana whites generally demonstrated willingness to submit to Union controls over the economy. But an education system for Black Americans, funded by federal dollars, supervised by Unionists, and protected by military occupation, represented an entirely new and threatening institution within Louisiana society. Education offered Black Americans a crucial tool of self-mastery; it announced an equality of persons previously anathema to the South.

Even before Willey's report, Banks tried to articulate an essential connection between land and education. In a letter to the provost marshals of St. James and St. John Parishes on June 27, 1864, he expressed that "it is indispensable to the cultivation of the soil, that schools for colored children shall be maintained. The policy of the Government demands this, and nothing will be allowed to interfere with its success. If persons resist them, they will be removed." Banks understood the systemic interdependence that tethered Black labor to Black education. "Unless laborers are assured that the education of their children will be provided for, they become discontented, and will be allowed to remove to Parishes where such provisions are made." From the beginning of his education system, one of Banks's principal aims was to stymie the flood of Black labor from rural areas to urban centers. He understood that Black Americans would rarely remain where their labor and visions of household autonomy, including education, were disrespected. He also understood that respect for Black education and Black labor meant respect for white teachers as part of the military's project of racial uplift and social equality. "It is for this reason that whenever provision for teachers is required by the Board of Education, it must be accorded with respectful and courteous reception." Statements such as these demonstrated that emancipated Black people could find support in the ranks of Union occupation, but they revealed the prevalence of white hostility as well.[52]

Captain J. M. White, commander of company C in the disgruntled 93rd USCT, sent Provost Marshal Stearns the "sincere thanks and heartfelt gratitude of several members of my company to you for the interest you took and the exertion you have made to secure the welfare of the suffering laborers on Smith's plantation and believe me captain I am highly gratified to find you ready to assist even the neglected contraband." As an officer in a Black regiment, White witnessed firsthand the difficulty Black Americans faced as citizens-in-becoming. "I am now led to believe I have at last found a man who is willing to heed the petitions of the hitherto downtrodden race," he told Stearns. "Please to say to them for me," Stearns replied, "that what I have done for their race has been no more than *my duty*, & not deserving of any special thanks." His only regret was his lack of "some *civil* authority in order to have the power to redress wrongs that I could not otherwise remedy, for this here to for [sic] grievously wronged race of people." Stearns humbly attested his personal moral duty but recognized that a lack of more definitive governmental power in southern civic life restrained his capacity as an individual Union officer to effect change on the ground level. Nevertheless, he thanked White for bringing to his attention "the evils" on the Wofford Plantation.[53]

Not enough men existed in the Union army, however, to dispel such evils in Union-occupied Louisiana. Several hundred families of Black soldiers remained in New Orleans in May 1865, Union commissary officer Colonel E. G. Beckwith reported, "living in miserable holes and crowded rooms in much poverty and want, and are continually applying for aid at the free market." Most were from rural areas and suffered greatly from smallpox. Lieutenant Colonel J. S. Crosby responded that the war was over and soldiers' families were not entitled to further support. "Some provision for these people is absolutely necessary to their welfare, and ought to be made independent of this charity, which has been so much abused, and which is of such enormous proportion." As many had endured during the war, Union military policy continued to impair Black families and households after the cessation of hostilities.[54]

As a fledging, haphazard labor bureaucracy flowered under the auspices of Union authority, the military produced an altered but not alternative social environment for Black laborers. Black Americans—as refugees, soldiers, laborers, family members, students, and emerging citizens—participated in manifold ways, eagerly aligning with Union command while upbraiding the army for shortcomings. In many instances, Union governmental policy attenuated the power of white planters and enhanced the personal autonomy of formerly enslaved Black Americans. However, Union support for Black people in occupied Louisiana was qualified. Military necessity came first. Black laborers faced imposing demands from Union officials, who used Black people to fill recruitment quotas and construct public works. Union ranks held men with conflicting personal feelings and policy initiatives concerning Black people, and the army faced an equally diverse public—a combustible environment that oftentimes compromised the potential of occupation to reshape southern society.

Paradoxically, while the Union army dismantled slavery and experimented with various policies of Black labor, mobility, and education, the army also often reinforced the material foundations of white citizens rather than those of formerly enslaved people. Despite intermittent moments of internal opposition, especially regarding Black recruits or Black schools, the army catered to whites as citizen-beneficiaries of Union protection. While loyalty management tactics such as restriction of contraband trade or oath requirements circum-scribed white participation in society, Union occupation was primarily a con-servative action that did not permanently disrupt the material foundations of white Americans or their social power over Black Americans.

Occupation recalibrated but did not reconstitute democracy. Union troops freed enslaved people, but imposed specific boundaries on their labor, mobil-ity, and autonomy within the restabilized world of occupation. They protected white property as much as they confiscated it for military purposes and en-acted no comprehensive redistribution of land and resources directly to Black people. On the radical pages of remade national law like the Emancipation Proclamation or the Thirteenth Amendment, the American democratic family was reforged to include the Black American. However, in the social landscape of occupied territory itself, the administrating hand of the army guided as well as restrained formerly enslaved people. Consequently, at liberty's gate these new Americans-in-becoming experienced freedom mingled with exclusion on what the unforgiving overseer Enos Smith called "small pieces of ground." Attenuated access to the material foundation of American democracy like-wise compromised the potential of Union occupation to reorder society. The careful, uneven dismantling of slavery was beginning and end to a revolution in southern society, not only because southerners remained culturally unre-constructed, but also because occupation as a system of government practice reshaped the boundaries of American citizenship on the basis of loyalty, not necessarily racial equality. After the zenith of armed military occupation during the Civil War, the federal government neglected sizable interventions into ra-cial democracy for a century. Yet within the parameters of Union-occupied Louisiana, formerly enslaved laborers contended for a better physical world that they could make with their own hands.[55]

6

Partial though Disputed

DEMOCRACY, POWER & OCCUPATION IN CONFEDERATE LOUISIANA

William T. Palfrey, a planter from a wealthy family in St. Mary Parish, was distraught in early 1864 as he issued a report of conditions in his region to Nathaniel Banks. From late 1862 until fall 1863, Confederate and Union forces had captured and recaptured the parish, the effect of which "has been to lay waste nearly the whole country." Palfrey wrote that for more than fifty miles across his parish, "there is not a plantation that is in a condition to make a crop." He made a long list of ruination. "There is no fencing standing of any consequence, and most of the buildings are dilapidated or gone. Many have been pulled down to make shanties, others to furnish fuel. There is no cane left for seed. The forage has been pressed for the armies, and the mules & horses taken for the same purpose. The engines & machinery in many sugar houses have been destroyed, the negroes have some been forced into the army as conscripts, others [taken] from their former owners, or are of their own accord wandering without employment or means of support through the country." More egregiously for a man of means like Palfrey, "Families or heads of families have been compelled to fly from their homes, and many who have been accustomed to the enjoyment of affluence or at least a sufficient competency, are reduced to want & privation." The purpose of Palfrey's report was to alert Banks to the difficulties involved in building an efficient labor system in southern Louisiana. But his report also signaled the cost of Confederate war. Half of his parish, which Palfrey called the "garden spot of Louisiana," was "in the partial though disputed possession of the Confederates." Much of the damage he described occurred not just in battle but as a direct result of Confederate military forces and the policies of the Confederate state government. As Palfrey and many Louisianans experienced, the Confederate state—despite its efforts to protect the southern household—prioritized military operations to the detriment of personal rights, household property, and social order. Moreover the state government often exercised tactics of social control similar to the Union's program of military occupation.[1]

As Union armies severed the geography of the South, they generated two prominent changes in Confederate statecraft. First, in response to territorial losses, internal pressures, and military threats on Richmond, the Confederate government developed a more centralized state, more substantial than even its northern counterpart. The southern government imposed higher taxes, implemented the war's first draft, introduced social welfare initiatives, and instituted a host of police programs, including a pass system for travel—all instances in which individual rights were subordinated to national survival. Second, as a result of these government interferences, the geographically and politically fractionalized South pursued state and local alternatives to Richmond and Union troops. Southerners intent on survival more than national allegiance demonstrated flexible loyalties in their local responses to government power. This incidental decentralization revealed the limitations of Confederate state-making. No governmental platform could fully triumph without a secure material base.[2]

When the Union military seized New Orleans, Confederates in Louisiana scrambled to stabilize their territory. After the fall of Baton Rouge, Governor Moore and the government moved the capital to Opelousas, then again to Shreveport. Rebel troops under former presidential candidate John C. Breckinridge attacked Baton Rouge in August but failed to retake the city. Throughout 1862 and into 1863, Confederates mounted vigorous defenses of and offensives into the Lafourche and Teche regions west of New Orleans, as Palfrey could lamentably attest. After the fall of Vicksburg and Port Hudson in July 1863, Confederate soldiers and civilians in the Trans-Mississippi West were cut off from the Confederate mainland. In response to territorial loss and increasing material privation, Confederate Louisiana established a paradoxical social order—one both highly militarized and coercive yet also committed to social welfare initiatives—that frequently called on themes of household protection even as it pared down the material and patriarchal foundations of the southern slaveholding household.[3]

The Confederate state government of Louisiana, headed initially by Thomas Moore, then by the military/political figure Henry Watkins Allen, interacted closely with and often in subordination to Generals E. Kirby Smith and Richard Taylor, who coordinated Confederate resistance in the Trans-Mississippi region with the governors of Texas, Louisiana, and Arkansas. Allen and Smith created a series of bureaucratic endeavors to manage the Confederate war in Louisiana. Although Taylor preferred audacious offensive strategies, Smith spread Confederate forces out and concentrated them only to oppose Union invasions, most notably the Red River Campaign in the spring of 1864. He also utilized construction projects and natural landscape obstacles to blunt Union movements. With a more organized and localized war front, a general lack of Union reinforcements to the Trans-Mississippi, and the overall incompetence of Butler and Banks as field commanders, Confederate forces in Louisiana managed to dominate large portions of the state until the end of the war. Mostly isolated after summer 1863, Confederate Louisiana was a strange, crowded place where state authorities and local residents wrestled and relied on one another as they negotiated controversial topics like allegiance, desertion, confiscation, slavery, finances, and defense.[4]

While political and military figures in Louisiana struggled to manage a war society, Louisiana men and women of varying class backgrounds experienced dramatic upheaval. Their experience with wartime government and military occupation differed significantly from that of their eastern counterparts, who enjoyed more social cohesion and the protection of more competent Confederate armies. Dysfunction typified the wartime lives of Louisianans. Wealthy planters from the lush plantation country along the waterways of southern Louisiana streamed northward after Union ships appeared on the coast. Evacuating with as much material and enslaved property as they could, these elites sought relatively safe ground in northern Louisiana or eastern Texas.[5] They chafed under coercive measures from the Louisiana state government that conscripted enslaved labor for defense projects. Other planters did not flee but made alliances with the enemy, much to the consternation of state leaders like Moore. Poorer southerners were as likely to reject Confederate authority as Union oversight. Acadians in the Teche region seemed to fight a guerrilla war as much for their own communities as for or against a national government. Apart from persistent internal division within the Confederate high command and the serious battlefield blunders that southerners made, civilian discontent undermined the stability of the Confederate republic in the western theater. The war debilitated the social consensus needed to cinch together the disparate classes of the South, and Confederate Louisiana, despite protracted social aid programs, exemplified that disintegration.[6]

Although many Louisianans derogated national and state governments, most still weaponized their cultural values of race and self-mastery, especially in the form of guerrilla resistance, which increased in the final years of the war in Louisiana. Where guerrilla bands organized to protect their households, attack liberated plantation workers, or even raid surrounding communities without much regard to loyalty, they signaled a failure of state sovereignty, the growing incapacity of Confederate armies to safeguard southern territory. But guerrilla activity also represented the rebellious voice of the people, or at least male patriarchs, in continued revolt against the cultural upheaval of the war. Male guerrilla warriors reasserted their self-mastery and violently targeted Black Americans and their white allies, foreshadowing the violence of Reconstruction. Guerrilla warfare demonstrated how a democracy at war could foster armed factions in support of national and local political agendas, not just, as some scholars suggest, a destructive free-for-all.[7]

Even before the U.S. flag flew over New Orleans, more than a few southerners expressed frustration with the national government or chafed under Confederate control. New Orleans business owner William J. Dewey found his trade destroyed by the "disastrous change" since secession. The Confederacy, he charged, was "a slavery despotism" that suppressed free speech. After the fall of New Orleans, Confederates in the state felt abandoned by their national government because it had drained the state of men and materiel, Governor Moore explained to Richmond. He warned that "a dormant disloyalty has awakened." In the months immediately following Union invasion, Confederate Louisiana was highly disorganized. Most Louisiana volunteers were stationed far from home. The Union army captured much of the state's military supplies. Confederates lost access to vital waterways and railroads in the south and the roads north and west were choked with displaced Louisianans. Enslaved people abandoned plantation properties in droves or refused to yield to southern masters any longer.[8]

Just as Union commanders like Butler emphasized loyalty to the United States as the primary qualification for citizenship and martial protection, Confederate leaders in Louisiana issued their own injunctions of allegiance to south-erners. "The occupation by the enemy of a portion of the territory of our State imposes upon us new and unaccustomed responsibilities," Moore announced from Opelousas in mid-June 1862. First was economic abstinence. As the "Commercial Depot of the State . . . freighted with the every-day transactions of all classes of our citizens," occupied New Orleans could no longer serve its cultural and economic mission of "binding our urban and rural population together by the strong bands of mutual dependence and reciprocal benefit." Moore explicitly forbade trade with the enemy. "There cannot be a war for arms and a peace for trade between two people at the same time," he directed. "To each loyal Citizen of Louisiana and of the Confederacy, every citizen of the country hostile to us is an enemy. We cannot barter our products for theirs." Even communication with fellow southerners in occupied territory was impru-dent, Moore stated, because it might damage the Confederate cause or bring harm to those citizens under occupation. "Absolutely non-intercourse, the en-tire suspension of communication by visit or for trade, is the only safe rule for our guidance." Faced with enemy occupation, Confederates on both sides of the Union lines had to deprive the occupiers of material goods.[9]

As part of these trade restrictions, Moore commanded that Louisianans only transact with Confederate money. Confederate bills "constitute a cur-rency that measures the value of all our property, and that custom and loyalty recognize them as a legal tender. They are received and paid as such by all pa-triots." Refusal to buy and sell using Confederate money would paralyze the government, he warned, but he also enlisted the imagery of devastated land and aggrieved dependents to drive his argument home. "The refusal to take Confederate money does a direct injury to our sacred cause, fans the latent spark of treason, and gives indirect aid and comfort to the ruthless enemy who invades our soil, ravages our coasts, insults our mothers, wives, and daughters, and tyrannizes over our conquered cities." For those who ignored his directive, "such refusal affords a presumption of disloyalty."[10]

Second, Moore commanded strict allegiance to the Confederate cause and rejection of all oaths of loyalty that Union authorities might proffer. Every oc-cupied southerner must watch for opportunities by which the Union might "trammel him in the rendition of those services which his country demands." Knowing fully the expectation of the enemy command for loyalty oaths, Moore proclaimed that "whoever now . . . voluntarily place[s] himself in the power of the enemy by entering their lines, throws a shade upon his loyalty to his Government." Signing an oath "is treachery to our cause." Occupied citizens were not prisoners of war, the governor reasoned. They had no duty to abide by the rules of military parole. "The passport," he then declared, "shall not be a shelter from duty." Some residents of southern Louisiana apparently traveled into New Orleans out of curiosity, obtained passes from the Union provost marshal, departed Union lines again, then used the parole section of the pass to distance themselves from supporting the Confederacy. A man who did so "cannot claim that he holds himself bound by the stipulation not to give aid and support to this Government, and thus avoid military duty . . . which is treason unmasked." Moore did not equivocate about the responsibilities of Louisiana citizens and the powers of the state Confederate government. "The Confederacy and the State recognize but two classes—its friends and its foes," he articulated. "All considerations of blood and friendship must give way, all apprehensions for the safety of property must be disregarded. Obedience to the laws and acquiescence to the policy of the Government will be the cheerful homage that every true man will make. Those who are not true must be deprived of the power to harm." From Moore's perspective, governmental authority was more important than personal liberty, property, or strategies of household survival. Legislative acts passed in June 1863 further reinforced the primacy of Confederate loyalty by requiring that all elected officials take an oath of allegiance to the Confederacy, as well as all voters who were suspected of disloyalty.[11]

The year following Moore's demanding decree, the fiery secessionist minister Benjamin Palmer also inveighed against those who took a Union oath or traded with the enemy. Confederates who committed these acts, even under occupation, fell into two categories, he argued. The first were those "never true to our cause" or "destitute of all principle." Others, however, were still loyal in their hearts but, facing coercion, took the oath "as one of the necessities of war." But for these still-loyal pragmatists, Palmer had little patience. Oaths were a sacred instrument that none should make light of, he insisted. Even if some Confederates did not hold any fealty to the Union when they took the oath in order to obtain protection and rations, their action still produced "foul calumny" against those who died honorably for the Confederacy. "The inability of the Confederacy for the time being to protect them, is viewed as dissolving the bond between them and it," Palmer criticized, "and, like traders in the market, they bargain with another party, purchasing protection with loyalty."

Palmer demanded that household heads, however few truly loyal Confederate patriarchs might have remained in Union-occupied Louisiana, "say to the Federal authorities we have recovered our manhood and withdraw our allegiance unjustly and cruelly extorted at our hands." Only then could they reclaim their "dishonored name." Only by renouncing their apostasy could household heads fulfill their obligations to God, country, home, and family. In summary, true patriotism was no mere contract, and loyal Confederates should stop taking the oath of allegiance in Union-held areas.[12]

Nationally, Confederates looked to occupied Louisiana as a testament to Confederate resolve. On January 13, 1863, the Confederate House of Representatives issued two joint resolutions to commend the Confederate population under occupation in Louisiana. Congress celebrated "the course pursued by the true men and women of the Confederacy, who, falling within the lines of the enemy, have resisted all appeals to their pecuniary interest and refused . . . to perjure themselves or to foreswear their own government by taking an oath of allegiance . . . it regards with peculiar satisfaction the conduct of those citizens of Louisiana, who, by refusing the oath and openly registering themselves enemies to the United States in the immediate presence and in defiance of Butler's military authorities, have borne most noble testimony to the martyr-like courage and patriotic spirit and Christian faith of our people." Their resistance also inspired a grateful nation. "Such conduct has secured them the present respect and sympathy of all good people, it will be esteemed, in the future, a most honorable claim upon the gratitude of their country, and the highest evidence of their devotion to truth and principle."[13]

David French Boyd, son of a wealthy Virginia lawyer and legislator and himself a faculty member of Louisiana State Seminary, never doubted Louisianans' loyalty, he informed his friend Union general William Sherman. Even though he was a prisoner-of-war in April 1864, Boyd estimated nine-tenths of the southern people "are more determined today than ever before; and they will fight to the last." This was surely an exaggeration, but his own resolve was clear. "When General Lee has taken the *Oath of Allegiance to Mr. Lincoln* then I will consider the propriety of my doing so" and "so will it be with a large majority of those who are now struggling for their existence, not merely national, but personal and individual." To quit the war at that moment, he alleged—to relinquish "our birth-right"—would be "dishonor and disgrace."[14]

To secure loyalty and defend the birthright of Louisiana, Confederate leaders adopted increasingly bureaucratic strategies. Aside from Governor Henry Allen, perhaps no other Confederate figure in Louisiana or the whole of the Trans-Mississippi wielded as much power as Kirby Smith. Smith was a West Point graduate and Mexican War veteran who had served under Zachary Taylor as well as Winfield Scott. After winning a notable victory at the Battle of Richmond during Bragg's failed 1862 invasion of Kentucky, Smith was promoted to the rank of lieutenant general and given command of the Trans-Mississippi Department in early 1863. Whereas the Confederacy never quite became a totalitarian state, despite stern measures from Davis and others, "Kirby Smithdom" came closest to unquestioned autocracy. Historian Paul Escott refers to Smith as "an American proconsul on American soil" who "wielded a kind of imperial power . . . as the agent of the state." In northwestern Louisiana and eastern Texas, Smith and other Confederate leaders set about creating war industries: small arms, powder, cannon, textiles, and other articles. With little contact with the rest of the Confederacy, Smith needed his own source of supplies, currency, and public authority. He established a subtreasury and a post office under his own command and sold interest-paying bonds to fund his department. He established sixteen executive and military departments and expended much effort in impressing cotton from planters before they could sell it to private buyers for specie.[15]

In mid-August 1863, Smith called for a conference of all civil and military leaders in the Trans-Mississippi Department to meet in Marshall, Texas, which was the second of such meetings. "We hope to unite all our patriotic citizens in a vigorous support of the Confederate and State authorities in the defense of our families and homes," the Confederate governors of Louisiana, Texas, Arkansas, and Missouri collectively announced. Though Smith was "clothed with more than usual powers," the governors assured southerners that he was guided by "a profound respect for law and the constitutional rights of the citizen" and he would exercise his power "within the bounds of the Constitution and the law . . . for the common good." That common good might entail inconvenience for some people, but the leaders called on patriotism and common sense "to produce a cheerful endurance of the hardships to be expected in a war for our very existence as a nation." To secure that national existence, Confederate civil-military leaders once more enlisted themes of household—women were to "tend the loom and even follow the plow" and boys too young for military service should "guard the homes their fathers are defending on the frontier." If every southerner in the Trans-Mississippi District remembered their courage, intelligence, and energy, the announcement proclaimed, soon they would be reunited with their countrymen and women to the east.[16]

A few months after the second Marshall conference, Confederate Louisiana elected a new governor, Henry Allen, who would embody perhaps more than any other Confederate figure the careful if disproportionate balance between powerful state authority and the common people. Allen was an impressive figure. He practiced law in Mississippi, fought in the Texas Revolution, traveled and published widely, and, by all accounts, wielded excellent rapport with common people and wealthy planters alike. Still recovering from severe leg wounds sustained at the Battle of Baton Rouge, Allen embarked on a five-week tour of northern Louisiana and the Red River Valley just after his November 1863 election. He was inaugurated on January 26, 1864, while standing on crutches. In his first message to the legislature, Allen called for a mounted State Guard of five hundred men to arrest vandals who committed atrocities and plundered on the northern border of the state "where neither military or civil law" ruled. He also called for a stronger militia law and declared the militia would never be sent out of the state. In a conspicuous display of the reciprocal nature between state and people, Allen recommended that cotton cards be extended free of charge to every Louisiana woman above the age of 18.[17]

As leader of Confederate Louisiana, Allen made clear that household concerns and family safety were of paramount importance to his government. While he promised cooperation with and loyalty to President Davis, Allen also declared that "my people must be protected in all their constitutional and legal rights." To this end, in the summer of 1864 he encouraged Louisiana citizens to immediately appeal to the court system when their rights or property were "violated under pretence [sic] of military authority." Around the same time, he ordered commissioners to begin collecting testimony from southern citizens "concerning the conduct of the enemy during their brief and inglorious occupancy of a part of West Louisiana." Perhaps Allen was inspired by his previous literary publications or maybe he was motivated by the governors' call from the second Marshall conference for an "all-pervading patriotic public opinion." Either way, the result, published in April 1865 as the *Official Report Relative to the Conduct of Federal Troops in Western Louisiana,* was perhaps the most successful propaganda of the Confederate war. Much like General Butler, Governor Allen apparently extended relief to families regardless of their political allegiance and by the end of the war the governor's contingent fund had paid out over $11,000 to destitute families and wounded soldiers.[18]

To recruit home defense forces, supply their war effort, stabilize social order, and confront Union forces, Confederate leaders in Louisiana like Moore, Smith, Taylor, and Allen escalated bureaucratic programs and coercive techniques. Recruitment remained of central importance throughout the war because Confederate Louisiana needed military units for defense, confiscation, and enforcement of laws. "The Confederate Government had no soldiers, no arms and munitions, and no money, within the limits of the district," Richard Taylor lamented when he arrived in Louisiana in August 1862. He may have exaggerated somewhat, but not much. Measures to increase the ranks included severe punishments for deserters and those who harbored them. On January 3, 1863, Governor Moore approved the "Act to Raise an Army for the defense of the State of Louisiana"—no more than 20,000 men for twelve months, with a $50 bounty paid at enlistment and eighty acres distributed at the war's end. On the same day the legislature passed a new militia act, setting age limits of service between seventeen and fifty, exempting railroad engineers, track masters, professors, students, and one justice of the peace per parish. Some Louisianans condemned the act as too sweeping and its punishments too severe, especially as the Confederate conscription act then in practice required only those up to age thirty-five join the armed forces. Others considered drastic action necessary. "To protect them against lawless violence, as well as the treasonable schemes of disaffected persons, it becomes the duty of all good citizens to co-operate with the Martial as well as the Civil Authorities," one newspaper declared.[19]

In May 1863, the legislature repealed the militia act and passed a new one. Any person failing to respond to the call of the militia would be court-martialed and fined between $50 and $5,000 or face a jail term of ten to ninety days. Exemptions now included mayors and treasurers, civilians in occupied regions, newspaper editors, every head of a family consisting of ten white persons, overseers on plantations where no men resided, presidents of incorporated railroad companies and employees needed to run trains, millers, and tanners with over five hundred hides.[20] After Allen's inaugural address, the legislature authorized his State Guard, paid them the same as Confederate regulars, and referred to them as "conservators of the peace." Yet another militia act meted out the death penalty to anyone who deserted or encouraged desertion. On April 18, 1864, Allen surrendered power over the militia when the Confederate Congress stipulated that all state militias were now under national control. He also declared to his "citizen soldiers" that "every man who has failed to comply with his order shall be arrested, and brought into camp." These state efforts to register and recruit were no small actions. Henry Lawrence, a wealthy resident of Brashear City, wrote, "Our Military demands that all persons under 55 over 45 shall register[.] I presume it is to know the name and whereabouts of every man in the state. The office is crowded by Hundreds and no one can get in handy to be registered." In addition to the troubles of recruiting soldiers and keeping them in the ranks, Confederate authorities struggled to obtain supplies for these units from the local environment. When many southerners refused to sell property and supplies for Confederate bills, Confederate officials oftentimes simply confiscated local property. As the crisis of war deepened, both in terms of material privation and contested law and order, Louisiana witnessed escalating dissent that coincided with increasingly robust Confederate statist action.[21]

The more desperate that the Confederate state government became to place uniformed men in the field, the more that local Louisiana residents resented government interference. The duty of the state government was to protect and defend, many believed, not enact invasive measures on the people. A Rapides Parish petition to Governor Moore in December 1862 complained that, because of conscription, few men remained to "assist the sick, the afflicted and the poor families in our midst." From Monroe, Sarah Wadley lamented, "This country on this side the Mississippi is almost in a state of anarchy." In September 1863, a military friend of the family informed them that Confederate guards had recently stationed themselves outside of a church in Shreveport and arrested every man that exited. "What an outrage to humanity!" Wadley exclaimed. "Such we must think, though perpetrated in our own country. They were in search of conscripts." Her brother Willie hoped to join Robert E. Lee's army, but his family feared that conscription officers from Shreveport would apprehend Willie before he could reach Virginia. Union soldier Danville Chadbourne saw only boys and no men in Brashear City, he wrote in a letter home. Confederate conscription was so severe that the government would take any man, "no matter how old a man is if he has good front teeth so he can tear of the end of the catridge, so sais [sic] one of their parolled soldiers."[22]

Wadley's indignation reflected a larger dissatisfaction with government conscription, forcing Confederate leaders in Louisiana to spend a great deal of time recruiting, conscripting, and rounding up deserters. Kirby Smith created a Conscript Bureau in 1863. He also prohibited substitutions in the Trans-Mississippi region in July of that year, several months before the Confederate Congress likewise outlawed the practice of substitution. In February 1864, the legislature passed "An Act to Punish Persons for Harbouring Deserters" that leveled a fine of up to $1,000 and a year in jail to any convicted of harboring or aiding a deserter. Another measure adopted that month forbid speaking, printing, or writing any words to subvert the Confederate government, stipulated punishment for any person who obstructed enlistment, and prohibited aid to the Union. Two additional acts from the state legislature on February 6 empowered the governor to resist extralegal impressment of Louisiana property by the Confederate government in Richmond and also imposed heavy fines on officers or persons responsible for such impressment.[23]

Thousands of desertions indicated that common support for the Confederate state government was hardly uniform. Newspaper notices published in the Shreveport *Semi-Weekly News* in June 1862 offered $30 for apprehended deserters. On August 29, 1863, Major Louden Butler published a similar reward for thirty-three deserters from the 19th Louisiana Volunteers in the *Caddo Gazette*. Winn, Jackson, Union, and adjoining northern parishes became rife with deserters, draft dodgers, and jayhawkers. Smith detailed Richard Taylor with clearing out these troublesome parishes in late 1863. Taylor and Governor Allen estimated some eight thousand deserters and draft evaders in the southern parts of Louisiana. Taylor urged Confederate commanders and local police officials in Mississippi to seek out and return numerous Louisiana deserters who sought refuge in neighboring states. As the war continued, many locals and deserters joined bushwhacker bands—men seemingly opposed to everyone but themselves. Compelled from one side by the Confederate state of Louisiana and on the other by invading Union forces, bushwhacker bands signaled the triumph of personal and local community allegiances over national ideologies. Louisianans also spurned the bloated Confederate military bureaucracy within the state and despised corrupt officials who confiscated and sold cotton or other goods for personal gain, which perhaps gave them more incentive to abandon the ranks.[24]

Throughout his command of the Trans-Mississippi District, Smith was concerned with collecting cotton, which only increased in value as it grew scarcer, especially in the once cotton-rich region he commanded, before it disappeared to the enemy through capture or trade. Despite having no authority to impress cotton from Confederate citizens for sale or trade, Smith acted on what he believed was military necessity. Confederate Secretary of the Treasury C. C. Memminger considered confiscation of cotton to be unlawful for anything other than immediate military needs. Funding the war effort through cotton impressment did not constitute a pressing military exigency, Memminger argued. Most other Confederate officials sided with Smith, as the Confederate government could not easily supply the Trans-Mississippi Department. Subsequently, Smith established his own Cotton Bureau in August 1863 following the second Marshall conference. As state governors and local officials bickered with Smith over conscription and confiscation policies in the Trans-Mississippi, they illustrated one of the most potent disconnects between military and civil authorities in the war.[25]

Long before the contentions over recruitment and military control in Confederate Louisiana, the civil-military leaders of the state made it clear that private property and market concerns were secondary to depriving Union forces of potential material gains. When the Union navy arrived in April 1862, numerous southern residents and Union troops reported cotton ablaze on the levees of the Mississippi River. Ironically, Confederates destroyed the property they had seceded from the Union to protect. This was a common tactic in warfare prior to and long after the Civil War but for Louisiana Confederates, especially wealthy planters who occupied the fertile riverside soil of the Mississippi, protecting their cotton product became a preeminent mission during the war. When Confederate military figures burned cotton, such an action represented not just a military tactic to prevent the Yankee enemy from acquiring valuable goods, but also literally indicated a failure of the Confederate state to protect southern people and property.[26]

By early 1863 it was Confederate state policy to destroy any goods, especially cotton, that might fall into Union hands. Between the secession of the state and the fall of New Orleans, Nelson McStea, a British subject and cotton factor, left a dizzyingly trail of receipts for cotton purchases throughout southern Louisiana. He worked closely with local farmers and planters to acquire cotton, then left it on the premises until he could return. When he could, he secured various permissions from the Confederate state government to ship the cotton. Yet prosperous factors like McStea and plantation owners like John Burnside and John M. Andrews were stunned at how readily the Confederate military burned their product to prevent it from falling to Union forces. On the first day of May 1863, a Confederate colonel arrived on Houmas Plantation with orders from General Mansfield Lovell to burn the some two thousand bales of cotton on site. The manager, Hopkins Seale, persuaded the officer to leave by promising to move the cotton further upriver. Three days later, however, another Confederate official arrived with a battalion of soldiers and burned 288 bales of cotton. A week after that, Capt. E. A. Scott appeared with an escort of men and burned 1,839 bales of cotton belonging to McStea, two sheds of lumber valued at $1,368, and hundreds of cotton bales belonging to others. When Seale protested and offered to produce evidence that McStea and Burnside (owner of Houmas Plantation) were British citizens, Scott "said he did not care to see, that he was himself well aware of the fact, but this he did not care a Damn and that he would carry out his orders no matter what occurred." To the dismay of men like McStea, unrepentant state military officials continued such destructive actions throughout the war.[27]

Historians can track state action and the woes of property owners by using the receipts that military authorities like Captain Scott left in the wake of their destructive measures. Outraged citizens, especially wealthy businessmen, also produced depositions outlining their losses. "I have this day burned (594) bales of cotton on S. M. Davis Pitts field plantation under orders from Col. J. T. Harrison to burn all cotton [in] Concordia Parish" read the receipt of Captain John J. Peek on July 12, 1863. The following day Peek burned 240 bales on the plantation of W. B. Page. These bales were notable because not only did they belong to McStea, but they were also draped with the British flag for protection. Later that year, Confederate troops burned more of McStea's cotton near Yazoo City, Mississippi. A business associate named George McFarland who witnessed the event wrote that these troops "were by no means discreet or discriminating in selecting what was likely to fall into the hands of the enemy, they burned indiscriminately all they could find." Several days later, McFarland traveled to another nearby plantation and placed the British flag over thirty-four bales of cotton that McStea had purchased. He left a letter with the plantation owner "to show the *paper* & the *flag* to either Confederate or Federal authority who might attempt to burn the cotton and if the 'flag' failed to protect it to take a receipt from the party who might burn it." The historical record does not reveal what became of these bales but McFarland's actions are illustrative of responses that individuals made to Union and Confederate seizure policies.

For many people in the Department of the Gulf, both Union and Confederate regimes were institutions of occupation and coercion.[28]

The Palfrey family experienced widespread destruction on their St. Mary Parish property. "The brigade returned to their campsite on my place & resumed their usual habit of depredation," wrote John Palfrey in November 1862. Soon after he found his house occupied by none other than Richard Taylor and staff for several days. The following month, the brigade under Confederate general Alfred Mouton was still on his plantation, "destroying my property; robbing and plundering me of my negro cabins." Palfrey even moved his enslaved people to his son's plantation further from the fighting. On December 19, Confederate forces finally pulled out of the area. "They have left my plantation, devastation & desolation behind them. No discipline among them & no regard to private property." Similarly, in Monroe the following spring, Sarah Wadley reported that "one or two companies of our men were going about burning the cotton a week or two ago, but the citizens were at that time very much opposed to it and a good deal was hidden away." Louisiana residents like Palfrey and Wadley opposed the material cost of Confederate war because it wrecked the material security of their households.[29]

To fund its defense of the state and provide relief to citizens through redistribution of food and wealth, the Confederate state made more strenuous demands on property holders and increased extraction of natural resources. Daniel Dudley Avery, patriarch of the Avery-Marsh family in St. Mary Parish, paid $301.87 in parish and state taxes in 1861. The following year, he paid $90 in Confederate war taxes in addition to $270.88 in parish taxes, a moderate but not negligible increase even after state taxes were suspended for the war's duration. Appointed superintendent of St. Mary Parish salt mines in September of 1862, Avery was tasked with producing as much salt for the war effort as possible. Even before his official appointment, Avery was calling on St. Mary residents for powder to fuel his own mining operations. One local woman regretfully informed him she had no powder to spare. "I am so very scarce of the article & have such constant calls for it from every part of the state that I fear it will be impossible for me to accommodate you." Over time, such demands from the Confederate state and its emissaries would only grow and those demands drained resources from the homes and properties of beleaguered Louisiana citizens.[30]

In an effort to reduce tensions between state and people, the state legislature suspended tax payments in 1862 and 1863. Moore wanted to end the suspension in 1864, as the lack of funding in the government had reached drastic proportions, but Henry Allen extended the moratorium on taxes—excluding state licenses on trades, occupations, and professions—until 1865. Property owned by soldiers and sailors was protected from seizure or taxation, but the legislature also enforced the arrest and imprisonment of anyone who refused to accept state-issued bonds and Confederate currency. Treasury notes were the only means of revenue for the state in 1863. These financial efforts to allevi-ate pressure on common Louisiana households were one of the most effective means of preserving loyalty among the people. As Kirby Smith complained to the War Department in the final year of the war, Confederate tax collectors "spread discontent and dissatisfaction widely among our producers at home."[31]

Throughout his tenure as governor, Allen continued to make financial is-sues central to governance. In his inaugural speech in 1864, he claimed treasury notes were not all that devalued, and he blamed scarcity, not inflation, for the high prices afflicting the state. He publicly encouraged greater production of goods to alleviate the state's scarcity problems. He argued that state money should be called in and Confederate currency alone dominate the market, even suggesting state bonds should be traded for state notes to incentivize people to surrender them. Sale of state bonds opened on February 23, 1864, but in a year's time the state had collected less than $600,000. Disappointed with bond sales, Allen hit upon an extremely successful idea—a state store to sell price-controlled goods and accept state treasury notes, which withdrew notes from circulation and improved both the financial situation of the state market and the physical conditions of the people. "The goods had been imported from Mexico and paid for in cotton," he assured the legislature. The store was an immense success, producing nearly $400,000 in profit in 1864 and over $1.5 million in 1865.[32]

Meanwhile, Confederates authorities endeavored to continue the war effort with every available means. In January 1865, Allen urged the Louisiana legisla-ture to appoint and pay syndics to operate abandoned plantations throughout the state. In the northwestern part of the state, salt mines began producing massive amounts to supply the Confederate armies in the area and the needs of the civilian population. In accordance with Allen's appropriation of $700,000 to distribute at least two cotton or wool cards to Louisiana women, by January 1865, Allen's agents had distributed fifteen thousand pairs of cotton cards to soldier's families (at a cost of $10 per pair). In June 1864, he oversaw the construction of machinery to manufacture cotton cards at Minden. To produce more medicine in the state, the governor called for a geological survey to uncover natural resources in Louisiana. Allen also established a state laboratory in February 1864, with Dr. Bartholomew Egan as superintendent, to produce medicine for the state. Egan purchased the Mt. Lebanon Female College and eighty-four acres of land for the state. He distributed a circular to Louisiana residents urging them to plant medical plants such as corn for alcohol and turpentine leaves and castor beans for oil.[33]

The state government took extensive measures to reduce alcohol production and provide financial and material relief to Southern families. On June 20, 1863, the state legislature forbade the production, sale, or trade of alcohol of any kind. Allen celebrated this measure, blaming alcohol for crime and demoralization. Informants were entitled to half of the $5,000-$15,000 fine given to those who produced alcohol, which accompanied a jail term of three months. Restricting the creation of alcohol in the state was primarily a material, not a moral measure, for it preserved vital breads, grains, corn, and sugar. As conscription laws gobbled up more men throughout the war, private and parish level donations to provide for families dissipated and the state was forced to assume more responsibility. On January 3, 1863, the state legislature appropriated $5 million for family aid—$5 a month for each child under twelve and $10 for wives. Before long, the state began distributing food as well as money. Disabled veterans received $11 a month from the state. The legislature also established funds for hospitals.[34]

Ultimately, the general welfare state within Confederate Louisiana delivered material goods to loyal Confederates in exchange for more expansive state knowledge of those citizens. In one example from the summer of 1864, Allen wrote to the superintendent of the State Penitentiary, "You are hereby authorized to loan the looms in your charge to planters in Eastern Louisiana, giving preference to such as are most likely to take proper care of them & keep them out of the hands of the enemy." His order required special knowledge about enemy movements and Southern loyalties. To receive state protection and material, Louisianans had to adhere to Confederate authority, just as those under Union occupation. As one Rapides Parish woman complained, Confederate women could not receive a pension from the state "without first making oath before some civil officer, signing this printed certificate and then have it endorsed by some responsible persons." Allen attempted to alleviate as many

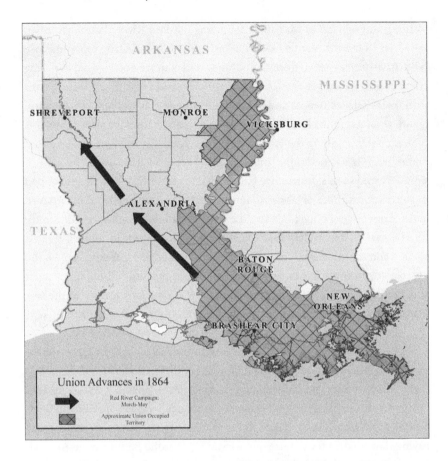

such concerns as possible. Civil-military leaders like Allen and Smith demonstrated that fighting a war on Louisiana soil required greater government intervention among the people and the economy, yet their administration of social relief programs also illustrated that they, to some extent, understood the reciprocal nature between government power and responsibility to the people.[35]

With the confiscation of slave labor, however, Allen and other state leaders strained Confederate allegiance the most. The Confederate state government posed a threat to slavery as impressment disrupted the plantation system and signaled the state's willingness to violate property rights in the name of military defense. After his property was ransacked by vandals, Robert Hyman demanded that James Calvert Wise, quartermaster general of the Confederate Army in the Trans-Mississippi, return eight enslaved people to him to begin planting and repairs. In May 1864, following the Red River Campaign, Allen called on Louisiana planters who had escaped enemy destruction and those "who have been expelled from their homes, and who are not engaged in raising crops of grain" to enter the Red River parishes and assist in cultivating corn with their enslaved people and livestock. Although this was not a direct command, several months later Allen reissued his exhortation for slave labor, this time for defenses along the Red River. In dire tones, he referenced "desolated homes" and "blackened ruins" that evidenced the consequences of Union invasion. To avoid such a destructive fate again and carefully noting that he hoped to avoid impressment of labor, Allen urgently requested one-third of enslaved males from ten parishes in central Louisiana. Citing the authority of Smith, Allen assured slaveholders that the enslaved laborers would be well treated and fed and returned after sixty days. But, he concluded somberly, "Unless the negroes are promptly sent forward, they will be impressed—the country must be defended." Richard Taylor pondered, "It was a curious feature of the war that the Southern people would cheerfully send their sons to battle, but kept their slaves out of danger."[36]

Scores of receipts in the Slave Payroll Index reveal that the Confederate state government of Louisiana paid hundreds of slaveholders for the labor of their enslaved people on state military sites like Fort Macomb, Fort Livingston, Fort Jackson, Fort St. Philip, New Iberia Ordinance Works, Port Hudson fortifications, and Camp Moore. As early as March 1861, the state government was paying slaveholders for the use of enslaved labor at the Baton Rouge Arsenal. In August 1862, the New Orleans, Opelousas & Great Western Railroad used state funds to pay slaveholders for labor, including a payment of $88.81 to L. J. Dodge for boarding some enslaved laborers. The state paid over $1,100 to nine slaveholders in 1863 to rent slave labor for the defenses around Shreveport. Later that year, H. M. Blake received $20 from the quartermaster department of a Confederate division for the teamster service of his eighteen-year-old enslaved man Esquire. State projects could also include agricultural endeavors. "Sent five negro men to Brashear City at the requisition of Capt. E. W. Fuller, to assist in trimming a lot of cane," John Palfrey wrote in the summer of 1862. Owners could be remunerated for enslaved people who died during state work. But any enslaved person convicted of bearing arms against the state was put to death without compensation to the owner.[37]

During the war enslaved people experienced deadly coercion from slaveholders more frequently. On February 1, 1863 twenty enslaved laborers attempted to escape down river from Fort Taylor where they were coerced to work. Fifteen of the laborers commandeered a boat while the others departed on foot away from Confederate lines. A Confederate officer stationed at the fort reported to his commanding officer, Lt. Col. George W. Logan, that "after repeated orders to halt and return to shore . . . the Guard fired upon them; whereupon most of those in the boat jumped into the River and four of their bodies were this morning found dead." The other runaways managed to get ashore, where one was pursued and caught after receiving a wound to the leg. Accompanying the report was a list of the enslaved people and their owners. Of the four bodies that washed ashore, only one, Tuck, was found to have bullet wounds. The others—Big Jim, Eli, and Hampton—had drowned. In total, only eight of the original twenty safely escaped Confederate lines. Perhaps these enslaved people dashed for freedom when they heard of the Emancipation Proclamation or maybe they hoped to reach Union lines that approached in spring 1863. Union movements, as many Louisiana planters and state authorities well understood, constantly disrupted slavery. As John Ransdell wrote to Moore a few months later, "Things are just now beginning to work right—the negroes hated awfully to go to work again. Several have been shot and probably more will have to be."[38]

For their part, enslaved Black people under Confederate occupation—for the system of slavery was a violent coercive enterprise dependent on continual state regulation—chose a variety of responses to their wartime situations. Some, like the laborers at Fort Taylor, fled if they found themselves on the fringes of Confederate lines. Others, forced northward and eastward as their masters fled Union advances, waited until freedom was more obtainable. "Father gave all the negroes choice yesterday evening," Sarah Wadley wrote in her diary as the family prepared to leave for Georgia in August 1863. He "told them they might go . . . to a place of safety or they might bundle up their things and go to the Yankees." Perhaps to the family's surprise, all of the enslaved people chose to remain with their white owners. "Some were not sincere," however, Wadley wrote, for one of her neighbors believed he saw several with Union forces a short time later.[39]

Like common Confederate Louisianans who made flexible choices under the pressures of war, enslaved people had any number of reasons for choosing to remain among their enslavers. Perhaps they desired to stay near kinfolk or perhaps they were safeguarding whatever property they claimed. Some maybe hoped to wait until masters fled so that they could take over abandoned land. Enslaved people were not ignorant of the contingencies of war either. No doubt many were aware that life within the Union lines could prove arduous and threatening. Just days before Wadley's father offered his enslaved property a decision about their future, one nearby enslaved man named Prince urged the patriarch to purchase him. Prince declared, "One reason I want to get away from Monro is because these black folks that come back say the Yankees takes all the young looking fellows and puts them in the army, and I've no notion of going in the army." Still others may have been waiting to see if the Union could in fact win the war. A victorious Confederacy, some enslaved people might have feared, would have horrifying punishments in store for Black traitors. Whatever the response of enslaved people to Confederate policies and local circumstances, they negotiated a wartime system of slavery with increasingly fluctuating parameters. Their careful, daring, and sacrificial decisions might deliver them to freedom or spell their doom.[40]

Despite the social welfare benefits that many could possibly reap from state leaders and programs, Confederate Louisianans were often dispirited by government corruption, the ineffectual attempts of their civil-military leaders to defend the state, as well as by confiscation of enslaved labor—all of which highlighted the extent to which government measures encroached on the material stability and self-mastery of the southern household. Historian John Winters estimated that corrupt Confederate commissary officers "appropriated nearly one third of every ration requisition, sold it, and pocketed the proceeds." Unwilling to accept Confederate notes as payment as early as 1862, some Baton Rouge merchants simply closed their stores, generating "much inconvenience and trouble generally, and great injury and loss to the lower classes." On April 29, 1862, Baton Rouge mayor B. F. Bryan, the City Council, and the Committee of Safety announced, "In the present perilous condition of public affairs, it behooves all good citizens and true patriots to act together in all measures calculated to promote the public welfare as well as to prevent among the poorer classes of our community want, suffering and distress." Bryan encouraged, not commanded, that all merchants and traders immediately reopen their stores and accept Confederate money and "sell their goods at reasonable prices." Any merchant who did not comply with this strong suggestion "will be regarded as wanting in fidelity and patriotism, and it may become necessary in such cases, that this committee should take further and more decisive action in the premises." However, the mayor also assured that no merchant was compelled to sell more merchandise than Confederate money was worth—a prevention against hoarders who sought to buy up as much goods as possible with reduced currency.[41]

Citizens in war-torn portions of Louisiana also expressed dismay at their ruined homes and lands, and desolation pushed many southerners further from Confederate allegiance. In the fall of 1864, Sarah Wadley traveled to see a nearby friend in northeastern Louisiana and recorded her shocked observations of the countryside. "I have seldom seen a more desolate looking country ... the houses were of the poorest sort, far between, often deserted and always ruinous, with people as miserable looking and as scarce as their cabins." On her return journey that evening she met "the most ragged and miserable looking man I ever saw" and a field of corn was "the only flourishing thing about his domain." Henry Lawrence's wife, Frances, lamented the federal presence around her house in Brashear City. "They have a battery in [my] garden, the mules and wagons pass thro it every day no fence. . . . Oh it seems such a pity to witness the waste tents are front of our house, and a large fort put up on the point of the Island just opposite this house." The Confederate government had failed to protect her household. "There is [sic] only 3 Houses left on Berwick side Bay," Henry Lawrence wrote during the later years of the war. "Had we only remained there the possibilities are we would have been the Richest of the Rich in place of poverty stricken." During the Red River Campaign, William Stewart's regiment easily captured and destroyed Fort DeRussy in Avoyelles Parish as they marched north along the river. Residents of Pineville "blow a great deal about Fort DeRussy or Fort Humbug as they call it," he wrote. "They say it cost 15 million and which we took in less than an hour and have pretty effectually devoted to Destruction." He also reported crowds of enslaved people "swinging aprons hats & Bonnets" as Union soldiers passed. Likewise, he noted how numerous poor white women exited their dwellings "waiving [sic] handkerchiefs or bonnets." He saw one house flying the U.S. flag. "I should think," he wrote happily, "among the poorer classes doubtless much Unionism." A month later, he wrote "So far today we seem to be passing through a region of loyalty—

Whites—men, women & children as well as drakes welcome us from Verandas as well as assemblages on the beach—with waving of handkerchiefs & other demonstrations." Sarah Wadley worried that Kirby Smith "has extraordinary powers bestowed on him, powers equal to those of the President." She feared the creation of a separate confederation west of the Mississippi River. "If this be so we must get away as soon as possible. Oh it is dreadful! . . . Our enemies are those that are in the midst of us, with the Yankees we can cope." As the war continued, and elites and corrupt officials tightened their grip on Confederate Louisiana, some citizens like Wadley were less inclined to maintain allegiance to the cause.[42]

While the government scrambled to curtail desertion, maintain social order, and wage the war, local communities organized their own responses to the war. Stunned by the loss of New Orleans, the great communication center of the state, northern Louisiana parishes established numerous "committees of safety" to provide special messenger service between the parishes. In Natchitoches Parish, local authorities paid slave owners $25 a month for slave labor to work on the defenses along the Red River. The state legislature empowered the executive committee at Shreveport to seize any property or material necessary for defense, including slave labor, with adequate compensation made. It also authorized police juries to appropriate money and levy taxes to aid the river defense program. Confederate associations rose in many parishes after August 1863 to unite and organize citizens. These associations encouraged patriotism with public meetings and speeches where information was transmitted and false information disputed. Caddo Parish residents organized and headquartered their association in Shreveport on September 10, 1863. It featured four committees—one for correspondence, one to arrange meetings of the people to hear speakers, another for the organization of public defense, and one to remove women and children in case of invasion into the parish. They organized enslaved labor to erect defenses in and around the town of Shreveport. Near Opelousas, local southern citizens organized to fight off jayhawker bands.[43]

Faced with increasing privation as the war continued, many Louisianans with little means of subsistence depended on community and state aid to get by. With many of the men gone to war, southern communities oftentimes pledged to take care of their own. In 1862, the St. Tammany Police Jury appropriated $20,000 for supporting families of local soldiers. A year later, the state assumed responsibility for their care. One Catholic church collected $750 and sent it to Governor Allen to be "distributed amongst the destitute." J. H. Sullivan, a member of the Cotile Ward Police Jury in Rapides Parish, wrote to Allen in early 1865 that numerous families in his ward were suffering for lack of food and some had even "lost every male member, large enough to work in the war." He pleaded for a "load of corn" to be sold at cost to the destitute families. "The entire neighborhood would assist" in unloading and storing it, Sullivan promised. That same month, two scouts reported to a Union officer that "discontent and insubordination" were widespread among Confederate soldiers and civilians because of the "destitution of the soldiers' families." Many outcries for corn or other food supplies reached Allen in the closing months of the war. Another Rapides citizen, W. H. Rogers, complained that conscription resulted in "more families left without heads than in any other parish."[44]

Confederate leaders were increasingly dismayed at discontent in Louisiana. Thomas Moore privately confessed that he was stunned at the conduct of people in Rapides Parish. "Who would have thought that my own parish would have had the bad of all the bad in disloyalty, or taking the oath?" General Taylor also found his efforts to rally civilian morale greatly stymied by a lack of trust. "The people think or affect to think that our State has been neglected by the government in Richmond," he complained, "and because soldiers are not sent to defend them they are unwilling to do anything to defend themselves." Given the rate of desertion and the persistent guerrilla campaigns in Louisiana, that last statement rang a little hollow. "In lower part of the State," he continued, "this feeling is almost universal, and of course I as the representative of the government am abused on all sides for not accomplishing impossibilities." For a people unwilling to defend themselves, Taylor found himself under significant pressure. Perhaps the foremost impossibility he faced, even if he and other Confederate state authorities never quite realized it, was to militarily defend the state without subordinating the physical property and social fabric of local communities to a coercive government.[45]

Louisianans who suffered under Confederate rule may not have been pro-Union, but privation increasingly detached them from Confederate nationalism. Despite lengthy pontifications about national loyalty and personal honor from the state, many rural white southerners in occupied Louisiana considered

Confederate state agendas of little importance compared to their material situations. Sometimes local identities were more important than national sacrifice and survival was more important than loyalty. In the middle region of the state, which exchanged hands more often, common Louisianans inhabited what James Scott might call a "non-state space" where the authority and structure of the state was less developed. Some resistant Louisiana men proved this by taking up arms in defense of local autonomy. Persistent irregular activity in places like Winn, Union, and Jackson Parishes undermined Confederate authority in those regions and weakened the government's war effort. Both Union and Confederate authorities struggled to exact absolute loyalty out of southerners because the nature of household war meant that support for family and community often superseded grand political demonstrations of national loyalty. As historians Jarret Ruminski and David Ballantyne have demonstrated, southerners in the tumultuous western regions of the Confederacy might easily express Confederate loyalty, align themselves with Union edicts, or defy both to provide for or defend their households.[46]

No Civil War combatant proved more controversial than the guerrilla fighter. From the early days of the war, Union commanders and the northern public made it clear that guerrilla warfare had no place in a civilized society. As Andrew Lang has argued, Union troops enacted violent reprisals against guerrillas not just as survival mechanisms in wartime but as acts of regulation or cleansing a disorderly southern society. To the west of the Mississippi, Confederate commanders and local communities had been waging a vehement guerrilla war against the Union since 1862 (and even earlier in Missouri). But guerrillas did not just oppose Union forces, they enforced or challenged Confederate authority as well. Ostensibly, guerrilla troops, both those formally sanctioned by the Confederate Congress and those sponsored by communities for local defense, targeted Union military objectives. Yet on a national and local level, guerrillas also served a social purpose. As Mark Grimsley notes, guerrilla forces "enforced the secessionist political order in occupied regions where the Confederate government could exert no direct influence" by plaguing stalwart bastions of Unionists and threatening any wayward Confederate who dared stray from the cause. Also, some guerrilla troops seemed to fight for no one but themselves. Men without perceived loyalty to North or South represented the worst kind of moral character in a war between two national ideologies.[47]

The first function of Confederate guerrilla forces was to oppose Union advances and frustrate their lines of communication and supply. Kirby Smith increasingly relied on guerrilla units such as those under command of Captain Joseph Lea to battle Union raids, rout local jayhawkers, and attack Union supply lines (especially plantations). These tactics of war were as ancient as they were common. But Union and Confederate military regimes did not recognize irregular bands without national loyalty as important demonstrations of personal or rural community defense almost entirely separate from the sprawling national conflict over national sovereignty. Jayhawkers, as many Confederates called them, often did not sign oaths of allegiance to the Union yet still attacked Confederate forces. In the eyes of both Union and Confederate nation-states, these were outlaws even worse than irregular warriors, but this assumption failed to consider the social location of local belligerents and their non-national identities. To be sure, some guerrillas, jayhawkers, or irregulars were simply outlaw bandits plundering the fluid wartime world of Louisiana. Some even attacked federal supply lines only to sell stolen goods back to the Union. But others—especially bands of escaped Black laborers who operated in the Confederate interior—were not bloodthirsty criminals without loyalty or mission. Their allegiances simply were not legible to the dueling nation-states intent on the classic assumptions of nineteenth-century warfare: territorial integrity and national allegiance.[48]

Confederate Louisiana officials were quick to demonize the actions of local Unionists who fought an irregular war against the Confederate state. Confederate soldiers and locals in St. Mary Parish executed a white jayhawker who supposedly planned to incite a slave rebellion in May 1863. A year earlier, when Moore issued his lengthy call to loyalty, he included a diatribe against Unionists in Confederate Louisiana. Tories, as he called them "can be tolerated no longer; if they did not wish to live under the Confederate Government, they were warned by its President a year ago that they were at liberty to depart. . . . They cannot live here and disregard our laws. They can neither hold property nor enjoy liberty if they disown the Government which protects the one and insures the other." Not all Unionists were bushwhackers, but the constellation of wartime identities in Louisiana included southerners who endeavored to undermine the Confederate cause. "All citizens should report to the nearest authorities the names and the proof or grounds of suspicion," Moore directed in 1862. "Strangers must give a satisfactory account of themselves, the doubtful must be closely watched, the disloyal must be imprisoned, and when found guilty of treason must be held liable to the penalty due to that capital crime." Three years later, Allen was equally unforgiving. He called on "all good citizens to suppress and restrain these violations of law and outrages upon private property." For a nation presumably dedicated to resisting the tyranny of the North and Black Republicanism, Confederate Louisiana repeatedly demonstrated authoritarian tendencies.[49]

Confederates in Louisiana best embodied this antidemocratic disposition through their harsh treatment of Unionists in their midst. Somewhere between five thousand and ten thousand Louisiana Unionists took up arms for the Union military or resisted Confederate power in some way. Dennis Haynes, an Irish immigrant who had lived in Rapides Parish since 1860, was one of numerous Unionists who tried to organize military units to oppose the Confederacy and suffered extensive physical punishment and household destruction as a result. When Confederates discovered his Unionist sympathies in late 1863, "they sent a squadron of cavalry to capture me, with several of the neighboring rebels for guides." Once captured, Haynes was placed in jail for "high treason" and subjected to harsh treatment, including broken bones in his chest and right arm that he sustained in an escape attempt. When he finally did escape, he relied on Unionist households to hide and supply him while partisans scoured the woods for him. Any Union man, Haynes wrote, that "stayed at home, and was caught was 'shot with bullets as thick as they could stick in him,' as was the usual phrase of those villains."[50]

Another much more essential function that guerrillas performed in southern communities, which military commanders seemed to overlook in their careful negotiations with southern locals, was that of community and household protection. As early as 1861, many local Louisianans were interested only in guarding their property and local communities, not in marching off to other fronts in the Confederacy. As the war intensified, nationalist allegiance did not subordinate these feelings. "After the coming engagement," Edward Palfrey wrote to his father from Vicksburg in 1862, "I will immediately return home if I can do so. . . . I desire to join some Guerrilla party at home for the protection of our property seized upon by vagrant scouting and foraging parties from the federal forces." A community leader named Dr. Ready contacted General Banks in early 1863 asking for permission to organize a home defense unit.

Banks informed him that military statutes forbid any such organization and instead encouraged local men to join the Union army, as "the troops so enlisted would not be called to service beyond the lines of the Department." In East Feliciana Parish, Ellen Power noted how local defense units or Confederate guerrillas warded off wayward Union troops from southern homes. "Some soldiers passed by here with a Yankee prisoner," she wrote in July of 1863, "and they killed one at Mrs. Fluker's because he would not surrender." A few weeks later, another Union deserter stayed the night in the home of one of her neighbors. Though he was attacked by vandals, Robert Hyman refused to leave his home. He was "determined to stay in it until compelled to leave."[51]

Deserters threatened the peace and property of rural Louisiana residents just as much as formal war. Just the previous month, seven Union troops had entered Power's home and "behaved like thieves, searched the house, and killed & carried away all the chickens and turkeys they could find. They seemed frightened did not stay long, they found my preserves I had hid, & carried them off." While not physically harmed, Power described an experience in which her personal autonomy and private property were violated, an experience that numerous Louisiana residents witnessed during the war. At least five Union troops broke into the home of Sarah Wadley's friend Mr. Fithol and pointed guns at him and his wife while demanding gold. One St. Landry Parish Unionist helped a band of Union troops kill the planter John Lyons "on the threshold of his own door." Local southern defense units, often operating in the bush to avoid Union patrols and Confederate conscription officers, endeavored to curtail such attacks on Louisiana households. When their military duties extended to bushwhacking Union troops, however, Union occupation authorities were quick to castigate community irregulars and punish local communities.[52]

Faced with such a treacherous wartime landscape, Confederate women had more reason than national loyalty to support guerrilla forces. "Let us burn in our houses, rather than be murdered in the woods," declared Sarah Morgan. Especially in rural areas that had more frequent contact with guerrilla forces, southern white women could have easily shared a social responsibility to supply their menfolk. They could have also shared a communal view of southern armed forces as a public resource. Their men departed households filled with women and children to perform martial service to the Confederate state and the local community. Those men left home wearing clothes southern women had made and carrying food southern women had prepared. Those men left a material and social void in the patriarchal households they departed. For those Confederate men serving in local partisan bands instead of the faraway formal armies, their first concern was community defense. Confederate women continued to look to them as community and household leaders. Since Banks no doubt understood the social connections between guerrilla men and southern white women, he forbade women to enter the Union lines around Port Hudson and Baton Rouge in June 1863. To those who insisted on entering, they were forbidden to leave again. He was also probably not surprised a month later when "a lady came through the pickets looking for a guerrilla leader," as he informed General George Andrews during the campaign. A war on guerrillas was a war on southern community as well, a community that consisted of numerous rebellious women intent on maintaining a domestic supply line.[53]

In late January 1864, Union men captured a Confederate soldier and partisan named Peter Bromon who illustrated the complexities of irregular Confederate resistance and the local support that sustained or opposed it. Union authorities discovered that Bromon had supposedly piloted the captured Union gunboat *Diana* before Union forces seized Brashear City in 1863. A local resident named Ichabod Lewis told the provost marshal that Bromon freely admitted that he piloted the captured ship, was a warrant officer in the Confederate navy, and also was a local scout for General Mouton. Bromon boldly infiltrated Union lines to discover their troop strength and find out what the federals knew about nearby Confederate forces. "The Picket told him the Rebels were near Tigerville and allowed him to pass into the Union lines[;] after gaining what information he could, he made a detour, and took a skiff at Flat Lake, returned, and gave the necessary information to General Mouton," which the general used "for concerted action" with local irregulars. Another Louisiana local reported that he saw Bromon and a Black man named Berry Mathias spying on ship movements one evening in January 1864.[54]

Union officials interviewed Mathias and a Black man named Tom Brewer, both of whom revealed a network of local Confederate support in the St. Mary Parish area. Brewer had lived on a plantation owned by a man named Bateman for three years, he testified. One Sunday night in January, Bateman woke Brewer in his cabin and told him to cross a nearby bayou, find Peter Bromon, and "take a letter and an [U.S.] overcoat to him." Brewer suspected that it was a plot to return him to slavery, and he refused to go. In the morning, Bateman successfully pressured Brewer. On finally seeing the letter Bromon seemed enthusiastic, Brewer told the provost marshal at Brashear City, and "he then asked me to row him over the Bayou, but I would not come inshore again, fearing he wanted to retain me." Brewer even refused to carry Bromon's response and departed without him. "Soon after Peter Bromon came over the bayou, and soon afterwards old Man Bateman came to me and said 'You, take this letter to my Daughter Mrs[.] Alexander.'" Still suspicious, Brewer hesitantly relented. The daughter read the letter and dispatched Brewer yet again to carry the letter to her husband, who was in Pattersonville. Mr. Alexander read the letter and immediately wanted to find a local friend, so he instructed Brewer to wait in the yard of a man named Wadsworth. But Brewer had had enough. "Knowing that something was wrong by all the people being excited, I fearing that they wanted to get me into the clutches of Peter Bromon, and run me off, I made for home." Without Brewer, Bromon turned to Berry Mathias to help him in his secret bayou mission. Brewer reported that he had hoped to warn Mathias away but Bromon secured the man's assistance first.[55]

Berry Mathias had been living in Pattersonville for several months as of January 1864, he told Union officials. He knew Peter Bromon through, as he referred to him, "the so called 'Capt' Bateman of the Confederate service." Mathias testified that he was in Bateman's employ, though he did not stipulate what his job was, and that Bateman had on occasion paid him in clothing and provisions. He traveled with Broman and Bateman for several days as they intersected with other Confederates, but he claimed to be ignorant of their larger mission.[56]

Within days, federal officials interviewed a local white man named William Drews, whose run-in with Confederate irregulars in the previous year, including Bromon, provided a startling sample of Confederate vigilante coercion and household violence. Traveling home along Bayou Long near Napoleonville (in neighboring Assumption Parish) on the evening of March 27, 1863, Drews was captured by Confederate soldiers in three boats. One officer was inclined to release Drews, but the officer in command—as well as Bromon, whom Drews recognized—disagreed. The rebels, Drews later told Union authorities, "treated [him] with severity and told he must go on with the party." With Drews as their prisoner, the group of rebels proceeded to a store owned by one John Pipser—"whose opinions, and public expression, have always been in favor of the Union"—ransacked it and carried the contents into their boats. Drews testified that Bromon was "taking an active part therein." Following the attack, two boats of the waterborne rebels made their way to Drews's home, "which they made a perfect wreck of, taking all, or destroying everything of value therein." It was Bromon, Drews claimed, that led the way. The Confederate raiders then deposited some of their plunder and Bromon near his own home on the Atchafalaya River before releasing Drews in Franklin, Louisiana (probably twenty–thirty miles from where he was captured). "During the whole of the trip," Drews told Union provost marshal authorities, "the officer commanding the Confederates deferred in all things to the opinion of said Bromon, who was acting as the actual leader of the party, but gave no military orders[;] the Confederates treated him as their good friend he urging them on to be quick for fear of capture by the U.S. gunboats." Once ashore, Bromon promised his fellow rebels that he would soon pilot a steamboat to seize further goods from Drews's household. The irregulars were excited by the prospect.[57]

Bromon and his companions demonstrated that guerrilla war was a community war and a household war. Irregulars targeted the Union military as well as local Unionists. They relied on dense information networks that included men, women, and however compelled, free and enslaved Black people. They operated within occupied territory itself, revealing how porous Union control could be at times. The experience of William Drews also displayed the heaviest cost of guerrilla war, for it was southern civilians that endured the most deleterious effects of irregular offensives. Regardless of national or local loyalties, guerrilla units in Louisiana precipitated an increase of violence in the state. Irregulars not only diluted Confederate nationalism in some war-weary regions, but also invited more aggressive Union responses that destroyed property and disrupted communities. Further, guerrilla activity undermined the Confederate war effort on the international scene because it compromised southern claims to legitimate sovereignty among the community of civilized nations.[58]

By the end of the war, the Confederates had some forty thousand soldiers spread out in the Trans-Mississippi Department. Many Louisianans continued to move into Texas and civilian demoralization was high. Union raids captured enslaved people and supplies the Confederates could not afford to lose. Lack of pay increased desertion dramatically in early 1865. As one Rapides Parish resident wrote to Henry Allen, many soldiers' families were in "deplorable conditions" without money, food, or shoes. "When the soldier goes home and sees that his bosom companion and helpless one are thus neglected and left with-out the commonest necessaries of life it is not to be wondered at that he vow not to serve his country only at the point of the bayonet." A few months later, William Stewart noted that "the Confederate Army seems to have entirely lost confidence in themselves . . . they do not fight as they did."[59]

When news of Lee's surrender came in April, Kirby Smith urged his troops to continue resistance. Rebels attempted a dismal river offensive late in the month by sending the steam ram *W. H. Webb* down the Mississippi River and into the Gulf, but it was trapped by federal ships. The ram ran aground and burned, and the Confederate crew dispersed into the bush. In a proclamation issued on April 21, Smith urged his soldiers to "sustain the holy cause," but little fighting spirit remained. On April 29, a large meeting of southern leaders from Louisiana, Texas, Arkansas, and Missouri, as well as thousands of soldiers and civilians, convened in Shreveport. Smith's army continued to evaporate. On May 8, Lieutenant Colonel John T. Sprague, envoy of General John Pope sta-tioned in St. Louis, appeared before Smith and requested his surrender. Smith and Confederate state governments claimed they would accept surrender only on lenient terms, and they appointed Allen to be the arbiter of peace in Louisi-ana. "I shall stay at the helm of state just as long as I am needed by my people," Allen wrote wearily, "and then I shall seek a home as an exile in a strange land."[60]

Smith's ambivalence to surrender and Allen's pursuit of peace generated some confusion among Louisianans. Officers lost control of the army, desert-ers walked off by the hundreds, and unpaid and underfed soldiers raided gov-ernment property with impunity. A "general pillage of governmental depots and Quartermasters' post" ensued as soldiers seized supplies of clothing and Confederate money. A crowd of women gathered around the state store in Natchitoches and barred all entry. These supplies had been left by "a class of men who . . . appeared to be the leeches sucking away the life-blood of the army in the Trans-Mississippi Department, by their incapacity, negligence, or corruption," Allen's daughter and biographer wrote a year after the war. Angry Confederate troops "robbed all the government stores and depots, distributing the contents as fairly and equitably as they could, among themselves." This was a final reminder that, for war-weary southerners, personal loyalties were often more important than grand national allegiances. Smith moved his headquar-ters to Houston, Texas, on May 18, leaving Lieutenant General Simon Buckner in charge of the army at Shreveport. This action obviated the need for Allen to continue as agent between Confederate and Union commands. Buckner signed terms of surrender in New Orleans on May 26. On June 2, Kirby Smith surrendered in Galveston Harbor and Henry Allen stepped down as governor.[61]

In response to expanding Union military incursions and the material exigencies of war, the Confederate state government of Louisiana fashioned an increasingly authoritarian state both in alliance with and in opposition to local Confederates. Despite frequent appeals from nineteenth-century conservatives to a division between the standing army and civilian control of America's democratic government, this separation of powers appeared mostly on paper and rarely manifested in reality during the war. In Confederate Louisiana, state control was preeminent from the beginning of the war and only strengthened as the state government increasingly relied on the military to enforce its decrees and secure the state from Union invasion. Although he governed perhaps as wisely as any wartime governor could, the rise of Henry Allen, a Confederate military officer, to the office of governor effectively fused civilian government and military power. Allen and Kirby Smith relied on civil-military bureaucracies to collect cotton, issue material aid, and conscript troops. Military commanders like Smith and Richard Taylor expressed dismay with civilian discontent and did not hesitate to wrestle with Confederate municipal and state authorities to ensure military order. More than any other wartime location perhaps, Confederate Louisiana revealed that under the pressure of war, the structure of American democracy yielded to powerful statist dictates.

For their part, Confederate civilians often responded to the war by privileging local interests over national unity. Men and women who faced certain material devastation unless they signed a loyalty oath were less concerned with ideological purity than they were with personal survival. Regardless of what state officials believed, personal survival strategies were just as important as national allegiance to locals and far more motivating. Still, white Louisianans were hardly Unionists just because they criticized the Confederacy, avoided conscription, or took a loyalty oath to the Union. Many white and Black southerners in Louisiana waged local wars against each other, revealing in microcosm the divided communities and households of the Civil War era.

Conclusion

DEMOCRACY DELAYED

Sometime in late 1863 or early 1864, Thomas Knox traveled with some northern associates near Vidalia, Louisiana (across the river from the garrison town of Natchez). He and his companions witnessed many planters eager to plant and harvest crops, if "it did not involve them in any trouble with their neighbours or the Rebel authorities." One Louisiana planter, who was also a judge, lamented "the severity of the storm which was passing over the South" and feared that the Confederacy would fail. "The fortune of war has materially changed my circumstances," the planter-judge confessed to Knox and his companions. "My n——s used to do as I told them, but that time is passed. Your Northern people have made soldiers of our servants, and will, I presume, make voters of them. In five years, if I continue the practice of law, I suppose I shall be addressing a dozen negroes as gentlemen of the jury." This defeated southerner plainly laid out the script of southern social change, which correlated to Union military occupation. His social relationships, with white neighbors, civil government, and Black dependents were utterly altered. Communal white power had shifted to isolated individuals subject to national loyalty and local Rebel vengeance. Elite wealthy planters faced stern military regulations and complex labor negotiations. This man also witnessed the social transformation of enslaved people from field hands to armed soldiers and contract laborers. The ballot box, the jury pool, and the American body politic appeared to be open to them in the dawning months of 1865. As a subject of Union military occupation, the planter well knew that occupation had empowered such social transformations by establishing the political mechanisms necessary for their accomplishment.[1]

But it was one of Knox's northern travel companions who reoriented the planter's fateful postwar vision. "If you had a negro on trial," one of the northerners replied, "that would be correct enough. Is it not acknowledged everywhere that a man shall be tried by his peers?" The southern planter-judge admitted that he had not considered this point before. "He said he would insist upon having negroes admitted into court as counsel for negroes that were to be tried by a jury of their race. He did not believe they would ever be available as labourers in the field if they were set free, and thought so many of them would engage in theft that negro courts would be constantly busy." Moments before, the planter had assumed that Union victory was complete and social transformation assured. Then he changed his mind. The seeds of racial control and separation began to flower even before Union occupation melted. Occupied Louisiana, as a test site for Reconstruction and a battleground for the rights of Black Americans, made bold promises but also produced profound limitations. Black self-emancipation and Union occupation steadily eroded slavery as a system of labor within white patriarchal households, but Union authorities did not or perhaps could not erase prominent features of slavery's racial ontology. White supremacy remained.[2]

By the time of this conversation, Knox himself had already passed a gloomy prophecy. "When the Southern states are fairly 'reconstructed,' and political control is placed in the hands of the ruling race, every effort will be made to maintain the old policy." By old policy he meant white racial control over Black laborers in a political world where Black Americans had little to no civil or material rights. "If possible," he continued, "the negroes will not be permitted to possess or cultivate land on their own account. To allow them to hold real estate will be partially admitting their claim to humanity. No true scion of chivalry can permit such an innovation, so long as he is able to make successful opposition." Having spent nearly three years in the Mississippi Valley during the war, Knox realized that lingering racial resentments boiled under the protective veneer of military occupation. Albert Stearns, the tireless provost marshal from New York, agreed. At his various stations in southern Louisiana, Stearns recalled numerous postharvest celebrations when Black laborers danced and sang to the delight of nearby occupation troops. "The slaves' sun of happiness seemed at meridian height," Stearns later wrote. Under Union occupation, though their suffering was not entirely eliminated, they often stood between the agonies of slavery in the past and the terrors of white supremacist violence to come.[3]

By the summer of 1864, the Union offensive campaigns against Atlanta and Richmond fully transitioned the Union war effort to slash-and-burn hard war policies and the final reduction of Confederate armies. These aggressive operations reduced the previous reliance on a strategy of occupied territory to conquer the Confederacy. Unlike their campaigns in the western theater in 1862–1863, by 1864 Grant and Sherman were far less concerned with depositing garrisons as they moved through the South. When Banks failed to provide the third offensive arm to Grant and Sherman with his Red River Campaign, Union high command organized the Military Division of West Mississippi, with Major General E. R. S. Canby commanding, which superseded Banks. By the fall, Banks was replaced as commander of the Department of the Gulf with Major General Stephen Hurlbut, who was disinclined to cooperate with the sometimes radical-leaning civil government under Michael Hahn. When Hahn resigned in March 1865, Unionist Louisiana planter James Madison Wells became governor. He embraced former Confederates and dismantled many radical initiatives in the state government.[4]

With Reconstruction came immediate groundswells of conservative opposition. Just before the February 1864 election in occupied Louisiana, Banks claimed, "The creation of a State is not a matter of voting merely. It must be a growth, representing in its course all the elements of society." But in every area of the Border States and occupied South where Lincoln had hoped that Unionism would prevail and pave the way for a peaceful Reconstruction, these regions proved to be little more than "halfway houses toward real restoration," as historian Mark Wahlgren Summers writes. Former Confederates, Dennis Haynes wrote, swore that "as soon as the Federal army leaves the country, they intend to kill or run off all the returned refugees." Occupation strengthened southern hatred of the North. Such resistance added to the constitutional quandary over the legitimacy of governmental authority that even some Radical Republicans hesitantly pondered in the Reconstruction years. Republican leaders were increasingly divided over the capacity of national government to shape American society.[5]

While Congress debated Reconstruction policy, Louisiana conservatives remembered the power of violence and street-level resistance to curtail government authority. Reconstruction in Louisiana and elsewhere cast darkness over the federal project to recreate the South in the image of free labor ideology and Republican government. General William Emory—who commanded the dwindling occupation regime in Louisiana from 1871 to 1875—noted that conservative belligerents made repeated efforts "to influence the action of that body," but President Ulysses Grant expressed reluctance to intervene in Louisiana's civil government. White conservatives in Louisiana reversed the Union tactics of the Civil War and frequently occupied areas of the state, most notably the state house itself in 1874 after the Battle of Liberty Place. Armed Democrats patrolled the streets of Baton Rouge and Monroe on election day in 1876. The following year, white vigilantes, echoing the days of secession, occupied police stations and other state government institutions. The Civil War spilled over into the wars of Reconstruction, spelling misery and persecution for Black Americans.[6]

Hundreds of household attacks hovered behind the headlines of major conflicts like the Battle of Liberty Place. In late 1865, a white overseer named Battice (perhaps a misspelling of Baptiste) Como shot at and drove away a Black worker named Aesop on a plantation in St. Martin Parish. Aesop and another Black laborer soon appeared asking for jobs at a nearby plantation where Union soldiers were stationed. Only a few days before, Union corporal J. B. Burdick had seized a government horse, an Enfield rifle, and a carbine from Como. In that expedition, he also had a conversation with a nearby property owner who informed Burdick that Como and "a number of men in the naborhood have bin laying [sic] around his negro cabins the night trying to shoot some of his negros." Perhaps Como had purloined a government horse and guns for this very reason. Burdick bore witness to a continued household war.[7]

Burdick's report also demonstrated that for many southerners, including white Unionists, not enlisted in the formal ranks of the military, the Civil War was hardly over. Irregular war, though harder to trace in the historical record, spelled out more immediate consequences for many local people in the South than did grand battles. Appomattox did not end the war, but only shifted its most prominent locale from celebrated battlefields to a scattered host of local sites across the South. Many southerners, Black and white, had been fighting a national war in such locations for years and the violence and strife would only continue. For many local white southerners far from formal battlefields and halls of decision making, occupation represented the national government's most pressing aggression. When men like Baptiste Como fought realigned economic and racial relationships, they opposed a lingering vestige of military occupation itself. Even white Unionists in Louisiana often rallied to undermine occupation's most radical potentialities. White Unionists were generally not animated by commiseration with Black Americans, nor did a lasting biracial coalition emerge in Louisiana, despite the large presence of free people of color, that was strong enough to continue the cultural transformation begun by occupation.[8]

For many Black southerners, occupation was a conflicted reality that produced familiar restraints alongside notable freedoms. Even as Black Americans experienced an incredible surge in their political participation after the war, the roots of postwar exclusion for Black people developed during the war itself, when occupation commanders fostered a conservative state government based on white cooperation and Black subservience. Postwar convict labor not only resembled the habit of southern states to use Black labor on public works projects, but also reflected the policy of forced Black labor on Union field works and local levees. The racial violence of Jim Crow America took root in white opposition to Union occupation forces in the Civil War and the social changes they oversaw. Equally important, Union occupation administrators established the earliest blueprints of postwar racial separation within occupied regions. In April 1863, for instance, the 176th New York published a copy of its regimental journal that endorsed the labor regime in Union-occupied Louisiana as a suitable environment for "commendable" Black laborers. Not only did Union occupation fail to effectively incubate a biracial democracy during the war, but Union forces retreated too soon after the war to prevent the loss of those essential gains made in favor of Black democratic inclusion during the war.[9]

The halcyon days of Republicans' national reimagining withered quickly after 1865, most notably because the vision of the Republican Party largely extended to political solutions like the Fourteenth and Fifteenth Amendments and not so much to material solutions on the ground. Reconstruction was a complex series of political and personal negotiations, not only in Congress and in southern state houses but also in the households and communities of the occupied South. Federal projects intended to aid the development of autonomous Black households, namely the Freedmen's Bureau, were underfunded, understaffed, and deeply contested from the outset. For years, one of the most triumphant historiographic perspectives about the Civil War was that it represented a new birth of freedom, primarily via emancipation as a national project. W. E. B. DuBois was the strongest proponent of this argument, though Lincoln himself might deserve credit as the father of this view. More recently, historical works, including this one, question the extent to which the Union military and emancipation empowered Black people during the years of war and reconstruction.[10]

In the middle of the war, loyal Louisianan Thomas Durant wrote President Lincoln with the firm idea that agricultural production in Louisiana "cannot be carried on without the labor of Slaves[;] the slaveholders consider the [Emancipation] Proclamation as effecting the ruin of the state, as well as their own." Durant's words called attention to the explicit connection between the well-being of the national state and the welfare of individual households. Former Confederates and their offspring never really gave up a culture war against Yankees they imagined were bent on destroying their way of life and reducing white people to the status of Black people. Long after the war drew to a close at Appomattox, decades of Black codes, Jim Crow violence, and segregation remained as testament to one of the central values of the Confederacy: the racial social order of white America, built from the ground up in slaveholding households since the days of colonial settlement. Military occupation in Louisiana had tested, even undermined, that household order of racial, gender, and labor hierarchy. Yet in many ways, the war of occupation reified the antebellum tradition of white over Black, male over female, and employer over employee.[11]

But how did military occupation and military government, Union and Confederate, change the household in Louisiana from 1861 to 1865? Most importantly, military forces and policies transitioned the occupied household away from a regime of slavery and coercive production. In its place, Union authorities established a series of free labor systems and recruitment practices that offered nominal levels of autonomy and respect for Black Americans, even if those systems reproduced much of the material dependency among Black laborers that defined slavery. When spring 1865 brought the formal war to a close, the Union had won the war in Louisiana but failed to change the underlying southern social order because the Union bureaucracy was unable to translate its numerous initiatives into a functional reconstruction society. Conservative militias in turn exercised their own coercive dominance over Black families in Louisiana. Yet even if occupation did not annihilate white supremacy or permanently enshrine equal Black citizenship, it did forever interrupt the national mythology of the United States as solely a white man's democracy.[12]

In a war that redefined American social relationships, the war of occupation in Louisiana reaffirmed that female civilians in modern wars were hardly innocent bystanders. While Black and white women did not become fully included in the American body politic as voters or political representatives, civil-military authorities witnessed the enhanced political presence of American women in occupied Louisiana and their capacity to challenge the male-dominated social order around them. Southern women, as well as the numerous Union women who resided in the South or traveled with the Union army, demonstrated their valuable material contributions to society and flexed their considerable social influence over policy decisions. These actions occurred in a military setting, and southern women, especially white women, considered themselves to be domestic combatants. Military commanders concurred on this point. White and Black women also faced one another in new labor negotiations. Whereas enslaved Black women had once been occupied domestic subjects within slaveholder households, after the war, white women balked at the autonomy of Black women. With so many men killed and permanently maimed by the war, female-headed households proliferated. Politically, women remained simultaneously liminal but influential; socially, the war—especially in occupied regions like Louisiana—permanently reconfigured their relational status with men, family, and the state. For years after the war, the household and the nature of household order would remain a hotly debated subject in high politics and local disputes.[13]

As they dealt with emancipated people and rebellious women, civil-military bureaucracies in Civil War Louisiana also demonstrated that government and the governed shared a mutually constitutive relationship. Wartime governments in the state benefited from local support throughout the war. Confederate communities in Louisiana dispatched legions of men and streams of supplies to the war. They patrolled local loyalties and surveilled the enslaved population. They also waged an ongoing guerrilla war on beleaguered Union forces, even as they grumbled under the increasing intrusion of the Confederate state government. While Union authorities expanded their territorial reach and instituted a matrix of regulations in occupied Louisiana, they depended on liberated Black Americans for labor and production, recruited reinforcements from among the southern population, staffed numerous bureaucratic positions with loyalists, and traded with local merchants. The people of Louisiana—Black and white, male and female, loyal and disloyal—proved that they could, to some degree, measure or shape the centralizing power of the state. They negotiated with state bureaucracy, depleted state supplies for their own means, and blunted state oversight by fleeing to the bush or hiding cotton.

On a more conceptual scale, military occupation tested democracy and revealed the extent to which Americans were willing to experiment with social engineering. Occupation simultaneously illustrated a dramatic escalation of U.S. invasion power even as many Americans expressed a conservative hesitancy about the radical potential of that power. Though the Union army did not construct a long-lasting colonial regime in the South, occupation provided a glimpse of what a "forced democracy" might have looked like. But Union soldiers balked at extensive departures from the ideal of republicanism that originally animated many to take arms against aristocratic slave power. As the intervention of war came to its formal military end, the army, as Andrew Lang writes, "had to check its domestic influence if the limited constitutional principles of Union were to be preserved." Once the South was defeated on the battlefield, the North never implemented a sustained regime of violent change comparable to the French Revolution, the Haitian Revolt, or the European Revolutions of 1848. By exercising rationalized restraint against white southerners, the Union army halted a complete transfiguration of the South's social landscape under the schema of a totally mobilized state. Much of the nation was unwilling to significantly break with conservative American political tradition, broadly reconsider constitutional limitations, or violate property rights by redistributing land. Subsequently, the Radical vision of the Republican Party—always in competition with the more conservative economic wing of the party—eventually dwindled and allowed independent free labor yeoman households to fall under the command of rising industry barons.[14]

Though radical restructuring was restrained, Union military occupation and Confederate government in Louisiana did demonstrate that nationhood and national belonging are malleable processes, not unchanging organic conditions. The real work of occupation occurred not on the front line or solely in the hands of military figures who burned cotton or confiscated property, but in the daily contests between household occupants and the statist military bureaucrats. Southern households, borrowed hallways of power, reappropriated desks of military bureaucracy—these were the sites of regulation and restraint where military figures dispensed policy, appraised loyalties, and managed an endless line of southern residents. Individual occupation figures could intercede to effect change or they could collect bribes and exploit labor. Occupation authorities might find gratefully relieved citizens or endlessly antagonistic enemies. Bureaucracy therefore empowered and yet circumscribed individual efforts for social change. In the minds of governments blue and gray, they worked to preserve democracy and social order, or what they believed to be democracy's most desirable form.[15]

Notes

1. Benjamin Palmer, *The Oath of Allegiance to the United States*, 8. Throughout the text, I have retained the original spelling, phrasing, punctuation, and emphasis of the primary sources, except where additional words, marked in brackets, are necessary to clarify meaning.

2. Palmer, *The Oath of Allegiance to the United States*, 8. See also Faust, *The Creation of Confederate Nationalism*, 78–79; Farmer, *The Metaphysical Confederacy*.

3. Palmer, *The Oath of Allegiance to the United States*, 19, 21.

4. Palmer, *The Oath of Allegiance to the United States*, 17; Glymph, *The Women's Fight*, 6; Berry, "Afterword: From Household to Personhood in America," in Frank and Whites, *Household War*, 287–90.

5. Ash, *When the Yankees Came*, x, 77; Johnson, *Red River Campaign*, 43–48, 89–100, 225–41; Joiner, *Through the Howling Wilderness*, xix–xxiii, 57–78, 131, 161, 177–85.

6. For a detailed analysis of the southern household order, see Fox-Genovese, *Within the Plantation Household*; Grossberg, *Governing the Hearth*; McCurry, *Masters of Small Worlds*; Bardaglio, *Reconstructing the Household*; Glymph, *Out of the House of Bondage*. For how Confederate policies created internal problems, see Williams, *Bitterly Divided*; McCurry, *Confederate Reckoning*; Sacher, *Confederate Conscription and the Struggle for Southern Soldiers*. For the politics of women's activity during the war, see Whites, *The Civil War as a Crisis in Gender*; Edwards, *Scarlett Doesn't Live Here Anymore*; Whites and Long, eds., *Occupied Women*, 1–13; Frank and Whites, *Household War*, 1–13; Faust, *Mothers of Invention*. On the destruction of slavery and war strategy, see Siddali, *From Property to Person*; Oakes, *Freedom National*; Martinez, *Confederate Slave Impressment in the Upper South*.

7. Whites and Long, eds., *Occupied Women*, 1–13. See also McCrary, *Abraham Lincoln and Reconstruction*; Powell, *New Masters*; Edling, *A Revolution in Favor of Government*, and *A Hercules in the Cradle*; Rao, "The New Historiography of the Early Federal Government," 98; Downs, "The Civil War and the American State," 350–71.

8. Collins, *Martial Law and English Laws*, 13–17, 27, 57, 85–86, 110, 227; O'Brien and Diefendorf, *General Orders of the War Department*, Vol. I, 394; Ash, *When the Yankees Came*, 58–59, 84; Downs, *After Appomattox*, 76; Siddali, *From Property to Person*, 1–11. See also Paludan, "The

American Civil War Considered as a Crisis in Law and Order"; Moore, "The Provost Marshal Goes to War," 62–71; Moore, "Union Army Provost Marshals in the Eastern Theater," 120–26.

9. Stearns, *Reminiscences of the Late War,* 5–6 (second quote on 5), 13 (first quote), 14 (third quote); Butler, *Butler's Book,* 896 (fourth quote); Higginson, *Cheerful Yesterdays,* 243–45; Brown, *The Negro in the American Rebellion,* 181–82 (fifth and sixth quote).

10. Whites and Long, eds., *Occupied Women,* 1–13; Frank and Whites, *The Household War,* 1–10; Glymph, *The Women's Fight,* 1–15; Daly, *The War after the War.*

11. McCurry, *Confederate Reckoning,* 9.

12. Whites and Long, eds., *Occupied Women,* 1–13; Frank and Whites, eds., *Household War,* 1–10.

13. Frank and Whites, eds., *Household War,* 1–10 (quote on 1); Whites and Long, eds., *Occupied Women,* 1–13. See also McCurry, *Confederate Reckoning;* Ruminski, *The Limits of Loyalty;* Ballantyne, "'Whenever the Yankees Were Gone, I was a Confederate,'" 36–67, and "Whose Hearth and Home?," 53–77.

14. Jefferson Davis's Farewell Address, Senate Chamber, U.S. Capitol, January 21, 1861, https://jeffersondavis.rice.edu/archives/documents/jefferson-davis-farewell-address; Georgia Declaration of Causes, https://www.battlefields.org/learn/primary-sources/declaration-causes -seceding-states; Benjamin Palmer, *The South: Her Peril and Her Duty,* 6–8; Moore, *Special Message of Thomas O. Moore. See also* James M. McPherson, *For Cause and Comrades: Why Men Fought in the Civil War;* Glymph, *The Women's Fight,* 22–23.

15. Sutherland, "Guerrilla Warfare, Democracy, and the Fate of the Confederacy," 259–61, 277–78.

16. Robertson, *The Red River Campaign and Its Toll,* 57–59; Beilein, *Bushwhackers;* Stith, *Extreme Civil War;* Sutherland, *A Savage Conflict;* McKnight and Myers, eds., *The Guerrilla Hunters;* Beilein and Hulbert, eds., *The Civil War Guerrilla.*

17. The standard political and military histories of Louisiana during the Civil War remain Bragg, *Louisiana in the Confederacy* and Winters, *The Civil War in Louisiana. See also* Johnson, *Red River Campaign;* White, *The Freedmen's Bureau in Louisiana;* Kerby, *Kirby Smith's Confederacy;* Dawson, *Army Generals and Reconstruction;* Hewitt, *Port Hudson;* Joiner, *One Damn Blunder from Beginning to End;* Prushankin, *A Crisis of Confederate Command;* Frazier, *Fire in the Cane Field* and *Thunder across the Swamp;* Cutrer, *Theater of a Separate War.*

18. Edwards, *Gendered Strife and Confusion,* 5; McCurry, *Confederate Reckoning.* For other excellent examples of community studies and social history, see Fisher, *War at Every Door;* Inscoe and McKinney, *The Heart of Confederate Appalachia;* McKenzie, *Lincolnites and Rebels;* Pierson, *Lt. Spalding in Civil War Louisiana;* Bynum, *The Long Shadow of the Civil War.*

19. Ash, *When the Yankees Came,* 89; Grimsley, *The Hard Hand of War;* Browning, *Shifting Loyalties;* Downs, *After Appomattox;* Lang, *In the Wake of War,* 1–14; Siddali, *From Property to Person,* 120–25; Sheehan-Dean, *The Calculus of Violence,* 1–11, 41–50, and *Reckoning with Rebellion,* 1–13. See also Edelstein, *Occupational Hazards;* Stirk, *The Politics of Military Occupation;* Reardon, *With a Sword in One Hand and Jomini in the Other;* Witt, *Lincoln's Code;* Blair, *With Malice Toward Some;* Dilbeck, *A More Civil War;* Clampitt, *Occupied Vicksburg;* Mathisen, *The Loyal Republic;* McCurry, *Women's War.*

20. Fox-Genovese, *Within the Plantation Household;* Clinton and Silber, eds., *Divided Houses;* Whites, *The Civil War as a Crisis in Gender;* Schwalm, *A Hard Fight For We;* Edwards, *Scarlett Doesn't*

Live Here Anymore; Faust, *Mothers of Invention;* Silber, *Gender and the Sectional Conflict;* McCurry, *Confederate Reckoning;* Whites and Long, eds., *Occupied Women;* McCurry, *Women's War;* Glymph, *Out of the House of Bondage* and *The Women's Fight;* Frank and Whites, eds., *Household War.*

21. McKnight and Myers, eds., *The Guerrilla Hunters,* 5; Foote, "Rethinking the Confederate Home Front," 446–65 (quote on 448). See also Fellman, *Inside War;* Grenier, *The First Way of War;* Sutherland, *A Savage Conflict;* Neely, "Guerrilla Warfare, Slavery, and the Hopes of the Confederacy," 376–412; Beilein, *Bushwackers;* Stith, *Extreme Civil War;* Bynum, *The Long Shadow of the Civil War,* x, 2, 9.

22. Bensel, *Yankee Leviathan,* 1–17; Neely, *Southern Rights,* 7–10. See also Vandiver, *Jefferson Davis and the Confederate State;* Thomas, *The Confederacy as a Revolutionary Experience;* Faust, *The Creation of Confederate Nationalism;* Escott, *After Secession,* and *Military Necessity;* Rable, *The Confederate Republic;* Quigley, *Shifting Grounds;* Bonner, *Confederate Political Economy;* McCurry, *Confederate Reckoning;* Pierson, *Free Hearts & Free Homes;* Balogh, *A Government Out of Sight;* Summers, *The Ordeal of Reunion;* Zuck, *Divided Sovereignties.*

1. TO RID THE COMMUNITY OF SUSPICIOUS PERSONS: THE MILITANT CONFEDERATE COMMUNITY IN SECESSION-ERA LOUISIANA

1. Winters, *The Civil War in Louisiana,* 3–4; *The Daily Picayune,* January 27, 1861; Richardson, *The Secret Service, the Field, the Dungeon, and the Escape,* 42; Sacher, "'Our Interest and Destiny Are the Same,'" 267.

2. For other discussions of divided loyalties and exacting wartime decisions, see Robertson, *The Red River Campaign and Its Toll,* 54; Ruminski, *The Limits of Loyalty,* 36–37; Ballantyne, "Whose Hearth and Home?," 53–77.

3. Sacher, *A Perfect War of Politics,* xi–xiv.

4. Stone, *Brokenburn,* 19.

5. Moore quote in Bragg, *Louisiana in the Confederacy,* 20–23; Sacher, *A Perfect War of Politics,* 259; McCrary, *Abraham and Reconstruction,* 54; Buman, "Two Histories, One Future," 276–281; Baggett, *The Scalawags,* 54–56; Watson, *Life in the Confederate Army,* 121–123.

6. Bragg, *Louisiana in the Confederacy,* 23; McCrary, *Abraham Lincoln and Reconstruction,* 54; *Acts Passed by the Fifth Legislature of the State of Louisiana, Second Session, held and Begun in the City of Baton Rouge, on the 21st of January, 1861,* 3–4.

7. Bragg, *Louisiana in the Confederacy,* 40–44.

8. Winters, *The Civil War in Louisiana,* 7–8; Stone, *Brokenburn,* 14, 20; Bragg, *Louisiana in the Confederacy,* 42. See also Stone, *Brokenburn,* 35–36; C. B. Thomas to Benjamin J. Lassing, January 7, 1864, Mss. 30, Historic New Orleans Collection (hereafter cited as HNOC); Watson, *Life in the Confederate Army,* 157–58.

9. Richardson, *The Secret Service,* 40–41.

10. Russell, *My Diary North and South,* 230, 253. For a similar disparaging account from a foreigner, see Stone, *Brokenburn,* 27.

11. Richardson, *The Secret Service,* 48–49 (first and third quotes); Palmer, *The South, Her Peril, and Her Duty,* 7–8, 16 (second quote); Monroe, "Bishop Palmer's Thanksgiving Day Address,"

107, 113; Winters, *The Civil War in Louisiana,* 8. See also Stone, *Brokenburn,* 24–25; Stearns, *Reminiscences of the Late War,* 15; Nguyen, "Keeping the Faith," 165–67.

12. Polk, *Extracts from the Journal of the Twenty-Third Annual Convention of the Protestant Episcopal Church,* 3, 11–12; Nguyen, "Keeping the Faith," 168. For an extensive look at southern defenses of a divinely ordained racial and gendered social order, see Farmer, *The Metaphysical Confederacy.*

13. Obert and Mattiacci, "Keeping Vigil," 600–616. For another perspective on how informal militias and vigilance committees used violence and coercion in cooperation with the formal state to discipline and conquer the western frontier of North America, see Dunbar-Ortiz, *Loaded.* See also Abrahams, *Vigilant Citizens;* Kirkpatrick, *UnCivil Disobedience.*

14. Sacher, *A Perfect Storm of Politics,* 259–79; McCrary, *Abraham Lincoln and Reconstruction,* 22–25. See also Grimsted, *American Mobbing.*

15. Richardson, *The Secret Service,* 57, 59–60. See also Pierson, *Mutiny at Fort Jackson,* 51–55.

16. Russell, *My Diary,* 230–33. See also Winters, *The Civil War in Louisiana,* 33–34.

17. Russell, *My Diary,* 239–40; Edwards, "The Thin Blue Line," 26–27. See also Derbes, "Prison Productions."

18. Russell, *My Diary,* 227, 253–54.

19. New Orleans *Daily Picayune,* June 11, 1861; Bragg, *Louisiana in the Confederacy,* 87–88; Winters, *The Civil War in Louisiana,* 22–28, 36–43.

20. Samuel G. Risk to Henry Bier, July 15, 1861, Henry Bier Correspondence, Mss. 6, HNOC; New Orleans *Daily Crescent,* September 6, 1861; Marianne Edwards letters, December 26, 1862, Mss. 1850, Louisiana and Lower Mississippi Valley Collections (hereafter cited as LLMVC); Bragg, *Louisiana in the Confederacy,* 87.

21. Southwood, *"Beauty and Booty,"* chapter 10 (quotes on 77); Bragg, *Louisiana in the Confederacy,* 89–91; Pierson, *Mutiny at Fort Jackson,* 56; New Orleans *Daily Crescent,* August 5, 15, 16, 1861; New Orleans *Price-Current,* October 5, 1861. See also LeGrand, *The Journal of Julia LeGrand,* 37–38.

22. Richardson, *The Secret Service,* 42; Russell, *My Diary,* 277.

23. Russell, *My Diary,* 229; *Sugar Planter,* January 26, 1861, page 2.

24. Russell, *My Diary,* 231–32, 239; Wyatt-Brown, *Southern Honor,* 34–45; Winters, *The Civil War in Louisiana,* 74–75; New Orleans Civil War Letter, Mss. 3309, LLMVC. See also LeGrand, *The Journal of Julia LeGrand,* 36–38.

25. Russell, *My Diary,* 250; Nathaniel Banks to William Seward, March 6, 1863, Department of the Gulf, Letter Sent, Volume 1, Entry 1738, Part 1, RG393, National Archives and Records Administration (hereafter cited as NARA); Shugg, *Origins of Class Struggle in Louisiana,* 171–176; Pierson, *Mutiny at Fort Jackson,* 38–39. See also Banks to Seward, March 27, 1863, Department of the Gulf, Letter Sent, Volume 1, Entry 1738, Part 1, RG393, NARA.

26. Bragg, *Louisiana in the Confederacy,* 62–63; Winters, *The Civil War in Louisiana,* 28–31; New Orleans *Daily Crescent,* September 30, 1861; Pierson, *Mutiny at Fort Jackson,* 61; U.S. War Department, *The War of the Rebellion* (hereafter cited as OR), Ser. IV, Vol. I, 753.

27. Russell, *My Diary,* 233, 239; McCrary, *Abraham Lincoln and Reconstruction,* 59; Pierson, *Mutiny at Fort Jackson,* 51. See also Stone, *Brokenburn,* 28; Robertson, *The Red River Campaign and Its Toll,* 29.

28. Richardson, *The Secret Service*, 53; Russell, *My Diary*, 227–29; Bragg, *Louisiana in the Confederacy*, 40. See also Hamilton, "The Confederate Sequestration Act."

29. Grivot quoted in Bragg, *Louisiana in the Confederacy*, 47; Russell, *My Diary*, 263–64; Stone, *Brokenburn*, 44; the *South-Western*, Wednesday, January 9, 1861, no. 22, page 2; *Sugar Planter*, Saturday, January 26, 1861, page 2; Tunnard, *A Southern Record*, 10–11; *Annual Report of the Adjutant General of the State of Louisiana for the Year Ending December 31, 1861, to the Governor*, 9–11; Winters, *The Civil War in Louisiana*, 21–22. See also *Shreveport Weekly News*, April 22, 1861.

30. *Sugar Planter*, January 26, 1861, page 2; Alexander Pugh Diary, February 22, April 18, April 20, 1861, Mss. 354, LLMVC; Alexandria *Constitutional*, January 5, 1861, quoted in Shugg, *Origins of Class Struggle in Louisiana*, 29.

31. Shreveport *South-Western*, August 21 and 28, 1861; Bragg, *Louisiana in the Confederacy*, 61–62. See also Winters, *The Civil War in Louisiana*, 72–73; Ash, *When the Yankees Came*, 3–5. For an example later in the war, see King, *No Pardons to Ask, Nor Apologies to Make*, 126.

32. New Orleans *Daily Picayune*, December 15, 1860; Shreveport *South-Western*, January 9, 1861; Stone, *Brokenburn*, 32; Ballantyne, "Whose Hearth and Home?," 56; Ash, *When the Yankees Came*, 11. See also Russell, *My Diary*, 279.

33. "Letter from the Atchafalaya Country," in the New Orleans *Daily Picayune*, July 6, 1861.

34. Stone, *Brokenburn*, 18; Russell, *My Diary*, 264–65.

35. Bragg, *Louisiana in the Confederacy*, 88; "Letter from the Atchafalaya Country," in the New Orleans *Daily Picayune* July 6, 1861; *Sugar Planter*, January 26, 1861, page 2; East Baton Rouge Parish Volunteer Fund letter, Mss. 1415, LLMVC; Winters, *The Civil War in Louisiana*, 77; Buman, "Two Histories, One Future," 283–87.

36. New Orleans *Daily Crescent*, September 16, 1861; Stone, *Brokenburn*, 18–19, 46–47; R. W. Stanley to Henry Bier, August 14, 1861, Henry Bier Correspondence, Mss. 6, HNOC. See also Winters, *The Civil War in Louisiana*, 26; Bond, *A Maryland Bride in the Deep South*, 201; Mary E. Stratton letter, January 27, 1861, Mss. 703, HNOC.

37. St. Tammany Parish Militia Slave Patrol Order, Mss. 4900, LLMVC; Winters, *The Civil War in Louisiana*, 31; Ripley, *Slaves and Freedmen in Civil War Louisiana*, 5–9.

38. Russell, *My Diary*, 293; New Orleans *Daily Crescent*, August 5, 1861; Hamilton, "The Confederate Sequestration Act"; McCrary, *Abraham Lincoln and Reconstruction*, 59–60, 79–80; Ballantyne, "Whose Hearth and Home?," 56–57; LeGrand, *The Journal of Julia LeGrand*, 49. For an extended analysis of Unionists in Louisiana, see Wetta, *The Louisiana Scalawags*, chapters 2 and 3; Butler, *True Blue*, introduction and chapter 1.

39. Bragg, *Louisiana in the Confederacy*, 25–26, 28. See Bragg, *Louisiana in the Confederacy*, 28–31; Winters, *The Civil War in Louisiana*, 12–13; Hyde, *Pistols and Politics*, 91; Shugg, *Origins of Class Struggle in Louisiana*, 167–68; Rable, *The Confederate Republic*, 59–63.

40. Richardson, *The Secret Service*, 72–77; Shugg, *Origins of Class Struggle in Louisiana*, 161–63, 170; Ballantyne, "Whose Hearth and Home?," 56. See also Alexandria *Constitutional*, March 9, 1861.

41. Russell, *My Diary*, 243, 250–52; McCrary, *Abraham Lincoln and Reconstruction*, 57–65.

42. Bragg, *Louisiana in the Confederacy*, 67–71; Russell, *My Diary*, 250; *Acts Passed by the Sixth Legislature of the State of Louisiana at Its First Session Held and Begun in the City of Baton Rouge on the 25th of November, 1861*, 45–46; Solomon, *The Civil War Diary of Clara Solomon*, 131; Winters, *The Civil War in Louisiana*, 55. For other examples of cash-poor Louisiana citizens, see Stone,

Brokenburn, 19; Sarah Lois Wadley diary, November 24, November 28, and December 13, 1860, Documenting the American South.

43. Bragg, *Louisiana in the Confederacy*, 72; New Orleans *Price Current*, March 22, 1862; New Orleans *Daily Picayune*, April 7, 1862.

44. Bragg, *Louisiana in the Confederacy*, 43–44; 93–94; *Acts Passed by the Sixth Legislature*, 12, 34, 40, 205–12; Pierson, *Mutiny at Fort Jackson*, 56–57; Hamilton, "The Confederate Sequestration Act"; McCrary, *Abraham Lincoln and Reconstruction*, 77–78. McCrary claims the stay law did pass, but only for the rural parishes.

45. Quote in Shugg, *Origins of Class Struggle in Louisiana*, 73–76, 78; *Acts Passed by the Sixth Legislature*, 68–69; Surdam, "Union Military Superiority and New Orleans's Economic Value to the Confederacy," 396–97. See also *OR*, Ser. III, Vol. 2, 725–27, 752.

46. Bragg, *Louisiana in the Confederacy*, 80–82; Russell, *My Diary*, 280; Surdam, "Union Military Superiority and New Orleans's Economic Value to the Confederacy," 399–404.

47. Pierson, *Mutiny at Fort Jackson*, 40–43, 51–53; Russell, *My Diary*, 250; Winters, *The Civil War in Louisiana*, 57–73; Quigley, *Shifting Grounds*, 197–98, 214.

48. Maj. Gen. Mansfield Lovell testimony, *OR*, Ser. I, Vol. 6, 556, 559–61; Buman, "Two Histories, One Future," 290.

49. Maj. Gen. Mansfield Lovell testimony, *OR*, Ser. I, Vol. 6, 561. See also Pierson, *Mutiny at Fort Jackson*, 15–30.

50. Winters, *The Civil War in Louisiana*, 34–35; Bell, *Revolution, Romanticism, and the Afro-Creole Protest Tradition in Louisiana*, 229–32; Ripley, *Slaves and Freedmen in Civil War Louisiana*, 103–5; *Official Copy of the Militia Law of Louisiana, adopted by the State Legislature, January 23, 1862*, 3; Hollandsworth, *The Louisiana Native Guards*, 8; Mills, "Patriotism Frustrated," 443–444. See also Glymph, "I'm a Radical Black Girl," 371–72.

51. *OR*, Ser. III, Vol. II, 728–31; New Orleans *Daily Crescent*, February 25, 1862; Bragg, *Louisiana in the Civil War*, 65–66.

52. *OR*, Ser. I, Vol. 6, 856–58, 860–61; Bragg, *Louisiana in the Confederacy*, 101–2; Pierson, *Mutiny at Fort Jackson*, 51, 57; Ash, *When the Yankees Came*, 14–15. See also King, *No Pardons to Ask, Nor Apologies to Make*, 1–3, 8; B. B. Smith diary, May 5, 1862, Tulane University Digital Library (hereafter cited as TUDL); Charles East, ed., *Sarah Morgan: The Civil War Diary of a Southern Woman*, 47–57 (hereafter cited as *Sarah Morgan Diary*).

53. *OR*, Ser. I, Vol. 6, 861; Pierson, *Mutiny at Fort Jackson*, 59–60.

54. Pierson, *Mutiny at Fort Jackson*, 7–21, 35–36, quote on 15.

2. DISORDER & DOMINION: BENJAMIN BUTLER & HIS WAR
OF OCCUPATION

1. Siddali, *From Property to Person*, 110–12; Grimsley, *The Hard Hand of War*, 7–11; McCrary, *Abraham Lincoln and Reconstruction*, 66–67; Bensel, *Yankee Leviathan*, 94–95. See also Blair, "Friend or Foe," 27; Downs, *After Appomattox*, 1–10; Rable, "Fighting for Reunion," 355–356.

2. Goss, *The War within the Union High Command*, xv–xvi, 140–42; Long, "(Mis)Remembering General Order No. 28" in Whites and Long, eds., *Occupied Women*, 21–30; Louis Gerteis,

for instance, refers to Butler's contraband policy in particular as "legal and practical rather than moral." Gerteis, *From Contraband to Freedman,* 13.

3. Holzman, *Stormy Ben Butler,* 228; Trefousse, *Ben Butler,* quotes on 177 and 256 respectively; West, *Lincoln's Scapegoat General,* xi–xiii, quote on xiii; Nash, *Stormy Petrel,* 7, 300, quote on 7; Nolan, *Benjamin Franklin Butler;* Hearn, *When the Devil Came Down to Dixie,* 1–3; Leonard, *Benjamin Franklin Butler,* xiv–xix, quote on xviii. For unfavorable assessments of Butler's character, see Holzman, *Stormy Ben Butler,* 10–11, 47, 232; Trefousse, *Ben Butler,* 122–134, 166–177; Nash, *Stormy Petrel,* 15–17, 173–177; Palmer and Carter, "Bruce Catton's Uncivil War on Benjamin Butler," 261–275; Lowenthal, *A Yankee Regiment in Confederate Louisiana,* 108; George Whittlesey, December 20, 1862, George Whittlesey letters, Mss. 2449, LLMVC.

4. Lowenthal, *A Yankee Regiment in Confederate Louisiana,* 25, 33; Long, "(Mis)Remembering General Order No. 28" in Whites and Long, eds., *Occupied Women,* 21–30; McCurry, *Confederate Reckoning,* 110; Sheehan-Dean, *The Calculus of Violence,* 110–14.

5. Grimsley, *The Hard Hand of War,* 1–10; Ripley, *Slaves and Freedmen in Civil War Louisiana,* 25–46.

6. Siddali, *From Property to Person,* 2–8.

7. Nolan, *Benjamin Franklin Butler,* x, 29–32, 46–47, 50–51, 56–61; Siddali, *From Property to Person,* 21–23, 52–53; Goss, *The War within the Union High Command,* 26–28, 140–42; Campbell, "There Is No Difference between a He and a She Adder in Their Venom," 9.

8. Butler, *Butler's Book,* 226–288; McCrary, *Abraham Lincoln and Reconstruction,* 70, 76. See also Butler, *Private and Public Correspondence of General Benjamin F. Butler* (hereafter cited as Correspondence), ed. Marshal, Vol. I, 43.

9. *OR,* Ser. 2, Vol. 1, 752; Ser. 1, Vol. 2, 52; Leonard, *Benjamin Franklin Butler,* 61–77; Campbell, "There Is No Difference between a He and a She Adder in Their Venom," 9–10; Nolan, *The Damnedest Yankee,* 97; Manning, *Troubled Refuge,* 32; Hearn, *When the Devil Came Down to Dixie,* 28–36; Siddali, *From Property to Person,* 8, 49–53, 136–41; Sheehan-Dean, *The Calculus of Violence,* 120–21; Goss, *The War within the Union High Command,* 36–37, 48, 80–83.

10. McCrary, *Abraham Lincoln and Reconstruction,* 77, 85–96, quote on 77; Goss, *The War within the Union High Command,* 140–42.

11. McCrary, *Abraham Lincoln and Reconstruction,* 69–71; Butler, *Correspondence,* Vol. I, 30; Siddali, *From Property to Person,* 52–53; Sheehan-Dean, *The Calculus of Violence,* 52–57, 120–21; Ripley, *Slaves and Freedmen in Civil War Louisiana,* 35–39, 102–6; Nolan, *The Damnedest Yankee,* 83; Gerteis, *From Contraband to Freedmen,* 65.

12. Leonard, *Benjamin Franklin Butler,* 84–86; McCrary, *Abraham Lincoln and Reconstruction,* 70; Surdam, "Union Military Superiority and New Orleans's Economic Value to the Confederacy," 406–8; Nolan, *The Damnedest Yankee,* 62–63, 85, 120.

13. Butler to Stanton, April 29, 1862, *OR,* Ser. I, Vol. 6, 503–505; Hearn, *When the Devil Came Down to Dixie,* 61–64; Bragg, *Louisiana in the Confederacy,* 103–106; Winters, *The Civil War in Louisiana,* 85–99; Butler, *Butler's Book,* 359–372; Morgan, *Sarah Morgan Diary,* 59.

14. Butler to Stanton, April 29, 1862, *OR,* Ser. I, Vol. 6, 503–505; Winters, *The Civil War in Louisiana,* 97–102; Hearn, *The Capture of New Orleans,* 244–248; Butler, *Correspondence,* Vol. I, 428.

15. Winters, *The Civil War in Louisiana,* 97–102; Hearn, *When the Devil Came Down to Dixie,* 72–75; Sheehan-Dean, *The Calculus of Violence,* 88; Parton, *General Butler in New Orleans,* 279–

82; Scott, "The Glory of the City Is Gone," 45–46. See also Alfred A. Parmenter Papers, May 13/ May 21, 1862, TUDL; B. B. Smith diary, May 2, May 3, May 4, May 8, May 14, and May 15, 1862, TUDL; Lowenthal, *A Yankee Regiment in Confederate Louisiana*, 61.

16. Butler, *Correspondence*, Vol. I, 433–36; Butler, *Butler's Book*, 373–85; B. B. Smith diary, May 16, 1862, TUDL. For an analysis of Butler's military operations, see Cutrer, *Theater of a Separate War*, chap. 10.

17. Winters, *The Civil War in Louisiana*, 134–35; New Orleans *Daily Picayune*, June 8, 1862; B. B. Smith diary, May 10 and May 21, 1862, TUDL; Edwards, "The Thin Blue Line," 49–50.

18. Butler, *Butler's Book*, 440; Butler, Special Orders No. 70, June 5, 1862, *OR*, Ser. I, Vol. 15, 469; Butler, *Correspondence*, Vol. I, 573–77; Hearn, *When the Devil Came*, 134–38. See also *OR*, Ser. I, Vol. 15, 465–68.

19. Grimsley, *Hard Hand of War*, 23–32; Sheehan-Dean, *The Calculus of Violence*, 84–89; Nolan, *The Damnedest Yankee*, 156–60. See also, Storey, "War's Domestic Corollary: Union Occupation Households in the Civil War South" in Frank and Whites, eds., *Household War*, 155–179.

20. Butler, *Butler's Book*, 437–44 (first quote on 440, second quote on 442); Haugen, "Patriotic Fervor," 192–93, 212–20; *New York Herald*, June 19, 1862.

21. Butler, *Butler's Book*, 539. For other evidence that Butler saw his role as protector of southern women and households, as long as they met respectable criteria, see Butler, *Butler's Book*, 423–25.

22. Butler, *Butler's Book*, 443–46; Nolan, *The Damnedest Yankee*, 156–60.

23. Hearn, *When the Devil Came Down to Dixie*, 42–43; Sheehan-Dean, *The Calculus of Violence*, 84–92. See also Nolan, *The Damnedest Yankee*, 166–68.

24. Leonard, *Benjamin Franklin Butler*, 90–91; Butler, *Butler's Book*, 418; Campbell, "There Is No Difference between a He and a She Adder in Their Venom," 5–24; Brill, "I Had the Men from the Start," 319–28; Edwards, "The Thin Blue Line," 62–64; Long, "(Mis)Remembering General Order No. 28" in Whites and Long, eds., *Occupied Women*, 17–32.

25. McCrary, *Abraham Lincoln and Reconstruction*, 76, 81; Sarah Butler to Harriet Heard, May 15, 1862, in Butler, *Correspondence*, Vol. I, 487; Storey, "War's Domestic Corollary" in Frank and Whites, eds., *Household War*, 157–58; Brill, "I Had the Men from the Start," 321–22. See also Butler's letters to his daughter about decorum and civility, March 25, 1861, Butler, *Correspondence*, Vol. I, 14; Nolan, *The Damnedest Yankee*, 81, 103; Edwards, "The Thin Blue Line," 62–64; Bond, *A Maryland Bride in the Deep South*, 219–20.

26. Campbell, "The Unmeaning Twaddle about Order 28," 11–30, and "There Is No Difference between a He and a She Adder in Their Venom," 17–18; McCurry, *Confederate Reckoning*, 104–16; Long, "(Mis)Remembering General Order No. 28," in Whites and Long, eds., *Occupied Women*, 17–32.

27. Grimsley, *The Hard Hand of War*, 38–39; Campbell, "The Unmeaning Twaddle about Order 28," 12, 20–21. See also McCurry, *Confederate Reckoning*, 110; Feimster, "Keeping a Disorderly House in Civil War Kentucky," 302–3; Brill, "I Had the Men from the Start," 321–23.

28. Monroe quotes in McCrary, *Abraham Lincoln and Reconstruction*, 80–82; Beauregard quote in McCurry, *Confederate Reckoning*, 111; Leonard, *Benjamin Franklin Butler*, 92–93; Long, "(Mis)Remembering General Order No. 28" in Whites and Long, eds., *Occupied Women*, 17–18; Butler, *Butler's Book*, 420, 425; B. B. Smith diary, May 22, 1862, TUDL.

29. McCurry, *Confederate Reckoning*, 110–16; Hearn, *When the Devil Came Down to Dixie*, 105–7; Butler, *Butler's Book*, 420; Campbell, "There Is No Difference between a He and a She Adder in Their Venom," 13; Long, "(Mis)Remembering General Order No. 28" in Whites and Long, eds., *Occupied Women*, 17–32.

30. Butler, *Butler's Book*, 405–6; Leonard, *Benjamin Franklin Butler*, 89–90; Nolan, *The Damnedest Yankee*, 163–65; Butler, *Correspondence*, Vol. I, 433; Doyle, "Nurseries of Treason," 164; Surdam, "Union Military Superiority and New Orleans's Economic Value to the Confederacy," 398–99.

31. McCurry, *Confederate Reckoning*, 110–14; Palmer, *The Oath of Allegiance to the United States, Discussed in Its Moral and Political Bearings*, 10–11; Campbell, "There Is No Difference between a He and a She Adder in Their Venom," 20–21.

32. Long, "(Mis)Remembering General Order No. 28" in Whites and Long, eds., *Occupied Women*, 17–32; Brill, "I Had the Men from the Start," 322–23; Butler, *Butler's Book*, 415–19, 450–52, 511–12.

33. Campbell, "The Unmeaning Twaddle about Order No. 28," 21–25, and "There Is No Difference between a He and a She Adder in Their Venom," 18–19; McCurry, *Confederate Reckoning*, 115–16; Nolan, *The Damnedest Yankee*, 169–70; Doyle, "Nurseries of Treason," 163; Leonard, *Benjamin Franklin Butler*, 97.

34. Bragg, *Louisiana in the Confederacy*, 117; Annie Jeter Carmouche memoir, 43, 40, LLMVC; Capers, *Occupied City*, 91; Marianne Edwards letters, December 26, 1862, LLMVC; Nolan, *The Damnedest Yankee*, 174–175; Nguyen, "Keeping the Faith," 168–170; Butler, General Orders No. 27, May 13, 1862, *OR*, Ser. I, Vol. 15, 426. See also Brackett, "Rewriting Domesticity, War, and Confederate Defeat," 42–43, 47–48; Hunter, "Late to the Dance," 303–304; Scott, "The Glory of the City Is Gone," 62; Van Alstyne, *Diary of an Enlisted Man*, 158.

35. McCrary, *Abraham Lincoln and Reconstruction*, 78–79; Nolan, *The Damnedest Yankee*, 174–76; Butler, *Correspondence*, Vol. II, 152–53; Butler, *Butler's Book*, 387–95, 403, 425–36; Leonard, *Benjamin Franklin Butler*, 122; B. B. Smith diary, May 11 and May 12, 1862, TUDL.

36. Butler, *Butler's Book*, 387–95, 403, 425–36; McCrary, *Abraham Lincoln and Reconstruction*, 78–79; Marianne Edwards letters, December 26, 1862, LLMVC; Goodwyne, "Business as Usual," 52–54; Lowenthal, *A Yankee Regiment in Confederate Louisiana*, 61–62. See also Nolan, *The Damnedest Yankee*, 183–86.

37. Butler, *Correspondence*, Vol. I, 435–36, 440; Military Commission, United States vs. A. B. Bacon, Sitting of May 15, 1862, Entry 1390, Part 4, RG 393, NARA; Hearn, *When the Devil Came Down to Dixie*, 100; Benjamin Butler to Jonas French, August 25, 1862, Entry 1390, Part 4, RG 393, NARA; McCrary, *Abraham Lincoln and Reconstruction*, 76–77; Ash, *When the Yankees Came*, 73–75.

38. Campbell, "The Unmeaning Twaddle about Order 28," 18, 21–22; McCurry, *Confederate Reckoning*, 110–16.

39. Butler to Weitzel, November 6, 1862, in Butler, *Correspondence*, Vol. II, 456–57; Lathrop, "The Lafourche District in 1862," 175–201.

40. Butler to Weitzel, November 6, 1862, in Butler, *Correspondence*, Vol. II, 457–58.

41. Butler to Weitzel, November 6, 1862, in Butler, *Correspondence*, Vol. II, 457–58.

42. Siddali, *From Property to Person*, 105–8. See also Hoffer, *Plessy v. Ferguson*, 17–18; Nolan, *The Damnedest Yankee*, 77.

43. Butler to Phelps, July 23 and July 30, 1862, Department of the Gulf, Letter Sent, Volume 1, Entry 1738, Part 1, RG393, NARA; Leonard, *Benjamin Franklin Butler*, 98–105; Gerteis, *From Contraband to Freedman*, 66–73; West, *Lincoln's Scapegoat General*, 176–85; Pritchard, "Moving toward Freedom?," 39–41.

44. McCrary, *Abraham Lincoln and Reconstruction*, 83–86; Butler, *Correspondence*, Vol. II, 153–54. Even after the war, Butler wrote that Phelps was a "crank upon the slavery question," Butler, *Butler's Book*, 488.

45. Leonard, *Benjamin Franklin Butler*, 105–8; McCrary, *Abraham Lincoln and Reconstruction*, 86–92; Chase to Butler, July 31, 1862, in Butler, *Correspondence*, Vol. II, 131–35; New Orleans *Daily Delta*, August 5, 1862; Messner, "Black Violence and White Response," 21–23, 27–31. See also Sheehan-Dean, *The Calculus of Violence*, 132–36, 155.

46. McCrary, *Abraham Lincoln and Reconstruction*, 89–92; Leonard, *Benjamin Franklin Butler*, 108–9; Hollandsworth, *The Louisiana Native Guards*, 16–17, 38.

47. Siddali, *From Property to Person*, 154–57; Sprague, *History of the 13th Infantry Regiment of Connecticut Volunteers*, 67; Oakes, *The Scorpion's Sting*, 16–17.

48. Butler, *Butler's Book*, 521–23; McCrary, *Abraham Lincoln and Reconstruction*, 91–94; Gerteis, *From Contraband to Freedman*, 68–72; Hollandsworth, *The Louisiana Native Guards*, 19–20.

49. McCrary, *Abraham Lincoln and Reconstruction*, 94–95, 108; Messner, "Black Violence and White Response," 31–34; Nolan, *The Damndest Yankee*, 199–205. See also Goodwyne, "Business as Usual"; Butler, *Butler's Book*, 521–23.

50. Butler, *Butler's Book*, 543–44.

51. Butler, *Butler's Book*, 545.

52. Butler, *Butler's Book*, 545–46; Sheehan-Dean, *The Calculus of Violence*, 146–52; McCurry, *Confederate Reckoning*, 257–59, 261–62; Oakes, *The Scorpion's Sting*, 104–7. See also Proclamation by the Confederate President, General Order No. 111, *OR*, Ser. 2, Vol. 5, 795–797.

53. Leonard, *Benjamin Franklin Butler*, 96–98; Campbell, "There Is No Difference Between a He and a She Adder in Their Venom," 23–24; Brown, *The Negro in the American Rebellion*, 177; Scott, "The Glory of the City Is Gone," 63–64; Hollandsworth, *Pretense of Glory*, 89, 95–99.

54. Butler, *Butler's Book*, 538.

55. Butler, *Butler's Book*, 540.

56. Butler, *Butler's Book*, 541; Lowenthal, *A Yankee Regiment in Confederate Louisiana*, 103.

57. Grimsley, *Hard Hand of War*, 1–10; McCrary, *Abraham Lincoln and Reconstruction*, 108–9.

58. Siddali, *From Property to Person*, 140–41; Zuck, *Divided Sovereignties*, 1–31.

3. ADMINISTERING (RE)UNION: COERCION & POLICY IN THE RANKS OF UNION OCCUPATION

1. William B. Allyn letter, November 25, 1862, Mss. 2941, LLMVC. See also Scott, "The Glory of the City Is Gone," 51–52; Cutrer, *Theater of a Separate War*, 183, 185; Howe, *Passages from the Life of Henry Warren Howe*, 59; Lowenthal, *A Yankee Regiment in Confederate Louisiana*, 62, 106, 125, 172, 204, 255.

2. William B. Allyn letter, November 25, 1862, LLMVC. See also Howe, *Passages from the Life of Henry Warren Howe*, 59.

3. Union Soldier Letter, April 22–24, 1863, Mss. 51, HNOC. See also Scott, "The Glory of the City Is Gone," 53–54; Duganne, *Camps and Prisons*, chap. 15; Howe, *Passages from the Life of Henry Warren Howe*, 59; Johns, *Life with the Forty-Ninth Massachusetts Volunteers*, 167–73; Martin Williston Papers, January 29, 1863, TUDL.

4. Sheehan-Dean, *The Calculus of Violence*, 92–94.

5. Ash, *When the Yankees Came*, 56–67, 76–92; Butler, *Butler's Book*, 540.

6. Lowenthal, *A Yankee Regiment in Confederate Louisiana*, 246, 255; Ballantyne, "Whose Hearth and Home?," 64–65; B. B. Smith diary, May 12, May 13, and June 17, 1862, TUDL. For examples of hospitable relationships, see Roland, *Louisiana Sugar Plantations during the Civil War*, 120.

7. McCrary, *Abraham Lincoln and Reconstruction*, 73.

8. Baton Rouge Civil War Broadside Collection, September 14, 1863, March 17, 1863, July 17, 1862, January 10, 1863, March 28, 1863, August 19, 1863, September 2, 1863, November 24, 1863, December 22, 1863, July 29, 1862, LLMVC. See also Scott, "The Glory of the City Is Gone," 59–60.

9. Butler, *Butler's Book*, 379–80; Winters, *The Civil War in Louisiana*, 73–74; A. J. Jonas to J. Tarbell, July 4, 1864; [J. W. Brown?] to Albert Stearns, April 8, 1864; S. E. Shepard to R. A. Cameron, February 21, 1865; H. Fitter to Provost Marshal at Brashear City, December 2, 1864; S. E. Shepard appointment contract, April 10, 1865; R. E. Jackson to E. J. Lewis, October 4, 1864; R. A. Cameron to E. J. Lewis, October 18, 1864; Nicholas W. Day to Albert Stearns, April 1, 1864; E. M. Wheelock to Albert Stearns, April 26, 1864; A. J. Bush testimony, November 6, 1864; R. A. Cameron to R. E. Jackson, February 1, 1865; S. E. Shepard to C. A. Miller, February 21, 1865; Q. J. Whitman to S. E. Shepard, April 28, 1865; C. L. Harris to E. J. Lewis, December 1, 1864; Bowen to Albert Stearns, March 31, 1864; Order to Brashear City Provost Marshal, July 27, 1864; Brashear City relief list, May 11, 1864; W. Cozzens to Albert Stearns, July 5, 1864; A. D. Barke to Brashear City Provost Marshal, September 28, 1863; Thomas M. Tucker to Albert Stearns, November 6, 1863; W. D. Miller to J. A. P. Hopkins, May 9, 1863; John McNeil, General Order No. 11, June 3, 1864; R. E. Jackson to Albert Stearns, June 6, 1864, Entry 1519, Department of the Gulf, Letters Received, Box 12, Part 4, RG 393, NARA. Bowen to Elias Dewey, December 1863; Nathaniel Banks, Special Order No. 8, April 4, 1864; N. T. Martin letter, September 21, 1864; Order to C. G. Brooks, April 24, 1865, Part 4, Entry 1515; Weed & Co contract with John D. Johnson, September 2, 1862; Patrick Conroy to Jonas French, undated, Entry 1390, Part 4; Provost Marshal Headquarters to Winslow Roberts, August 3, 1863, Entry 1516, Department of the Gulf, Letters Received, Box 2, Part 4, RG 393, NARA.

10. R. E. Jackson to Albert Stearns, June 6, 1864; Henry S. Pierson to Albert Stearns, January 8, 1864; Bowen to Albert Stearns, September 4, 1863, all in Entry 1519, Department of the Gulf, Letters Received, Box 12, Part 4, RG 393, NARA; William Smith letters, December 21 and December 29, 1862, TUDL; John De Forest, *A Volunteer's Adventures*, 39–40.

11. Mills H. Barnard letters, June 14, 1863, LLMVC. See also James T. Wallace diary, March 24, 1865, SHC.

12. Davis and Tremmel, *Parole, Pardon, Pass and Amnesty Documents of the Civil War*, 43–44; Butler, *Correspondence*, Vol. I, 574–76; McCrary, *Abraham Lincoln and Reconstruction*, 95–97;

Blair, *With Malice toward Some,* 128–59, quote on 129; Ruminski, *The Limits of Loyalty,* 42, 50; Wyatt-Brown, *Southern Honor,* 55–59. See also Ash, *When the Yankees Came,* 46; Zuck, *Divided Sovereignties,* 27–29.

13. Davis and Tremmel, *Parole, Pardon, Pass and Amnesty Documents of the Civil War,* 5–7.

14. John McNeil, General Order No. 11, June 3, 1864, Entry 1519; H. O. Bradley to St. Charles Provost Marshal, August 3, 1864, Part 4, Entry 1515, RG 393 NARA; Haynes, *A Thrilling Narrative,* 55–56 (quotes on 55); Sherman to Irwin, March 28, 1863, *OR,* Ser. I, Vol. 15, 696. See also Nicholas W. Day to Albert Stearns, April 1, 1864, Entry 1519; Patrick Conroy to Jonas French, undated, Entry 1390, Part 4, RG393, NARA; Scott, "The Glory of the City Is Gone," 52; Bosson, *History of the Forty-Second Regiment Infantry,* 241; Hepworth, *The Whip, Hoe, and Sword,* 23. For discussions over flexible loyalties among southerners under occupation, see Ballantyne, "Whose Hearth and Home?," 55–56; Ballantyne, "Whenever the Yankees Were Gone, I Was a Confederate," 49–50, and *Shifting Loyalties,* 4–5, 35, 129, 149–72; King, *No Pardons to Ask, Nor Apologies to Make,* 97–98; Lowenthal, *A Yankee Regiment in Confederate Louisiana,* 73.

15. Statement of Francis H. Brinkman and Francis Silwersser, November 6, 1862, Entry 1390, Part 4, RG393, NARA. See also L. O. Domell to Burke, January 5, 1865, Entry 1678, Part 4, RG393, NARA; George Shepley, Special Order No. 4, September 2, 1862; Special Order No. 46, March 3, 1863, Special Executive Orders: 1862–1864, Microfilm P1975–036, Louisiana State Archives (hereafter cited as LSA); Sheehan-Dean, *The Calculus of Violence,* 104–5; Blair, *With Malice toward Some,* 137–47; Rubin, *A Shattered Nation,* 94–99; Letter from Henry G. Gore to Isa Lund, March 11, 1863, in Alfred S. Lippman letters, 1848–1866, TUDL.

16. Henry L. Pierson to George S. Darling, April 18, 1864, Entry 1516, Department of the Gulf, Letters Received, Box 2, Part 4, RG 393, NARA. See also Wyatt-Brown, *Southern Honor,* 55–59; Inscoe and McKinney, *The Heart of Confederate Appalachia;* McKenzie, *Lincolnites and Rebels;* Ballantyne, "Whose Hearth and Home?" and "Whenever the Yankees Were Gone, I Was a Confederate"; Ruminski, *The Limits of Loyalty,* 42.

17. Sterkx, *The Free Negro in Antebellum Louisiana,* 106–108; Joseph Ballister to Jonas French, December 11, 1862; William M. and Sarah A. Pickard letter, November 15, 1864, Part 4, Entry 1515; N. G. Retterton to Jonas French, December 6, 1862; Albert Baldwin to Jonas French, November 3, 1862, Entry 1390, Part 4, RG393, NARA. See also, J. Curry to Benjamin Butler, May 10, 1862, Entry 1390, Part 4, RG393, NARA.

18. J. H. Burris letter, undated 1862; Henry Baggett letter, undated 1862; Letter to Benjamin Butler, November 11, 1862; Sillvester Cameron to Jonas French, July 25, 1862, Entry 1390, Part 4, RG393, NARA. See also Daniel Conway to Jonas French, June 3, 1862, Entry 1390, Part 4, RG393, NARA.

19. Peter Becker to Jonas H. French, October 27, 1862; Maurice Adams to Jonas French, December 1, 1862; E. Baxter to Jonas French, October 25, 1862; D. Carrothers to Jonas French, May 27, 1862; Louis Carella to Jonas French, July 3, 1862, all in Entry 1390, Part 4, RG393, NARA. See also Elisha Bills to Jonas French, August 26, 1862; G. W. Henry to Jonas French, September 4, 1862; E. T. Burnham to Jonas French, October 9, 1862; J. P. Bishop to Jonas French, October 11, 1862; Samuel Winn to Jonas French, October 23, 1862; J. M. Birou to Jonas French, October 21, 1862; A. F. Cochran to Jonas French, June 27, 1862; C. J. Cushman to Jonas French, August 19, 1862, all in Entry 1390, Part 4, RG393, NARA; Edwards, "The Thin Blue Line," 45–46.

20. Fred Courret to Weitzel, September 5, 1862; Frederic Collins to Jonas French, June 4, 1862, Entry 1390, Part 4, RG393, NARA.

21. James Bowen to J. L. King, August 12, 1863; St. John the Baptist Parish Provost Marshal to George S. Darling, January 24, 1865; Harai Robinson to George S. Darling, August 6 and August 23, 1864; F. A. Starring to George Darling, October 25, 1864; James Bowen to John P. Lowell, August 12, 1863; To Commanding Officer of Provost Guard Brashear City, July 27, 1864, Entry 1519; C. H. Miller Circular, November 2, 1864, Entry 1516, Department of the Gulf, Letters Received, Box 2, Part 4, RG 393, NARA.

22. George Shepley, Special Order No. 55, March 27, 1863, Special Executive Orders: 1862–1864, Microfilm P1975–036, LSA; B. Robinson to J. Hopkins, May 8, 1863; James Duane to J. Hopkins, May 9, 1863; W. D. Miller to J. Hopkins, May 9, 1863; Hy White to J. Hopkins, May 9, 1863, Entry 1519, RG393, NARA. See also Butler, *Butler's Book,* 382, 449; J. Elliot Smith to Stephen Hoyt, February 13, 1864, Mss. 654, HNOC.

23. Albert Stearns to Halibird, November 28, 1863, Entry 1668, Box 1, Part 4, RG393, NARA; George Shepley, Special Order No. 3, September 1, 1862; Special Order No. 42, October 17, 1862; Special Order No. 36, February 19, 1863; Special Order No. 24, September 19, 1862; Special Order No. 26, September 19, 1862, Special Executive Orders: 1862–1864, Microfilm P1975–036, LSA.

24. George Shepley, Special Order No. 54, November 11, 1862; Special Order No. 56, November 13, 1862; Special Order No. 60, November 22, 1862; Special Order No. 61, November 26, 1862; Special Order No. 62, November 26, 1862; Special Order No. 63, November 26, 1862; Special Order No. 64, November 27, 1862; Special Order No. 68, November 28, 1862; Special Order No. 73, December 11, 1862; Special Order No. 81, December 22, 1862; Special Order No. 91, December 31, 1862; Special Order No. 5, January 6, 1863; Special Order No. 7, January 7, 1863; Special Order No. 9, January 10, 1863; Special Order No. 23, February 4, 1863; Special Order No. 26, February 6, 1863; Special Order No. 18, January 28, 1863, Special Executive Orders: 1862–1864, Microfilm P1975–036, LSA. See also Special Order No. 38, October 13, 1862; Special Order No. 65, November 27, 1862; Special Order No. 90, December 30, 1862; Special Order No. 1, January 3, 1863; Special Order No. 22, February 3, 1863; Special Order No. 49, March 10, 1863; Special Order No. 58, April 2, 1863; Special Order No. 64, May 2, 1863; Special Order No. 112, June 25, 1863; Special Order No. 123, July 18, 1863; Special Order No. 125, September 10, 1863; Special Order No. 135, September 25, 1863; Special Order No. 137, October 2, 1863; Special Order No. 145, November 3, 1863; Special Order No. 158, December 10, 1863; Special Order No. 2, January 2, 1864; Special Order No. 12, February 9, 1864, Special Executive Orders: 1862–1864, Microfilm P1975–036, LSA.

25. George Shepley, Special Order No. 26, September 19, 1862; Special Order No. 89, December 29, 1862; Special Order No. 25, February 5, 1863; Special Order No. 43, February 28, 1863; Special Order No. 113, June 26, 1863, Special Executive Orders: 1862–1864, Microfilm P1975–036, LSA.

26. Rable, *Damn Yankees!,* 1–8, 49–67; McCurry, *Confederate Reckoning,* 111–12; Blair, *With Malice toward Some,* 128–59. See also, Zuck, *Divided Sovereignties,* 28; Ash, *When the Yankees Came,* 114.

27. George Shepley, Special Order No. 71, December 2, 1862; Special Order No. 60, April 4, 1863; Special Order No. 163, December 17, 1863, Special Executive Orders: 1862–1864, Microfilm P1975–036, LSA; E. Everett to Albert Stearns, September 9, 1864; R. E. Jackson to E. J. Lewis, October 4, 1864; George B. Drake to P. C. Haines, September 29, 1864, Entry 1519, RG393, NARA.

28. Grimsley, *The Hard Hand of War,* 174; Sheehan-Dean, *The Calculus of Violence,* 96–99, 120–26; Blair, *With Malice toward Some,* 131–37; Poche, *A Louisiana Confederate,* 219; McIntyre, *Federals on the Frontier,* 223; Lowenthal, *A Yankee Regiment in Confederate Louisiana,* 69; De Forest, *A Volunteer's Adventures,* 19.

29. Chase B. Child to Jonas French, June 7, 1862, Entry 1390, Part 4; George Shepley, Special Order No. 23, September 18, 1862, Special Executive Orders: 1862–1864, Microfilm P1975–036 LSA; Davis and Tremmel, *Parole, Pardon, Pass and Amnesty Documents,* 43; P. J. Conway to Jonas French, July 15, 1862, July 18, 1862; Augite Costa to Jonas French, July 31, 1862, Entry 1390, Part 4, RG393, NARA; Sheehan-Dean, *The Calculus of Violence,* 1–11, 180–81. See also C. N. Couant to T. C. Stafford, June 5, 1862; Property list of Charles M. Conrad, undated 1862, Entry 1390, Part 4, RG393, NARA.

30. George Shepley, Special Order No. 42, October 17, 1862, Special Executive Orders: 1862–1864, Microfilm P1975–036, LSA; James Bowen to George Darling, February 12, 1864; F. A. Starring circular, April 26, 1865; C. H. Miller report, December 30, 1864; B. Boggs to C. H. Miller, December 19, 1864, Entry 1516, Box 2, Part 4, RG393, NARA. See also circulars from August 25, 1864; September 6, 1864; March 8, 15, and 17, 1865; William N. Williams to George S. Darling, February 27, 1864; Extract from the Police Jury Law Parish of St. John the Baptist La. Section Fifth, undated, all in Entry 1516, Box 2, Part 4, RG 393, NARA; H. Fitter to Provost Marshal at Brashear City, December 2, 1864, Entry 1519, RG393, NARA; George Shepley, Special Order No. 3, September 1, 1862, Special Executive Orders: 1862–1864, Microfilm P1975–036, LSA; Order of Provost Marshal Edward Page, January 5, 1863, printed in *The Era,* February 15, 1863, page 4; A. Elfield to D. C. Houston, February 15, 1864, *OR,* Ser. I, Vol. 34, pt. 2, 331–32; Carpenter, *History of the Eighth Regiment Vermont Volunteers,* 40–41.

31. August Rohn to Jonas French, October 23, 1862; J. J. Bryant to Nathaniel Banks, December 27, 1862; John A. Matthews to Jonas French, November 10, 1862; William Brown to Jonas French, October 23, 1862, all in Entry 1390, Part 4, RG393, NARA. See also Will Coppell to British Consulate, June 6, 1862, Entry 1390, Part 4, RG393, NARA.

32. General Services Administration, *Hard Labor;* George Shepley, Special Order No. 3, September 1, 1862 (first quote); Special Order No. 6, September 4, 1862; Special Order No. 11, September 10, 1862, all in Special Executive Orders: 1862–1864, Microfilm P1975–036, LSA; Lowenthal, *A Yankee Regiment in Confederate Louisiana,* 73 (second quote). See also George Shepley, Special Order No. 16, September 12, 1862, and Special Order No. 21, September 18, 1862, all in Special Executive Orders: 1862–1864, Microfilm P1975–036, LSA.

33. George Shepley, Special Order No. 17, September 15, 1862; Special Order No. 37, October 11, 1862; Special Order No. 28, September 23, 1862; Special Order No. 77, May 19, 1863; Special Order No. 48, October 24, 1862; Special Order No. 49, October 27, 1862; Special Order No. 74, December 11, 1862; Special Order No. 75, December 11, 1862; Special Order No. 76, December 12, 1862; Special Order No. 78, December 18, 1862; Special Order No. 2, January 2, 1863; Special Order No. 4, January 6, 1863; Special Order No. 29, February 11, 1863; Special Order No. 34, February 17, 1863; Special Order No. 38, February 21, 1863; Special Order No. 53, March 19, 1863; Special Order No. 63, May 1, 1863; Special Order No. 65, May 4, 1863; Special Order No. 72, May 13, 1863; Special Order No. 6, January 16, 1864, all in Special Executive Orders: 1862–1864, Microfilm P1975–036, LSA; James Cogan to Benjamin Butler, May 7, 1862, Entry 1390, Part 4, RG393,

NARA. See also Special Order No. 36, October 4, 1862; Special Order No. 40, October 15, 1862; Special Order No. 41, October 16, 1862; Special Order No. 43, October 17, 1862; Special Order No. 45, October 20, 1862; Special Order No. 55, November 12, 1862; Special Order No. 58, November 17, 1862; Special Order No. 80, December 22, 1862; Special Order No. 6, January 6, 1863; Special Order No. 27, February 6, 1863; Special Order No. 31, February 16, 1863; Special Order No. 42, February 28, 1863; Special Order No. 85, June 1, 1863; Special Order No. 15, February 11, 1864, all in Special Executive Orders: 1862–1864, Microfilm P1975–036, LSA.

34. George Shepley, Special Order No. 12, September 10, 1862; Special Order No. 52, November 11, 1862; C. H. Schaefer to R. F. Braden, February 8, 1865, Entry 1668, Box 1, Part 4, RG393, NARA; George Shepley, Special Order No. 69, May 11, 1863, Special Executive Orders: 1862–1864, Microfilm P1975–036, LSA. See also George Shepley, Special Order No. 59, November 21, 1862; Special Order No. 69, November 29, 1862, Special Executive Orders: 1862–1864, Microfilm P1975–036, LSA; Derbes, "Prison Productions," 40–64.

35. George Shepley, Special Order No. 120, July 9, 1863, and Special Order No. 144, October 31, 1863, both in Special Executive Orders: 1862–1864, Microfilm P1975–036, LSA; Provost Marshal to J. S. Eakins, September 17, 1864; Provost Marshal to J. S. Eakins, October 8, 1864; Harai Robinson to Keeper of Police Jail, October 19, 1864; Provost Marshal Headquarters to Keeper of Police Jail, January 14, 1865; R. A. Alexander to Police Jail, February 22, 1865; C. H. Schaefer to R. F. Braden, February 6, 1865, all in Entry 1668, Box 1, Part 4; R. A. Cameron to R. E. Jackson, February 1, 1865, Entry 1519, NARA. See also Provost Marshal to J. S. Eakins, February 14, 1865, and Silas Harmon to R. F. Braden, April 18, 1865, both in Entry 1668, Box 1, Part 4, RG393, NARA; Paine, *A Wisconsin Yankee in Confederate Bayou Country,* 49.

36. Pemberton, "Enforcing Gender," 151–59, 166–68; Long, "(Mis)Remembering General Order No. 28" in Whites and Long, eds., *Occupied Women,* 17–32.

37. Pemberton, "Enforcing Gender," 151–59, 166–68; Foucault, *Discipline & Punish,* 298. For examples of Union officers and soldiers under arrest in the Department of the Gulf, see Bacon, *Among the Cotton Thieves,* chaps. 1 and 2; Paine, *A Wisconsin Yankee,* chap. 5; Alfred A. Parmenter Papers, May 13, 1862, TUDL; David W. James diary, February 25, 1864, TUDL; N. P. Banks to Thomas Durant, August 31, 1863, Nathaniel P. Banks letter book, Mss. 2326, LLMVC.

38. Butler, *Butler's Book,* 387–95, 403, 425–36; Leonard, *Benjamin Franklin Butler,* 88–89; *OR,* Ser. I, Vol. 15, 462–63, 538–39, 558, 607; De Forest, *A Volunteer's Adventures,* 21; Winters, *The Civil War in Louisiana,* 126–27, Denison quote on 126; Hunter, "The Politics of Resentment," 190, 198; Scott, "The Glory of the City Is Gone," 49–50. Butler claimed 32,400 families were provided for, and "these were all poor whites; the blacks were otherwise provided for." Butler, *Butler's Book,* 393.

39. James Bowen to George Darling, February 8, 1864, Entry 1516, Department of the Gulf, Letters Received, Box 2, Part 4, RG 393, NARA; Thomas W. Sherman, General Order No. 21, July 20, 1864, Entry 1519, RG393, NARA. See also B. B. Smith diary, May 27, 1862, TUDL.

40. Obert and Mattiacci, "Keeping Vigil," 606; Banks to Bowen, May 2, 1863, Department of the Gulf, Letter Sent, Volume 1, Entry 1738, Part 1, RG393, NARA; May 5, 1863, Josephine Moore diary, Frank Little Richardson Papers, SHC; George Shepley, Special Order No. 81, May 23, 1863, Special Executive Orders: 1862–1864, Microfilm P1975–036, LSA. See also Sheehan-Dean, *The Calculus of Violence,* 203–20; Blair, *With Malice toward Some,* 147–50, 159.

41. Ash, *When the Yankees Came,* 114; Bell, *Revolution, Romanticism, and the Afro-Creole Protest Tradition in Louisiana,* 123–36; Civil War New Orleans Orphanages 1863 receipts, Mss. 3913, LLMVC; George Shepley, Special Order No. 59, April 4, 1863; Special Order No. 78, May 20, 1863; Special Order No. 118, July 2, 1863; Special Order 128, September 18, 1863; Special Order 142, October 24, 1863; Special Order No. 159, December 11, 1863; Special Order 8, January 29, 1864; Special Order 22, February 26, 1864, Special Executive Orders: 1862–1864, Microfilm P1975–036, LSA; Post Head-Quarters Relief List, Brashear City, May 11, 1864, Entry 1519, RG393, NARA.

42. Michot, "War Is Still Raging in This Part of the Country," 172–173; Nolan, *The Damnedest Yankee,* 171–176.

43. James Bowen to Captain Lovell, August 27, 1863; James Bowen to George S. Denison, September 12, 1863, Entry 1519; James Bowen to George Darling, March 9, 1864; Stephen A. Hurlbut Circular, November 26, 1864; Special Order No. 3, January 27, 1865, Entry 1516, Department of the Gulf, Letters Received, Box 2, Part 4, RG 393, NARA. See also James Bowen to George S. Darling, April 11, 1864, Entry 1516, Box 2, Part 4; Albert Stearns to N. W. Day, February 8, 1864, Entry 1668, Box 1, Part 4, RG393, NARA; Order of Provost Marshal Edward Page, January 5, 1863 in *The Era,* February 15, 1863, page 4. See also Marten, "The Making of a Carpetbagger," 147–48.

44. Baton Rouge Civil War Broadside Collection, August 17, 1863, LLMVC. See also Alfred A. Parmenter Papers, June 27, 1862, TUDL.

45. Baton Rouge Civil War Broadside Collection, August 17, 1863; Hermitage Plantation receipts, March 23, 1864, April 13, 1864, May 20, 1864, June 3, 1864, August 22, 1864, June 4, 1864, September 14, 1864, October 19, 1864, Hermitage Plantation papers, SHC; George Shepley, Special Order No. 50, November 1, 1862, Special Executive Orders: 1862–1864, Microfilm P1975–036, LSA; Van Alstyne, *Diary of an Enlisted Man,* 73–74.

46. Lang, *In the Wake of War,* 83–97.

47. Banks to C. Grover, March 17 and 18, 1863, Department of the Gulf, Letter Sent, Volume 1, Entry 1738, Part 1, RG393, NARA; James Bowen to George Darling, April 1 and 4, 1864, Entry 1516, Department of the Gulf, Letters Received, Box 2, Part 4; James Bowen, Special Order No. 28, March 15, 1864; James Bowen to George Darling, March 16, 1864; N. C. Mitchell to George Darling, November 8 and 10, 1864, Entry 1516, Department of the Gulf, Letters Received, Box 2, Part 4, RG 393, NARA.

48. McCrary, *Abraham Lincoln and Reconstruction,* 76–77; Banks to Jerrard, April 29, 1863; Banks to S. H. Stafford, March 2, 1863; Banks to C. Grover, March 17, 1863; Banks to 1st New Hampshire Commanding Officer, July 24, 1863; Banks to Lewis M. Beck, July 24, 1863, Department of the Gulf, Letter Sent, Volume 1, Entry 1738, Part 1, RG393, NARA. See also Van Alstyne, *Diary of an Enlisted Man,* 170–71; Hollandsworth, *The Louisiana Native Guards,* 37–38; Paine, *A Wisconsin Yankee,* 74–75.

49. William H. Stewart diary, March 14 and 19, 1864, June 7, 1864, SHC; De Forest, *A Volunteer's Adventures,* 73, 76; Pellet, *History of the 114th Regiment,* 73; Ash, *When the Yankees Came,* 190–94; Johnson, *Red River Campaign,* 236, 268–72. See also James T. Wallace diary, April 3, 1864, SHC; Sarah Lois Wadley diary, April 15, 1864, Documenting the American South; Dollar, "The Red River Campaign, Natchitoches Parish, Louisiana," 411–32; *OR,* Ser. I, Vol. 34, pt. 3, 307; Johns, *Life with the Forty-Ninth Massachusetts Volunteers,* 190–92; J. Harvey Brown, April 27, 1863, J. Harvey Brown letters, TUDL.

50. William H. Stewart diary, March 15 and 19, April 3, 7, 8, and 14, 1864, SHC; Grimsley, *The Hard Hand of War*, 185, 202–4, 213; Sheehan-Dean, *The Calculus of Violence*, 97–99. See also Sutherland, "Guerrilla Warfare, Democracy, and the Fate of the Confederacy," 290; Moors, *History of the Fifty-second Regiment Massachusetts Volunteers*, 44–45; Stevens, *History of the Fiftieth Regiment of Infantry Massachusetts Volunteer Militia*, 86–89; Smith, *Leaves from a Soldier's Diary*, 32–33.

51. Civil War Broadside Collection, January 10, 1863, January 2, 1864, LLMVC; James V. Pitt to James M. Gee, December 26, 1864, Entry 1678, Part 4, RG393, NARA; Ripley, *Slaves and Freedmen in Civil War Louisiana*, 93. See also James T. Wallace diary, March 24, 1865; Ellen Louise Power diary, June 23, 1863, SHC; LeGrand, *The Journal of Julia LeGrand*, 47.

52. Frank, "The Union War on Women" in McKnight and Myers, eds., *The Guerrilla Hunters*, quote on 176; William H. Stewart diary, March 14, 19, and 25, 1864, April 3, 1864, SHC; Grimsley, *The Hard Hand of War*, 202–4. See also Frank, *The Civilian War*; Stearns, *Reminiscences of the Late War*, 11, 26; Ash, *When the Yankees Came*, 190; Beecher, *Record of the 114th Regiment, N.Y.S.V.*, 148–49; Poche, *A Louisiana Confederate*, 55–56.

53. Michot, "War Is Still Raging," 162; A. Robinson to John Burke, December 21, 1864; John Burke to Rayne, December 16, 1864; D. O. Domell to J. Burke, October 18, 1864; Letter to J. Burke, December 13, 1864; J. H. Bayou to J. Burke, January 6, 1865, Entry 1678, Part 4; C. L. Harris to Albert Stearns, July 11, 1864, Entry 1519, RG393, NARA. See also Leonard, *Benjamin Franklin Butler*, 94–95; Ash, *When the Yankees Came*, 45–46, 79, 83; Banks to Commanding Officer at Plaquemine, La., January 20, 1864, and Banks to E. G. Beckwith, February 8, 1864, both in Nathaniel P. Banks letter book, LLMVC.

54. W. D. Miller to J. A. P. Hopkins, May 9, 1863, Entry 1519, RG393, NARA. See also the *Times-Picayune*, January 4, 1863, page 3; LeGrand, *The Journal of Julia LeGrand*, 59; Paine, *A Wisconsin Yankee*, 120–21; Ewer, *The Third Massachusetts Cavalry in the War for the Union*, 54; Howe, *Passages from the Life of Henry Warren Howe*, 36.

55. Nathaniel Banks to H. M. Porter, March 24, 1863; Banks to Thomas W. Sherman, April 6, 1863; Banks to L. Goodrich, June 2, 1863; Banks to Commanding Officer Baton Rouge, September 18, 1863; A.A.A. General to Chief of Police, September 18, 1863, all in Entry 1738, Department of the Gulf, Letter Sent, Volume 1, Part 1, RG393, NARA. See also George L. Andrews to C. P. Stone, January 11, 1864, *OR*, Ser. I, Vol. 34, pt. 2, 56; Kinsley, *Diary of Christian Soldier*, 96, 98; William Smith letters, March 23, 1863, TUDL.

56. George Wheaton to unnamed officer, October 22, 1863, Entry 1519, RG393, NARA; Nathaniel Banks, General Order No. 21, March 7, 1863, *OR*, Ser. I, Vol. 15, 690–91. See also Sheehan-Dean, *The Calculus of Violence*, 96–99, 106, 207–20; Stearns, *Reminiscences of the Late War*, 14, 18–19, 25; Duganne, *Camps and Prisons*, 29–30; Morgan, *Sarah Morgan Diary*, 91.

57. Michot, "War Is Still Raging," 163, 173; Sutherland, *A Savage Conflict*, 73–74, 215–17; Frazier, *Fire in the Cane Field*, 158, 165–68; De Forest, *A Volunteer's Adventures*, 28–29; Edmonds, *Yankee Autumn in Acadiana*, 233–35; Gudmestad, "Elusive Victory," 97–98. See also Frazier, "Out of Stinking Distance," in *Guerrillas, Unionists, and Violence on the Confederate Home Front*, ed. Sutherland, 155; Sheehan-Dean, *The Calculus of Violence*, 97–99; B. B. Smith diary, June 2, June 25, and July 25, 1862, TUDL; *Sarah Morgan Diary*, 86–89.

58. Lang, *In the Wake of War*, 105–28; Michot, "War Is Still Raging," 160; B. B. Smith diary,

June 7, June 8, June 9, June 12, and June 13, 1862, TUDL. See also Sheehan-Dean, *The Calculus of Violence*, 72–81; Blair, *With Malice toward Some*, 150; Michael Fellman, *Inside War*, 38–43, 52–65; Stith, *Extreme Civil War*, chap. 4; Beilein, *Bushwhackers*, 165–88.

59. Office of Provost Marshal General to Winslow Roberts, August 27, 1863; Henry L. Pierson to George S. Darling, March 28, 1864, Entry 1516, Department of the Gulf, Letters Received, Box 2, Part 4, RG 393, NARA; Michot, "War Is Still Raging," 166–68. For an example of desertion from Union to Confederate ranks, see Affidavit of Alfred Stewart, February 3, 1864, Entry 1519, RG393, NARA.

60. Charles Darwin Elliot diary, March 19, 1864, #5457-z, SHC; Russel P. Turst to John Burke, November 19, 1864, Entry 1678, Part 4; Emile H. Brie to Jonas H. French, October 9, 1862; Statement of Thomas Castill, June 10, 1862, Entry 1390, Part 4; Albert Stearns to J. Tarbell, November 6, 1863; R. A. Cameron to E. J. Lewis, October 23, 1864; Nicholas W. Day to Albert Stearns, April 1, 1864, Entry 1519, RG393, NARA; George Shepley, Special Order No. 93, June 8, 1863, Special Order No. 101, June 12, 1863, Special Executive Orders: 1862–1864, Microfilm P1975–036, LSA; Michot, "War Is Still Raging," 174. See also Shepley, Special Order No. 119, July 9, 1863, Special Executive Orders: 1862–1864, Microfilm P1975–036, LSA. See also Powers, *The Story of the Thirty Eighth Regiment of Massachusetts Volunteers*, 129–30.

61. George Shepley, Special Order No. 32, September 29, 1862, Special Executive Orders: 1862–1864, Microfilm P1975–036, LSA; W. W. Bullock to J. H. French, October 6, 1862, Entry 1390, Part 4, RG393, NARA; George Shepley, Special Order No. 122, July 16, 1863, Special Executive Orders: 1862–1864, Microfilm P1975–036, LSA.

62. Regulations for the Patrol of the Parish of St. John the Baptist, Left Bank, undated, Entry 1516, Department of the Gulf, Letters Received, Box 2, Part 4, RG 393, NARA. See also Order of Provost Marshal Edward Page, January 5, 1863, published on February 15, 1863, in *The Era*, page 4.

63. James Bowen to George S. Darling, February 10 and 19, 1864, and Provost Marshal Headquarters Order to George Darling, February 20, 1864, both in Entry 1516, Department of the Gulf, Letters Received, Box 2, Part 4, RG 393, NARA; George Shepley, Special Order No. 12, February 9, 1864; Special Order No. 13, February 10, 1864; Special Order No. 14, February 11, 1864; Special Order No. 18, February 13, 1864; Special Order No. 19, February 19, 1864, all in Special Executive Orders: 1862–1864, Microfilm P1975–036, LSA; Banks to Shepley, February 9, 1864, Banks to Bowen, February 9, 1864, Banks to Alfred Rougelot, February 11, 1864, all in Nathaniel P. Banks letter book, LLMVC; Baggett, *The Scalawags*, 111–17.

64. Robertson, *The Red River Campaign and Its Toll*, 83–84; Johnson, *Red River Campaign*, 45–47, 83–85, 97–98, 109–10.

65. Banks to Grieff, Dewes, Durell, Graham, and others, February 18, 1864, Nathaniel P. Banks letter book, LLMVC; Ripley, *Slaves and Freedmen in Civil War Louisiana*, 170–76; Dawson, *Army Generals and Reconstruction*, 14–18; Hunter, "Late to the Dance," 305–6; Hollandsworth, *Pretense of Glory*, 162–71, 214–15, 219–20. For a more optimistic presentation of the Unionist Louisiana State Convention, see Reidy, *Illusions of Emancipation*, 232.

66. Lang, *In The Wake of War*, 182–209.

67. Michot, "War Is Still Raging," 183–84.

4. SENTINELS OF THE HOUSEHOLD WAR: BLACK & WHITE WOMEN
CONFRONT OCCUPATION

1. Kerber, *No Constitutional Right To Be Ladies*, xx–xxiv; Whites and Long, eds., *Occupied Women*, 1–13; Blair, *With Malice toward Some*, 128–29, 132, 136, 148, 158–59; McCurry, *Women's War*, 1–19 and *Confederate Reckoning*, 1–10, 85–132; Glymph, *Out of the House of Bondage*, 1–11, and *The Women's Fight*, 1–15; Ash, *When the Yankees Came*, 42–45, 61, 71, 197–203.

2. Kerber, *No Constitutional Right To Be Ladies*, xxiii–xxiv; Krowl, "For Better or for Worse," in Clinton and Silber, eds., *Southern Families at War*, 35–48; Glymph, *The Women's Fight*, 19–25. Historians have also uncovered considerable political participation by southern women during the antebellum era. This political presence informed and fueled their wartime activity as well. See Baker, "The Domestication of Politics," 620–47; McGerr, "Political Style and Women's Power," 864–85; Varon, *We Mean To Be Counted*; Sacher, "The Ladies Are Moving Everywhere," 439–57.

3. McCurry, "Women Numerous and Armed," in Waugh and Gallagher, eds., *Wars within a War*, 1–5; Murrell, "Of Necessity and Public Benefit," in Clinton and Silber, eds., *Southern Families at War*, 77–93; quote from Currans, *Marching Dykes, Liberated Sluts, and Concerned Mothers*, 2. See also Whites, *The Civil War as a Crisis in Gender*, 1–14; Brill, *The Weaker Sex in War*, 119.

4. McCurry, "Women Numerous and Armed," in Waugh and Gallagher, eds., *Wars within a War*, 8–9; Glymph, *The Women's Fight*, 22–23; 69–85; 202–220.

5. Hunter, *To 'Joy My Freedom*, 2–3. See also Rosen, *Terror in the Heart of Freedom*.

6. Manning, *Troubled Refuge*, 215–31, 283–84; Blair, *With Malice toward Some*, 132–34; Glymph, *The Women's Fight*, 210–214, 221–241.

7. McCurry, *Confederate Reckoning*, 106; Hunter, *To 'Joy My Freedom*, 1–13; Blair, *With Malice toward Some*, 154; Hepworth, *The Whip, Hoe, and Sword*, 40–41. For a discussion of public space as a personal resource, see Currans, *Marching Dykes, Liberated Sluts, and Concerned Mothers*, 3–4.

8. Whites and Long, eds., *Occupied War*; Frank and Whites, eds., *Household War*.

9. Annie Jeter Carmouche memoir, 40–43, 48, 54–55, LLMVC. See also Descriptive List of Property and Report of Mary J. Cohen, September 24, 1862, Report of Heloise Cenas, undated, and C. A. Curtis to Butler, undated, Entry 1390, Part 4, RG393, NARA.

10. Carmouche memoir, 37, LLMVC.

11. Blair, *With Malice toward Some*, 154–55; Marianne Edwards letters, December 26, 1862, LLMVC. See also Sacher, "'The Ladies Are Moving Everywhere," 451–52; Whites, "Forty Shirts and a Wagonload of Wheat," 56–78.

12. Brackett, "Rewriting Domesticity, War, and Confederate Defeat," 61–77; LeGrand, *The Journal of Julia LeGrand*, 128, 130–31; *The Era*, February 15, 1863, page 1, page 4; *The Era*, June 6, 1863, page 2; Bond, *A Maryland Bride in the Deep South*, 260.

13. Carmouche letters, January 20, 1864, and November 26, 1864, LLMVC.

14. Norman Murray to Brashear City Provost Marshal, October 10, 1863, Entry 1519, Box 2; Costa to French, undated, Entry 1390, Part 4, RG393, NARA. See also H. Stiler to Office Supervising Special Agent Treasury Department, January 20, 1865, Part 4, Entry 1515, RG393, NARA.

15. John Hawkes letter, January 23, 1863, Mss. 1265, LLMVC; Nathaniel Banks to E. E. Shelton, June 26, 1863; July 25, 1863; July 24, 1863, Department of the Gulf, Letter Sent, Volume 1,

Entry 1738, Part 1, RG393, NARA; Ballantyne, "Whenever the Yankees Were Gone, I Was a Confederate," 51–52. See also Blair, *With Malice toward Some*, 152–53; Nicholas Day to Albert Stearns, January 7, 1864, Entry 1519, Box 2, RG393, NARA; Sprague, *History of the 13th Infantry Regiment of Connecticut Volunteers*, 122; Laurel Tucker to Bowen, August 14, 1863, N. P. Banks order, August 14, 1863, and Banks to S. B. Holabird, all in Nathaniel P. Banks letter book, LLMVC.

16. Annie Jeter Carmouche memoir, 26, 29–31, LLMVC.

17. Edwards letters, December 26, 1862, LLMVC. Apparently the Batchilden family owned somewhere around 150 enslaved people. See also Robertson, *The Red River Campaign and Its Toll*, 56.

18. Sutherland, *A Savage Conflict*, 70–75; Ellen Bragg quote in Frazier, "Out of the Stinking Distance" in *Guerrillas, Unionists, and Violence on the Confederate Home Front*, 155; Annette Koch quote in DeCuir, *Yankees on the Tchefuncte*, 5.

19. LeGrand, *The Journal of Julia LeGrand*, 40, 42–43, 45, 59 (quote on 59); Edwards, "The Thin Blue Line," 53–55; Lowenthal, *A Yankee Regiment in Confederate Louisiana*, 106, 159; De Forest, *A Volunteer's Adventures*, 30. See also Morgan, *Sarah Morgan Diary*, 67–68; Bond, *A Maryland Bride in the Deep South*, 212; Glymph, *The Women's Fight*, 210–214.

20. April 6, 12, 27, 1863, Martha Josephine Moore diary, Folder 6, Volume 2, in the Frank Liddell Richardson Papers #631, SHC; Nguyen, "Keeping the Faith," 173–74; Morgan, *Sarah Morgan Diary*, 69.

21. Stearns, *Reminiscences of the Late War*, 21; Michot, "War Is Still Raging in This Part of the Country," 171–172; Carmouche memoir, 48, LLMVC; Grimsley, *The Hard Hand of War*, 46; Lowenthal, *A Yankee Regiment in Confederate Louisiana*, 128, 230; LeGrand, *The Journal of Julia LeGrand*, 60, 157, 164. For a Confederate example, see King, *No Pardons to Ask, Nor Apologies to Make*, 124–25.

22. Edwards letters, January 27, 1863; Unnamed Union General to Nathaniel Banks, July 23, 1863, Department of the Gulf, Letter Sent, Volume 1, Entry 1738, Part 1, RG393, NARA. See also Stearns, *Reminiscences of the Late War*, 14–15.

23. Huber, "The Battle of the Handkerchiefs," 48–53; Edwards letters, August 6, 1863, LLMVC.

24. Huber, "The Battle of the Handkerchiefs," 48–53; Edwards letters, August 6, 1863, LLMVC; Brackett, "Rewriting Domesticity," 70–73; Hollandsworth, *Pretense of Glory*, 98; Southwood, "*Beauty and Booty*," 278–81; LeGrand, *The Journal of Julia LeGrand*, 137–44.

25. Hearn, *When the Devil Came Down to Dixie*, 73–74; Southwood, "*Beauty and Booty*," 40, 42, 152; McCurry, *Confederate Reckoning*, 106–7; Long, "(Mis)Remembering General Order No. 28," 21, 27–28; Harrison, *The Rhetoric of Rebel Women*, xi–xvi; Brackett, "Rewriting Domesticity," 39–77; William H. Stewart diary, March 23, 1864, SHC. See also Ellen Louise Power diary, July 18, 1863, SHC; Edwards, "The Thin Blue Line," 82.

26. Carmouche memoir, 23, LLMVC; Winters, *The Civil War in Louisiana*, 27–28; Sutherland, *A Savage Conflict*, 71; Whites, "Forty Shirts and a Wagonload of Wheat," 56–78; Ballantyne, "Whose Hearth and Home?," 60.

27. Knox, *Camp-Fire and Cotton-Field*, 218–26; Camp, *Closer to Freedom*, 129–30; Baton Rouge Civil War Broadside Collection, January 10, 1863, and January 23, 1864, LLMVC. See also Luskey, *Men Is Cheap*.

28. Powell, *The Accidental City,* 97–99; Usner, *Indians, Settlers, and Slaves in a Frontier Exchange Economy,* 202–3; Hunter, *To 'Joy My Freedom,* 10, 13, 16–17.

29. East, *Baton Rouge: A Civil War Album,* 64–69; Ash, *When the Yankees Came,* 152, 165; Manning, *Troubled Refuge,* 97–149.

30. Hunter, *To 'Joy My Freedom,* 7–10, 20; Glymph, *The Women's Fight,* 221–241; Schwalm, "Between Slavery and Freedom," in Whites and Long, eds., *Occupied Women,* 137–154.

31. Manning, *Troubled Refuge,* 97–149; Carmouche memoir, 30–31, LLMVC; Glymph, *Out of the House of Bondage,* 1–17. See also O'Donovan, *Becoming Free in the Cotton South,* 120–121.

32. Marianne Edwards letters, December 26, 1862, LLMVC; Martin Williston Papers, December 28, 1862–January 2, 1863, TUDL. Butler did use Black spies to identify hidden weapons in New Orleans. Biographer James Parton wrote that Butler "had a spy in every house, behind every rebel's chair as he sat at table." Parton, *General Butler in New Orleans,* 493. See also Pritchard, "Moving toward Freedom?," 34, 68–69.

33. Marianne Edwards letters, December 26, 1862, LLMVC.

34. Marianne Edwards letters, December 26, 1862, LLMVC. For other confrontations in which Black people, especially women, overcame white household order, see Stone, *Brokenburn,* 170–71, 182; Glymph, "I'm a Radical Black Girl," 367–77; Sprague, *History of the 13th Infantry Regiment of Connecticut Volunteers,* 184. For an example of "Women Pedlar Merchants," see David W. James diary, January 5, 6, and 7, 1864, TUDL.

35. Thomas W. Conway to George H. Hanks, April 25, 1864, Entry 1519, Department of the Gulf, Letters Received, Box 2, RG393, NARA.

36. Conway to Hanks, April 25, 1864, Entry 1519, RG393, NARA.

37. Butler to Haggerty, May 27, 1862, Entry 1738; Oliver A. Pence and C. C. Pence to Albert Stearns, September 9, 1864, Entry 1519, Box 2; E. D. Beach to French, November 11, 1862, Entry 1390, Part 4; Banks to Bowen, May 9, 1863, Department of the Gulf, Letter Sent, Volume 1, Entry 1738, Part 1, RG393, NARA. See also McCurry, *Women's War*; Glymph, *The Women's Fight.*

38. Campbell, "The Unmeaning Twaddle about Order 28," 11–30; Nathaniel Banks to Gen. Emory, July 5, 1863, Department of the Gulf, Letter Sent, Volume 1, Entry 1738, Part 1, RG393, NARA. See also Glymph, *The Women's Fight,* 210–214, 221–241.

39. Long, "(Mis)Remembering General Order No. 28" in Whites and Long, eds., *Occupied Women,* 17–32; McCurry, *Confederate Reckoning,* 107.

40. Marianne Edwards letters, December 26, 1862, LLMVC; Sheehan-Dean, *Calculus of Violence,* 52–57.

41. Butler, *Correspondence,* Vol. II, 35–36; Moses Bates to George Shepley, August 29, 1862, Louisiana State Penitentiary, Misc. Papers 1862, George Foster Shepley Papers, Collection 117, Box 5, Collections of the Maine Historical Society; Bates to French, September 6, 1862, and Aimee Costillon to Stafford, undated, both in Entry 1390, Part 4, RG393, NARA. See also Edwards, "The Thin Blue Line," 66–67; LeGrand, *The Journal of Julia LeGrand,* 195. Special thanks to John Bardes for sharing resources from the MHS collection with me.

42. Hunter, *To 'Joy My Freedom,* 13; Blair, *With Malice toward Some,* 151–53; Feimster, "General Benjamin Butler and the Threat of Sexual Violence during the American Civil War," 126–34; Sheehan-Dean, *The Calculus of Violence,* 295, 306–13. For discussions of rape and sexual assault as war tactics in later centuries, see DeLargy, "Sexual Violence and Women's Health in War" in

Cohn, ed., *Women and Wars,* 54–79; Goldstein, *War and Gender,* chapter 6. The U.S. Congress did establish rules against rape and a number of other crimes against civilians on March 3, 1863, in Senate Bill 511. Before the passage of that law, U.S. courts-martial followed British common law or the laws of the state in which the case was heard. Barber and Ritter, "Dangerous Liaisons," 4–5; Barber and Ritter, "Physical Abuse . . . and Rough Handling," in Whites and Long, eds., *Occupied Women,* 49.

43. Julia to Francis Emily Brashear Lawrence, October 20, 1864, SHC; Henry Watkins Allen proclamation, February 13, 1864, Governor's Communications, 1860–1864, LSA; Ellen Louise Power diary, May 23, 1863, SHC; John Hawkes letter, January 23, 1863, Mss. 1265, LLMVC. Historian Laura Edwards writes that rape "graphically communicated propertied white men's anxieties about their public power." Edwards, *Gendered Strife and Confusion,* 12.

44. Francis Emily Brashear Lawrence to Hannah, March 15, 1863, SHC; William H. Stewart diary, March 15 and 20, 1864, SHC; *The Era,* February 15, 1863, page 4; Messner, "Black Violence and White Response," 24.

45. Lowry, *Sexual Misbehavior in the Civil War,* 162–63.

46. Lowry, *Sexual Misbehavior in the Civil War,* 162–63; Murphy, *I Had Rather Die,* 80.

47. Murphy, *I Had Rather Die,* 14–17, 19–20; Feimster, "Rape and Justice in the Civil War"; Barber and Ritter, "Physical Abuse . . . and Rough Handling," in Whites and Long, eds., *Occupied Women,* 56–57; Feimster, "What If I Am a Woman" in Downs and Masur, eds., *The World the Civil War Made,* 249–68; Somerville, *Rape and Race in the Nineteenth-Century South,* 111–12, 132–33, 191. See also Hodes, *White Women, Black Men: Illicit Sex in the Nineteenth-Century South;* Fischer, *Suspect Relations.*

48. Ash, *When the Yankees Came,* 79, 85–86. For instances of consensual sex between Union soldiers and prostitutes, southern white women, or formally enslaved women, see Edmonds, *Yankee Autumn,* 6–7; Capers, *Occupied City,* 204–5; West, *Lincoln's Scapegoat General,* 167–68; Scott, "The Glory of the City Is Gone," 59–60; Lowenthal, *A Yankee Regiment in Confederate Louisiana,* 106, 235; Roland, *Sugar Plantations during the Civil War,* 99–100.

49. Murphy, *I Had Rather Die,* 80; Lowry, *Sexual Misbehavior in the Civil War,* 162–3; Barber and Ritter, "Dangerous Liaisons," 7, 11–12.

50. Mitchel, *The Vacant Chair,* 104–6; Ash, *When the Yankees Came,* 146, 158–59, 197–98, 200–202; Beck, "Gender, Race, and Rape during the Civil War"; Feimster, "Rape and Justice in the Civil War." Feimster argues that President Lincoln's General Orders No. 100 (Lieber's Code) essentially defined rape in "women-specific terms as a crime against property, as a crime of troop discipline, and as a crime against family honor." See also Brownmiller, *Against Our Will,* 88, 416; Rable, *Civil Wars,* 161.

51. Lowry, *Sexual Misbehavior in the Civil War,* 162–63.

52. John H. Crowder letters, April 27, 1863, SHC; Lowry, *Sexual Misbehavior in the Civil War,* 162–63; Murphy, *I Had Rather Die,* 65–66; Barber and Ritter, "Physical Abuse . . . and Rough Handling," in Whites and Long, eds., *Occupied Women,* 64; Hollandsworth, *The Louisiana Native Guards,* 28. For a Confederate example similar to Crowder's perspective, see King, *No Pardons to Ask, Nor Apologies to Make,* 19.

53. Weitzel to Banks, February 9, 1863, Department of the Gulf, Letter Sent, Volume 1, Entry 1738, Part 1, RG393, NARA; Lowry, *Sexual Misbehavior in the Civil War,* 163; Sheehan-Dean, *The*

Calculus of Violence, 168–69; Barber and Ritter, "Dangerous Liaisons," 7, 11–12; Kinsley, *Diary of Christian Soldier*, 119; Edwards, "The Thin Blue Line," 70.

54. See Somerville, *Rape and Race in the Nineteenth-Century South*, 72–73, 86–88, 102–3, 124–25, 143–46. For another perspective, see Haumesser, *The Democratic Collapse*, 156–58.

55. Michot, "War Is Still Raging," 170–171; Lowry, *Sexual Misbehavior in the Civil War*, 161; Feimster, "What If I Am a Woman," 256–62. See also Barber and Ritter, "Dangerous Liaisons," 5; Faust, *Mothers of Invention*, 200; Somerville, *Rape and Race in the Nineteenth-Century South*, 147–50; Haumesser, *The Democratic Collapse*, 158.

56. Lowry, *Sexual Misbehavior in the Civil War*, 161; Sheehan-Dean, *The Calculus of Violence*, 306–13; Barber and Ritter, "Dangerous Liaisons," 4.

57. Feimster, "General Benjamin Butler and the Threat of Sexual Violence during the American Civil War," 132, and "What If I Am a Woman," 256–57. See also Ash, *When the Yankees Came*, 197–98; Glymph, *The Women's Fight*, 109; Taylor, *Embattled Freedom*, 85–86.

58. Feimster, "Rape and Justice in the Civil War"; Barber and Ritter, "Dangerous Liaisons," 11–12; Daly, *The War after the War*, 41–42; Barber and Ritter, "Physical Abuse . . . and Rough Handling," in Whites and Long, eds., *Occupied Women*, 51, 56; see also 205–6 fn. 9.

59. See Currans, *Marching Dykes, Liberated Sluts, and Concerned Mothers*, 4.

5. SMALL PIECES OF GROUND: BLACK FAMILIES & FREEDOM UNDER OCCUPATION

1. Knox, *Camp-Fire and Cotton-Field*, 197.

2. Knox, *Camp-Fire and Cotton-Field*, 197; Brown, *The Negro in the American Rebellion*, 184–85; Stearns, *Reminiscences of the Late War*, 13–14.

3. Ash, *When the Yankees Came*, chap. 5; Manning, *Troubled Refuge*, 102–6, 132–46; Gerteis, *From Contraband to Freedman*, 65–181; Wayne, *The Reshaping of Plantation Society*, chap. 2; Ripley, *Slaves and Freedmen in Civil War Louisiana*, chaps. 3 and 4; Rodrigue, *Reconstruction in the Cane Field*; Taylor, *Embattled Freedom*, 112–18; Silkenat, *Scars on the Land*, 158–167.

4. Berry, "From Household to Personhood in America," in Frank and Whites, *Household War*, 289.

5. Stanley, *From Bondage to Contract*, 19–23, 60–76; McCurry, *Confederate Reckoning*, 14–17; Manning, *Troubled Refuge*, 39–41; Pritchard, "Moving toward Freedom?," 2, 6, 8 fn. 10; Bynum, "Disordered Households" in Frank and Whites, eds., *Household War*, 221–247.

6. Conway, *The Freedmen of Louisiana: Final Report*, 3–4; Mellen, *Report Relative to Leasing Abandoned Plantations and Affairs of the Freed People*, 4–5; Messner, "Black Violence and White Response," 24–25; Manning, *Troubled Refuge*, 102–6, 140–46; Scott, *Degrees of Freedom*, 35–36; Knox, *Camp-Fire and Cotton-Field*, 215–17; Gerteis, *From Contraband to Freedman*, 88, 160; Roland, *Louisiana Sugar Plantations during the Civil War*, 78–80, 115–16; (Allen), *Official Report Relative to the Conduct of Federal Troops in Western Louisiana*, 67 (hereafter cited as *Official Report*); De Forest, *A Volunteer's Adventures*, 17, 31. See also Behrend, *Reconstructing Democracy*, chap. 1.

7. Nathaniel Banks, General Order No. 12, January 29, 1863, *OR*, Ser. I, Vol. 15, 666–67; General Order No. 23, February 3, 1864, *OR*, Ser. I, Vol. 34, pt. 2, 227–31 (see especially Sections IV,

XIV, and XVIII); General Orders No. 92, July 9, 1864, Entry 1519, Department of the Gulf, Letters Received, Box 12, Part 4, RG393, NARA; Hollandsworth, *Pretense of Glory*, 92–95, 158–60; Reidy, *Illusions of Emancipation*, 34–35. See also Duganne, *Camps and Prisons: Twenty Months in the Department of the Gulf*, 64–68;

8. Capers, *Occupied City*, 121, 224–25; Gerteis, *From Contraband to Freedman*, 83–85; Ripley, *Slaves and Freedmen in Civil War Louisiana*, 49–50; LeGrand, *The Journal of Julia LeGrand*, 228–29. Mellen, *Report Relative to Leasing Abandoned Plantations and Affairs of the Freed People*, 8–9. The four Home Colonies were McHatton Home Colony in Baton Rouge, the Ross and McCutcheon Home Colony in St. Charles Parish, the General Bragg Home Colony in Lafourche Parish, and the Sparks Home Colony in Jefferson Parish. Conway, The Freedmen of Louisiana: *Final Report*, 3, 5.

9. Ripley, *Slaves and Freedmen in Civil War Louisiana*, 160–80, 203; Wilson, "Education as a Vehicle of Racial Control," 157; Pritchard, "Moving toward Freedom?," chap. 2.

10. Stone, *Brokenburn*, 28, 33, 37–38, 40.

11. Ellen Louise Power diary, May 25, 1863, SHC; Francis Emily Brashear Lawrence to Hannah Lawrence, March 15, 1863, Brashear and Lawrence Family Papers, SHC. See also John H. Ransdell journal, May 13, 1863, Mss. 5, HNOC.

12. Ransdell to Thomas O. Moore, May 24, 1863, quoted in Whittington, "Concerning the Loyalty of Slaves in North Louisiana in 1863," 491–92; *Louisiana Democrat* (Alexandria), June 3, 1863, quoted in Whittington, "Concerning the Loyalty of Slaves in North Louisiana in 1863," 488; LeGrand, *The Journal of Julia LeGrand*, 58. See also Wish, "Slave Disloyalty under the Confederacy," 438–39; Taylor, "Slavery in Louisiana during the Civil War," 30; Behrend, *Reconstructing Democracy*, 25–41; Col. Elisha B. Smith to Lt-Col. Richard B. Irwin, April 24, 1863, *OR* Ser. I, Vol. 15, 709.

13. Butler, *Butler's Book*, 488; Leonard, *Benjamin Franklin Butler*, 99–100; George Shepley, Special Order No. 19 and Special Order No. 20, September 16, 1862; Special Order No. 22, September 18, 1862, all in Special Executive Orders: 1862–1864, Microfilm P1975–036, LSA; Harai Robinson Circular, September 6, 1864, Entry 1516, Department of the Gulf, Letters Received, Box 1, Part 4, RG 393, NARA; Pritchard, "Moving toward Freedom?," 43; Sprague, *History of the 13th Infantry Regiment of Connecticut Volunteers*, 53, 59–60. See also Shepley, Special Order No. 25, September 20, 1862; Special Order No. 30, September 24, 1862; Special Order No. 35, October 3, 1862, all in Special Executive Orders: 1862–1864, Microfilm P1975–036, LSA; Ripley, *Slaves and Freedmen in Civil War Louisiana*, 40–46; Sarah Lois Wadley diary, July 13, 1862; Stevens, *History of the Fiftieth Regiment of Infantry*, 119; Danville S. Chadbourne, January 13, 1863, D. S. Chadbourne letters, Mss. 1128, LLMVC. For a considerable study of Black labor on public works in antebellum Louisiana, see Hall, "Public Slaves and State Engineers," 531–76.

14. A. M. Bradshore to George E. Abbott, March 21, 1864; George A. Hanks to Albert Stearns, July 18, 1864, Entry 1519, Department of the Gulf, Letters Received, Box 2, Part 4, RG 393, NARA; George Shepley, Special Order No. 57, November 13, 1862, Special Executive Orders: 1862–1864, Microfilm P1975–036, LSA; Siddali, *From Property to Person*, 56–57. For other examples of Black labor on military projects, including from Black troops, see Report of Lt. Col. Uri B. Pearsall, August 1, 1864, *OR*, Ser. I, Vol. 34, pt. 1, 253–56; D. N. Welch to S. B. Holabird, March 21, 1864, *OR*, Ser. I, Vol. 34, pt. 2, 679.

15. Siddali, *From Property to Person*, 50–54, 61–62, 79–82, 107; James Bowen, General Orders No. 12, February 2, 1863, Entry 1516, Department of the Gulf, Letters Received, Box 1, Part 4, RG 393, NARA; Hahn, *A Nation under Our Feet*, 102–15; Grimsley, *The Hard Hand of War*, 144–51; Ripley, *Slaves and Freedmen in Civil War Louisiana*, 40–68.

16. Ripley, *Slaves and Freedmen in Civil War Louisiana*, 50–51; Bell, "Self-Emancipating Women, Civil War, and the Union Army in Southern Louisiana and Lowcountry Georgia," 1, 3–9; Glymph, "I'm a Radical Black Girl," 368–69.

17. Ripley, *Slaves and Freedmen in Civil War Louisiana*, 91–92; William H. Whitney Letters, September 20, 1863, LLMVC; New Orleans *Daily Delta*, August 5, 1862; George Shepley, Special Order No. 8, September 4, 1862; Special Order No. 18, September 15, 1862, Special Executive Orders, 1862–1864, LSA; Court Summary of P. B. Marmillion, April 21, 1863, Entry 1516, Department of the Gulf, Letters Received, Box 1, Part 4, RG 393, NARA. See also Brown, *The Negro in the American Rebellion*, 181–82; Stearns, *Reminiscences of the Late War*, 15; War Department, Adjutant General's Office, General Orders No. 113, March 19, 1864, Mss. 1493, Box 3, United States Army Collection, LLMVC.

18. R. E. Jackson to E. J. Lewis, December 16, 1864; Albert Stearns to C. L. Harris, June 15, 1864; R. E. Jackson to Lieutenant Newton, November 26, 1864; Edward J. Lewis to Harai Robinson, September 20, 1864, Entry 1519, Department of the Gulf, Letters Received, Box 2, Part 4, RG 393, NARA; Lang, *In the Wake of War*, 82–104. See also Johns, *Life with the Forty-Ninth Massachusetts Volunteers*, 192; McIntyre, *Federals on the Frontier*, 216; Alfred A. Parmenter Papers, June 27, 1862, TUDL; David W. James diary, December 2, 3, and 4, 1863, TUDL.

19. Banks to Bowen, March 3, 1863, Department of the Gulf, Letter Sent, Volume 1, Entry 1738, Part 1, RG393, NARA; Messner, "Black Violence in Louisiana," 22–23; Pemberton, "Enforcing Gender," 151–175; Edwards, "The Thin Blue Line," 22–23. See also Brown, *The Negro in the American Rebellion*, 178–82; Conway, *The Freedmen of Louisiana: Final Report*, 6, 15–16; Glymph, "I'm a Radical Black Girl," 376.

20. Ripley, *Slaves and Freedmen in Civil War Louisiana*, 61–62; Thomas W. Conway to Provost marshal, Parish of St. Mary, October 31, 1864; Thomas W. Conway to Provost marshal Parish of St. Mary, August 16, 1864; Albert Stearns to C. L. Harris, September 6, 1864, and C. L. Harris to Albert Stearns, September 6, 1864, Entry 1519, Department of the Gulf, Letters Received, Box 2, Part 4, RG 393, NARA; Hahn, *A Nation under Our Feet*, 89–102.

21. Ripley, *Slaves and Freedmen in Civil War Louisiana*, 106–9; William H. Whitney Letters, September 20, 1863, LLMVC. See also Smith and Luke, eds., *Soldiering for Freedom*; Kinsley, *Diary of Christian Soldier*, 172; Bosson, *History of the Forty-Second Regiment Infantry*, 264–65; Johns, *Life with the Forty-Ninth Massachusetts Volunteers*, 343.

22. Albert Stearns to R. A. Cameron, September 8, 1864; Valgrand Verret and August Verret affidavit, September 8, 1864; C. L. Harris to Albert Stearns, September 9, 1864, all in Entry 1519, Department of the Gulf, Letters Received, Box 2, Part 4, RG 393, NARA. See also Albert Stearns to commanding officer of the 18th Regiment New York Cavalry, September 8, 1864; Stearns, *Reminiscences of the Late War*, 29–30.

23. Ripley, *Slaves and Freedmen in Civil War Louisiana*, 109–13; Office Superintendent Recruiting Service to Winslow Roberts, September 29, 1863, Entry 1516, Department of the Gulf, Box 1, RG 393, NARA. See also Stearns, *Reminiscences of the Late War*, 22–23.

24. Yeatman, *Report to the Western Sanitary Commission,* 8; Conway, The Freedmen of Louisiana: *Final Report,* 6–7; Ripley, *Slaves and Freedmen in Civil War Louisiana,* 113–18; Gerteis, *From Contraband to Freedman,* 107–11; Hollandsworth, *The Louisiana Native Guards,* chap. 7.

25. Gerteis, *From Contraband to Freedman,* 114–15, quote on 114; Winters, *The Civil War in Louisiana,* 238; Taylor, "Slavery in Louisiana during the Civil War," 32; Moors, *History of the Fifty-second Regiment Massachusetts Volunteers,* 158 (second quote). See also Ransdell to Moore, June 3, 1863, in Whittington, "Concerning the Loyalty of Slaves in North Louisiana in 1863," 498; Wish, "Slave Disloyalty under the Confederacy," 444, 446; Andrews to Stone, February 5, 1864, *OR,* Ser. I, Vol. 34, pt. 2, 247; Poche, *A Louisiana Confederate,* 195–96.

26. William H. Stewart diary, March 23, 1864, #2873-z, SHC; Ellen Louise Power diary, August 2, 1863, SHC; Lang, *In the Wake of War,* 158–81. See also Stearns, *Reminiscences of the Late War,* 16; Cutrer, *Theater of a Separate War,* 205–206, 219–20.

27. Scott, "The Glory of the City Is Gone," 66–68 (first quote on 66); J. Harvey Brown, January 30, 1863, J. Harvey Brown papers, TUDL (second and third quotes); Ripley, *Slaves and Freedmen in Civil War Louisiana,* 115–16. See also King, *No Pardons to Ask, Nor Apologies to Make,* 92; Lowenthal, *A Yankee Regiment in Confederate Louisiana,* 113; LeGrand, *The Journal of Julia LeGrand,* 59–60.

28. Thomas W. Conway to Provost Marshal Headquarters in Brashear City, April 23, 1864, Entry 1519, Department of the Gulf, Letters Received, Box 2, Part 4, RG 393, NARA.

29. Foner, *Reconstruction: America's Unfinished Revolution,* 164–65; Stanley, *From Bondage to Contract,* chaps. 1 and 2.

30. Karen Bell notes, for example, that the Labor Bureau hired 139 women, 111 men, and 72 children to work plantations in Terre Bonne Parish from November 1863 to February 1864. Bell, "Self-Emancipating Women," 7–9; U.S. Census Bureau, New Orleans, Louisiana, 1860; Glymph, *Out of the House of Bondage,* 8 (first quote); Yeatman, *Report to the Western Sanitary Commission,* 8 (second quote); Johns, *Life with the Forty-Ninth Massachusetts Volunteers,* 342–43 (third quote); Taylor, *Embattled Freedom,* 112–18. See also Jones, *Labor of Sorrow, Labor of Love,* 43–76; Smith, *Leaves From a Soldier's Diary,* 46–47; Glymph, "I'm a Radical Black Girl," 364–365; Schwalm, "Between Slavery and Freedom" in Whites and Long, eds., *Occupied Women,* 137–38.

31. Halcomb Williams Provost Marshal Labor Contract, March 28, 1864, Entry 1519, Department of the Gulf, Letters Received, Box 2, Part 4, RG 393, NARA; Yeatman, *Report to the Western Sanitary Commission,* 16; Hunter, *Bound in Wedlock,* 148–50; Pritchard, "Moving toward Freedom?," 119–26. See also labor contracts with Jas. Keller, undated 1864; Emma V. Linten, March 1, 1864; Allen and Green Employers, March 26, 1864; M. McCann, March 26, 1864; Ovid E. Smith, undated 1864; Norbert Bodin, March 25, 1864; R. Keser, undated 1864; Peter Haws, undated 1864; Smith and Prime, March 20, 1864 all in Entry 1519, Letters Received, Box 2, Part 4, RG393, NARA; Hahn, *A Nation under Our Feet,* 68–82; Manning, *Troubled Refuge,* 87–95; Ripley, *Slaves and Freedmen in Civil War Louisiana,* 146–59; O'Donovan, *Becoming Free in the Cotton South,* 1–11, 59–60; Malone, *Sweet Chariot,* 205–17.

32. W. L. Minn to Major Porter, October 13, 1863; J. L. Billiu to Provost Marshal, December 26, 1862, Entry 1519, Department of the Gulf, Letters Received, Box 2, Part 4, RG 393, NARA. See also George Shepley, Special Order No. 51, November 1, 1862, Special Executive Orders:

1862–1864, Microfilm P1975–036, LSA; Ripley, *Slaves and Freedmen in Civil War Louisiana*, 22–24.

33. Adam Hawthorn to Albert Stearns, undated, Entry 1519, Department of the Gulf, Letters Received, Box 2, Part 4, RG 393, NARA. See also Berlin and Rowland, eds., *Families and Freedom*, 63–64.

34. Oliver A. Pence to Albert Stearns, September 9, 1864; S. W. Cozzens to H. M. Pater, October 15, 1863; Thomas W. Conway to Provost Marshal of St. Mary Parish, November 5, 1864; George H. Hanks to James Bowen, April 4, 1864, all in Entry 1519, Department of the Gulf, Letters Received, Box 2, Part 4, RG 393, NARA; Ripley, *Slaves and Freedmen in Civil War Louisiana*, 57. See also John S. Clark to Bowen, September 6, 1863, and Clark to Jacob Baker, January 15, 1864, both in Nathaniel P. Banks letter book, LLMVC.

35. Page to Butler, May 27, 1862, in Butler, *Correspondence*, Vol. I, 524–25; McCrary, *Abraham Lincoln and Reconstruction*, 83; James McMillan, General Order No. 1, July 17, 1862, Mss. 3416, Box 3, United States Army Collection, LLMVC. See also Polycarpe Fortier to Benjamin Butler, June 4, 1862, in Butler, *Correspondence*, Vol. I, 553–54; Pritchard, "Moving toward Freedom?," 64–65.

36. Edwin Wheelock to Albert Stearns, July 23, 1864, and E. J. Lewis to R. E. Jackson, December 14, 1864, both in Entry 1519, Department of the Gulf, Letters Received, Box 2, Part 4, RG 393, NARA (Jackson's reply to Lewis is contained on this document); *United States v. Emilie L. Schiff*, Entry 1920, Box 12, RG393, NARA. See also S. E. Shepard to Thomas Conway, January 19, 1865, Entry 1519, Box 2, Part 4; Thomas Conway to George S. Darling, March 17, 1865, Entry 1516, Letters Received, Box 1, Part 4, RG 393, NARA; Powell, *New Masters*, 30–31.

37. E. R. S. Canby to R. E. Jackson, July 30, 1864, Entry 1519, Department of the Gulf, Letters Received, Box 2, Part 4, RG 393, NARA; Schwalm, "Between Slavery and Freedom," in Whites and Long, eds., *Occupied Women*, 146–48.

38. J. Schuyler Crosby to Thomas Conway, August 18, 1864; George A. Hanks to George S. Darling, July 29, 1864, Entry 1516, Department of the Gulf, Letters Received, Box 1, Part 4, RG 393, NARA; Ripley, *Slaves and Freedmen in Civil War Louisiana*, 52, 151–52. See also Knox, *Camp-Fire and Cotton-Field*, 218; Taylor, *Embattled Freedom*, 124–26, 129–33.

39. John Ransdell to Thomas O. Moore, May 24, 1863, and May 26, 1863, quoted in Whittington, "Concerning the Loyalty of Slaves in North Louisiana in 1863," 491–95; Hunter, *Bound in Wedlock*, 123–24, 152, 158, 162, 166–68. See also Roland, *Louisiana Sugar Plantations during the Civil War*, 51, 99, 109; Lathrop, "The Lafourche District in 1862: Invasion," 182–83, 187–92. For an alternative Union perspective of free labor and the presence of Black homes and families, see Hepworth, *The Whip, Hoe, and Sword*, 28–29.

40. Jas. M. White to Albert Stearns, August 24, 1864, Entry 1519; W. W. Mason to Albert Stearns, August 23, 1864, Entry 1519, Department of the Gulf, Letters Received, Box 2, Part 4, RG 393, NARA. See also Hollandsworth, *The Louisiana Native Guards*, 30–31. The Wofford Plantation that appears in this exchange of letters is most likely the Avoca Plantation, located in St. Mary Parish and owned by the family of Elizabeth Alzira Wofford, who married Jared Young Sanders, previously a soldier in the 26th Louisiana Regiment, in 1868. See Jared Young Sanders Family Papers, LLMVC.

41. See also O'Donovan, *Becoming Free in the Cotton South*, 2, 10–11; Gutman, *The Black Family in Slavery and Freedom*, 9–11; Berlin and Rowland, eds., *Families and Freedom*, 60–62.

42. Butler to Scott, May 27, 1861, *OR*, Ser. I, Vol. 2, 52–54; Hepworth, *The Whip, Hoe, and Sword*, 141–43; Ripley, *Slaves and Freedmen in Civil War Louisiana*, 151–59. See also Gutman, *The Black Family in Slavery and Freedom*, xx–xxi, 9–11, 21–24; De Forest, *A Volunteer's Adventures*, 77.

43. Albert Stearns Provost Marshal Memorandum, undated, 1864; General Order No. 92, July 9, 1864, Entry 1519, Department of the Gulf, Letters Received, Box 2, Part 4, RG 393, NARA; Banks to Hanks, May 5, 1863, Department of the Gulf, Letter Sent, Volume 1, Entry 1738, Part 1, RG393, NARA.

44. Testimony of William Talbot, Mary Jones, John Willis, Morning Willis, John Marshal, and Sophy Jones all in *United States v. Emilie L. Schiff,* February 7, 1865, Entry 1920, Department of the Gulf, Letters Received, Box 12, Part 4, RG 393, NARA.

45. Testimony of Mary Jones, John Willis, Albert Gaillard, Morning Willis, Sophy Jones, and William Talbot all in *United States v. Emilie L. Schiff,* February 7, 1865, Entry 1920, Department of the Gulf, Letters Received, Box 12, Part 4, RG 393, NARA; Hahn, *A Nation under Our Feet*, 82–89. See also Sheehan-Dean, *The Calculus of Violence*, 146–52, 160–61; Knox, *Camp-Fire and Cotton-Field*, 202; Berlin and Rowland, eds., *Families and Freedom*, 57–59.

46. Testimony of William Talbot, John Marshal, and John Willis all in *United States v. Emilie L. Schiff,* February 7, 1865, Entry 1920, Department of the Gulf, Letters Received, Box 12, Part 4, RG 393, NARA; Cohen, *At Freedom's Edge*, 3–13.

47. Cohen, *At Freedom's Edge*, 3–13; Charles Darwin Elliot diary, March 19, 1864, SHC; testimony of Mary Jones and John Willis both in *United States v. Emilie L. Schiff,* February 7, 1865, Entry 1920, Department of the Gulf, Letters Received, Box 12, Part 4, RG 393, NARA. See also Power, "A Vermonter's Account of the Red River Campaign," 363.

48. S. E. Shepard to S. Jones, March 8, 1864; S. E. Shepard to S. Jones, March 13, 1865, Entry 1519, Department of the Gulf, Letters Received, Box 2, Part 4, RG 393, NARA. See also Taylor, "Slavery in Louisiana during the Civil War," 30–31; Stearns, *Reminiscences of the Late War*, 17; Carpenter, *History of the Eighth Regiment Vermont Volunteers*, 92–96; Murray, *History of the Ninth Regiment, Connecticut Volunteer Infantry*, 114; Letter from Henry G. Gore to Isa Lund, March 11, 1863, in Alfred S. Lippman letters, 1848–1866, TUDL.

49. Nathaniel Banks, General Order No. 64, August 29, 1863, *OR*, Ser. I, Vol 26, 704; General Order No. 38, March 22, 1864, *OR*, Ser. 3, Vol. 4, 193–94; E. M. Wheelock to G. S. Darling, April 15, 1864, Entry 1516, Box 1; E. M. Wheelock to Albert Stearns, April 15, 1864, Entry 1519, Department of the Gulf, Letters Received, Box 2, Part 4, RG 393, NARA; Wheelock quote in Wilson, "Education as a Vehicle of Racial Control," 162; Manning, *Troubled Refuge*, 84–87, 108–9; Winters, *The Civil War in Louisiana*, 397–99; Ripley, *Slaves and Freedmen in Civil War Louisiana*, 126–45, 185–88. By the end of 1864, the Board of Education released a report listing 15,840 Black students in ninety-five schools throughout occupied Louisiana. This represented a little less than half of the eligible school-age children, many of whom did not attend the entire academic year, and New Orleans boasted a disproportionate percentage of the teachers, schools, and students when compared to rural parishes. *Report of the Board of Education for Freedmen*, 21; Wilson, "Education as a Vehicle of Racial Control," 161–62; Crouch, "Black Education in Civil War and Reconstruction Louisiana," 292–93. See also Brady, "Trials and Tribulations," 5–20; Rufus Kinsley, *Diary of Christian Soldier*, 109.

50. W. B. Stickney to Albert Stearns, April 11, 1864, Entry 1519; Report of Albert Stearns,

March 23, 1864, Entry 1668, Box 1, Part 4; Albert Stearns to Board of Education, August 20, 1864, Entry 1668, Box 1, Part 4; E. W. Wheelock to Albert Stearns, August 27, 1864, Entry 1519; E. W. Wheelock to Albert Stearns, April 26, 1864, Entry 1519; Board of Education for Freedmen to George S. Darling, September 16, 1864, Entry 1516, Box 1; E. M. Wheelock to Albert Stearns, June 25, 1864, Entry 1519, Letters Received, Box 2, Part 4, RG 393, NARA; Wilson, "Education as a Vehicle of Racial Control," 165–67; Brady, "Trials and Tribulations," 7–9; Stearns, *Reminiscences of the Late War,* 23.

51. Enos W. Smith to Albert Stearns, August 1, 1864, Entry 1519, Box 2; Nathan Willey to Provost Marshal St. James Parish, March 17, 1865, Entry 1516, Department of the Gulf, Letters Received, Box 1, Part 4, RG 393, NARA.

52. Nathaniel Banks to Provost Marshal of St. James & St. John Baptiste Parish, June 27, 1864, Entry 1516, Letters Received, Box 1, Part 4, RG 393, NARA; Wilson, "Education as a Vehicle of Racial Control," 164–65.

53. Jas. M. White to Albert Stearns, August 23, 1864; Albert Stearns to Jas. M. White, August 25, 1864, Entry 1519, Letters Received, Box 2, Part 4, RG 393, NARA.

54. Steven Hahn et al., *Freedom: A Documentary History of Emancipation, 1861–1867,* 598–615, 663–65, quotes on 614–15.

55. Lang, *In the Wake of War,* 220–25, 233–35.

6. PARTIAL THOUGH DISPUTED: DEMOCRACY, POWER & OCCUPATION IN CONFEDERATE LOUISIANA

1. Report of William Palfrey to Nathaniel Banks, February 17, 1864, Palfrey Family Papers, LLMVC. For similar instances of destruction and negotiation a year earlier, see Edmonds, *Yankee Autumn in Acadiana;* Ewer, *The Third Massachusetts Cavalry in the War for the Union,* chap. 5.

2. Neely, *Southern Rights,* 1–6; Ripley, *Slaves and Freedmen in Civil War Louisiana,* 14–19; Downs, "The Civil War and the American State," 358; McCurry, *Confederate Reckoning,* 1–10, 39–40. Michael Fellman used the term "survival lies" to refer to the malleable self-presentations of southerners who experienced guerrilla war, occupation, and devastation. Fellman, *Inside War,* 44–52.

3. Winters, *The Civil War in Louisiana,* 111–23, 221; Ballantyne, "Whose Hearth and Home?," 57–58; Lathrop, "The Lafourche District in 1862: Confederate Revival," 300–302, 311–19; Cutrer, *Theater of a Separate War,* 184–85, 192; Carpenter, *History of the Eighth Regiment Vermont Volunteers,* 97–106; Ewer, *The Third Massachusetts Cavalry in the War for the Union,* 134–35. See also Kerby, *Kirby Smith's Confederacy,* chaps. 3 and 5; Johnson, *Muskets and Medicine,* chap. 16; Powers, *The Story of the Thirty-Eighth Regiment of Massachusetts Volunteers,* chap. 5.

4. Escott, *Military Necessity,* 11–31; Winters, *The Civil War in Louisiana,* 111–23, 221; Kerby, *Kirby Smith's Confederacy,* 20–28; Parrish, *Richard Taylor,* 1–5; Robertson, *The Red River Campaign and Its Toll,* 17–18. See also Escott, *After Secession;* Prushankin, *A Crisis of Confederate Command;* King, *No Pardons to Ask, Nor Apologies to Make,* 107, 119.

5. See, for example, Haynes, *A Thrilling Narrative,* 14; Sternhell, *Routes of War,* 98–100; George Whittlesey, May 12, 1863, LLMVC.

6. Escott, *Military Necessity*, 175–77. See also Gallagher, *The Confederate War*; Sheehan-Dean, *Why Confederates Fought*; Owsley, *State Rights in the Confederacy*; Powell and Wayne, "Self Interest and the Decline of Confederate Nationalism," in Owens and Cooke, eds., *The Old South in the Crucible of War*; Beringer et al., *Why the South Lost the Civil War*; McCurry, *Confederate Reckoning*; Quigley, *Shifting Grounds*, chaps. 4 and 5; Whites and Long, eds., *Occupied Women*, 4–5.

7. Winters, *The Civil War in Louisiana*, 304, 323, 411–12; Frazier, "Out of Stinking Distance," in Sutherland, ed., *Guerrillas, Unionists, and Violence on the Confederate Home Front*, 168–69; Sutherland, *A Savage Conflict*, chap. 6; Kerby, *Kirby Smith's Confederacy*, 44–50; Sutherland, "Guerrilla Warfare, Democracy, and the Fate of the Confederacy," 261. Other studies of guerrilla war in the Civil War and as a tradition of American warfare include Fellman, *Inside War*; Grenier, *The First Way of War*; Beilein, *Bushwackers*; Neely, "Guerrilla Warfare, Slavery, and the Hopes of the Confederacy"; Stith, *Extreme Civil War*; McKnight and Myers, eds., *The Guerrilla Hunters*.

8. Dewey quote in Pierson, *Mutiny at Fort Jackson*, 55–56; Moore quote in Sacher, "Our Interest and Destiny Are the Same," 270–274, 277, quote on 274; Winters, *The Civil War in Louisiana*, 149–54; Ballantyne, "Whenever the Yankees Were Gone, I Was a Confederate," 37; Cutrer, *Theater of a Separate War*, 184–85; Ewer, *The Third Massachusetts Cavalry in the War for the Union*, 74. See also Moore to Randolph, *OR*, Ser. I, Vol. 15, 773–74; Taylor, "Discontent in Confederate Louisiana," 411–12; LeGrand, *The Journal of Julia LeGrand*, 39–40, 43, 45–46, 150.

9. Moore, "Address to the People of Louisiana," June 18, 1862, in Butler, *Correspondence*, Vol. II, 16–17; Ballantyne, "Whose Hearth and Home?," 60–63. See also Alfred A. Parmenter Papers, June 27, 1862, TUDL.

10. Moore, "Address to the People of Louisiana," in Butler, *Correspondence*, Vol. II, 20–21. See also Bensel, *Yankee Leviathan*, 151–53.

11. Moore, "Address to the People of Louisiana," in Butler, *Correspondence*, Vol. II, 17–18; Bragg, *Louisiana in the Confederacy*, 190–93. See also Haynes, *A Thrilling Narrative*, 84.

12. Palmer, *The Oath of Allegiance to the United States*, 6–7, 19–22; Bragg, *Louisiana in the Confederacy*, 201–7; Ballantyne, "Whenever the Yankees Were Gone, I Was a Confederate," 50–51; Poche, *A Louisiana Confederate*, 187. See also Davis and Tremmel, *Parole, Pardon, Pass and Amnesty Documents of the Civil War*, 47–48; Ruminski, "Tradyville," 511–37.

13. "Joint Resolutions, Expressing opinion of Congress in relation to the conduct citizens of Louisiana within the lines, and in the presence of the enemy," January 13, 1863, https://babel.hathitrust.org/cgi/pt?id=du11.ark:/13960/t4nk45p25&view=1up&seq=1.

14. David F. Boyd to William T. Sherman, April 7, 1864, SHC. See also Poche, *A Louisiana Confederate*, 14.

15. Prushankin, *A Crisis in Confederate Command*, 5–15; Escott, *Military Necessity*, 98–100; Kerby, *Kirby Smith's Confederacy*, 51–54.

16. "To the People of Louisiana, Texas, Arkansas, and Missouri, and the Allied Indian Nations," August 18, 1863, *OR*, Ser. I, Vol. 53, 892–94; Escott, *Military Necessity*, 107–13. See also *OR*, Ser. 1, Vol. 22, pt. 2, 1004–10.

17. Dorsey, *Recollections of Henry Watkins Allen*, 17–35, 238–39; Means, "Guy Mannering Travels North," 85–100; Winters, *The Civil War in Louisiana*, 317–19, quote on 317; Simpson and Cassidy, "The Wartime Administration of Governor Henry W. Allen," 257–69.

18. Allen quotes in Simpson and Cassidy, "The Wartime Administration of Governor Henry W.

Allen," 265–68; Dorsey, *Recollections of Henry Watkins Allen*, 241, 246–47; Allen, *Official Report*; Quigley, *Shifting Grounds*, 197–98. For examples of Allen's social welfare distributions, see Henry W. Allen to Col. James C. Wise, April 29, 1864, D. C. Dellier receipt, January 17, 1865, T. W. Mieure order, March 4, 1865, all in James Calvert Wise Papers, Mss. 3239, Box 1, LLMVC; Dorsey, *Recollections*, 251–56.

19. Taylor quote in Parrish, *Richard Taylor*, 245–46; Winters, *The Civil War in Louisiana*, 149–67, 304–5; Bragg, *Louisiana in the Confederacy*, 140–50; Taylor, "Discontent in Confederate Louisiana," 413–15; *Louisiana Democrat*, July 31, 1862, quote in Robertson, *The Red River Campaign and Its Toll*, 49–50; Quigley, *Shifting Grounds*, 187–98.

20. Bragg, *Louisiana in the Confederacy*, 140–50; Winters, *The Civil War in Louisiana*, 305–6.

21. Winters, *The Civil War in Louisiana*, 305–6, 317–18; Bragg, *Louisiana in the Confederacy*, 140–50, 162–63; Henry Effingham Lawrence to Francis Lawrence, undated, SHC; Shugg, *Origins of Class Struggle in Louisiana*, 182; Sacher, *Confederate Conscription and the Struggle for Southern Soldiers*, 173. See also McIntyre, *Federals on the Frontier*, 225; Ruminski, *The Limits of Loyalty*, chap. 4.

22. Taylor, "Discontent in Confederate Louisiana," 415 (first quote); Sarah Lois Wadley diary, September 2, 1863 (second and third quotes); Danville S. Chadbourne, April 9, 1863, LLMVC (fourth quote); Bragg, *Louisiana in the Confederacy*, 140–50; Winters, *The Civil War in Louisiana*, 305–6; Sacher, *Confederate Conscription and the Struggle for Southern Soldiers*, 102–103.

23. Kerby, *Kirby Smith's Confederacy*, 88–95; Winters, *The Civil War in Louisiana*, 149–67, 305; Bragg, *Louisiana in the Confederacy*, 244–64; Parrish, *Richard Taylor*, 246–47; Ballantyne, "Whenever the Yankees Were Gone, I Was a Confederate," 43–44; Sacher, *Confederate Conscription and the Struggle for Southern Soldiers*, 40–42, 73, 77–78, 133–34. See also Watson, *Life in the Confederate Army*, 163–64; King, *No Pardons to Ask, Nor Apologies to Make*, 133.

24. Shreveport *Caddo Gazette*, August 29, 1863; Shugg, *Origins of Class Struggle in Louisiana*, 179–82; *OR*, Ser. I, Vol. 26, pt. 2, 194–95, 215, 240; Parrish, *Richard Taylor*, 247, 419–22; Kerby, *Kirby Smith's Confederacy*, 91; Winters, *The Civil War in Louisiana*, 305–6; Taylor, "Discontent in Confederate Louisiana," 421–22; Haynes, *A Thrilling Narrative*, 5, 9, 16, 31, 34, 45, 69, 84. See also Noe, *Reluctant Rebels*, 169; King, *No Pardons to Ask, Nor Apologies to Make*, 36–37, 128–29; Lowenthal, *A Yankee Regiment in Confederate Louisiana*, 159, 164, 227; Fairclough, *The Revolution That Failed*, 29–30.

25. Escott, *Military Necessity*, 106–13; Kerby, *Kirby Smith's Confederacy*, chap. 4; Poche, *A Louisiana Confederate*, 191.

26. Grimsley, *The Hard Hand of War*, 157, 165–66; Smith, "The Defense of The Red River" in *Battles and Leaders of the Civil War*, 374; Lufkin, *History of the Thirteenth Maine Regiment*, 76. See also Robertson, *The Red River Campaign and Its Toll*, 64.

27. Butler, *Butler's Book*, 385–86; Winters, *The Civil War in Louisiana*, 103; Ballantyne, "Whose Hearth and Home?," 61–62; Hurt, *Agriculture and the Confederacy*, 93–94; Knox, *Camp-Fire and Cotton-Field*, 259; Deposition of Hopkins M. Seale, January 21, 1864, Folder 24 and E. A. Scott receipt, Folder 22, Houmas Plantations Records, SHC. See also deposition of John M. Andrews, May 20, 1862, Folder 22; Fairclough, *The Revolution That Failed*, 30–31.

28. John J. Peek receipts for burned cotton, July 12 and 13, 1863; George McFarland to J. R. Value, December 4 and 8, 1863, all in Folder 23, Houmas Plantations Records, SHC; David W.

James diary, October 4, 1863, TUDL. According to Thomas Knox, he was selling cotton at $.60 a pound in February 1864, but the price fluctuated frequently during the war. That same month on the other side, Felix Poche wrote that Confederate officials paid $.25 per pound in Confederate currency—though some speculators could garner 20 or even 30 cents in gold. Knox, *Camp-Fire and Cotton-Field,* 262; Poche, *A Louisiana Confederate,* 89. For examples of Louisianans flying foreign flags, see Bentley, *History of the 77th Illinois Volunteer Infantry,* 248; Edmonds, *Yankee Autumn in Acadiana,* 101.

29. November 4, 6, and 12, and December 10 and 19, 1862, Palfrey Account Books, Mss. 334. H:22, Vol. 18, Plantation Diary, Palfrey Papers, LLMVC; Sarah Lois Wadley diary, April 12, 1864. See also Poche, *A Louisiana Confederate,* 6.

30. Daniel Dudley Avery tax receipts, October 9, 1862; R. S. Burke to Daniel Avery, September 10, 1862; O. Moore to Daniel Avery, August 12, 1862, Avery Papers, SHC; Parrish, *Richard Taylor,* 420–21. See also Simpson and Cassidy, "The Wartime Administration of Governor Henry W. Allen," 264–65; Henry W. Allen, Special Order No. 113, April 28, 1864, James Calvert Wise Papers, Mss. 3239, Box 1, LLMVC.

31. Bragg, *Louisiana in the Confederacy,* 190–93; quote in Smith to Seddon, February 11, 1865, *OR,* Ser. I, Vol. 48, pt. 1, 1381–1382. See also Haynes to Boggs, February 8, 1865, and Smith to Gray, February 11, 1865, *OR,* Ser. I, Vol. 48, pt. 1, 1382–1384.

32. Kerby, *Kirby Smith's Confederacy,* 263–67; Bragg, *Louisiana in the Confederacy,* 194; Simpson and Cassidy, "The Wartime Administration of Governor Henry W. Allen," 260–61, 267–68; Gentry, "White Gold," 232–40. See also Cutrer and Parrish, eds., *Brothers in Gray,* 246, 251, 253–54.

33. Kerby, *Kirby Smith's Confederacy,* 267–68; Bragg, *Louisiana in the Confederacy,* 220–30; Simpson and Cassidy, "The Wartime Administration of Governor Henry W. Allen," 261–64; Winters, *The Civil War in Louisiana,* 408–9; Kerby, *Kirby Smith's Confederacy,* 258–63; Taylor, *Destruction and Reconstruction,* 114. See also Ransdell to Moore, June 13, 1863, in Whittington, "Concerning the Loyalty of Slaves in North Louisiana, 1863," 502; Letter to James C. Wise, March 11, 1864, and Henry W. Allen, unnumbered Special Order, April 28, 1864, both in James Calvert Wise Papers, Mss. 3239, Box 1, LLMVC.

34. Bragg, *Louisiana in the Confederacy,* 238, 242; Simpson and Cassidy, "The Wartime Administration of Governor Henry W. Allen," 265–266; Kerby, *Kirby Smith's Confederacy,* 87.

35. Henry Allen to William Lockwood, July 6, 1864, Henry Watkins Allen Papers, Mss. 2867, LLMVC; Priscilla Allen to Henry W. Allen, January 17, 1865, James Calvert Wise Papers, Mss. 3239, Box 1, LLMVC. See also Allen to Wise, June 21, 1864, James Calvert Wise Papers, Mss. 3239, Box 1, LLMVC.

36. Robert C. Hyman to James Wise, May 21, 1864, James Calvert Wise Papers, Mss. 3239, Box 1, LLMVC; Henry W. Allen, Governor of Louisiana, "To Refugee Planters of Louisiana" and "To the Planters and Slave-owners of Louisiana"; Taylor, *Destruction and Reconstruction,* 123–124, quote on 124. See also McCurry, *Confederate Reckoning,* chapter 7; K. M. Clark to Wise, April 17, 1865, James Calvert Wise Papers, Mss. 3239, Box 1, LLMVC.

37. Bragg, *Louisiana in the Confederacy,* 213–215; Domby and Sheridan, "Slave Rolls Project: Index," version 0.5, July 14, 2020, adamhdomby.com/SlaveRolls, Slave Payroll 5641, 5689, 5683, and 5554, Confederate Slave Payrolls, RG 109, War Department Collection of Confederate Records, NARA; William Palfrey, June 3, 1862, Vol. 18, Plantation Diary, Palfrey Account Books, LL-

MVC; Sheehan-Dean, *The Calculus of Violence,* 115–116; Ballantyne, "Whose Hearth and Home?," 61. See also Sarah Lois Wadley diary, February 29, 1864; Levine, *Confederate Emancipation.*

38. D. Castleberg to G. W. Logan, February 2, 1863, Folder 3, George Logan Papers, SHC; Ransdell to Moore, May 26, 1863 in Whittington, "Concerning the Loyalty of Slaves in North Louisiana in 1863," 494. See also Parrish, *Richard Taylor,* 423; Cutrer, *Theater of a Separate War,* 222; Kerby, *Kirby Smith's Confederacy,* 56–57; Poche, *A Louisiana Confederate,* 199; Behrend, *Reconstructing Democracy,* 18. For a list of sixty-nine enslaved people killed during the construction of Fort DeRussy, see Mayeux, *Earthen Walls, Iron Men,* Appendix E.

39. Sarah Lois Wadley diary, August 29, 1863. For other examples see Stone, *Brokenburn,* 15.

40. Fairclough, *The Revolution That Failed,* 34–37; Wadley diary, August 27, 1863. See also May 26 and July 13, 1862. See also Browning, *Shifting Loyalties,* chapter 4; Ruminski, *The Limits of Loyalty,* chap. 5; Behrend, *Reconstructing Democracy,* 20–25. For an alternative Confederate perspective of slave loyalty, see Taylor, *Destruction and Reconstruction,* 210.

41. Winters, *The Civil War In Louisiana,* 25; Parrish, *Richard Taylor,* 419–21; Baton Rouge Civil War Broadside Collection, April 29, 1862, LLMVC; Taylor, *Destruction and Reconstruction,* 227, 235; Knox, *Camp-Fire and Cotton-Field,* 262. See also Robertson, *The Red River Campaign and Its Toll,* 59–60.

42. Sarah Wadley Lois diary, September 7, 1864; Francis Emily Brashear Lawrence to Hannah, March 15, 1863, and Henry E. Lawrence to Francis Lawrence, undated, Brashear and Lawrence Family Papers, SHC; William H. Stewart diary, March 19, March 20, and April 3, 1864, SHC; Sarah Lois Wadley diary, September 2, 1863; Ballantyne, "Whenever the Yankees Were Gone, I Was a Confederate," 37–38. See also Ludwell, *Red River Campaign,* 91–94; Joiner, *Through the Howling Wilderness,* 27–34, 41–43, 58–62; Taylor, *Destruction and Reconstruction,* 136; Poche, *A Louisiana Confederate,* 131; J. Harvey Brown, September 5, 1863, J. Harvey Brown letters, TUDL.

43. Bragg, *Louisiana in the Confederacy,* 140–50, 160–63; *Shreveport Semi-Weekly News,* September 15 and 25, and October 16, 1863; Winters, *The Civil War in Louisiana,* 304–7; Ash, *When the Yankees Came,* 97–107. Unfortunately, these Confederate associations left few records. Historians must be content with references to their existence rather than direct records of their operations. C. B. Thomas, Chaplain of St. James Hospital, lamented that he had few or no copies of pamphlets published by the Southern Rights Association because Confederate printers and editors had trouble procuring paper. Thomas to Lassing, January 7, 1864, HNOC.

44. DeCuir, *Yankees on the Tchefuncte,* 7; D. C. Dellier receipt, January 17, 1865, J. H. Sullivan to Henry W. Allen, January 20, 1865, and W. H. Rogers to Allen, March 7, 1865, all in James Calvert Wise Papers, Mss. 3239, Box 1, LLMVC; Capt. S. M. Eaton to Lt. Col. C. T. Christensen, *OR,* Ser. I, Vol. 48, pt. 1, 625; Kerby, *Kirby Smith's Confederacy,* 57–87; Ash, *When the Yankees Came,* 177–81; Noe, *Reluctant Rebels,* chap. 8. For appeals to the governor for food as civilian relief, see J. R. Andrews to Allen, March 1, 1865, A. H. Pierson to Allen, March 10, 1865, E. E. Smart to Allen, April 8, 1865, C. E. Hosea to Allen, April 10, 1865, K. M. Clark to Wise, April 17, 1865, all in James Calvert Wise Papers, Mss. 3239, Box 1, LLMVC.

45. Moore to Wise, June 26, 1864, James Calvert Wise Papers, Mss. 3239, Box 1, LLMVC; Taylor quotes in Parrish, *Richard Taylor,* 246–47. See also Gentry, "White Gold," 239–240; Ballantyne, "Whose Hearth and Home?," 58–60; Cutrer, *Theater of a Separate War,* 192; Fairclough, *The Revolution That Failed,* chap. 2.

46. Scott, *Seeing Like a State*, 183–91; Ruminski, *The Limits of Loyalty*, 74–76, 178–92; Ballantyne, "Whose Hearth and Home?," 62–64; Ballantyne, "Whenever the Yankees Were Gone, I Was a Confederate," 37–39; Browning, *Shifting Loyalties*, 4–5, 149–72. See also McKenzie, *Lincolnites and Rebels*, 140.

47. Ash, *When the Yankees Came*, 47–53, 125–26; Lang, *In the Wake of War*, 105–28; quote from Mark Grimsley, *The Hard Hand of War*, 112; Sheehan-Dean, *The Calculus of Violence*, 72–81, 95–110. See also Charles Darwin Elliot diary, March 19, 1864, SHC; Sheehan-Dean, *Reckoning with Rebellion*, 41.

48. Winters, *The Civil War in Louisiana*, 305–8, 393–94; Lathrop, "The Lafourche District in 1862," 230–44.

49. Winters, *The Civil War in Louisiana*, 307; Moore, "Address to the People of Louisiana," in Butler, *Correspondence*, Vol. II, 18–21; Allen, "Annual Message," 8.

50. Haynes, *A Thrilling Narrative*, xv–xvi, 13–21, 25–33, 65–66; Tunnell, *Crucible of Reconstruction*, 10; Hunter, "The Politics of Resentment," 186; Butler, *True Blue*; Ash, *When the Yankees Came*, chap. 4. See also Lathrop, "Disaffection in Confederate Louisiana," 310, 315–16; Ballantyne, "Whose Hearth and Home?," 58–60; King, *No Pardons to Ask, Nor Apologies to Make*, 37, 127.

51. Edward Palfrey to John Palfrey, June 3, 1862, Palfrey Papers, LLMVC; Banks to Ready, February 20, 1863, Department of the Gulf, Letter Sent, Volume 1, Entry 1738, Part 1, RG393, NARA; Ellen Louise Power diary, July 4, 1863, SHC; Hyman to Wise, May 21, 1864, James Calvert Wise Papers, Mss. 3239, Box 1, LLMVC; Sutherland, "Guerrilla Warfare, Democracy, and the Fate of the Confederacy," 270–73; Ballantyne, "Whose Hearth and Home?," 58–59; Sacher, *Confederate Conscription and the Struggle for Southern Soldiers*, 60. See also Hollandsworth, *The Louisiana Native Guards*, 8; Sacher, "Our Interests and Destiny Are the Same," 279; Frazier, "Out of Stinking Distance," in Sutherland, ed., *Guerrillas, Unionists, and Violence on the Confederate Home Front*, 60; Kerby, *Kirby Smith's Confederacy*, 44–50.

52. Ellen Louise Power diary, July 4, 1863, SHC (first quote); Sarah Lois Wadley diary, August 31, 1863; Taylor, "Discontent in Confederate Louisiana," 424–27; Robertson, *The Red River Campaign and Its Toll*, 67, 60–61; Ballantyne, "Whose Hearth and Home?," 62–64 (second quote on 67); Allen, *Official Report*, 33; Kerby, *Kirby Smith's Confederacy*, 91–92.

53. Morgan, *Sarah Morgan Diary*, 101; Nathaniel Banks to Captain Goodrich, June 13, 1863; Banks to W. H. Emory, June 19, 1863; Banks to George L. Andrews, July 15, 1863, all in Entry 1738, Department of the Gulf, Letter Sent, Volume 1, Part 1, RG393, NARA; Foote, "Rethinking the Confederate Home Front," 453; Frank and Whites, eds., *Household War*, 1–10. See also Haynes, *A Thrilling Narrative*, 24, 26–29, 31, 33, 45; Streater, "'She-Rebels' on the Supply Line," in Whites and Long, eds., *Occupied Women*, 88–102; Corsan, *Two Months in the Confederate States*, 31; King, *No Pardons to Ask, Nor Apologies to Make*, 66.

54. Affidavit of Francis Mora, January 31, 1864; Affidavit of Ichabod N. Lewis, February 3, 1864; Affidavit of Michael McCarm, February 6, 1864, Entry 1519, RG393, NARA. See also Beecher, *Record of the 114th Regiment, N.Y.S.V.*, 139–40.

55. Affidavit of Tom Brewer, January 30, 1864, Entry 1519, RG393, NARA.

56. Affidavit of Berry Mathias, January 30, 1864, Entry 1519, RG393, NARA.

57. Affidavit of William Drews, February 3, 1864, Entry 1519, RG393, NARA.

58. Lang, *In the Wake of War*, 105–28; Sheehan-Dean, *The Calculus of Violence*, 72–81, 103–4; Sutherland, *A Savage Conflict*, xii–xiii, 267–79; Sheehan-Dean, *Reckoning with Rebellion*, 38–50. See also Stearns, *Reminiscences of the Late War*, 18–19; Haynes, *A Thrilling Narrative*, 8–9, 11, 13, 26–28, 30, 65–68, 72.

59. Priscilla Allen to Henry W. Allen, January 17, 1865, James Calvert Wise Papers, Mss. 3239, Box 1, LLMVC; William H. Stewart diary, April 7 and 28, 1865, SHC; Bragg, *Louisiana in the Confederacy*, 300–310; Kerby, *Kirby Smith's Confederacy*, chap. 9; Poche, *A Louisiana Confederate*, 232; Lowenthal, *A Yankee Regiment in Confederate Louisiana*, 243–43; Cutrer and Parrish, eds., *Brothers in Gray*, 259–60; Fairclough, *The Revolution That Failed*, 31–34.

60. Smith quote in *OR*, Ser. I, Vol. 48, pt. 2, 1284; Bragg, *Louisiana in the Confederacy*, 300–310; William H. Stewart diary, May 1, 1865, SHC; Dorsey, *Recollections of Henry Watkins Allen*, 293–94; Damico, "Confederate Soldiers Take Matters into Their Own Hands," 195–97. See also *OR*, Ser. I, Vol. 41, pt. 4, 1140–1141; Rable, "Fighting for Reunion," 347–77.

61. Dorsey, *Recollections of Henry Watkins Allen*, 294–96; Thomas C. Manning to Allen, May 10, 1865, James Calvert Wise Papers, Mss. 3239, Box 1, LLMVC; Bragg, *Louisiana in the Confederacy*, 300–310; Kerby, *Kirby Smith's Confederacy*, chap. 9. See also Damico, "Confederate Soldiers Take Matters into Their Own Hands," 190, 194, 201–5; Kerby, *Kirby Smith's Confederacy*, 401; Stone, *Brokenburn*, 345; Taylor, "Discontent in Confederate Louisiana," 423–24; Clampitt, "The Breakup," 498–534.

CONCLUSION: DEMOCRACY DELAYED

1. Knox, *Camp-Fire and Cotton-Field*, 215–16.

2. Knox, *Camp-Fire and Cotton-Field*, 216; Conway, *Final Report*, 17; Hoffer, *Plessy v. Ferguson*, 17; Ballantyne, "Whose Hearth and Home?," 65–66; Gerteis, *From Contraband to Freedman*, 48, 66, 154.

3. Knox, *Camp-Fire and Cotton-Field*, 206; Stearns, *Reminiscences of the Late War*, 28; Hepworth, *The Whip, Hoe, and Sword*, 49–60; Messner, "Black Violence and White Response," 37. For discussions of emancipation's fractured legacy in America, see Manjapra, *Black Ghost of Empire*; Alexander, *The New Jim Crow*; Rael, *Eighty-Eight Years*. For contrasting opinions about the nature of abolition, emancipation, and American biracial democracy, see Wilentz, "The Emancipators' Vision," 58–61; Masur, *Until Justice Be Done*; Wilentz, *No Property in Man*.

4. Dawson, *Army Generals and Reconstruction*, 19–23; Johnson, *Red River Campaign*, 283–84; Baggett, *The Scalawags*, 140–46; Banks to Stanton, April 6, 1865, *OR*, Ser. I, Vol. 34, pt. 1, 212; Hollandsworth, *Pretense of Glory*, 223–24; Wetta, *The Louisiana Scalawags*, 3, 12–13, 92–100.

5. Banks to Grieff, Dewes, Durell Graham, and others, February 18, 1864, Nathaniel P. Banks letter book, LLMVC (first quote); Summers, *The Ordeal of the Reunion*, 27–35 (second quote on 30); Haynes, *A Thrilling Narrative*, 86; Fairclough, *The Revolution That Failed*, 37–40, chap. 10; Behrend, *Reconstructing Democracy*, chap. 7.

6. Dawson, *Army Generals and Reconstruction*, 147–53, 234, 245, Emory quoted on 151; Daly, *The War after the War*, 4, 9–16, 20, 109–10, 141–42, 150–52.

7. J. B. Burdick to Captain Newton, November 3, 1865, Entry 1519, RG393, NARA. See also Bynum, *The Long Shadow of the Civil War*; Bynum, "Disordered Households" in Frank and Whites, eds., *Household War*, 221–240.

8. Downs, *After Appomattox*, 1–10; Rosen, *Terror in the Heart of Freedom*, 1–19; Dawson, *Army Generals and Reconstruction*, 1–18; Butler, *True Blue*, 2–12; Tunnell, *Crucible of Reconstruction*, 8–25, 33–50; Daly, *The War after the War*, 98–99. See also Hahn et al., *Freedom: A Documentary History of Emancipation, 1861–1867*, 820–21; Pritchard, "Moving toward Freedom?," chap. 5.

9. Manning, *What This Cruel War Was Over*, 94; Hoffer, *Plessy v. Ferguson*, 19–22; Ripley, *Slaves and Freedmen in Civil War Louisiana*, 102–22, 130–43; Lang, *In the Wake of War*, 182–235.

10. See DuBois, *Black Reconstruction*; Robinson, *Bitter Fruits of Bondage*; Foner, *The Second Founding*. For the alternative perspective in recent historiography, see Manning, *Troubled Refuge*; Daly, *The War after the War*; Pritchard, "Moving toward Freedom?," 10, 12, 15.

11. Durant to Lincoln, October 1, 1863, quoted in Robertson, *The Red River Campaign and Its Toll*, 78; Lowenthal, *A Yankee Regiment in Confederate Louisiana*, 273; Bynum, *The Long Shadow of the Civil War*.

12. See Lang, *In the Wake of War*, 1–14; Sheehan-Dean, *The Calculus of Violence*, 1–11, 15–20, 28; Frank and Whites, eds., *Household War*, 1–10.

13. McCurry, *Women's War*, 15–62, 86–92, 104–123; Whites, *The Civil War as a Crisis in Gender*, 160–98; Frank and Whites, eds., *Household War*, 1–10; Jacobson, "Women 'after' Wars" in Cohn, ed., *Women and Wars*, 225–28; Bell, "Self-Emancipating Women," 15–16; Hunter, *To 'Joy My Freedom*, 4–20; Glymph, *Out of the House of Bondage*, 2, 6, 99–100, 130–34, 140–45, 166; Edwards, *Gendered Strife and Confusion*, 34–35, 107, 145–47, 177–83; Stanley, *From Bondage to Contract*, x–xii, 24, 39–40, 138–41. See also O'Donovan, *Becoming Free in the Cotton South*; Rosen, *Terror in the Heart of Freedom*; Farmer-Kaiser, *Freedwomen and the Freedmen's Bureau*; Jones, "Women, Gender, and the Boundaries of Reconstruction," 111–31.

14. Lang, *In the Wake of War*, 210–35, quote on 213; Sheehan-Dean, *The Calculus of War*, 1–11; White, *The Freedmen's Bureau in Louisiana*, 44, 63; Grimsley, *The Hard Hand of War*, 218; Bensel, *Yankee Leviathan*, 91–93; Summers, *The Ordeal of Reunion*, chap. 3; Ash, *When the Yankees Came*, 25.

15. See Bensel, "Valor and Valkyries," 386–93.

Bibliography

PRIMARY SOURCES: MANUSCRIPT COLLECTIONS

Documenting the American South (all digital)
Annual Message of Governor Henry Watkins Allen, to the Legislature of the State of
    Louisiana
Sarah Lois Wadley diary

Historic New Orleans Collection, New Orleans
C. B. Thomas letter, January 7, 1864
Henry Bier Collection, 1861–1862
John H. Ransdell papers, 1840–1961
Mary E. Stratton letter, January 27, 1861
Letter from J. Elliot Smith to Stephen Hoyt, February 13, 1864
Union Soldier's letter, April 22–24, 1863

**Louisiana and Lower Mississippi Valley Collections, Louisiana State University,
Baton Rouge**
Alexander Franklin Pugh Papers, 1859–1865
Annie Jeter Carmouche Papers, 1853–1915
Baton Rouge Civil War Broadside Collection, 1860–1864
Civil War New Orleans Orphanages Receipts, 1863
D. S. Chadbourne Letters, 1862–1863
East Baton Rouge Parish Volunteer Fund Letter, 1861
George W. Whittlesey Letters, 1862–1863
Henry Watkins Allen Papers, 1820–1866
Henry Watkins Allen Inaugural Address, January 25, 1864
Henry Watkins Allen, *To Refugee Planters of Louisiana*, 1864
Henry Watkins Allen, *To the Planters and Slave-owners of Louisiana*, 1864

James Wise Calvert Papers, 1860–1917
John Hawkes Letter, 1863
Journal of the Louisiana Constitutional Convention, 1861
Mills H. Barnard Letters, 1862–1912
Marianne Edwards Letters, 1855–1866
Nathaniel P. Banks Letter Book, 1863–1864
New Orleans Civil War Letter
Palfrey Family Papers, 1776–1918
St. Tammany Parish Militia Slave Patrol Order, 1862
Thomas Overton Moore Letter, 1862
United States Army Collection, 1806–1911
William B. Allyn Letter, November 25, 1862
William H. Whitney Letters, 1863–1864

Louisiana State Archives, Baton Rouge
George Shipley Special Executive Orders, 1862–1864
Governor's Communications, 1860–1864

Maine Historical Society, Portland
George F. Shipley Papers, 1860–1903

National Archives and Records Administration, Washington, D.C.
RG 105: Records of the Bureau of Refugees, Freedmen, and Abandoned Lands
RG 109: Confederate Slave Payrolls, War Department Collection of Confederate
    Records
RG 153: Records of the Office of the Judge Advocate General (Army), Court Martial
    Case Files, 1809–1884
RG 393: U.S. Army Continental Commands, 1821–1920

Southern Historical Collection, UNC, Chapel Hill
Annual Message of Governor Henry Watkins Allen, to the Legislature of the State of
    Louisiana, January 1865. Printed at the Office of the Caddo Gazette.
Avery Family of Louisiana, 1796–1951
Brashear and Lawrence Family Papers, 1802–1897
Charles Darwin Elliot Diary and Surveyor Field Books, 1863–1864
David French Boyd Letter, 1864
Ellen Louis Power Diary, 1862–1863
Frank Liddell Richardson Papers, 1851–1869

George William Logan Papers, 1861–1865
Hermitage Plantation Papers, 1864
Houmas Plantations and William Porcher Miles Materials Collection, 1760–1927
James T. Wallace Diary, 1862–1865
John H. Crowder Papers, 1862–1873
William H. Stewart Diary, 1863–1865

Tulane University Digital Library
Alfred A. Parmenter Papers, 1861–1862
Alfred S. Lippman Letters, 1848–1866
B. B. Smith Diary, 1862
Bartlett Family Papers, 1860–1884
David W. James Diary, 1863–1864
J. Harvey Brown Papers, 1861–1864
Lansing Porter Family Papers, 1861–1863
Martin L. Williston Papers, 1862–1866
William A. Smith Letters, 1862–1863

NEWSPAPERS

Constitutional (Alexandria)
Sugar Planter (Baton Rouge)
Weekly Gazette and Comet Baton Rouge)
Guardian-Journal (Homer, Louisiana)
Daily Crescent (New Orleans)
Daily Delta (New Orleans)
Daily Picayune (New Orleans)
De Bow's Review (New Orleans)
Era (New Orleans)
Price-Current (New Orleans)
Times-Picayune (New Orleans)
Herald (New York)
Caddo Gazette (Shreveport)
Semi-Weekly News (Shreveport)
South-Western (Shreveport)

PUBLISHED PRIMARY SOURCES

Acts Passed by the Fifth Legislature of the State of Louisiana, Second Session, held and Begun in the City of Baton Rouge, on the 21st of January, 1861. Baton Rouge: J. M. Taylor, State Printer, 1861.

Acts Passed by the Sixth Legislature of the State of Louisiana at its First Session Held and Begun in the City of Baton Rouge on the 25th of November, 1861. Baton Rouge: Tom Bynum, State Printer, 1861.

Adjutant General's Office. Annual Report of the Adjutant General of the State of Louisiana for the Year Ending December 31, 1861, to the Governor. Baton Rouge, 1861.

Bacon, Edward. Among the Cotton Thieves. Detroit: The Free Press Steam and Job Publishing House, 1867.

Beecher, Harris H. Record of the 114th Regiment, N.Y.S.V. Norwich, New York: J. F. Hubbard Jr., 1866.

Bentley, William H. History of the 77th Illinois Volunteer Infantry, Sept. 2, 1862–July 10, 1865. Peoria: Edward Hine, Printer, 1883.

Bering, John A., and Thomas Montgomery. History of the Forty-Eighth Ohio Veteran Volunteer Infantry. Hillsboro, OH: Highland News Office, 1880.

Bond, Priscilla. A Maryland Bride in the Deep South: The Civil War Diary of Priscilla Bond. Edited by Kimberly Harrison. Baton Rouge: Louisiana State University Press, 2006.

Bosson, Charles P. History of the Forty-Second Regiment Infantry, Massachusetts Volunteers, 1862, 1863, 1864. Boston: Mills, Knight & Co., 1886.

Brown, William Wells. The Negro in the American Rebellion, His Heroism and His Fidelity. Boston: A. G. Brown & Co., 1880.

Butler, Benjamin Franklin. Autobiography and Personal Reminiscences of Major-General Benj. F. Butler: Butler's Book: A Review of His Legal, Political, and Military Career. Boston: A. M. Thayer & Co., 1892.

———. Private and Public Correspondence of General Benjamin F. Butler. Edited by Jessie Ames Marshal. Norwood, Massachusetts, 1917.

Carpenter, Thomas W. History of the Eighth Regiment Vermont Volunteers, 1861–1865. Boston: Press of Deland & Barta, 1886.

Confederate States of America House of Representatives. Joint Resolutions Expressing Opinion of Congress in Relation to the Conduct of Certain Citizens of Louisiana Within the Lines, and in the Presence of the Enemy. Richmond, Virginia, 1863.

Conway, Thomas W. The Freedmen of Louisiana: Final Report of the Bureau of Free Labor, Department of the Gulf, to Major General E. R. S. Canby, Commanding. New Orleans: Printed at the New Orleans Times Book and Job Office, 1865.

Corsan, W. C. Two Months in the Confederate States: An Englishman's Travels through *the South.* Edited by Benjamin H. Trask. Baton Rouge: Louisiana State University Press, 1996.

Cutrer, Thomas W., and T. Michael Parrish, eds. *Brothers in Gray: The Civil War Letters of the Pierson Family.* Baton Rouge: Louisiana State University Press, 1997.

De Forest, John Williams. *A Volunteer's Adventures: A Union Captain's Record of the Civil War.* Edited by James H. Croushore. Baton Rouge: Louisiana State University Press, 1996.

Domby, Adam H., and Patrick Sheridan. "Slave Rolls Project: Index," version 0.5, July 14, 2020, adamhdomby.com/SlaveRolls.

Dorsey, Sarah A. *Recollections of Henry Watkins Allen, Brigadier-General Confederate States Army, Ex-Governor of Louisiana.* New York: M. Doolady, 1866.

Duganne, A. J. H. *Camps and Prisons: Twenty Months in the Department of the Gulf.* New York: J. P. Robens, Publisher, 1865.

East, Charles, ed.: *The Civil War Diary of a Southern Woman.* New York: Simon & Schuster, 1991.

Ewer, James K. *The Third Massachusetts Cavalry in the War for the Union.* Maplewood, MA: William G. J. Perry Press, 1903.

Haynes, Dennis E. *A Thrilling Narrative: The Memoir of a Southern Unionist.* Edited by Arthur W. Bergeron. Fayetteville: University of Arkansas Press, 2006.

Hepworth, George. *The Whip, Hoe, and Sword: Or, The Gulf Department in '63.* Boston: Walker, Wise, and Co., 1864.

Higginson, Thomas Wentworth. *Cheerful Yesterdays.* Cambridge, MA: Riverside Press, 1898.

Howe, Henry Warren. *Passages from the Life of Henry Warren Howe, Consisting of Diary and Letters Written During the Civil War, 1861–1865.* Lowell, MA: Courier-Citizen Co., Printers, 1899.

Johns, Henry T. *Life with the Forty-Ninth Massachusetts Volunteers.* Washington, D.C.: Ramsey & Bisbee, Printers and Binders, 1890.

Johnson, Charles Beneulyn. *Muskets and Medicine: Or, Army Life in the Sixties.* Philadelphia: F. A. Davis Co., 1917.

King, William Henry. *No Pardons to Ask, Nor Apologies to Make: The Journal of William Henry King, Gray's 28th Louisiana Infantry Regiment.* Edited by Gary D. Joiner, Marilyn S. Joiner, and Clifton D. Cardin. Knoxville: University of Tennessee Press, 2006.

Kinsley, Rufus. *Diary of Christian Soldier: Rufus Kinsley and the Civil War.* Edited by David C. Rankin. Cambridge: Cambridge University Press, 2004.

Knox, Thomas W. *Camp-Fire and Cotton-Field: A New York Herald Correspondent's View of the American Civil War.* Leonaur, 2008.

LeGrand, Julia. *The Journal of Julia LeGrand, New Orleans 1862–1863.* Edited by Kate Mason Rowland and Julia Ellen Waitz. HardPress Publishing, 2012.

Lufkin, Edwin B. *History of the Thirteenth Maine Regiment from Its Organization in 1861 to Its Muster-Out in 1865.* Bridgton, ME: H. A. Shorey & Sons, Publishers, 1898.

McIntyre, Benjamin F. *Federals on the Frontier: The Diary of Benjamin F. McIntyre, 1862–1864.* Edited by Nannie M. Tilley. Austin: University of Texas Press, 1963.

McMyler, James J. *History of the 11th Wisconsin Veteran Volunteer Infantry.* New Orleans, 1865.

Mellen, William P. *Report Relative to Leasing Abandoned Plantations and Affairs of the Freed People in First Special Agency.* Washington, D.C.: McGill & Witherow, Printers and Stereotypers, 1864.

Moore, Thomas O. *Special Message of Thomas O. Moore, Governor of the State of Louisiana, to the General Assembly, December 1860.* Baton Rouge: J. M. Taylor, State Printer, 1860.

Moors, J. F. *History of the Fifty-second Regiment Massachusetts Volunteers.* Boston: Press of George H. Ellis, 1893.

Murray, Thomas Hamilton. *History of the Ninth Regiment, Connecticut Volunteer Infantry, "The Irish Regiment," in the War of the Rebellion, 1861–65.* New Haven, CT: The Price, Lee & Adkins Co., 1908.

O'Brien, Thomas M., and Oliver Diefendorf. *General Orders of the War Department, Embracing the Years 1861, 1862 & 1863, Vol. I.* New York: Derby & Miller, 1864.

Official Copy of the Militia Law of Louisiana, adopted by the State Legislature, January 23, 1862. Baton Rouge: Tom Bynum, State Printer, 1862.

Official Journal of the Proceedings of the Convention of the State of Louisiana. New Orleans: J. O. Nixon, Printer to the State Convention, 1861.

Official Report Relative to the Conduct of Federal Troops in Western Louisiana, During the Invasions of 1863 and 1864. Compiled from Sworn Testimony, Under Direction of Governor Henry W. Allen. Shreveport: BWS Printing Establishment, 1865.

Paine, Halbert Eleazer. *A Wisconsin Yankee in Confederate Bayou Country: The Civil War Reminiscences of a Union General.* Edited by Samuel C. Hyde, Jr. Baton Rouge: Louisiana State University Press, 2009.

Palmer, Benjamin Morgan. *The South, Her Peril, and Her Duty: A Discourse, Delivered in the First Presbyterian Church, New Orleans, on Thursday, November 29, 1860.* New Orleans: True Witness & Sentinel, 1860.

———. *The Oath of Allegiance to the United States, Discussed in its Moral and Political Bearings.* Richmond: MacFarlane & Fergusson, 1863.

Parton, James. *General Butler in New Orleans: History of the Administration of the Department of the Gulf in the Year 1862: With an Account of the Capture of New Orleans, and a Sketch of the Previous Career of the General, Civil and Military.* New York: Mason Brothers, 1864.

Pellet, Elias Porter. *History of the 114th Regiment, New York State Volunteers.* Norwich, NY: Telegraph & Chronicle Power Press Print, 1866.

Poche, Felix Pierre. *A Louisiana Confederate: Diary of Felix Pierre Poche.* Edited by Edwin C. Bearss. Natchitoches: Louisiana Studies Institute, 1972.

Polk, Leonidas. *Extracts from the Journal of the Twenty-Third Annual Convention of the Protestant Episcopal Church, in the Diocese of Louisiana, Containing an Extract from the Address of the Rt. Rev. Leonidas Polk, D.D., Bishop of the Dioceses. Also, the Report of the Committee on the State of the Church, with the Resolution Thereupon Adopted.* New Orleans: Printed at the Bulletin Book and Job Office, 1861.

Powers, George Whitefield. *The Story of the Thirty-Eighth Regiment of Massachusetts Volunteers.* Cambridge, MA: Dakin & Metcalf, 1866.

Report of the Board of Education for Freedmen, Department of the Gulf, for the year 1864. New Orleans: Printed at the Office of the True Delta, 1865.

Richardson, Albert Deane. *The Secret Service, The Field, The Dungeon, and The Escape.* Hartford: American Publishing Company, 1865.

Russell, William Howard. *My Diary North and South.* Boston: T.O.H.P. Burnham, 1863.

Smith, Edmund Kirby. "The Defense of the Red River," in *Battles and Leaders of the Civil War: Being for the Most Part Contributions by Union and Confederate Officers.* New York: Century Co., 1887.

Smith, George G. *Leaves from a Soldier's Diary: The Personal Record of Lieutenant George G. Smith Co. C, 1st Louisiana Regiment Infantry Volunteers [White] During the War of the Rebellion.* Putnam, CT: Macdonald & Williams, Printers, 1906.

Solomon, Clara. *The Civil War Diary of Clara Solomon: Growing Up in New Orleans, 1861–1862.* Edited by Elliott Ashkenazi. Baton Rouge: Louisiana State University Press, 1995.

Southwood, Marion. *"Beauty and Booty," the Watchword of New Orleans.* New York: M. Doolady, 1867.

Sprague, Homer B. *History of the 13th Infantry Regiment of Connecticut Volunteers, During the Great Rebellion.* Hartford, CT: Case, Lockwood & Co., 1867.

Stearns, Albert. *Reminiscences of the Late War.* New York, 1881.

Stevens, William B. *History of the Fiftieth Regiment of Infantry Massachusetts Volunteer Militia in the Late War of the Rebellion.* Boston: Griffith-Stillings Press, 1907.

Stone, Kate. *Brokenburn: The Journal of Kate Stone, 1861–1868.* Edited by John Q. Anderson. Baton Rouge: Louisiana State University Press, 1955.

Taylor, Richard. *Destruction and Reconstruction: Personal Experiences of the Late War.* New York: D. Appleton & Co., 1879.

Tunnard, William H. *A Southern Record: The History of the Third Regiment Louisiana Infantry.* Fayetteville: University of Arkansas Press, 1997.

U.S. War Department. *The War of the Rebellion: A Compilation of the Official Records of the Union and Confederate Armies.* 128 vols. Washington, D.C.: Government Printing Office, 1880–91.

Van Alstyne, Lawrence. *Diary of an Enlisted Man.* New Haven, CT: Tuttle, Morehouse & Taylor Co., 1910.

Watson, William. *Life in the Confederate Army: Being the Observations and Experiences of an Alien in the South during the American Civil War.* New York: Scribner & Welford, 1888.

Whittington, G. P., ed. "Concerning the Loyalty of Slaves in North Louisiana in 1863. Letters from John H. Ransdell to Governor Thomas O. Moore, dated 1863." *Louisiana Historical Quarterly* 14, no. 4 (October 1931): 487–502.

Yeatman, James E. *Suggestions of a Plan of Organization for Freed Labor and the Leasing of Plantations along the Mississippi River: Under a Bureau or Commission to be Appointed by the Government: Accompanying a Report Presented to the Western Sanitary Commission.* St. Louis: Rooms Western Sanitary Commission, 1864.

———. *Report to the Western Sanitary Commission: In Regard to Leasing Abandoned Plantations, with Rules and Regulations Governing the Same.* St. Louis: Rooms Western Sanitary Commission, 1864.

SECONDARY SOURCES

Books

Abrahams, Ray. *Vigilant Citizens: Vigilantism and the State.* Cambridge: Polity Press, 1998.

Alexander, Michelle. *The New Jim Crow: Mass Incarceration in the Age of Colorblindness.* New York: The New Press, 2020.

Anderson, Benedict. *Imagined Communities: Reflections on the Origins and Spread of Nationalism.* New York: Verso Books, 2006.

Ash, Stephen V. *When the Yankees Came: Conflict and Chaos in the Occupied South, 1861–1865.* Chapel Hill: University of North Carolina Press, 1995.

Baggett, James Alex. *The Scalawags: Southern Dissenters in the Civil War and Reconstruction.* Baton Rouge: Louisiana State University Press, 2002.

Balogh, Brian. *A Government Out of Sight: The Mystery of National Authority in Nineteenth-Century America.* Cambridge: Cambridge University Press, 2009.

Bardaglio, Peter W. *Reconstructing the Household: Families, Sex, and the Law in the Nineteenth-Century South.* Chapel Hill: University of North Carolina Press, 1998.

Behrend, Justin. *Reconstructing Democracy: Grassroots Black Politics in the Deep South after the Civil War.* Athens: University of Georgia Press, 2015.

Beilein, Joseph M., Jr., and Matthew C. Hulbert, eds., *The Civil War Guerrilla: Unfolding the Black Flag in History, Memory, and Myth.* Lexington: University Press of Kentucky, 2015.

————. *Bushwhackers: Guerrilla Warfare, Manhood, and the Household in Civil War Missouri*. Kent, OH: Kent State University Press, 2016.

Bell, Caryn Cosse. *Revolution, Romanticism, and the Afro-Creole Protest Tradition in Louisiana, 1718–1868*. Baton Rouge: Louisiana State University Press, 1997.

Bensel, Richard F. *Yankee Leviathan: The Origins of Central State Authority, 1859–1877*. Cambridge: Cambridge University Press, 1990.

Bercaw, Nancy. *Gendered Freedoms: Race, Rights, and the Politics of Household in the Delta, 1861–1875*. Gainesville: University Press of Florida, 2003.

Beringer, Richard E., Herman Hattaway, Archer Jones, and William N. Still, Jr., eds. *Why the South Lost the Civil War*. Athens, GA: University of Georgia Press, 1986.

Berlin, Ira, et al., *Freedom: A Documentary History of Emancipation, 1861–1867*, Series I Volume I: *The Destruction of Slavery*. Cambridge: Cambridge University Press, 1986.

———— and Leslie S. Rowland. *Families and Freedom: A Documentary History of African-American Kinship in the Civil War Era*. New York: The New Press, 1997.

Blair, William. "Friend or Foe: Treason and the Second Confiscation Act. In *Wars within Wars*, edited by Gary W. Gallagher and Joan Waugh, 63–116. Chapel Hill: University of North Carolina Press, 2009.

————. *With Malice toward Some: Treason and Loyalty in the Civil War Era*. Chapel Hill: University of North Carolina Press, 2014.

Bonner, Michael Brem. *Confederate Political Economy: Creating and Managing a Southern Corporatist Nation*. Baton Rouge: Louisiana State University, 2016.

Bragg, Jefferson Davis. *Louisiana in the Confederacy*. Baton Rouge: Louisiana State University Press, 1941.

Brill, Kristen. *The Weaker Sex in War: Gender and Nationalism in Civil War Virginia*. Charlottesville: University of Virginia Press, 2022.

Browning, Judkin. *Shifting Loyalties: The Union Occupation of Eastern North Carolina*. Chapel Hill: University of North Carolina Press, 2011.

Brownmiller, Susan. *Against Our Will: Men, Women and Rape*. New York: Random House, 1975.

Butler, Clayton. *True Blue: White Unionists in the Deep South during the Civil War and Reconstruction*. Baton Rouge: Louisiana State University Press, 2022.

Bynum, Victoria E. *Unruly Women: The Politics of Social and Sexual Control in the Old South*. Chapel Hill: University of North Carolina Press, 1992.

————. *The Long Shadow of the Civil War: Southern Dissent and Its Legacies*. Chapel Hill: University of North Carolina Press, 2010.

Camp, Stephanie. *Closer to Freedom: Enslaved Women and Everyday Resistance in the Plantation South*. Chapel Hill: University of North Carolina Press, 2004.

Capers, Gerald M. *Occupied City: New Orleans under the Federals, 1862–1865*. Lexington: University of Kentucky Press, 1965.

Cashin, Joan E., ed. *The War Was You and Me: Civilians in the American Civil War*. Princeton: Princeton University Press, 2002.

Clampitt, Bradley R. *Occupied Vicksburg*. Baton Rouge: Louisiana State University Press, 2016.

Clinton, Catherine, ed. *Southern Families at War: Loyalty and Conflict in the Civil War South*. Oxford: Oxford University Press, 2000.

Clinton, Catherine, and Nina Silber, eds. *Divided Houses: Gender and the Civil War*. Oxford: Oxford University Press, 1992.

Cohen, William. *At Freedom's Edge: Black Mobility and the Southern White Quest for Racial Control, 1861–1915*. Baton Rouge: Louisiana State University Press, 1991.

Cohn, Carol, ed. *Women and Wars*. Cambridge: Polity Press, 2013.

Collins, John M. *Martial Law and English Laws, c.1500–c.1700*. Cambridge: Cambridge University Press, 2016.

Cornell, Saul. *The Other Founders: Anti-Federalism and the Dissenting Tradition in America, 1788–1828*. Chapel Hill: University of North Carolina Press, 1999.

Currans, Elizabeth. *Marching Dykes, Liberated Sluts, and Concerned Mothers: Women Transforming Public Space*. Urbana: University of Illinois Press, 2017.

Cutrer, Thomas W. *Theater of a Separate War: The Civil War West of the Mississippi River, 1861–1865*. Chapel Hill: University of North Carolina Press, 2017.

Daly, John Patrick. *The War after the War: A New History of Reconstruction*. Athens: University of Georgia Press, 2022.

Davis, William C. *Jefferson Davis: The Man and His Hour*. New York: Harper Collins, 1991.

Davis, John Martin, Jr., and George B. Tremmel. *Parole, Pardon, Pass and Amnesty Documents of the Civil War: An Illustrated History*. Jefferson, NC: McFarland & Company, Inc., Publishers, 2014.

Dawson, Joseph G. *Army Generals and Reconstruction: Louisiana, 1862–1877*. Baton Rouge: Louisiana University Press, 1982.

DeCuir, Randy. *Yankees on the Tchefuncte: The Civil War in Madisonville, Louisiana*. Amazon Publishing, 2013.

Dilbeck, D. H. *A More Civil War: How the Union Waged a Just War*. Chapel Hill: University of North Carolina Press, 2016.

Downs, Gregory P. *After Appomattox: Military Occupation and the Ends of War*. Cambridge, MA: Harvard University Press, 2015.

——— and Kate Masur, eds. *The War the Civil War Made*. Chapel Hill: University of North Carolina Press, 2015.

Downs, Jim. *Sick From Freedom: African American Illness and Suffering during the Civil War and Reconstruction*. Oxford: Oxford University Press, 2012.

DuBois, W. E. B. *Black Reconstruction in America*. New York: The Free Press, 1998.

Dunbar-Ortiz, Roxanne. *Loaded: A Disarming History of the Second Amendment*. City Lights Publishers, 2018.

East, Charles. *Baton Rouge: A Civil War Album*. Baton Rouge: Moran Industries, Inc., 1977.

Edelstein, David M. *Occupational Hazards: Success and Failure in Military Occupation*. Ithaca, NY: Cornell University Press, 2008.

Edling, Max M. *A Revolution in Favor of Government: Origins of the U.S. Constitution and the Making of the American State*. Cambridge: Oxford University Press, 2003.

———. *A Hercules in the Cradle: War, Money, and the American State, 1783–1867*. Chicago: University of Chicago Press, 2014.

Edmonds, David C, ed. *The Conduct of Federal Troops in Louisiana during the Invasions of 1863 and 1864*. Acadiana Press, 1988.

———. *Yankee Autumn in Acadiana: A Narrative of the Great Texas Overland Expedition through Southwestern Louisiana, October–December 1863*. Lafayette, LA: Center for Louisiana Studies, 2005.

Edwards, Laura F. *Gendered Strife and Confusion: The Political Culture of Reconstruction*. Urbana: University of Illinois Press, 1997.

———. *Scarlett Doesn't Live Here Anymore: Southern Women in the Civil War Era*. Carbondale: University of Illinois Press, 2004.

Escott, Paul D. *After Secession: Jefferson Davis and the Failure of Confederate Nationalism*. Baton Rouge: Louisiana State University Press, 1978.

———. *Military Necessity: Civil-Military Relations in the Confederacy*. Westport, CT: Praeger Security International, 2006.

Fairclough, Adam. *The Revolution That Failed: Reconstruction in Natchitoches*. Gainesville: University Press of Florida, 2018.

Farmer, James Oscar. *The Metaphysical Confederacy: James Henley Thornwell and the Synthesis of Southern Values*. Macon, GA: Mercer University Press, 1986.

Farmer-Kaiser, Mary. *Freedwomen and the Freedmen's Bureau: Race, Gender, and Public Policy in the Age of Emancipation*. New York: Fordham University Press, 2010.

Faust, Drew Gilpin. *The Creation of Confederate Nationalism: Ideology and Identity in the Civil War South*. Baton Rouge: Louisiana State University Press, 1988.

———. *Mothers of Invention: Women of the Slaveholding South in the American Civil War*. Chapel Hill: University of North Carolina Press, 2004.

Fellman, Michael. *Inside War: The Guerrilla Conflict in Missouri during the American Civil War*. New York: Oxford University Press, 1989.

Fischer, Kirsten. *Suspect Relations: Sex, Race, and Resistance in Colonial North Carolina*. Ithaca, NY: Cornell University Press, 2002.

Fisher, Noel C. *War at Every Door: Partisan Politics and Guerrilla Violence in East Tennessee, 1860–1869*. Chapel Hill: University of North Carolina Press, 1997.

Follett, Richard. *Sugar Masters: Planters and Slaves in Louisiana's Cane World, 1820–1860.* Baton Rouge: Louisiana State University Press, 2005.

Foner, Eric. *Reconstruction: America's Unfinished Revolution, 1863–1877.* New York: Harper Perennial, 2014.

———. *The Second Founding: How the Civil War and Reconstruction Remade the Constitution.* New York: W. W. Norton & Company, 2019.

Foucault, Michel. *Discipline and Punish: The Birth of the Prison.* New York: Vintage Books, 1995.

Fox-Genovese, Elizabeth. *Within the Plantation Household: Black and White Women of the Old South.* Chapel Hill: University of North Carolina Press, 1988.

Frank, Lisa Tendrich. *The Civilian War: Confederate Women and Union Soldiers during Sherman's March.* Baton Rouge: Louisiana State University Press, 2015.

———, and LeeAnn Whites, eds. *Household War: How Americans Lived and Fought the Civil War.* Athens: University of Georgia Press, 2020.

Frazier, Donald S. *Fire in the Cane Field: The Federal Invasion of Louisiana and Texas, January 1861–January 1863.* Buffalo Gap, TX: State House Press, 2009.

———. *Thunder across the Swamp: The Fight for the Lower Mississippi, February 1863–May 1863.* Buffalo Gap, TX: State House Press, 2011.

Gallagher, Gary W. *The Confederate War: How Popular Will, Nationalism, and Military Strategy Could Not Stave Off Defeat.* Cambridge, MA: Harvard University Press, 1999. General Services Administration. *Hard Labor: History and Archeology at the Old Louisiana State Penitentiary, Baton Rouge, Louisiana.* Fort Worth, TX: 1991.

Gerteis, Louis S. *From Contraband to Freedman: Federal Policy toward Southern Blacks, 1861–1865.* Westport, CT: Greenwood Press, Inc., 1973.

Giesberg, Judith. *Army at Home: Women and the Civil War on the Northern Home Front.* Chapel Hill: University of North Carolina Press, 2009.

Glymph, Thavolia. *Out of the House of Bondage: The Transformation of the Plantation Household.* Cambridge: Cambridge University Press, 2008.

———. *The Women's Fight: The Civil War's Battles for Home, Freedom, and Nation.* Chapel Hill: University of North Carolina Press, 2020.

Goldstein, Joshua S. *War and Gender.* Cambridge: Cambridge University Press, 2001.

Goss, Thomas J. *The War within the Union High Command: Politics and Generalship during the Civil War.* Lawrence: University Press of Kansas, 2003.

Grenier, John. *The First Way of War: American War Making on the Frontier.* Cambridge: Cambridge University Press, 2005.

Grimsley, Mark. *The Hard Hand of War: Union Military Policy toward Southern Civilians, 1861–1865.* Cambridge: Cambridge University Press, 1995.

Grimsted, David. *American Mobbing, 1828–1861: Toward Civil War.* New York: Oxford University Press, 1998.

Grossberg, Michael. *Governing the Hearth: Law and the Family in Nineteenth-Century America*. Chapel Hill: University of North Carolina Press, 1988.

Gutman, Herbert G. *The Black Family in Slavery and Freedom, 1750–1925*. New York: Pantheon Books, 1976.

Hahn, Steven. *A Nation under Our Feet: Black Political Struggles in the Rural South from Slavery to the Great Migration*. Cambridge, MA: Harvard University Press, 2003.

Hahn, Steven, et al., *Freedom: A Documentary History of Emancipation, 1861–1867*. Series 3: Volume 1: *Land and Labor, 1865*. Chapel Hill: University of North Carolina Press, 2008.

Harrison, Kimberly. *The Rhetoric of Rebel Women: Civil War Diaries and Confederate Persuasion*. Carbondale: Southern Illinois University Press, 2013.

Haumesser, Lauren N. *The Democratic Collapse: How Gender Politics Broke a Party and a Nation, 1856–1861*. Chapel Hill: University of North Carolina Press, 2022.

Hearn, Chester G. *The Capture of New Orleans, 1862*. Baton Rouge: Louisiana State University Press, 1995.

———. *When the Devil Came Down to Dixie: Ben Butler in New Orleans*. Baton Rouge: Louisiana State University Press, 1997.

Hewitt, Lawrence Lee. *Port Hudson: Confederate Bastion on the Mississippi*. Baton Rouge: Louisiana State University Press, 1987.

Hodes, Martha. *White Women, Black Men: Illicit Sex in the Nineteenth-Century South*. New Haven, CT: Yale University Press, 1997.

Hoffer, Williamjames Hull. *Plessy v. Ferguson: Race and Inequality in Jim Crow America*. Topeka: University of Kansas, 2012.

Hollandsworth, James G., Jr. *The Louisiana Native Guards: The Black Military Experience during the Civil War*. Baton Rouge: Louisiana State University Press, 1995.

———. *Pretense of Glory: The Life of General Nathaniel P. Banks*. Baton Rouge: Louisiana State University Press, 1998.

Holzman, Robert S. *Stormy Ben Butler*. New York: Collier Books, 1954.

Hunter, Tera W. *To 'Joy My Freedom: Southern Black Women's Lives and Labors after the Civil War*. Cambridge, MA: Harvard University Press, 1998.

———. *Bound in Wedlock: Slave and Free Black Marriage in the Nineteenth Century*. Cambridge, MA: Belknap Press of Harvard University Press, 2017.

Hurt, R. Douglas. *Agriculture and the Confederacy: Policy, Productivity, and Power in the Civil War South*. Chapel Hill: University of North Carolina Press, 2015.

Hyde, Samuel C., Jr. *Pistols and Politics: Feuds, Factions, and the Struggle for the Order in Louisiana's Florida Parishes, 1810–1935*. Baton Rouge: Louisiana State University Press, 2018.

Inscoe, John C., and Gordon B. McKinney. *The Heart of Confederate Appalachia: Western North Carolina in the Civil War*. Chapel Hill: University of North Carolina Press, 2000.

Johnson, Ludwell H. *Red River Campaign: Politics and Cotton in the Civil War.* Kent, OH: Kent State University Press, 1993.

Joiner, Gary D. *One Damn Blunder from Beginning to End: The Red River Campaign of 1864.* Wilmington, DE: Scholarly Resources Inc., 2003.

———. *Through the Howling Wilderness: The 1864 Red River Campaign and Union Failure in the West.* Knoxville: University of Tennessee Press, 2006.

———. *Mr. Lincoln's Brown Water Navy: The Mississippi Squadron.* Lanham, MD: Rowman & Littlefield Publishers, Inc., 2007.

Jones, Jacqueline. *Labor of Sorrow, Labor of Love: Black Women, Work, and the Family, from Slavery to the Present.* New York: Basic Books, 1985.

Jones, Martha S. *Birthright Citizens: A History of Race and Rights in Antebellum America.* Cambridge: Cambridge University Press, 2018.

Kerber, Linda K. *No Constitutional Right to Be Ladies: Women and the Obligations of Citizenship.* New York: Hill & Wang, 1998.

Kerby, Robert L. *Kirby Smith's Confederacy: The Trans-Mississippi South, 1863–1865.* Tuscaloosa: University of Alabama Press, 1972.

Kirkpatrick, Jennet. *UnCivil Disobedience: Studies in Violence and Democratic Politics.* Princeton, NJ: Princeton University Press, 2008.

Lang, Andrew. *In the Wake of War: Military Occupation, Emancipation, and Civil War America.* Baton Rouge: Louisiana State University Press, 2017.

Leonard, Elizabeth. *Benjamin Franklin Butler: A Noisy, Fearless Life.* Baton Rouge: Louisiana State University Press, 2020.

Levine, Bruce. *Confederate Emancipation: Southern Plans to Free and Arm Slaves during the Civil War.* Oxford: Oxford University Press, 2007.

Link, William A., and James J. Broomall, eds. *Rethinking American Emancipation: Legacies of Slavery and the Quest for Black Freedom.* Cambridge: Cambridge University Press, 2016.

Lowe, Richard. *The Texas Overland Expedition of 1863.* Fort Worth, TX: Ryan Place Publishers, 1996.

Lowenthal, Larry. *A Yankee Regiment in Confederate Louisiana: The 31st Massachusetts Volunteer Infantry in the Gulf South.* Baton Rouge: Louisiana State University Press, 2019.

Lowry, Thomas P. *Sexual Misbehavior in the Civil War: A Compendium.* Xlibris Corporation, 2006.

Luskey, Brian. *Men is Cheap: Exposing the Frauds of Free Labor in Civil War America.* Chapel Hill: University of North Carolina Press, 2020.

Malone, Ann Patton. *Sweet Chariot: Slave Family and Household Structure in Nineteenth-Century Louisiana.* Chapel Hill: University of North Carolina, 1992.

Manjapra, Kris. *Black Ghost of Empire: The Long Death of Slavery and the Failure of Emancipation.* New York: Simon & Schuster, 2022.

Manning, Chandra. *What This Cruel War Was Over: Soldiers, Slavery, and the Civil War.* New York: Knopf, 2007.

———. *Troubled Refuge: Struggling for Freedom in the Civil War.* New York: Vintage Books, 2016.

Martinez, Jaime Amanda. *Confederate Slave Impressment in the Upper South.* Chapel Hill: University of North Carolina Press, 2013.

Masur, Kate. *Until Justice Be Done: America's First Civil Rights Movement, from the Revolution to Reconstruction.* New York: W. W. Norton, 2021.

Mathisen, Erik. *The Loyal Republic: Traitors, Slaves and the Remaking of Citizenship in Civil War America.* Chapel Hill: University of North Carolina Press, 2018.

Mayeaux, Steven M. *Earthen Walls, Iron Men: Fort DeRussy, Louisiana, and the Defense of Red River.* Knoxville: University of Tennessee Press, 2007.

McCrary, Peyton. *Abraham Lincoln and Reconstruction: The Louisiana Experiment.* Princeton, NJ: Princeton University Press, 1978.

McCurry, Stephanie. *Masters of Small Worlds: Yeoman Households, Gender Relations, and the Political Culture of the Antebellum South Carolina Low Country.* New York: Oxford University Press, 1995.

———. *Confederate Reckoning: Power and Politics in the Civil War South.* Cambridge, MA: Harvard University Press, 2010.

———. *Women's War: Fighting and Surviving the American Civil War.* Cambridge, MA: Harvard University Press, 2019.

McKenzie, Robert Tracy. *Lincolnites and Rebels: A Divided Town in the American Civil War.* New York: Oxford University Press, 2006.

McKnight, Brian D., and Barton A. Myers, eds. *The Guerrilla Hunters: Irregular Conflicts during the Civil War.* Baton Rouge: Louisiana State University Press, 2017.

McPherson, James M. *For Cause and Comrades: Why Men Fought in the Civil War.* New York: Oxford University Press, 1997.

Mitchel, Reid. *The Vacant Chair: The Northern Soldier Leaves Home.* New York: Oxford University Press, 1995.

Murphy, Kim. *I Had Rather Die: Rape in the Civil War.* Afton, VA: Coachlight Press, 2014.

Nash, Howard P., Jr. *Stormy Petrel: The Life and Times of General Benjamin F. Butler, 1818–1893.* New York: Houghton Mifflin, 1965.

Neely, Mark E., Jr. *Southern Rights: Political Prisoners and the Myth of Confederate Constitutionalism.* Charlottesville: University Press of Virginia, 1999.

Noe, Kenneth W. *Reluctant Rebels: The Confederates Who Joined the Army after 1861.* Chapel Hill: University of North Carolina Press, 2010.

————. *The Howling Storm: Weather, Climate, and the American Civil War.* Baton Rouge: Louisiana State University Press, 2020.

Nolan, Dick. *Benjamin Franklin Butler: The Damnedest Yankee.* Novato, CA: Presidio Press, 1991.

Novack, William J. *The People's Welfare: Law and Regulation in Nineteenth-Century America.* Chapel Hill: University of North Carolina Press, 1996.

Oakes, James. *Freedom National: The Destruction of Slavery in the United States, 1861–1865.* New York: W. W. Norton & Company, 2013.

————. *The Scorpion's Sting: Antislavery and the Coming of the Civil War.* New York: W. W. Norton & Company, 2014.

O'Donovan, Susan Eve. *Becoming Free in the Cotton South.* Cambridge, MA: Harvard University Press, 2007.

Owsley, Frank Lawrence. *State Rights in the Confederacy.* Chicago: University of Chicago Press, 1925.

Parrish, Michael. *Richard Taylor: Soldier Prince of Dixie.* Chapel Hill: University of North Carolina Press, 1992.

Pierson, Michael D. *Free Hearts and Free Homes: Gender and American Antislavery Politics.* Chapel Hill: University of North Carolina Press, 2003.

————. *Mutiny at Fort Jackson: The Untold Story of the Fall of New Orleans.* Chapel Hill: University of North Carolina Press, 2016.

————. *Lt. Spalding in Civil War Louisiana: A Union Officer's Humor, Privilege, and Ambition.* Baton Rouge: Louisiana State University Press, 2016.

Potter, David M. *The Impending Crisis: 1848–1861.* New York: Harper Perennial, 1976.

Powell, Lawrence N. *New Masters: Northern Planters during the Civil War and Reconstruction.* New Haven, CT: Yale University Press, 1980.

————. *The Accidental City: Improvising New Orleans.* Cambridge, MA: Harvard University Press, 2012.

Prushankin, Jeffrey A. *A Crisis of Confederate Command: Edmund Kirby Smith, Richard Taylor, and the Army of the Trans-Mississippi.* Baton Rouge: Louisiana State University Press, 2005.

Quigley, Paul. *Shifting Grounds: Nationalism and the American South, 1848–1865.* New York: Oxford University Press, 2011.

Rable, George C. *Civil Wars: Women and the Crisis of Southern Nationalism.* Urbana: University of Illinois Press, 1991.

————. *The Confederate Republic: A Revolution against Politics.* Chapel Hill: University of North Carolina Press, 1994.

————. *God's Almost Chosen Peoples: A Religious History of the Civil War.* Chapel Hill: University of North Carolina Press, 2010.

———. *Damn Yankees! Demonization and Defiance in the Confederate South.* Baton Rouge: Louisiana State University Press, 2015.

Rael, Patrick. *Eighty-eight Years: The Long Death of Slavery in the United States, 1777–1865.* Athens: University of Georgia Press, 2015.

Reardon, Carol. *With a Sword in One Hand and Jomini in the Other: The Problem of Military Thought in the Civil War North.* Chapel Hill: University of North Carolina Press, 2012.

Reidy, Joseph P. *Illusions of Emancipation: The Pursuit of Freedom and Equality in the Twilight of Slavery.* Chapel Hill: University of North Carolina Press, 2020.

Ripley, C. Peter. *Slaves and Freedmen in Civil War Louisiana.* Baton Rouge: Louisiana State University Press, 1976.

Robertson, Henry O. *The Red River Campaign and Its Toll: 69 Bloody Days in Louisiana, March–May 1864.* Jefferson, NC: McFarland & Company, Inc., Publishers, 2016.

Robinson, Armstead L. *Bitter Fruits of Bondage: The Demise of Slavery and the Collapse of the Confederacy, 1861–1865.* Charlottesville: University of Virginia Press, 2005.

Rodrigue, John C. *Reconstruction in the Cane Field: From Slavery to Free Labor in Louisiana's Sugar Parishes, 1862–1880.* Baton Rouge: Louisiana State University Press, 2001.

Roland, Charles P. *Louisiana Sugar Plantations during the Civil War.* Baton Rouge: Louisiana State University Press, 1997.

Rosen, Hannah. *Terror in the Heart of Freedom: Citizenship, Sexual Violence, and the Meaning of Race in the Postemancipation South.* Chapel Hill: University of North Carolina Press, 2009.

Rubin, Anne Sarah. *A Shattered Nation: The Rise and Fall of the Confederacy, 1861–1868.* Chapel Hill: University of North Carolina Press, 2005.

Ruminski, Jarret. *The Limits of Loyalty: Ordinary People in Civil War Mississippi.* Jackson: University Press of Mississippi, 2017.

Sacher, John M. *A Perfect War of Politics: Parties, Politicians, and Democracy in Louisiana, 1824–1861.* Baton Rouge: Louisiana State University Press, 2003.

———. *Confederate Conscription and the Struggle for Southern Soldiers.* Baton Rouge: Louisiana State University Press, 2021.

Sandy, Laura R., and Marie S. Molloy, eds. *The Civil War and Slavery Reconsidered: Negotiating the Peripheries.* New York: Taylor & Francis Group, 2019.

Schafer, Judith K. *Becoming Free, Remaining Free: Manumission and Enslavement in New Orleans, 1846–1862.* Baton Rouge: Louisiana State University Press, 2003.

Schwalm, Leslie A. *A Hard Fight for We: Women's Transition from Slavery to Freedom in South Carolina.* Urbana: University of Illinois Press, 1997.

Scott, James C. *Seeing Like a State: How Certain Schemes to Improve the Human Condition Have Failed.* New Haven, CT: Yale University Press, 1998.

Scott, Rebecca J. *Degrees of Freedom: Louisiana and Cuba after Slavery.* Cambridge: Belknap Press of Harvard, 2008.

Sheehan-Dean, Aaron. *Why Confederates Fought: Family and Nation in Civil War Virginia.* Chapel Hill: University of North Carolina Press, 2007.

———. *The Calculus of Violence: How Americans Fought the Civil War.* Cambridge, MA: Harvard University Press, 2018.

———. *Reckoning with Rebellion: War and Sovereignty in the Nineteenth Century.* Gainesville: University of Florida Press, 2020.

Shugg, Roger W. *Origins of Class Struggle in Louisiana: A Social History of White Farmers and Laborers during Slavery and After, 1840–1875.* Baton Rouge: Louisiana State University Press, 1939.

Siddali, Silvana R. *From Property to Person: Slavery and the Confiscation Acts, 1861–1862.* Baton Rouge: Louisiana State University Press, 2005.

Silber, Nina. *Daughters of the Union: Northern Women Fight the Civil War.* Cambridge: Harvard University Press, 2005.

———. *Gender and the Sectional Conflict.* Chapel Hill: University of North Carolina Press, 2008.

Silkenat, David. *Scars on the Land: An Environmental History of Slavery in the American South.* Oxford: Oxford University Press, 2022.

Smith, John David, and Bob Luke, eds. *Soldiering for Freedom: How the Union Army Recruited, Trained, and Deployed the U.S. Colored Troops.* Baltimore: Johns Hopkins University Press, 2014.

Somerville, Diane Miller. *Rape and Race in the Nineteenth-Century South.* Chapel Hill: University of North Carolina Press, 2004.

Stanley, Amy Dru. *From Bondage to Contract: Wage Labor, Marriage, and the Market in the Age of Slave Emancipation.* Cambridge: Cambridge University Press, 1998.

Sterkx, H. E. *The Free Negro in Ante-bellum Louisiana.* Madison, NJ: Fairleigh Dickinson University Press, 1972.

Sternhell, Yael A. *Routes of War: The World of Movement in the Confederate South.* Cambridge, MA: Harvard University Press, 2012.

Stirk, Peter M. R. *The Politics of Military Occupation.* Edinburgh: Edinburgh University Press, 2009.

Stith, Matthew M. *Extreme Civil War: Guerrilla Warfare, Environment, and Race on the Trans-Mississippi Frontier.* Baton Rouge: Louisiana State University Press, 2016.

Summers, Mark Wahlgreen. *The Ordeal of Reunion: A New History of Reconstruction.* Chapel Hill: University of North Carolina Press, 2014.

Sutherland, Daniel E., ed. *Guerrillas, Unionists, and Violence on the Confederate Home Front.* Fayetteville: University of Arkansas Press, 1999.

———. *A Savage Conflict: The Decisive Role of Guerrillas in the American Civil War.* Chapel Hill: University of North Carolina Press, 2009.

Taylor, Amy Murrell. *Embattled Freedom: Journeys through the Civil War's Slave Refugee Camps.* Chapel Hill: University of North Carolina Press, 2018.

Thomas, Emory M. *The Confederacy as a Revolutionary Experience.* Englewood Cliffs, NJ: Prentice Hall, 1971.

Trefousse, Hans L. *Ben Butler: The South Called Him Beast!* New York: Octagon Books, 1974.

Tunnell, Ted. *Crucible of Reconstruction: War, Radicalism, and Race in Louisiana, 1862–1877.* Baton Rouge: Louisiana State University Press, 1984.

Usner, Daniel. *Indians, Settlers, and Slaves in a Frontier Exchange Economy: The Lower Mississippi Valley before 1783.* Chapel Hill: University of North Carolina Press, 1992.

Vandiver, Frank E. *Jefferson Davis and the Confederate State.* Oxford: Clarendon Press, 1964.

Varon, Elizabeth. *We Mean to Be Counted: White Women and Politics in Antebellum Virginia.* Chapel Hill: University of North Carolina Press, 1998.

———. *Disunion! The Coming of the American Civil War, 1789–1859.* Chapel Hill: University of North Carolina Press, 2008.

———. *Armies of Deliverance: A New History of the Civil War.* Oxford: Oxford University Press, 2019.

Waugh, Joan, and Gary W. Gallagher, eds. *Wars within a War: Controversy and Conflict over the American Civil War.* Chapel Hill: University of North Carolina Press, 2009.

Wayne, Michael. *The Reshaping of Plantation Society: The Natchez District, 1860–80.* Baton Rouge: Louisiana State University Press, 1983.

Welch, Kimberly. *Black Litigants in the Antebellum American South.* Chapel Hill: University of North Carolina Press, 2018.

West, Richard S. *Lincoln's Scapegoat General: A Life of Benjamin F. Butler, 1818–1893.* Boston: Riverside Press, 1965.

Wetta, Frank L. *The Louisiana Scalawags: Politics, Race, and Terrorism during the Civil War and Reconstruction.* Baton Rouge: Louisiana State University Press, 2013.

White, Howard Ashley. *The Freedmen's Bureau in Louisiana.* Baton Rouge: Louisiana State University Press, 1970.

Whites, LeeAnn. *The Civil War as a Crisis in Gender: Augusta, Georgia, 1860–1890.* Athens: University of Georgia Press, 1996.

———, and Alecia Long, eds. *Occupied Women: Gender, Military Occupation, and the American Civil War.* Baton Rouge: Louisiana State University Press, 2009.

Wilentz, Sean. *No Property in Man: Slavery and Antislavery at the Nation's Founding.* Cambridge, MA: Harvard University Press, 2018.

Williams, David. *Bitterly Divided: The South's Inner Civil War.* New York: The New Press, 2008.

Winters, John D. *The Civil War in Louisiana.* Baton Rouge: Louisiana State University Press, 1963.

Witt, John Fabian. *Lincoln's Code: The Laws of War in American History.* New York: Free Press, 2012.

Woolworth, Steven E. *Jefferson Davis and His Generals: The Failure of Confederate Command in the West.* Lawrence: University Press of Kansas, 1990.

Wyatt-Brown, Bertram. *Southern Honor: Ethics and Behavior in the Old South.* Oxford: Oxford University Press, 2007.

Zuck, Rochelle Raineri. *Divided Sovereignties: Race, Nationhood, and Citizenship in Nineteenth-Century America.* Athens: University of Georgia Press, 2016.

Journal Articles

Baker, Paula C. "The Domestication of Politics: Women and American Political Society, 1780–1920." *American Historical Review* 89, no. 3 (June 1984): 620–47.

Ballantyne, David T. "'Whenever the Yankees Were Gone, I Was a Confederate': Loyalty and Dissent in Civil War–Era Rapids Parish, Louisiana." *Civil War History* 63, no. 1 (March 2017): 36–67.

Barber, E. Susan, and Charles F. Ritter. "Dangerous Liaisons: Working Women and Sexual Justice in the American Civil War." *European Journal of American Studies* 10, no. 1 (2015): https://journals.openedition.org/ejas/10695.

Beck, Julie. "Gender, Race, and Rape during the Civil War." *The Atlantic,* February 20, 2014.

Bell, Karen Cook. "Self-Emancipating Women, Civil War, and the Union Army in Southern Louisiana and Lowcountry Georgia, 1861–1865." *Journal of African American History* 101, no. 1–2 (Winter-Spring 2016): 1–22.

Bensel, Richard F. "Valor and Valkyries: Why the State Needs Valhalla." *Polity* 40, no. 3, (July 2008): 386–93.

Brady, Patricia. "Trials and Tribulations: American Missionary Association Teachers and Black Education in Occupied New Orleans, 1863–1864." *Louisiana History: The Journal of the Louisiana Historical Association* 31, no. 1 (Winter 1990): 5–20.

Brill, Kristen. "'I Had the Men from the Start': General Benjamin Butler's Occupation of New Orleans." *Women's History Review* 26, no. 3 (2017): 319–28.

Campbell, Jacqueline G. "There Is No Difference between a He and a She Adder in Their Venom: Benjamin F. Butler, William T. Sherman, and Confederate Women." *Louisiana History: The Journal of the Louisiana Historical Association* 50, no. 1 (Winter 2009): 5–24.

———. "'The Unmeaning Twaddle about Order 28': Benjamin F. Butler and Confederate Women in Occupied New Orleans, 1862." *Journal of the Civil War Era* 2, no. 1 (March 2012): 11–30.

Clampitt, Brad R. "The Breakup: The Collapse of the Confederate Trans-Mississippi Army in Texas, 1865." *Southwestern Historical Quarterly* 108, no. 4 (April 2005): 498–534.

Crouch, Barry A. "Black Education in Civil War and Reconstruction Louisiana: George T. Ruby, the Army, and the Freedmen's Bureau." *Louisiana History: The Journal of the Louisiana Historical Association* 38, no. 3 (Summer 1997): 287–308.

Damico, John Kelly. "Confederate Soldiers Take Matters into Their Own Hands: The End of the Civil War in North Louisiana." *Louisiana History: The Journal of the Louisiana Historical Association* 39, no. 2 (Spring 1998): 189–205.

Derbes, Brett J. "Prison Productions: Textiles and Other Military Supplies at the Louisiana State Penitentiary in the Civil War." *Louisiana History: The Journal of the Louisiana Historical Association* 55, no. 1 (Winter 2014): 40–64.

Dollar, Susan E. "The Red River Campaign, Natchitoches Parish, Louisiana: A Case of Equal Opportunity Destruction." *Louisiana History: The Journal of the Louisiana Historical Association* 43, no. 4 (Autumn 2002): 411–32.

Doyle, Elisabeth Joan. "Nurseries of Treason: Schools in Occupied New Orleans." *Journal of Southern History* 26, no. 2 (May 1960): 161–79.

Feimster, Crystal. "General Benjamin Butler and the Threat of Sexual Violence during the American Civil War." *Daedalus* 138, no. 2 (Spring 2009): 201–2.

———. "Rape and Justice in the Civil War." *New York Times*, April 25, 2013.

———. "Keeping a Disorderly House in Civil War Kentucky." *Register of the Kentucky Historical Society* 117, no. 2 (Spring 2019): 301–22.

Foote, Lorien. "Rethinking the Confederate Home Front." *Journal of the Civil War Era* 7, no. 3 (September 2017): 446–65.

Gentry, Judith F. "White Gold: The Confederate Government and Cotton in Louisiana." *Louisiana History: The Journal of the Louisiana Historical Association* 33, no. 3 (Summer 1992): 229–40.

Glymph, Thavolia. "'I'm a Radical Black Girl': Black Women Unionists and the Politics of Civil War History." *Journal of the Civil War Era* 8, no. 3 (September 2018): 359–87.

Gudmestad, Robert. "Elusive Victory: The Union Navy's War along the Western Water." *Civil War History* 67, no. 2 (2021): 79–109.

Hall, Aaron R. "Public Slaves and State Engineers: Modern Statecraft on Louisiana's Waterways." *Journal of Southern History* 85, no. 3 (August 2019): 531–76.

Hamilton, Daniel W. "The Confederate Sequestration Act." *Civil War History* 52, no. 4 (December 2006), 373–408.

Haugen, Andrew. "Patriotic Fever, the Civil War Press, and the Execution of William B. Mumford." *Louisiana History: The Journal of the Louisiana Historical Association* 63, no. 2 (Spring 2022): 191–236.

Huber, Leonard V. "The Battle of the Handkerchiefs." *Civil War History* 8, no. 1 (March 1962): 48–53.

Hunter, G. Howard. "The Politics of Resentment: Unionist Regiments and the New Orleans Immigrant Community, 1862–1864." *Louisiana History: The Journal of the Louisiana Historical Association* 44, no. 2 (Spring 2003): 185–210.

———. "Late to the Dance: New Orleans and the Emergence of a Confederate City." *Louisiana History: The Journal of the Louisiana Historical Association* 57, no. 3 (Summer 2016): 297–322.

Jones, Catherine A. "Women, Gender, and the Boundaries of Reconstruction." *Journal of the Civil War Era* 8, no. 1 (March 2018): 111–31.

Lathrop, Barnes F. "Disaffection in Confederate Louisiana: The Case of William Hyman." *Journal of Southern History* 24, no. 3 (August 1958): 308–18.

———. "The Lafourche District in 1862: Militia and Partisan Rangers." *Louisiana History: The Journal of the Louisiana Historical Association* 1, no. 3 (Summer 1960): 230–44.

———. "The Lafourche District in 1862: Confederate Revival." *Louisiana History: The Journal of the Louisiana Historical Association* 1, no. 4 (Autumn 1960): 300–319.

———. "The Lafourche District in 1862: Invasion." *Louisiana History: The Journal of the Louisiana Historical Association* 2, no. 2 (Spring 1961): 175–201.

Marten, James. "The Making of a Carpetbagger: George S. Denison and the South, 1854–1866." *Louisiana History: The Journal of the Louisiana Historical Association* 34, no. 2 (Spring 1993): 133–60.

McGerr, Michael E. "Political Style and Women's Power, 1830–1930." *Journal of American History* 77, no. 3 (December 1990): 864–85.

Means, Emilia Gay Griffith. "Guy Mannering Travels North: Letters from Henry Watkins Allen, a Slaveholder to Command." *Louisiana History: The Journal of the Louisiana Historical Association* 40, no. 1 (Winter 1999): 85–100.

Messner, William F. "Black Violence and White Response: Louisiana, 1862." *Journal of Southern History* 41, no. 1 (February 1975): 19–38.

Michot, Steven S. "'War Is Still Raging in This Part of the Country': Oath-Taking, Conscription, and Guerrilla War in Louisiana's Lafourche Region." *Louisiana History: The Journal of the Louisiana Historical Association* 38, no. 2 (Spring 1997): 167–84.

Mills, Gary B. "Patriotism Frustrated: The Native Guards of Confederate Natchitoches." *Louisiana History: The Journal of the Louisiana Historical Association* 18, no. 4 (Autumn 1977): 437–51.

Monroe, Haskell. "Bishop Palmer's Thanksgiving Day Address." *Louisiana History: The Journal of the Louisiana Historical Association* 4, no. 2 (Spring 1963): 105–18.

Moore, Wilton P. "The Provost Marshal Goes to War." *Civil War History* 5, no. 1 (March 1959): 62–71.

———. "Union Army Provost Marshals in the Eastern Theater." *Military Affairs* 26, no. 3 (Autumn 1962): 120–26.

Nguyen, Julia Huston. "Keeping the Faith: The Political Significance of Religious Services in Civil War Louisiana, 1860–1865." *Louisiana History: The Journal of the Louisiana Historical Association* 44, no. 2 (Spring 2003): 165–83.

Neely, Mark E., Jr. "Guerrilla Warfare, Slavery, and the Hopes of the Confederacy." *Journal of the Civil War Era* 6, no. 3 (September 2016): 376–412.

Novack, William J. "The Myth of a 'Weak' American State." *American Historical Review* 113, no. 3 (June 2008): 752–72.

Obert, Jonathan, and Eleonora Mattiacci. "Keeping Vigil: The Emergence of Vigilance Committees in Pre–Civil War America." *Perspectives on Politics* 16, no. 3 (September 2018): 600–616.

Palmer, Paul C., and Nancy Carol Carter. "Bruce Catton's Uncivil War on Benjamin Butler. *Louisiana History: The Journal of the Louisiana Historical Association* 36, no. 3 (Summer 1995): 261–75.

Paludan, Phillip. "The American Civil War Considered as a Crisis in Law and Order." *American Historical Review* 77, no. 4 (October 1972): 1013–1034.

Pemberton, Sarah. "Enforcing Gender: The Constitution of Sex and Gender in Prison Regimes." *Signs* 39, no. 1 (Autumn 2013): 151–75.

Power, Sally P. "A Vermonter's Account of the Red River Campaign." *Louisiana History: The Journal of the Louisiana Historical Association* 40, no. 3 (Summer 1999): 355–64.

Rable, George C. "Fighting for Reunion: Dilemmas of Hatred and Vengeance." *Journal of the Civil War Era* 9, no. 3 (September 2019): 347–77.

Rao, Gautham. "The New Historiography of the Early Federal Government: Institutions, Contexts, and the Imperial State." *William and Mary Quarterly* 77, no. 1 (January 2020): 97–128.

Ruminski, Jarret. "'Tradyville': The Contraband Trade and the Problem of Loyalty in Civil War Mississippi." *Journal of the Civil War Era* 2, no. 4 (December 2012): 511–37.

Sacher, John M. "'The Ladies Are Moving Everywhere': Louisiana Women and Antebellum Politics." *Louisiana History: The Journal of the Louisiana Historical Association* 42, no. 4 (Autumn 2001): 439–57.

———. "'Our Interest and Destiny Are the Same': Governor Thomas Overton Moore and Confederate Loyalty." *Louisiana History: The Journal of the Louisiana Historical Association* 49, no. 3 (Summer 2008): 261–86.

Scott, Sean A. "'The Glory of the City Is Gone': Perspectives of Union Soldiers on New Orleans during the Civil War." *Louisiana History: The Journal of the Louisiana Historical Association* 57, no. 1 (Winter 2016): 45–69.

Simpson, Amos E., and Vincent Cassidy. "The Wartime Administration of Governor Henry W. Allen." *Louisiana History: The Journal of the Louisiana Historical Association* 5, no. 3 (Summer 1964): 257–69.

Surdam, David G. "Union Military Superiority and New Orleans's Economic Value to the Confederacy." *Louisiana History: The Journal of the Louisiana Historical Association* 38, no. 4 (Autumn 1997): 389–408.

Sutherland, Daniel E. "Guerrilla Warfare, Democracy, and the Fate of the Confederacy." *The Journal of Southern History* 68, no. 2 (May 2002): 259–92.

Taylor, Ethel. "Discontent in Confederate Louisiana." *Louisiana History: The Journal of the Louisiana Historical Association* 2, no. 4 (Autumn 1961): 410–28.

Taylor, Joe Gray. "Slavery in Louisiana during the Civil War." *Louisiana History: The Journal of the Louisiana Historical Association* 8, no. 1 (Winter 1967): 27–33.

Wilentz, Sean. "The Emancipators' Vision." *New York Review* 69, no. 20 (December 22, 2022): 58–61.

Wilson, Keith. "Education as a Vehicle of Racial Control: Major General N. P. Banks in Louisiana, 1863–64." *Journal of Negro Education* 50, no. 2 (Spring 1981): 156–70.

Wish, Harvey. "Slave Disloyalty under the Confederacy." *Journal of Negro History* 23, no. 4 (October 1938): 435–50.

Whites, LeeAnn. "Forty Shirts and a Wagonload of Wheat: Women, the Domestic Supply Line, and the Civil War on the Western Border." *Journal of the Civil War Era* 1, no. 1 (March 2011): 56–78.

THESES, DISSERTATIONS, AND BOOK CHAPTERS

Ballantyne, David T. "Whose Hearth and Home? White Civil War-Era Loyalties in Central Louisiana." In *The Civil War and Slavery Reconsidered: Negotiating the Peripheries,* edited by Laura R. Sandy and Marie S. Molloy, 53–77. New York: Taylor & Francis Group, 2019.

Brackett, Katherine. "Rewriting Domesticity, War, and Confederate Defeat: Julia LeGrand, Sensibility, and Literary Culture in the Nineteenth-Century South. Unpublished Master's Thesis, West Virginia University, 2012.

Buman, Nathan. "Two Histories, One Future: Louisiana Sugar Planters, Their Slaves, and the Anglo-Creole Schism, 1815–1865." Unpublished dissertation, Louisiana State University, 2013.

Downs, Gregory P. "The Civil War and the American State." In *Cambridge History of the Civil War, Vol. III,* edited by Aaron Sheehan-Dean, 350–71. Cambridge: Cambridge University Press, 2019.

Edwards, Stephen Jay. "The Thin Blue Line: Law and Order during the Federal Occupation of New Orleans, 1862–1865." Unpublished master's thesis, Texas Christian University, 2015.

Feimster, Crystal, "'What If I Am a Woman?': Black Women's Campaigns for Sexual Justice and Citizenship." In *The World the Civil War Made*, edited by Gregory P. Downs and Kate Masur, 249–68. Chapel Hill: University of North Carolina Press, 2015.

Frazier, Donald S. "'Out of Stinking Distance': The Guerrilla War in Louisiana." In *Guerrillas, Unionists, and Violence on the Confederate Home Front*, edited by Daniel Sutherland, 151–70. Fayetteville: University of Arkansas Press, 1999.

Goodwyne, Christopher James. "Business as Usual: The Gulf Department under the Administrations of Benjamin F. Butler and Nathaniel P. Banks." Unpublished master's thesis, Louisiana State University, 1985.

Powell, Lawrence N., and Michael S. Wayne. "Self-Interest and the Decline of Confederate Nationalism." In *The Old South in the Crucible of War*, edited by Harry P. Owens and James J. Cooke, 29–45. Jackson: University Press of Mississippi, 1983.

Pritchard, William Ryan. "Moving toward Freedom?: African-American Mobility and the Perils of Emancipation in Civil-War Era Louisiana, 1862–1867." Unpublished dissertation, University at Buffalo, 2016.

Index

Carroll Parish, 3

citizenship, 2, 10, 16, 18, 21–22, 42, 46, 75–76, 81–82, 84–85, 96, 113, 146, 151, 164–165, 167, 173, 186, 195, 199, 235

class conflict, 23, 26–30, 43–44, 46, 49, 58–59, 62–64, 113, 198–199, 216–217

Concordia Parish, 3, 209

Confederate Louisiana, 1–5, 12–14, 116, 129–130; destruction within, 196–197, 199, 210, 217–218; military operations, 129, 184, 190, 196–198, 203–204, 210; and religion, 19–20; and secession, 15–18, 31; and slavery, 27–28, 32–33, 40–41, 167–168, 213–216; state government, 34–38, 197–214, 216–217, 221–222, 226–228; and soldiers, 26–27, 29–30, 34–35, 205–207, 226–227; war production and defenses, 18–19, 28–29, 31–32, 39–44, 52, 203, 235–236

confiscation of property, 4, 9, 14, 33, 36, 46–49, 56, 72, 84, 86, 94, 100, 147, 178, 191, 198, 205, 208, 213, 216; Confiscation Acts, 5, 45, 69

conscription, 9, 14, 36, 89, 205–208, 219, 223, 228

contraband, 179, 182, 193; Butler's contraband policy, 47–50, 67–69; contraband camps, 123, 145–146, 164–165, 177; contraband labor, 145, 168–170, 173; contraband trade, 97, 101, 172, 184, 195

Conway, Thomas, 148–149, 173, 177–178, 182

corruption, 17, 36, 81, 167, 173; in Confederate Louisiana, 216, 227

cotton, 32, 38–40, 51, 100–109, 141, 148, 188, 190, 203–204, 207–212, 228, 236; Cotton Bureau, 208, 211–212

Crescent (Union steamer), 143

Daily Crescent (newspaper), 17, 33, 64

Darling, George, 89, 99, 102–103, 109

Davis, Jefferson, 9, 14–15, 27, 41, 49, 52, 54, 56, 62, 71–73, 153, 203–204

De Soto Parish, 3

democracy, 3, 10, 21, 33–34, 36, 45, 51, 81, 93, 106, 112–113, 161, 195, 228, 233, 235–237

Denison, George S., 71, 98, 101

Department of the Gulf, 13, 26, 46–48, 50–51, 74, 89, 100, 125, 138, 145, 170, 175, 210, 227, 231

desertion, 205, 207, 218–219, 226

Donaldsonville, 107–108, 184, 189

East Baton Rouge Parish, 32

East Feliciana, 168, 176, 223

Edwards, Marianne, 62–63, 137, 140, 142–143, 147–148, 151

emancipation, 4, 9, 45, 48–50, 67, 69–70, 80, 113, 133, 145, 150, 164–165, 168–172, 179, 182, 186, 192, 234; Emancipation Proclamation, 45, 72, 141, 164, 174, 195, 215, 234; self-emancipation, 230, 234

Emory, William, 232

Farragut, David, 44, 47, 52, 108

financial policy, 37–38, 100–101, 211–212

firemen, 90, 107

flags, 9, 19, 26, 44, 52–53, 141, 269–270n28

Fort Jackson and Fort St. Philip, 28, 40, 44, 51–52, 54, 59, 64, 96, 214

Fort Monroe, 47–48, 67, 186

free labor, 12, 27, 45, 48, 51, 65, 70–71, 74, 102, 108, 110, 145–149, 163–195, 230–236

free people of color, 6–7, 23, 27, 40–41, 65, 68, 70, 78, 100, 108, 112, 123, 126, 133, 138–139, 144–149, 155, 159, 161, 163–165, 176, 183–184, 226, 233

Freedmen's Bureau, 233

French, Jonas H., 6, 60, 87–89, 94–95, 152, 172

gender, 4, 11–12, 26, 58–59, 61–62, 68, 75, 88, 92, 98, 113, 131–136, 144, 149, 151–153, 156–161, 179–180, 186, 191, 234. *See also* household war; women (Black); women (white)

government, 1–5, 7, 11–14, 20, 42, 114, 165, 173, 177, 179–180, 187, 193–195, 216–217, 220–221, 229, 231–237; military government, 8,

slavery, 2, 4–10, 16, 25, 30, 36, 73, 79, 83, 93, 111, 133, 139–140, 145–150, 166–168, 188, 198–199, 210–216, 229–231, 234–236; and politics, 50, 63, 65, 67–70, 74–76, 80, 113; and refugees, 99–100, 113, 140, 145–146, 151, 171–172, 182–185, 189–190, 194; and secession, 19–20, 23; slaveholders, 4, 10, 30, 40, 67–68, 79, 132, 147, 163, 168, 182, 184, 210, 214–215, 234; and violence, 27–28, 57, 66, 71, 155–156, 159–160, 169, 215, 221; and war labor, 31, 45, 48–49, 163–165, 169–170, 179–180, 213–218

Smith, E. Kirby, 129, 198, 203, 207, 211, 218, 221, 227–228

smuggling. *See* trade: trade with the enemy

Solomon, Clara, 37

St. Bernard Parish, 41–42, 110

St. Charles Parish, 30, 85–86, 91, 94, 101–102

St. Helena Parish, 24

St. James Parish, 31, 101, 192

St. John the Baptist Parish, 89, 91, 94, 102, 110, 171, 175, 184, 192–193

St. Landry Parish, 3, 30–31, 33, 108, 136, 223

St. Martin Parish, 3, 127, 142, 176, 232

St. Mary Parish, 3, 78, 127, 154, 173, 181–183, 185–187, 190–191, 196, 210, 221, 224

St. Tammany Parish, 32, 85, 218

Stanton, Edwin, 52, 68–69

Stearns, Albert, 6, 109, 122, 127, 142, 170, 172, 174, 181, 186–187, 191–193, 230

Stewart, William H., 103–105, 144, 154, 176, 227

Stone, Kate, 17–18, 29–32, 167–168

stores, 42, 54, 63–64, 78, 101, 108, 172, 211, 216, 225, 227

Sugar Planter (newspaper), 29, 32

surrender, 65–66, 73, 82, 223; of federal property, 28; of forts Jackson and St. Philip, 43–44; of New Orleans, 51–53; of Confederate Louisiana, 227–228

Taliaferro, James G., 34–35, 43

taxation, 9, 36, 43, 46, 63, 71, 73–74, 81, 91–92, 99–100, 103, 113, 191–192, 197, 210–211, 218

Taylor, Richard, 129, 198, 205, 207, 210, 214, 219, 228

Tensas Parish, 3

Terrebonne Parish, 180, 185

Texas, 11, 19, 32, 38, 198, 203–204, 226–227

trade, 38, 43, 64, 80–81, 164, 176, 199, 211–212, 217–217, 236; trade with the enemy, 11, 42, 82, 100–107, 109, 125, 172, 195, 200–201, 208

Trans-Mississippi Department, 11–12, 16, 129, 197–198, 203–204, 207–208, 213, 220, 226–227

True Delta (newspaper), 17

Twiggs, David E., 19, 62

Union Parish, 207, 220

Unionists, 5, 16, 22, 28, 30, 41, 49, 80, 84, 100, 191–192, 220–222, 226, 228, 232–233

Vermillion Parish, 3

Vicksburg Campaign, 3, 11, 163, 197, 222

vigilance committees, 21–23, 30–31, 33, 35, 37, 40–42, 44, 216, 218, 242n13

violence, 11, 13, 21, 36, 41, 106, 143, 152, 205, 225–226; and language, 25–26; military violence, 57, 103–104; racial violence, 54, 69, 149, 169, 175–176, 199, 231–234

W. H. Webb (Confederate ram), 227

Wade-Davis Bill, 85

Wadley, Sarah, 206, 210, 215–218, 223

Weitzel, Godfrey, 65–67, 69, 158

Wells, James Madison, 34, 231

Western Sanitary Commission, 175, 179

Wheelock, Edwin, 191–192

Winn Parish, 3, 29–30, 207, 220

Wise, James Calvert, 213

Woman's Order, 57–62, 160

women (Black), 13, 15–16, 133, 164, 235–236; and education, 191–193; and free labor, 70, 78, 127, 145–146, 179–184, 186; and General Butler, 147–150; and historiography, 131–134; and the household, 146–148; and